Cooking with
Lydie Marshall

Illustrations by Stephanie Fleischer Osser

COOKING
WITH LYDIE
MARSHALL

Alfred A. Knopf
New York 1983

THIS IS A BORZOI BOOK PUBLISHED BY ALFRED A. KNOPF, INC.

Copyright © 1982 by Lydie Marshall
Illustrations Copyright © 1982 by Stephanie Fleischer Osser
All rights reserved under International and Pan-American Copyright Conventions.
Published in the United States by Alfred A. Knopf, Inc., New York,
and simultaneously in Canada by Random House of Canada Limited, Toronto.
Distributed by Random House, Inc., New York.

The recipes for "Apple Custard Pie," "Apple Gratin," "Chicken Bouillabaise,"
"Mussel Soup," "Plum Cake," and "Oyster Soup," originally appeared
in *The Pleasures of Cooking* by Cuisinart Cooking Club, Inc.

LIBRARY OF CONGRESS CATALOGING IN PUBLICATION DATA
Marshall, Lydie.
Cooking with Lydie Marshall.
Includes index.
1. Cookery, French. I. Title.
TX719.M3432   1982   641.5944   82-47832
ISBN 0-394-52022-X   AACR2

Manufactured in the United States of America

To Mrs. Charles B. Dunn, "Tatane,"
my first cooking teacher

ACKNOWLEDGMENTS

So many people have contributed to and influenced this book that it is impossible to thank them all here. All of my students and many friends have made important contributions, but some deserve special mention. I particularly want to thank Susan Geriak and Joan Danziger who typed and retyped the manuscript with such care. Sylvia Eckardt and Heidi Trachtenberg have tested most of the recipes—their help is gratefully acknowledged.

The encouragement and kindness of outstanding members of the profession were most welcome. I wish to thank especially Cecily Brownstone, Richard Olney, Julia Child, James Beard, and Mimi Sheraton, who have done so much for me.

Finally, I wish to thank that indispensable guide and mentor, my editor Judith Jones, whose experience and skill have determined the final form of this book.

Contents

Cooking with
Lydie Marshall

Introduction

When I started teaching cooking ten years ago, I planned to teach demonstration classes. That plan lasted a half an hour into the first class; the director-style armchairs bought especially for this purpose were folded and never used again. I realized then and there how much more fun and educational that participation classes would be. I could give individual attention to the needs of each student, and for the last ten years in my kitchen that is what I have been doing.

Again and again my students have asked me to write a cookbook. My answer was always: Why do we need yet another cookbook? I did not feel ready to contribute to the literature of cooking until I had something special to say and give. But little by little, after all the years of teaching, supervising, and helping students in class, I realized that I did have something to offer, particularly to all those people who couldn't cook with me in my own classes.

Not only is this book a summation of my teaching experience, it is also a summation of my own learning experiences from my students. I have noted many of the pitfalls my students run into, the kinds of directions that create anxiety, and I have tried to anticipate and to allay all their fears. I've worked out ways so that they don't attempt too much before they are ready, and I've tried to instill confidence, to enable them to develop their own judgment and sense of taste. My constant refrain in class is: "Don't worry, there's always a solution." I reiterate that they can't expect to learn everything immediately. If you are taking piano lessons, for instance, you're not going to play a Chopin mazurka the very first week. The same is true with cooking, but most people don't realize that.

I deliberately structured this book so that it embodies progressively more complex cooking techniques from one lesson to the next and so that every lesson offers menu suggestions that allow you to create delicious meals from an ever increasing repertoire. The twenty-two lessons represent about one year of classes in my cooking school, A La Bonne Cocotte (At the Good Cooking Pot).

The cooking I teach is influenced by my French background; but more than French cooking, I teach good home cooking. Alexandre Dumaine, one of the great chefs of France in the twentieth century, said "Il n'y a qu'une cuisine, la bonne." (There is only one kind of cooking, good cooking.)

I know that many of you who will cook from this book are already good cooks, as many of my students are, and that you are familiar with some of the techniques and recipes introduced. I hope you will enjoy making these familiar dishes, for I find they can be as challenging as new ones. It is the interpretation that counts. One never tires of seeing a new production of *Don Giovanni*, and similarly, another version of onion soup can reveal pleasures unknown before. However, I hope also to reach the cooks who are ready to experiment beyond basics. This book is for them, too.

I love to teach. During my childhood, I realized what teaching meant from a friend, a great teacher who helped me with my lessons, patiently coaching me along. Many years later, when I became a language teacher, I remembered her patience, putting herself at my level, explaining in simple words any complex idea.

I learned to cook by watching my mother, a natural cook who did not own a single cookbook. On very special occasions, she would make brioches and soufflés that were a delight to a child. Orphaned, I came to live in the United States with my aunt and uncle who adopted me. Tatane, my mother's sister, is another natural cook and she became my principal teacher. Just watching her and eating her food provided the kind of background that most good cooks in France have. But I really started cooking when I got married; it was fun to cook for my husband and his friends—they ate everything and thought I was great. I bought Julia Child's *Mastering the Art of French Cooking*, and it was as if my mother or my aunt were talking to me instead of Julia; all the recipes mentioned in the book were so familiar, I knew how they would taste before trying them.

My husband and I spent a year in Paris where I took cooking classes at Les Trois Gourmandes from Simone Beck and Louisette Bertholle. This was a welcome change from my own teaching at St. John's University. I learned from them how to verbalize techniques picked up from my aunt who cooked instinctively, but could not explain the reasons.

When we came to New York, we bought a small brownstone in Greenwich Village. My husband, with ulterior motives, renovated one floor as a beautiful, spacious kitchen, and in 1971, I was ready for the birth of A La Bonne Cocotte. My classes proved successful and I abandoned the teaching of French for the full-time teaching of cooking.

How This Book Works

There is an introduction to each lesson listing the recipes, techniques, and kitchen utensils introduced, followed by suggested menus drawn from that lesson and previous lessons, gradually building up a repertoire of menus. These menus are very flexible most of the time and usually omit a cheese or a tossed green salad course, simply to avoid repetitiousness in the listing of courses.

Each recipe in the lessons has a short introduction, often with a Special Instructions section that explains anything pertinent to the recipe that you need to know before you attempt to cook it. The recipe is then divided in steps to be followed as closely as possible. These steps are not arbitrarily placed; they are the result of a great deal of trial and error. The steps are there to minimize mistakes that can be made by a learning cook; however, once you have mastered the technique of the recipe and the flavor of the dish, you can prepare it as you choose and add your own interpretation to make it your own.

The lessons do become progressively more complex, but not all the recipes necessarily get more difficult. There will always be simple dishes to balance the work while you gradually learn more complicated techniques.

Don't always expect success the first time you try a complex technique, and do not tell yourself you can't do it. You will need practice to master it. For instance, in each class, I have two people learning to make puff pastry with me. We each make our own. I demonstrate, then I watch them try; there are some natural pastry makers, but in general, it is not the case. For most people, it is a question of doing it over and over again before becoming adept. But as with most things, you must practice regularly in order not to forget.

Cooking is learned through doing; the more you do, the better you do it. Not everyone is a natural cook, but anyone, willing to learn, can become a very good cook.

Special Kitchen Utensils

Most recipes in the book have a Special Kitchen Utensils section. The word *special* refers usually to the size of the pan. There is nothing special about a 9″ cast-iron skillet per se, but it is important for that recipe for the browning or the timing of the dish that it be 9″. I chose cast-iron skillets because they are the most readily available and less expensive than copper or stainless steel. But that does not mean you can't use your copper sauté pan if you have one. When using heavy-gauge stainless steel sauté pans with tight-fitting covers, leave the cover askew, otherwise the food will stew instead of braising.

Copper gratin pans are great if you can afford them, but Pyrex or Corning Ware will do very well. Use tin-plate baking molds if possible instead of aluminum because they season well and don't stick as much.

Why Do Recipes Fail?

Recipes fail for a variety of reasons. First of all, the quality of ingredients is hard to control, especially with vegetables and fruits. This is most difficult for suburban dwellers who have no garden and depend on supermarket vegetables. How frustrating it is: You cook an eggplant dish with great success once and the next time around it is disappointing, with a bitter taste. I have not been able to make really first-rate french fries in New York—they are never as good as my French french fries. I have been told by American farmers that irrigation is the culprit. Irrigated potatoes contain more water which dilutes the flavor of the potato but also gives high yield per acre. It is the age-old battle between quantity and quality. Quantity wins because that is where profit is. Vegetables are picked green to avoid spoilage because of the long interval between the time the vegetable is picked and the time it reaches the consumer. "We need more small farms that can get vegetables to consumers in a matter of hours," says Robert Rodale in his *Prevention Magazine,* and how right he is. A green bean does not wait to ripen on the day the farmer is allowed to sell. We, the consumers, need to put pressure on our local government and merchants to have green markets open every day during the growing seasons.

Some causes of failures are avoidable, however. The most common is misreading the recipe, or not reading it through. Also, sometimes, the cook just does not have the skills required for a dish. Don't, for instance, make puff pastry before knowing how to make a simple shortcrust pastry with success.

The climate can play tricks and provoke failures in baking. Not all flours are alike: Some are ground from soft wheat, some from hard wheat, and their behavior is quite different. I test all recipes with an all-purpose, unbleached flour from Gold Medal or Heckers. Variations in humidity will change the amount of flour needed in a specific recipe. Yeast doughs will rise faster during summer months when the weather is hot and humid than in winter.

Egg sizes can create a problem in dishes where the specific amount of ingredients is important. For most pastries, or baking, measure an egg by volume (a beaten egg should measure 1/4 cup).

Kitchen equipment accounts for some of the failures as well. The pot or pan or baking mold used may not have been the right shape, size or material. I don't mean that you need to own the identical pan mentioned in a recipe, but you need to be aware of the size and adjust the recipe accordingly.

Ovens behave differently and are a great source of frustration for a recipe writer. The bigger the oven, the longer the dish needs to cook. On the other hand, professional ovens, even though they are large, cook faster than home ovens because of the way they are built. I cook in a standard gas oven about 16" wide and 18" high, and the oven temperatures mentioned in this book are for this common type of oven. If you have a different size, just learn to make slight adjustments.

The more you practice cooking, the better you get at turning a failure into a success.

Composing Menus

Choose a menu that will fit into your schedule and not overtax you. A harassed, overworked cook cannot be a good host. Let the seasons dictate your choice of menus, be aware of what is available in the markets. Food journalists can be very helpful, so don't forget to read the food sections of your paper and magazines. At the same time, do not be overwhelmed by fads in food. Eat and cook what you like and what your family and friends like.

The next thing is to decide on the balance of ingredients in the menu. If you have a quiche for a first course, don't have a tart for dessert; choose a sherbet or fresh fruits instead. Portion sizes are a function of how many courses are planned and how rich the dishes will be. The portions mentioned in this book are small because each dish is a part of a menu. The more dishes in a menu, the smaller the portion is.

The difficulty of a menu does not depend necessarily on the complexity of one dish but on knowing how to orchestrate several dishes to make it a pleasant dinner for everyone. This is where anticipation of work is of prime importance. Keep last-minute preparations at a minimum, but on the other hand, don't sacrifice the dish by cooking it ahead of time if you know it is a detriment to the flavor or texture.

For a dinner party, if you need help choosing wines, ask a knowledgeable wine merchant in your area. For a wine connoisseur who wants fine bottles to shine at a dinner party, no elaborate dishes with complicated or startling tastes should be offered as the food should not compete with the wines.

Always try new recipes on your family and friends before attempting them on guests at a formal dinner party and always be sure to have one dish that never fails you.

If you want to impress, keep the dinner as simple as possible; some of my best meals are made with the simplest food.

Sometimes I enjoy cooking with my friends and for an informal dinner, I invite them early and we all cook; it's fun and saves me lots of work. You can do the same thing but remember that somebody has to be in charge; this means planning the meal and maybe directing others in the kitchen. You become a cooking teacher and chef for the occasion.

I would love to be with everyone who is learning to cook. Since this is impossible, I hope this book will be the next best thing and that each recipe will be more than a recipe to cook from. I want each cooking experience to be a step toward developing a confident and competent cook who loves to prepare meals for family and friends.

TECHNIQUES AND UTENSILS INTRODUCED

How to prepare salad greens, using a salad spinner

How to make a vinaigrette dressing

How to make vinegar in a wooden keg or 1-gallon
glazed crock

How to broil and peel peppers—essential,
a jelly-roll pan

How to make croutons and bread baskets

How to truss, baste, roast, deglaze, and cut up
a chicken, using a roasting pan 12″ x 16″ by 1½″
or two 12″ cast-iron skillets

How to render chicken fat

How to flambé, using a gas or electric range

How to make caramel, requiring a 1½–2 quart
heavy-bottomed saucepan

How to use a water bath

How to unmold baked desserts from a ring mold

How to whip cream cheese or heavy cream by hand
or with an electric mixer

Lesson 1

RECIPES

Tossed Green Salad with Vinaigrette

Homemade Vinegar

Tossed Green Salad with Leftover Meat

Red and Green Bell Pepper Salad with
a Vinaigrette Dressing

Zucchini Gratin with Cream and Swiss Cheese

Roast Chicken with Vegetables

Roast Chicken with Garlic

Roast Chicken with Pernod

Caramelized Pear Mousseline

Caramelized Apple Mousseline

Cream-Cheese Topping

Strawberries with Cream-Cheese Topping

Whipped Cream

Suggested Menus for Lesson 1

Roast Chicken with Garlic

Red and Green Bell Pepper Salad

Caramelized Pear Mousseline
with Whipped Cream

Roast Chicken with Vegetables

Tossed Green Salad
or
Sauté of Zucchini

Caramelized Apple Mousseline
with Cream-Cheese Topping

4-Course Menu

Red and Green Bell Pepper Salad
in Bread Baskets or with Croutons

Roast Chicken with Vegetables
or
Roast Chicken with Garlic
or
Roast Chicken with Pernod

Zucchini Gratin with Cream
and Swiss Cheese

Caramelized Pear or Apple
Mousseline with Whipped Cream or
Cream-Cheese Topping

A Light Dinner

Tossed Green Salad with
Leftover Meat

Strawberries with
Cream-Cheese Topping

For a Lunchbox

A Sandwich Filled with
Red and Green Bell Pepper Salad

Tossed Green Salad with Vinaigrette

Boston lettuce, chicory (sometimes called curly endive), and young spinach leaves are my favorite greens for a salad. I use them separately or mix them. In the spring, when young, tender watercress and arugula are on the market, I mix the two for a tossed salad. As soon as I buy the greens, I wash and dry them very carefully, being sure there is no grit left in the leaves. I dry them first in a salad spinner, then in paper towels. There is nothing worse than limp salad leaves, dressed in a waterlogged vinaigrette. Keep the salad in a plastic bag, tied at the top, leaving air in the bag. It stays fresh several days in the refrigerator. I use this system for parsley and keep it over a week in the refrigerator.

For the vinaigrette dressing, I use a light Italian olive oil available everywhere in supermarkets; I shy away from the expensive brands found in specialty stores. Most of the oils are too heavy-scented for the amount of oil needed to make a vinaigrette or a mayonnaise.

Buy plain red-wine vinegar or, even better, make your own, page 12. Buy plain Dijon-style mustard. If the oil, vinegar, and mustard are too strong, the flavors fight against each other. Stay as simple as possible when making a vinaigrette.

SERVES 6

1 head lettuce	½ cup olive oil
	¾ teaspoon salt
For about ½ cup vinaigrette	Freshly ground black pepper
1 clove garlic	1 tablespoon fresh herbs minced
1½ teaspoons Dijon-style mustard	(summertime)
2 tablespoons red-wine vinegar	

1. Wash the salad greens. Don't let them stand long in water; the vitamins get lost with prolonged standing in water.

2. Dry the leaves in a salad spinner and then pat dry in paper towels. Refrigerate until ready to toss the salad. Never toss a salad before dinnertime; the salad becomes soggy very quickly.

3. *Prepare the vinaigrette.*
   Mash the garlic clove either with a garlic press or by rubbing it across the ends of the tines of a fork held against a plate. Mix the mustard, garlic, and vinegar thoroughly with a fork, then slowly dribble in the oil, drop by

drop, stirring all the time with the fork. The sauce will stay creamy and will not separate. Season with salt and freshly ground pepper. In summer, add 1 tablespoon fresh herbs minced.

4. When ready to eat the salad, toss the greens in the vinaigrette with your hands; they are the best mixing tools. Taste for salt and pepper, or perhaps a little more seasoning with oil and/or vinegar.

For a warm vinaigrette. Prepare the vinaigrette in a mixing bowl set in a pan of simmering water to heat slightly, and serve right away.

Homemade Vinegar

Because we once found in our cellar a bottle of wine with a broken neck that had turned into vinegar, we have never since bought another bottle of vinegar.

Special instructions. To start making vinegar, you need 1 cup of unpasteurized vinegar (use a good French or Italian vinegar). Also, the wine you use to make vinegar must be unpasteurized and not treated with preservatives; otherwise, the alcohol will not turn into acetic acid which makes vinegar. Avoid American jug wines and the like, but any medium-priced imported table wine—French, Italian, or bottled California—will do; as long as it is dry, it will work. White, red, or both may be used.

Save the leftovers from the various wines you drink, fill bottles with them, and cork them for the next batch of vinegar.

Special kitchen utensil. Depending on how much vinegar you need, buy a 1–2-gallon wooden keg with an opening on top for aeration, or a 1-gallon glazed crock. (Go to an antique show and buy a glazed crock. It will do fine.) Cover the top with double-thickness cheesecloth and tie with a string around the crock.

1. If you are using a wooden keg, first make sure your keg is watertight. Fill it with water for 3 days and keep it in a sink or tub. It will probably leak at first, and then tighten up as the wood swells. Add water to keep it filled to the top. Empty out the water when the leaking stops.

2. Pour about 1 cup of unpasteurized wine vinegar into the keg or the crock and then fill with dry red or white wine or a mixture.

3. Let the keg sit for at least 3–4 months in a 70°F. temperature (the kitchen is fine). Do not plug the hole on the top of the keg. Cover it with cheese-cloth to let air circulate; do the same for the crock.

4. After 3–4 months, draw off some of the vinegar and taste it. If it is not vinegary enough, keep for another month or so in the keg or crock. There will be some evaporation of the vinegar, especially in the wintertime when there is not much humidity. When the vinegar is ready, pour out the vinegar from the top of the keg (you don't need a spigot) into a big mixing bowl. Leave about 1 cup of vinegar inside the keg or the crock and fill it once more with the corked leftover wines you kept or with wine just opened.

5. Pour the vinegar into a pitcher and fill bottles. Cork them tightly. (If you don't have a bottle corker, try to get tapered corks.) Before bottling, you may macerate different dry herbs or garlic in the vinegar for a week or two.

6. The vinegar will age in the bottle, so it is interesting to note the date on the bottle in case you want to keep it for several years. Store in a dark place on its side.

Note. When I make tarragon vinegar, I use only dry white wine to make the vinegar. Then I place 2 or 3 sprigs of fresh tarragon in each bottle of vinegar.

Tossed Green Salad with Leftover Meat

With leftover meat, cheese, and stale bread (for croutons), you can make a delicious, nutritious salad for dinner.

SERVES 4

1 head Boston lettuce or chicory	Several cherry tomatoes
½ rib celery	2 eggs
Leftover meat	Cheese: Swiss, goat, feta, etc.
2 tablespoons butter	½ cup bean sprouts
4 Tuscan peppers*	Vinaigrette, page 11
	Croutons, page 15

* These are found in supermarkets with the vinegars and oils; buy the hot variety called Tuscan peppers or pepperoncini.

1. Wash the salad leaves. Dry and reserve.

2. Dice ½ rib of celery (yields ⅓ cup).

3. Cut up leftover meat in bite sizes. Melt 2 tablespoons butter in a skillet. Sauté the meat for 1 minute or so to warm through.

4. Cut the Tuscan peppers in small strips. Split the cherry tomatoes in half.

5. Cover the eggs with cold water. Bring to a boil and cook for 10 minutes. Drain the water and cool the eggs under running cold water for 5 minutes.

6. Cut up leftover Swiss, blue, or goat cheese in bite sizes. If you have feta cheese, crumble it.

7. Toss all the vegetables, salad leaves, meat, and cheese together, then pour the vinaigrette over it and toss it with your hands. Taste for seasonings, adding more salt, pepper, oil, and vinegar, if necessary. Decorate the salad with sliced hard-boiled eggs and croutons.

Red and Green Bell Pepper Salad
with a Vinaigrette Dressing

A salad of green and red peppers seasoned with a vinaigrette makes a fine appetizer or vegetable course; served with garlicky croutons or, more elegantly, in bread baskets it's a lovely appetizer with drinks.

Special instructions. There are three main steps that can be done ahead of time:

- Cooking and peeling of the peppers
- Preparing the vinaigrette
- Shaping the croutons or bread baskets

Special kitchen utensil. A jelly-roll pan 16″ x 11″ x 1″.

SERVES 6

4 green bell peppers
4 red bell peppers
1 cup vinaigrette, page 11
½ teaspoon salt
Freshly ground black pepper

For croutons or bread baskets

A loaf of French bread about
    3½″ in diameter and 16″ long
8 tablespoons (1 stick) sweet
    butter
1 clove garlic

Cooking and peeling the peppers

Light the broiler.

1. Broil the peppers on a jelly-roll pan, 4″ below the heat. Be very careful not to burn the peppers; broiling takes about 15 minutes. Every 3–5 minutes, turn them so that all sides and ends puff up. The skin browns but not the meat. Watch carefully during the time it takes to broil the peppers. Remember, each pepper must be puffed up all over.

2. Remove the peppers from the oven and let rest for a minute or so, then transfer the peppers to 2 plastic bags, 4 in each bag, and close very tightly. Cool completely. Take out one pepper at a time and peel and seed on a plate. Discard the stem and seeds. Cut the peppers in strips (juliennes) ¼″ wide and 3″ long. I generally discard the juice that collects in the plastic bags because it tastes burnt; if not, reserve for later to add to the vinaigrette.

3. Prepare 2 batches of vinaigrette according to the recipe, page 11. Mix the pepper strips in 1 batch of vinaigrette. Taste and correct seasonings with salt and freshly ground pepper. Reserve the second batch of vinaigrette in a sauceboat for the table.

To eat the peppers as a vegetable

Warm the peppers and vinaigrette slowly in a water bath over low heat. The water bath can be a skillet filled with water. Place the bowl of peppers in the water bath. Cover the peppers and heat slowly until the peppers are warmed through. Serve with Roast Chicken, page 18.

To serve Red and Green Pepper Salad with croutons as an appetizer

Making croutons. Freeze the loaf of bread for 1 hour. This makes it easier to trim. Cut ½ loaf of bread in 1″ slices. Saw off the crust and cut each slice in 3, crosswise, and once in the middle, lengthwise. Just before dinnertime, dry the cubes of bread in the oven at 400°F. for several minutes, turning them on their sides once in a while to dry out and until they are lightly toasted. Brush melted butter over them and rub them with a garlic clove. Toss the croutons in the salad of peppers and serve.

To serve Red and Green Pepper Salad in bread baskets as an appetizer

1. *The bread baskets.* Freeze the loaf of bread for 1 hour; this makes it easier to trim. Cut the ends off the bread (to make bread crumbs, see note below at the end of this recipe), leaving a piece about 12″ long. Cut this into 1″ thick slices (if you are passing them around with drinks, cut the slices smaller—¾″ slices) and with a serrated knife, saw off the crust, then

run the blade of the knife, perpendicular to the bread, cutting out the inside 1½″ deep and ½″ from the edge. Scoop out the center piece of bread with a serrated spoon. Place the baskets on a cookie sheet and toast for about 15 minutes in the oven at 400°F., or until lightly brown. Check every so often to make sure they are not burning.

2. Melt 8 tablespoons sweet butter. (I prefer sweet butter. If it is unavailable, use lightly salted butter.) Brush butter inside and outside of the baskets. Reserve for the assembly. It is better not to refrigerate the baskets. Prepare them in the morning of the dinner, to be reheated later.

Just before dinnertime, preheat the oven to 400°F.

3. *The assembly.* Reheat the bread baskets (otherwise, the butter congeals on the bread and makes it unappetizing) in a 400°F. oven for 5 minutes, checking that they do not burn. Peel a garlic clove and rub it all over the hot baskets. (Don't rub the garlic on before reheating the bread; it would burn and smell bad.) Fill each basket with the peppers and the sauce. Serve with the reserved batch of vinaigrette in a sauceboat. Ladle more vinaigrette on top of the peppers and baskets.

Note on making bread crumbs. Toast the ends of the loaf to dry out the bread, grind them in the food processor, and freeze the crumbs.

Zucchini Gratin with
Cream and Swiss Cheese

The zucchini can be prepared ahead of time, then baked for dinner if you are serving it with the Roast Chicken that follows. Since it is baked at the same temperature as the chickens, there is no problem using only one oven.

Special kitchen utensils. A 12″ cast-iron skillet and a 1½-quart baking dish (Pyrex, Corning Ware, or a copper gratin pan).

SERVES 6

2 pounds small zucchini	Freshly ground black pepper
4 tablespoons chicken or goose fat, or 2 tablespoons butter and 2 tablespoons oil	½ cup freshly grated Swiss cheese (2 ounces)
2 cloves garlic, finely minced	⅔ cup heavy cream*
1 teaspoon salt	1–2 tablespoons butter

* Avoid the ultra-pasteurized heavy cream, if possible. Health-food stores generally carry the non-ultra-pasteurized. Substitute half-and-half if necessary.

1. Wash and dry the zucchini. Do not peel them. Cut off the ends, then cut them in ¼″ slices. Make 2 piles of zucchini to sauté in 2 batches. If they are sautéed all at once, the zucchini will steam up and get mushy instead of browning slightly.

2. Melt 2 tablespoons fat or 1 tablespoon butter with 1 tablespoon oil (the oil is there to prevent the butter from burning) over medium-high heat in a 9″ or 12″ skillet. When the fats are hot but not smoking, add 1 batch of zucchini. Sauté the zucchini, which means to shake and toss them in the skillet all the while, regulating the heat if necessary to prevent burning. It takes around 5–10 minutes or so for the zucchini slices to be golden and lose their whitish appearance. Transfer the first batch to a plate and reserve. Sauté the second batch of zucchini with the rest of the fats. Add more fat if the bottom of the skillet seems dry.

3. *Mincing garlic cloves.* Split each garlic clove in two lengthwise, then with one piece flat on the counter, holding it with one hand, slice the piece vertically lengthwise, leaving one end piece whole, then slice twice horizontally, then crosswise to mince.

4. Add the reserved zucchini to that in the skillet. Add also the minced garlic. Sprinkle on about ½ teaspoon salt, and grind fresh pepper over them. Cover and simmer for 10 minutes. (It can be eaten at this stage.)

5. Transfer half the zucchini slices to a buttered 1½-quart baking dish, sprinkle with ¼ teaspoon salt, and grate the Swiss cheese over the zucchini. (It is better to grate the cheese at the last minute, otherwise it packs down, which makes it difficult to sprinkle.) Spread the rest of the zucchini slices over the cheese, sprinkle on ¼ teaspoon salt, and grate cheese over the top. Pour over ⅔ cup heavy cream. (You can prepare the gratin ahead of time to this point and refrigerate covered; just remember to bring it back to room temperature before baking it.)

Preheat oven to 350°F.

6. Dot the top with tiny pieces of butter and bake in a 350°F. oven for about 35 minutes or until the top is golden brown.

For a Quick Sauté of Zucchini. Simply follow the recipe to step 5

Roast Chicken with Vegetables

Chicken roasted in the oven along with basic vegetables, such as carrots, onions, and potatoes, is a classic dish in French homes. In the Drôme, the region where I spend my summers, chicken is still considered Sunday fare. It should well be, since in the Drôme, as in rural regions everywhere, people still can obtain "ground-raised" chickens which are much more costly than cage-raised birds available in cities.

Despite the differences in the chickens, the following dish is much the same as one might find in a French farmhouse. Careful basting of the chicken and the vegetables is the key to the success of the dish.

Special kitchen utensils. Use a proper roasting pan to help you along. The shape and the size are the most important characteristics; the pan can be made of aluminum, Pyrex, cast iron, etc. A rectangular shape is ideal for roasting more than one chicken. The sides of the pan must not be higher than 2″ because high-sided pans tend to hold in the steam and therefore stew a chicken instead of roasting it. (This rule applies to all meats to be roasted.) The ideal size for the following recipe and for all the recipes in the book that call for roasting is 12″ x 16″ x 1½″. In lieu of a roasting pan, I have used two 12″ cast-iron skillets, interchanging them on two oven racks during the roasting period to ensure even roasting.

SERVES 6–8

Two 3½-pound chickens	2 carrots
2 teaspoons salt	2 yellow onions
Several grinds of the pepper mill	6 medium-size Russet potatoes
6 tablespoons sweet butter	About 1¼ cups water
2 tablespoons vegetable oil	A bunch of watercress

1. Wipe the chickens (outside and inside) with paper towels. Sprinkle ¼ teaspoon salt and freshly ground pepper in the cavity of each chicken. Cut off and freeze the fat around the opening of the cavity. When you have collected enough chicken fat, render it as described on page 20.

2. Melt 2 tablespoons butter and 1 tablespoon vegetable oil in each of two 12″ cast-iron skillets. When the fats are hot but not smoking, brown the chickens, breast side down first, then turn the chickens on their sides and backs to brown all over (about 20 minutes); always regulate the heat to prevent scorching the skin of the chickens.

3. While the chickens are browning, peel the carrots and slice thinly. Peel and quarter the onions. Peel the potatoes, rinse them under cold water, and dry them; cut them in half, lengthwise; then with each half flat side on the counter, slice lengthwise in 3 even strips. Then dice cross-

Technique: To truss a chicken

Place the chicken breast side
up with the tail toward you.
Cut a 3-foot-long piece of
kitchen string. Place the
center of the string under the
tail. Cross the two ends of
the string tightly on top of
the tail.

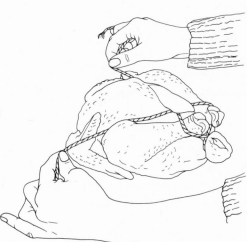

Then pass the string under
the ends of the drumsticks,
crossing the string over them
so it catches under the pointed
end of the breastbone. Bring
the string over each thigh
where it meets the body.

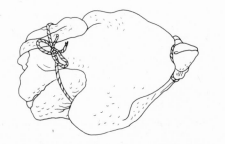

Turn the bird over, bring
the two ends of the string
together on the back catching
the wings tightly to the body,
and make a knot in the back.
Cut off the extra string ends.

wise into ½″ cubes for approximately 4 cups of potatoes. *It is important not to overload the pan with potatoes*; otherwise, the chicken will stew instead of roasting, since Russet potatoes exude water while cooking. Turn the prepared vegetables (about 7 cups in all) into a mixing bowl and season with 1½ teaspoons salt and 5–6 twists of freshly ground pepper. Toss the vegetables, using your hands to distribute the seasonings evenly.

4. Transfer the chickens to a large roasting pan about 12″ x 16″ x 1½″, breast side up, not touching each other.

5. Put half the vegetables in each skillet; stir them around over high heat with a pancake turner (steel spatula) for about 5 minutes to coat them with the remaining fats. Transfer the vegetables to the roasting pan, distributing them evenly around the chickens.

6. Over high heat, pour ⅓ cup water in each skillet, bring the water to a rolling boil for 30 seconds or so, and pour over the vegetables. (This technique is called deglazing. It gets up the drippings and aroma in the liquids, and it also cleans the skillet at the same time. After pouring off the liquid, I generally keep the skillet handle in my hand, go to the sink, scrub the skillet under very hot water without any detergent, then dry it immediately with paper towels.)

Preheat oven to 350°F.

7. Put the chickens in a 350°F. oven and roast for 1½ hours, basting the chickens every 15 minutes with the liquids in the pan and stirring the

---

Technique: To render chicken fat

MAKES 2 CUPS

   1 pound chicken fat
   ¼ cup water

Combine the fat and water in a kettle. Cook over low heat for ½ hour covered, then uncover and continue cooking until the fat is melted (about 1 hour). Strain the fat through a fine-mesh sieve lined with paper towels. The melted fat can be kept for several weeks in the refrigerator or several months in the freezer. Use the fat for browning vegetables or meat.

vegetables around. During 1½ hours, baste 6 times; pour ¼ cup water over the vegetables for the first 2 bastings. After 30 minutes of cooking, the potatoes will usually render enough liquids to continue basting without adding more water. From this point onward, add only enough water to keep about 1 cup of liquid in the pan.

8. Transfer one chicken to a cutting board (preferably grooved around the edge to catch the juices). Cut it in 8 pieces (illustration pages 96–97). Cut off the legs at the joint where the thigh joins the body. Cut the thighs and drumsticks apart at the joint. Cut off the wings where they join the body. Run the knife back along each side of the breastbone to cut off the breast meat. Reserve pieces on a preheated platter.

9. Pour the chicken juices back into the roasting pan and repeat with the second chicken. Remove the vegetables with a skimmer and decorate the chicken platter with them. Add watercress for decoration.

10. Bring the chicken juices in the roasting pan to a boil for 30 seconds, then turn off the heat. (There should be about 1¼ cups of liquids in the pan.) Whisk in vigorously the remaining 2 tablespoons butter. Pour the sauce into a preheated sauceboat and serve.

Roast Chicken with Garlic

This chicken from the Bordeaux region resembles the famous Provençal Chicken with Forty Cloves of Garlic. The amount of garlic you use is up to you—a nice-size chicken will feed 4 to 6 people served after a first course, and we manage to eat 24 cloves of garlic very easily—twice as much would not hurt a bit, since you really eat it as a vegetable. The cooking, of course, removes the very strong taste and leaves you with only buttery garlic to spread on the croutons. Use large, fresh, juicy cloves of garlic (about the size of a small American olive—avoid the kind so often found in supermarkets which is usually undersized and nearly always rather dried out).

Special kitchen utensil. A 12″ cast-iron skillet.

SERVES 4–6

5 slices French or Italian bread 1½″ thick	½ teaspoon salt
9 tablespoons sweet butter	Freshly ground black pepper
24 cloves garlic	2 tablespoons olive oil
4½-pound roasting chicken	1–1½ cups water
	1 bunch watercress

Preheat oven to 300°F.

1. *To make croutons.* Trim the crust off the bread. (Freezing it for an hour or so makes it easier to trim off the crusts.) To cut off the crust, use a bread knife and carefully saw around the edge to avoid crushing the bread. Cut into pieces about 1″ square. Dry these cubes in the oven at 300°F. for about 20 minutes. Remove squares of bread from oven. Melt 5 tablespoons of the butter, then brush it all over the croutons.

2. Parboil 12 cloves of the garlic (unpeeled) for 20 minutes to put inside the chicken. The garlic outside the chicken cooks enough in the oven, but the cloves inside will not be done enough unless parboiled.

3. Dry the chicken. Season the cavity of the chicken with salt and pepper and stuff it with half the croutons and 12 parboiled cloves of unpeeled garlic. Truss the chicken: see illustration, page 19.

4. Melt 2 tablespoons of the sweet butter and 1 tablespoon olive oil in a 12″ cast-iron skillet. Over medium to high heat, brown the chicken, starting breast side down; then brown the sides until they are golden. This should take about 20 minutes.

5. Turn the chicken breast side up, add the remaining garlic (12 large unpeeled cloves) to the pan, and season the chicken with ½ teaspoon salt and freshly ground pepper. Pour ½ cup water into the pan and place in a 300°F. oven on the middle rack, uncovered.

6. Every 20 minutes baste the chicken with the pan liquids, then pour ⅓ cup water into the pan. It must cook for about 1¾ hours to 2 hours, depending on your oven and the size of the chicken. At the end, the skin should be golden brown and crisp, with the flesh moist and tender.

7. Remove the chicken to a preheated carving platter. Cut up the chicken and surround it with the croutons and garlic, still unpeeled. Garnish with watercress.

8. Degrease the liquids in the roasting pan. There should be about 1 cup of juices left; if not, add enough water to make 1 cup of liquid. Bring to a boil for 1 minute or 2, stirring all the while. Turn off the heat, whisk in the remaining 2 tablespoons butter, and serve in a hot sauceboat.

9. Remove the peel from the garlic. (The peel will slip off easily.) Mash the garlic and spread it over the croutons like butter—its taste is mild.

Note on doubling the recipe. Either use 2 cast-iron skillets and place them next to each other on the middle rack of the oven, or transfer the 2 chickens to a roasting pan (12″ x 16″ x 1½″) at step 5, then pour ⅓ cup water in each skillet. Bring the liquids to a boil, scraping the sides and bottoms of the skillets, boil 30 seconds, then pour the liquids into the roasting pan.

Roast Chicken with Pernod

Constant basting is the key to a moist, tender roasted chicken. Read carefully the introduction to the Roast Chicken with Vegetables, page 18, and apply the same principles to this recipe. Pernod and Ricard are the two best-known brands of the anise-based apéritifs so dearly loved by Frenchmen in Provence, the southeastern region of France that includes the Riviera. Pernod is diluted with lots of water, because it is strong in flavor and alcohol. In cooking, it must be used sparingly. The following chicken is flambéed with only 1½ tablespoons of Pernod. The alcohol must burn. Do not pour Pernod over the chicken without flaming it first because it will give a disagreeably strong taste, instead of a subtle anise flavor minus the alcohol. Carefully follow the instructions, page 24.

Special kitchen utensils. A 12″ cast-iron skillet and a ladle or a small pan.

SERVES 4

3½-pound chicken	6 tablespoons sweet butter
1 teaspoon salt	1 tablespoon olive oil
Freshly ground black pepper	½ cup dry white wine
1 branch fennel or 1 rib celery	1–2 cups water
3 white bulbs of scallions	1½ tablespoons Pernod or Ricard

1. Wipe the chicken dry outside and inside with paper towels. Sprinkle ¼ teaspoon salt and freshly ground pepper in the cavity of the chicken. Cut up the fennel branch or the celery rib into ½″ slices. Mince the white bulbs of scallions and stuff the chicken. Truss (see illustration, page 19).

2. Melt 3 tablespoons butter and 1 tablespoon olive oil in a 12″ cast-iron skillet. When the fats are hot but not smoking, brown the chicken, breast side down first, then turn the chicken on its sides and back to brown all over (about 20 minutes); always regulate the heat to prevent scorching the skin of the chicken. Remove the chicken to a plate.

3. Discard the fat in the skillet. Add ½ cup wine and ½ cup water to the skillet and, over high heat, deglaze by stirring with a wooden spoon to get up the drippings (1 minute). Remove from the heat.

4. Return the chicken to the skillet, breast side up, with the juices that spewed out of the chicken. Sprinkle with ½ teaspoon salt and freshly ground pepper.

Preheat oven to 350°F.

Technique: To flambé

With a gas range.
Pour 1½ tablespoons **Pernod**
in a ladle. Heat the alcohol
in the ladle over a high flame
for 20–30 seconds, tip the
ladle toward the flame to ignite,
and pour over the chicken.
Don't boil the alcohol; it will
evaporate and you will not
have the pleasure of flam-
béing it.

With an electric range. Heat the
alcohol in a small pan (a pipkin)
and ignite it with a match.

5. Roast uncovered in a 350°F. preheated oven for 1½ hours, basting every 10 minutes as follows: Baste the chicken with the pan juices, then add more water in the pan. There should be only about a cup of pan juices at the finish.

6. Flambé the chicken with Pernod. Transfer the chicken to a cutting board with a groove around the edge to catch the juices. Carve into 8 pieces (illustration on pages 96–97). Pour the chicken juices back into the skillet; bring them to a boil for 30 seconds, stirring all the while. Turn off the heat and whisk in 3 tablespoons butter, cut up in small pieces. Taste and correct seasoning with ¼ teaspoon salt and freshly ground pepper, if necessary.

7. Serve the sauce in a preheated sauceboat. Serve the chicken with Fennel Purée if you wish, see page 311.

Caramelized Pear Mousseline

You can make a lovely and elegant dessert out of pear or apple sauce combined with eggs, then baked in a caramel-coated ring mold. If you are hesitant about making caramel, read carefully the Special Instructions given here.

Special instructions. Caramel is a syrup made with sugar and water cooked until the syrup reaches a temperature of 310°–370°F. When the syrup starts to change from a white opaque color to a light golden color and then rapidly goes to a deeper amber color, the caramel is ready to coat the mold.

If you cook the caramel syrup longer, it will turn black and become bitter. (If that happens to you, turn off the heat, fill the pan with hot water— it will spatter—and bring the water back to a boil to dissolve the burnt caramel. Discard.)

Sometimes the syrup while it is cooking will dry up into a white crust that does not want to dissolve. If so, pour ¼ cup boiling water into the pan and be careful—the syrup will spatter. Stir the water into the dry syrup and continue cooking until it is hot enough to change color and become caramel.

Special kitchen utensils. A 1½–2-cup heavy-bottomed saucepan and a 4-cup ring mold.

SERVES 8

For the caramel	For the pears
½ cup superfine sugar	8 pears (2½ pounds),
3 tablespoons water	preferably Bosc
	⅓ cup sugar
	8 tablespoons (1 stick) butter
	4 large eggs

1. *Cooking the caramel for a ring mold.* Combine ½ cup superfine sugar and 3 tablespoons water in a heavy saucepan. Bring to a boil over medium-high heat; continue cooking, stirring once in a while, until it changes color (about 8 minutes). As soon as the syrup colors to a light brown, swirl the syrup by tipping the pan to evenly color the caramel; continue cooking for 10 more seconds or so until the caramel colors to medium amber. Potholders in hands, quickly pour the caramel into the mold. Tip the mold in all directions until the caramel stops running and hardens. Reserve.

2. *Cooking the pears.* Peel, seed, and cut the pears into 1" cubes. Combine them with the sugar and butter in a 12" skillet and cook over medium-high heat until pears are soft and color slightly (about 30 minutes). With the back of a fork, mash into a coarse purée or purée in a blender or food processor for a finer texture. I prefer a coarser texture. Cool for 10 minutes.

Preheat oven to 350°F.

3. Beat 4 eggs into the cooled purée, one at a time. Pour the mixture into the caramel-lined mold. Place the mold in a water bath: a pan with simmering water to immerse the mold to about two-thirds of its height. Bake on the middle shelf of the oven for about 1 hour.

4. Remove the pan from the water bath. Pass the blade of a knife around the edges of the mousseline. Turn the ring mold upside down onto a serving platter. Wait about 30 minutes, then unmold. Eat at room temperature. If the dessert is prepared a day ahead of time, remove from the refrigerator several hours before eating it to bring it back to room temperature.

Note. Some of the caramel might stick to the mold. Place the mold in a water bath over medium heat, pour in ¼ cup water, and let the caramel soften. Stir and use it as extra caramel sauce for the dessert.

Caramelized Apple Mousseline

Cortland, Jonathan, Macoun, or Golden Delicious apples are excellent for this dessert. In the spring cook with Granny Smith apples.

Special instructions and kitchen utensil. See preceding recipe.

SERVES 8

For the apples	For the caramel
8 medium-size apples (2½ pounds)	½ cup superfine sugar
¼ cup water	3 tablespoons water
⅓ cup sugar	
8 tablespoons (1 stick) sweet butter	
2 tablespoons apricot preserves	
4 large eggs	

1. Peel, seed, and chop the apples coarsely. Combine them with water, ⅓ cup sugar, butter, and apricot preserves in a 12″ skillet and cook over medium-high heat until the apples turn into a near-purée, mashing them once in a while with a fork (about 20 minutes). Cool.

2. Follow the directions for Caramelized Pear Mousseline, page 25, for the caramel and the baking of the dessert.

Cream-Cheese Topping

A cream topping for fresh fruits as well as for fruit tarts or mousselines, this is a mixture of cream cheese, heavy cream, and sugar. Try to get fresh cream cheese free of preservatives.

MAKES 2 CUPS

½ pound fresh cream cheese* or ricotta cheese	*Apples:* Calvados, Armagnac, Cognac
1½ cup heavy cream	*Oranges/Lemons:* Cointreau, Grand Marnier, Triple Sec
¼ cup superfine sugar	*Pears:* Pear Liqueur or Brandy
1 tablespoon of a fruit brandy corresponding to the fruits used	*Raspberries/Strawberries:* Raspberry Liqueur or Brandy
	Cherries/Plums: Kirsch

* If fresh cream cheese is not available, use the packaged product and double the amount of heavy cream. Supermarket cream cheese is dense and needs more cream to whip it into a smooth mixture.

1. Place the mixing bowl in the freezer for 5 minutes, or 10 minutes in the refrigerator, so the heavy cream will not curdle before it is mixed thoroughly into the cream cheese and sugar.

2. Beat the cream cheese to aerate it in the cold mixing bowl at medium speed. Dribble the cream in, then add the sugar. Stop before all the sugar is incorporated and taste for sweetness. Then whisk in the fruit alcohol of your choice. The mixture should be neither too firm nor too runny. The consistency of rather stiff whipped cream is about right. Refrigerate until ready to serve the dessert.

Strawberries with Cream–Cheese Topping

SERVES 6

2 pints strawberries
2 tablespoons superfine sugar
1 teaspoon raspberry liqueur
   or Kirsch
Cream-Cheese Topping, page 27

1. Wash the strawberries, but do not hull them (it keeps more flavor in the strawberries that way). Sprinkle the sugar and liqueur over them (substitute Kirsch if the raspberry liqueur is not available). Let stand for 1 hour. Hull the strawberries.

2. Prepare the Cream-Cheese Topping, page 27.

3. Serve the strawberries in chilled champagne glasses with the Cream-Cheese Topping over them.

Whipped Cream

Unfortunately, today in most supermarkets whipping cream is ultra-pasteurized. Check your local health-food stores or cheese stores for pasteurized cream. Even better is the cream found on top of raw milk sold in health-food stores or bought from a local farmer.

Special instruction. If prepared ahead of time, transfer the whipped cream, called chantilly in French, to a fine-meshed strainer and place it over a mixing bowl in the refrigerator. The whipped cream will stay firm—some of the liquid will drip into the bowl.

1 cup heavy cream	1 tablespoon liqueur or fruit
¼ cup superfine sugar	brandy

1. Put your mixing bowl in the freezer to chill for 10 minutes—the colder it and the cream are, the lighter the whipped cream will be.

2. Whisk the cream slowly and speed up gradually. As soon as the cream starts to thicken, sprinkle in the sugar and the liqueur or fruit alcohol. Beat until fairly firm, but be careful not to beat the cream into butter.

TECHNIQUES AND UTENSILS INTRODUCED

How to make vegetable stock using a stockpot

How to peel broccoli

How to make a purée using a fine-mesh sieve

How to reheat a purée

How to roast and carve whole veal shanks,
and to braise osso bucco–style in a Dutch oven

All about chocolate: types, melting, and smoothing out

How to make a quick pastry cream custard

Lesson 2

Suggested Menus for Lesson 2

3-Course Menus

Braised Veal Shanks with Paprika

Rice Pilaf
or
Store-bought Green Pasta

Chocolate Sunflower

Roasted Whole Veal Shanks

Broccoli Purée
or
Split Pea Purée

Caramelized Apple Mousseline
(Lesson 1)

4-Course Menus

Vegetable Soup

Roasted Whole Veal Shanks

Broccoli Purée

Chocolate Sunflower

Broccoli Purée on Toast

Braised Veal Shanks with Paprika

Rice Pilaf

Caramelized Pear Mousseline
(Lesson 1)

A Light Dinner

Vegetable Soup

Fresh Spinach Leaves Salad (Lesson 1)
with Leftover Veal and a Warm
Vinaigrette Dressing

Fresh Fruits with a Pastry Cream

Vegetable Soup

My Aunt, Tatane, makes the best vegetable soup I have ever eaten. She lives in Sun City, Arizona, and from October to May, there are very few days when she and my uncle do not have vegetable soup for lunch.

To her, soup means vegetables cooked in water. She adds butter to each soup plate when served, then swirls it in the hot soup.

Potatoes are generally included to provide body to the soup, but the choice of other vegetables is a matter of preference, availability, or what's left over in the vegetable bin of the refrigerator.

Special kitchen utensil. A stockpot is a worthwhile investment for anyone who likes to cook. Heavy-gauge aluminum and stainless steel are among the best materials for a stockpot. Its size and shape are both important. For an average-size family, a 15-quart stockpot is ideal (10½" diameter and about 11" high); it just covers a standard-size burner.

SERVES 8

3 Russet potatoes (about 4 ounces each)	10 cups water
4 medium-size yellow onions	Freshly ground black pepper
4 carrots	2 tablespoons salt
4 ribs celery with their leaves	½ teaspoon dried thyme
2 cloves garlic	8 tablespoons (1 stick) sweet
A small bunch of fresh parsley	butter (1 tablespoon per person)

1. Peel the vegetables. Cut the potatoes in small cubes, quarter the onions, cut the carrots and celery into slices, and coarsely chop 2 garlic cloves and a small bunch of fresh parsley. Measure in cups the amount of prepared vegetables (about 10 cups for this recipe). Use the same amount of water.

2. Place the vegetables in a stockpot, grind fresh pepper, add 2 tablespoons salt and ½ teaspoon thyme, and toss the vegetables to distribute the seasoning evenly. Add water (about 10 cups). Cover and bring to a boil slowly, then simmer for over 1 hour, or until all the vegetables are soft (about 1½ hours in all).

3. Remove the vegetables with a slotted spoon and purée either in a food mill or in a processor, then pour the cooking water (the vegetable stock) over the purée to thin it out to the consistency you like in a soup. It can be prepared ahead of time. If so, use the whole amount of vegetable stock because the soup will thicken as it stands.

4. Reheat the soup until the first boil. It should be boiling hot. Taste and correct seasonings.

5. Pour into individual soup plates and float 1 tablespoon butter on top.

Pumpkin Soup

My October soup. Pumpkins are available everywhere during the month of October. They also will keep for several weeks cut into wedges, wrapped in plastic wrap in the refrigerator. A pumpkin is difficult to peel, so cut it in 2" thick wedges first. Butternut squash is a good substitute for pumpkin later on in the season.

Special kitchen utensil. A 15-quart stockpot.

SERVES 8

½ small pumpkin (about 5 pounds)	About 10 cups water
1 pound boiling potatoes	2 tablespoons salt
3 medium-size yellow onions	Freshly ground black pepper
	8 tablespoons sweet butter

1. Cut the pumpkin in wedges 2" wide in the middle. Lay a wedge of pumpkin flat on the counter and slice off the outer tough peel, using a 10" chef's knife. Remove the seeds and cut out the stringy membrane on the inside of each wedge, then cut it into ½" cubes (for 5 cups).

2. Peel the potatoes; cut into ½" cubes. Peel and chop the onions coarsely. Measure in cups the amount of prepared vegetables (about 10 cups for this recipe). Use the same amount of water.

3. *Cooking the soup.* Follow the directions of the Vegetable Soup, page 33.

Broccoli Purée

The most popular version of broccoli purée in the States is made by puréeing the broccoli with cream in the food processor. Forced through a fine-mesh sieve, the purée takes on a silky quality; butter, instead of cream, whipped into it intensifies the flavor of broccoli, and the purée keeps its lovely green color. The extra time required is well repaid, especially since the purée can be prepared ahead of time and reheated when needed.

It can also be served as an hors d'oeuvre in finger-size tart shells or spread on buttered toast, sprinkled with cheese, and gratinéed (see Variations at end of recipe).

Special instruction. Steps 1–5 may be completed 24 hours before serving.

Special kitchen utensil. A fine-mesh sieve.

SERVES 6 AS A VEGETABLE AND MAKES 4 CUPS PURÉE

5 quarts boiling water with	½ teaspoon salt, more if necessary
2 tablespoons salt	Freshly ground black pepper
2 bunches of broccoli (2–2½ pounds)	4 tablespoons sweet butter

1. Boil 5 quarts of water with 2 tablespoons salt with the cover on; it boils faster.

2. Discard the tough lower stems of the broccoli (approximately 2″ of the stem) and peel the stem ¼″ deep. Cut off the stems and split them lengthwise, then cut them crosswise in small cubes. Reserve the flowerets for later.

3. Boil the cubed broccoli stems until tender (about 15 minutes). Test them with a needle or skewer for doneness. If they are not tender, it will be very difficult to force through a fine-mesh sieve at step 5.

4. Add the broccoli flowerets in the same water until tender (at most 1 minute). Drain, rinse under cold water to stop the cooking, and drain well.

5. Purée the stems and flowerets in a vegetable mill or a processor (process at least 2 minutes). Then force through a sieve. Reserve the purée in a sieve over a bowl, covered with a plate, and refrigerate until 2 hours before dinner.

6. Reheat the purée, and season to taste with salt and freshly ground pepper. Remove from heat and whisk in 4 tablespoons sweet butter, 1 tablespoon at a time. Taste once more for additional salt and pepper, if necessary.

To reheat the purée. Place the pan in a skillet with water, and reheat over a medium flame, but be careful to add water to the skillet once in a while.

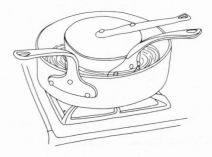

Technique: To use a fine-mesh sieve

A drum sieve. Place the sieve over a plate with the mesh side up. Put about ¼ cup (no more) of purée on the nylon mesh and force it through with a plastic scraper with rounded edges at one end, holding the scraper almost parallel to the mesh with one hand.

Once in a while, scrape the underside of the mesh to facilitate forcing through the purée.

Small Broccoli Purée Tarts

Broccoli purée should be served hot. Fill the tarts or spread it on croutons at the last minute before eating.

1. Prepare Shortcrust Pastry, pages 88–90, following directions for rolling out the dough and the baking.

2. Fill each tartlet with the purée, sprinkle on grated cheese, and pass under the broiler to melt the cheese.

A regular sieve. Secure it over a mixing bowl and force 2 tablespoons at a time of the purée with the back of a soup spoon (it works very well).

The Kitchen Aid colander-sieve. Fit the sieve into the mixing bowl. Fit the wooden paddle where the whisk generally is attached. Force through 2–3 tablespoons of the purée at a time at medium speed. Unfortunately, the sieve is aluminum and tends to discolor most vegetables.

Broccoli Purée as an Hors d'Oeuvre on Buttered Toast

1. Spread the purée on small pieces of buttered toast. Sprinkle lightly with grated Swiss cheese. (It is better to grate the cheese right on the toast. If the cheese is grated ahead of time, it packs down and one tends to put on too much cheese.)

2. Pass under broiler for half a minute or so, just enough to melt the cheese.

Split Pea Purée

I like to cook a pound of split peas at a time, even though it makes more purée than needed, so that I have the leftovers for a soup.

Special kitchen utensil. A 4-quart Dutch oven.

SERVES 8–10

1 pound split peas	2 medium-size carrots
1 medium-size onion with 2 cloves	½ teaspoon dried thyme
	1 bay leaf
1 small parsnip (for 1 cup of ½″ cubes)	Several sprigs of parsley
	2 teaspoons salt
1 rib celery	2 tablespoons sweet butter

1. Pour the peas out on a table and check through them for foreign objects (stones, stems, etc.).

2. Peel the vegetables. Cut the onion in half and stick a clove in each half. Cut the parsnip in ½″ cubes (1 cup) and slice the celery in thin slices. Cut carrots in thin slices.

3. Put the peas in a heavy 4-quart pot with a lid (a Dutch oven). Pour 1 quart of water over them and bury the vegetables in the peas. Add the thyme, bay leaf, parsley, and 2 teaspoons salt. Cover, bring to a boil, then simmer over medium-low heat for 1–1½ hours until the peas are tender. Check them once in a while, and stir. The peas will absorb the water. If there is any liquid left, drain the peas and vegetables.

4. When the peas are tender, remove the bay leaf and purée the peas, carrots, onion (cloves removed), celery, and parsnip with the food mill or the food processor (process in several batches).

5. Cover the purée if it is prepared ahead of time to keep it from drying out. Reheat in a water bath (a skillet filled with water one-third of the way up).

6. Off the flame, whisk in 2 tablespoons butter. Taste, then correct seasonings with salt.

Split Pea Soup

To 3 cups of purée, add 2 cups water and 1 teaspoon salt. Bring to a boil. Then swirl in 1 tablespoon butter in a soup plate.

Rice Pilaf

I use the long-grain rice when it accompanies a roast. When it is cooked, the grains are separate and fluffy. But if I mold the rice in a ring mold, I prefer the medium or short grain rice because cooked the grains are more moist and cling together more than long grains. It is then easier to unmold.

Special kitchen utensil. A 1½-quart heavy saucepan with a tight-fitting lid.

SERVES 6–8

1½ cups long-grain Carolina rice	6 tablespoons sweet butter
1 small yellow onion	1½ teaspoons salt
2½ cups boiling water	Freshly ground black pepper

1. Wash and drain the rice.

2. Mince the onion. Boil water in a kettle.

3. Melt 2 tablespoons butter in a 1½-quart heavy-bottomed saucepan with a lid. When the butter stops sizzling, stir the minced onion in the butter for a minute. Then add the rice; continue stirring the rice without coloring it (about 5 minutes).

4. Pour 2½ cups boiling water over the rice. Stir the rice; add 1½ teaspoons salt and freshly ground pepper. Bring the rice to a boil. Cover tightly. Reduce the heat to low and let cook for 20 minutes.

5. Reheat when needed in a water bath (a skillet filled one-third of the way up with water). Taste and correct seasonings with more salt and freshly ground pepper. Then add the remaining 4 tablespoons butter, fluffing the rice with the tines of a fork.

Roasted Whole Veal Shanks

Osso Bucco has become such a familiar dish in the United States that cooking veal shanks in a different fashion is almost unheard of. Yet, one very cold day, I ate roasted whole veal shanks at the home of a friend whose mother, Mrs. Maria Feldmeier, had come on a vacation from Germany. The shanks were delicious, moist and tender. They are roasted whole, then sliced.

It is prudent to order the hind shanks several days ahead of time, especially in supermarkets where only the better-known cuts of meats are on display.

The shanks should be 6″ long and weigh around 2¼ pounds each. There are lighter and heavier shanks, depending on the grade of the veal. I do not worry too much about the different timing for the roasting. Still, if they are less than 2 pounds each, roast for 1¼ hours, and if they are over 3 pounds, roast for 2 hours.

Special instruction. Present the roasted shanks whole on a bed of watercress to your guests or family. Then carve them into thin slices, holding the marrow bone straight up, slicing off the meat parallel to the bone. There is much more meat than it looks when the shanks are whole. Three shanks are more than enough for 8 people, but the leftover meat is delicious cold. Cut up in cubes and mixed with raw spinach, seasoned with a vinaigrette, it makes a lovely lunch or a light supper-salad.

Special kitchen utensils. Use 2 cast-iron skillets, 9″ and 12″, and an open roasting pan about 12″ x 16″ x 1½″.

SERVES 8

4 tablespoons butter and 2 tablespoons oil, or 6 tablespoons chicken fat (see page 20)	About ½ cup ¼″ bread cubes
	1 cup white wine
	About 1 teaspoon salt
3 veal hind shanks, about 2¼ pounds each	Freshly ground black pepper
	½ lemon, cut in wedges
2 medium-size yellow onions, thinly sliced	About 2–3 cups water to baste
	Watercress for decoration

1. Heat 2 tablespoons butter with 1 tablespoon oil (or use 3 tablespoons chicken fat) in each of two cast-iron skillets over medium heat until hot but not smoking. Brown 2 shanks in the 12″ skillet, and the third shank in the 9″ skillet. Brown on all sides evenly. Be sure to regulate the heat so that nothing burns. It will take about 20 minutes. Transfer the browned shanks to the roasting pan.

2. Add the onions and bread cubes to the skillets and sauté (tossing and stirring) for 5 minutes, until the bread and onions are lightly browned. Transfer the bread and the onions to the roasting pan around the shanks. Be careful that the onion slices are not on the meat, or they will burn.

3. Pour ½ cup white wine in each skillet over high heat and scrape (deglaze) the sides and bottom of the skillets until the wine boils for 30 seconds. Pour over the onions and bread.

Preheat oven to 400°F.

4. Sprinkle ½ teaspoon salt over the meat. Grind pepper twice over each shank. Add wedges of lemon. Place the roasting pan on the middle shelf of the 400°F. preheated oven.

5. Baste with the pan liquids about every 15 minutes for 1 hour. Then pour about ⅓ cup water as needed over the onions, adding only enough water to keep about a cup of liquid in the pan. Turn the shanks on their side every 30 minutes to roast evenly. The shanks will cook in 1½–2 hours.

6. *Presentation and carving.* Decorate a cutting board with watercress and transfer the shanks to the bed of watercress. Heat the liquids (including the onions and bread) in the roasting pan over high heat. Judge by sight if there is about a cup of liquid. If not, add ½ cup water and scrape (deglaze) the sides and bottom to dislodge any caramelized drippings. Bring to a boil. Taste and correct seasonings with salt and pepper. Serve in a preheated sauceboat.

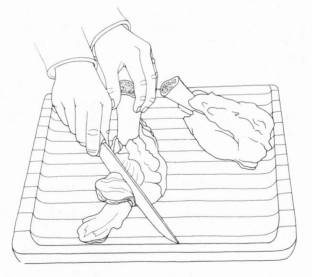

7. Present the shanks first on the bed of watercress. Then, holding the bone straight up, carve the meat parallel to the bone into slices. Scoop out the marrow from the bones.

8. *Presentation on individual plate.* Overlap 2 slices of meat in the center of the plate. Add a piece of marrow on top. Ladle 1 tablespoon of sauce over the meat and serve with Broccoli Purée, page 34.

Braised Veal Shanks with Paprika

Special kitchen utensil. A 6½-quart roaster with a lid (a Dutch oven) is a perfect pot in which to braise the shanks.

SERVES 6–8

5 tablespoons butter	½ cup dry white wine
1 tablespoon olive oil	2 teaspoons sweet paprika
8 pieces of veal shanks cut into	2 teaspoons salt
2″–3″ thickness as for osso bucco	Freshly ground black pepper
20 small white onions	1 cup heavy cream
3 tablespoons flour	2 cloves garlic, minced
1½ cups water	⅓ cup minced fresh parsley

1. Heat 2½ tablespoons butter and ½ tablespoon olive oil in each of two 9″ cast-iron skillets. When the fats are hot but not burning, brown the veal pieces, turning them a few times, until golden brown over medium heat. It takes about 30 minutes—do not burn.

2. Remove the meat from one skillet to a platter, and brown the onions in the fat of this skillet for 10 minutes at medium heat. Remove to a plate and reserve.

3. Transfer the meat back to the skillets. Sprinkle 1½ tablespoons of flour in each skillet, turning the meat to coat evenly. Over a medium flame, stir the meat, scrape the bottom for 1 minute, then add ¾ cup of water in each skillet, scraping the bottom all the while. Then add ¼ cup of dry white wine to each skillet. Bring to a boil. Transfer the meat to a heavy 6½-quart pot with a lid, sprinkle the paprika over the meat, and add 2 teaspoons salt and freshly ground pepper. Add the onions and the liquids in the skillets. Then cover and braise for 1½ hours at least, turning the meat once over so the top pieces go to the bottom to cover them with liquids.

4. Mix the minced garlic and parsley together. Reserve. Boil down 1 cup cream in a 9″ heavy-bottomed skillet to half its original volume. (Notice that I use a low-sided and wide-surface pan to reduce the cream. The cream reduces much faster than in a small, high-edged pan.) Remove the meat and onions to a preheated platter. Degrease the liquids. Cook for about 10 minutes over a low to medium flame to reduce the liquids to 2 cups. Then whisk in the reduced cream. Add the meat and onions and half the mixed parsley and garlic. Cover and reheat for 5 minutes.

5. Serve with buttered pasta or rice pilaf. Sprinkle the remaining parsley and garlic over the meat and rice.

6. *For an elegant presentation on individual plates.* Coil strands of cooked green pasta in the center of the plate and nest the meat in the center of the pasta.

Chocolate Sunflower

This is essentially a chocolate fudge cake served with a light custard for children and chocoholics. The fudge cake is put in the middle of a platter and the custard poured around the outside, hence the name.

Special instructions. It is essential you buy a good quality chocolate such as Lindt or Tobler. Any gourmet store has Tobler or Lindt chocolate, but if you cannot find it where you live, order from Maison Glass, 52 East 58th Street, New York, NY 10022.

Special kitchen utensil. Bake the chocolate cake in an 8″ round layer cake pan.

SERVES 8

Pastry Cream, page 44	2 large eggs
1 tablespoon Frangelico liqueur or brandy	½ cup chopped pecans
	⅔ cup superfine sugar
4½ ounces bittersweet chocolate (Lindt or Tobler)	1 tablespoon flour
	1 tablespoon butter to grease
4½ ounces sweet butter	cake pan

1. Prepare a batch of Pastry Cream. Add 1 tablespoon of Frangelico (a hazelnut-flavored after-dinner drink) or brandy.

2. Melt the chocolate in a pan set in a water bath (improvise a water bath with a low-sided pan such as a skillet one-third full of water) or double boiler uncovered. Be sure no moisture gets into the chocolate, otherwise it will "tighten," meaning "grainy." If so, smooth it out with 2 teaspoons shortening (Crisco). Allow it to cool to just above skin temperature. Test the temperature of the melted chocolate as follows: Dip your finger into the chocolate and touch it to your lower lip—if it feels warm, the chocolate is too warm to mix with the butter.

3. Knead the butter with the palm of your hand until smooth.

4. In a heavy mixer at medium speed, beat eggs and sugar until thick and foamy (about 8 minutes).

5. When the chocolate has cooled, whisk it into the butter. (The butter-

chocolate must be thick, not runny. If it is runny, refrigerate until cold, then beat the mixture to aerate it.)

6. Beat the chocolate and butter mixture into the eggs and sugar, tablespoon by tablespoon.

7. Fold in ½ cup chopped pecans, then sift 1 tablespoon flour on top of the batter and fold in by hand, using a rubber spatula.

   Preheat oven to 350°F.

8. Butter an 8″ round cake pan and line the bottom with buttered waxed paper (cut exactly to fit the bottom of the pan. Pour the batter into the mold and cover with buttered waxed paper, cut exactly to fit the top of the cake to keep it from drying out and place in a hot water bath about half as deep as the cake pan. Bake 1 hour at 350°F.

9. Remove pan from water bath. Remove the waxed paper and slide a knife around the edge of the pan to loosen the cake. Invert onto a serving platter with a large enough rim to accommodate the Pastry Cream and allow it to cool. Do not try to remove the mold at this point; wait until the cake is cool. Then unmold—the cake will be quite flat. Remove the waxed paper. The cake can be prepared in the morning of the dinner. If it is refrigerated, bring it back to room temperature (about 2 hours) before eating it.

10. Pour the Pastry Cream around the cake and serve.

Pastry Cream

This pastry cream (crème patissière) is not for fillings—the consistency is too loose. Serve over a chocolate or rum cake, or serve in parfait glasses with fresh fruits over it, or serve it as is, in glasses, to be drunk like an eggnog. Before making the pastry cream, assemble and measure all the ingredients so you have them at hand. When you do so, it does not take more than 15 minutes to prepare.

Special kitchen utensil. A 1½-quart saucepan.

SERVES 6–8

2 tablespoons cornstarch	3 cups milk
2 tablespoons flour	3 tablespoons butter
½ cup sugar	2 tablespoons liqueur
3 egg yolks	

1. Sift the cornstarch and flour into a 3-quart mixing bowl. Mix in the sugar. Reserve next to the stove.

2. Break 3 egg yolks in a bowl and beat lightly. Reserve next to the stove.

3. In a 1½-quart heavy-bottomed saucepan, bring 3 cups of milk to a *rolling* boil over medium heat.

4. Quickly pour half the boiling milk over the sugar, flour, and cornstarch. Whisk vigorously. Whisk in the beaten egg yolks.

5. Bring the other half of the milk back to a rolling boil, then pour into the custard mixture. Whisk over medium heat until the custard thickens. It binds within 10 seconds.

6. Remove from the heat, but continue whisking for a while to cool the custard. Transfer it to a mixing bowl to cool for 15 minutes. Meanwhile, cream 3 tablespoons butter with the heel of your hand. Start whisking 1 tablespoon of butter at a time into the custard. Whisk in 2 tablespoons liqueur of your choice. Cover with plastic wrap. Refrigerate overnight if you wish. Whisk again before serving.

TECHNIQUES AND UTENSILS INTRODUCED

How to make cream puff dough

How to fill a pastry bag and use it to shape puffs

How to make a mayonnaise by hand with a whisk
and with an electric mixer

How to remedy a curdled mayonnaise

How to braise meat for slow oven cooking: how to
seal a pot, how to use a clay pot

How to bind a sauce with a flour and butter paste

How to prepare apples properly for baking

Lesson 3

RECIPES

Cream Puff Dough

Cheese Puffs

Crudités:
    Celery Root Rémoulade
    Grated Carrots in a Vinaigrette
    Grated Red Cabbage in a Vinaigrette

Grated Carrots and Tuna Salad

Braised Spareribs with Winter Vegetables

Braised Fresh Pork Picnic Shoulder "Hollandaise"

Braised Beef with Vegetables

Braised Curried Veal Shoulder

Braised Chicken with Vegetables

Caramel Custard

Baked Apples on Toast

Apple Gratin

Suggested Menus for Lesson 3

3-Course Menu

Cheese Puffs

Braised Spareribs with Winter Vegetables
or
Braised Chicken with Vegetables
or
Braised Fresh Pork Picnic Shoulder
"Hollandaise"
or
Oven-Braised Beef with Vegetables

Baked Apples on Toast with
Cream-Cheese Topping (Lesson 1)

4-Course Menu

Cheese Puffs

Crudités:
Celery Root, Red Cabbage, Carrots

Braised Curried Veal Shoulder

Rice Pilaf (Lesson 2)

Caramel Custard

A Winter Lunch

Crudités:
Celery Root, Red Cabbage, Carrots

Caramel Custard

A Summer Lunch

Grated Carrots and Tuna Salad

Strawberries with Cream-Cheese Topping
(Lesson 1)

For a Lunchbox

Cold Beef Sandwich

Cream Puff Dough

Baked, poached, and deep-fried, cream puff dough is the base of hors d'oeuvre, potato puffs, cream puffs, éclairs, etc. It is certainly the quickest dough to prepare and to bake. You need a good strong arm to beat the dough to incorporate as much air as possible for the lightest puffs. A heavy-duty electric mixer, such as the Kitchen Aid mixer with the flat paddle, will be a good substitute for a weak arm.

Special kitchen utensil. A 3-quart pan.

MAKES 40 PUFFS

4 large eggs
1 cup plus 2 tablespoons water
½ teaspoon salt

7 tablespoons sweet butter
1 cup plus 1½ tablespoons flour

1. Break 4 eggs and mix in a glass measuring cup. It is important to have 1 cup of eggs; sometimes the eggs are not of the same size in the same box. If you need a bit more egg, break 1 extra egg, mix it, and use whatever is needed; then reserve the extra for the glaze.

2. Combine water, salt, and butter cut up in small pieces (to melt faster) in a 3-quart pan and bring to a boil slowly until the butter is melted.

3. Quickly, remove the pan from the heat and add all the flour at once; beat vigorously with a sturdy wooden spoon for a smooth dough, then reheat 1 minute over medium heat, stirring all the time. Remove from heat.

4. *Hand method.* Quickly add ½ cup eggs to the batter and beat it with as much strength as you can achieve until the dough is very smooth before adding ¼ cup eggs, again beating the eggs to incorporate into the dough. Then repeat with the last of the eggs. Now the dough should be just sticky enough to adhere to the wooden spatula and gradually drip back toward the pan. Beat the dough for 2 minutes against the sides of the pan to incorporate as much air as possible.

Electric mixer method. Quickly transfer the dough to the bowl of a heavy-duty mixer, add ½ cup beaten eggs and beat at medium speed until the eggs are incorporated into the dough. Beat in the remaining ½ cup eggs and continue beating until the dough is very smooth.

5. To shape: Follow the directions in the recipes.

Note on humidity. If you live in a dry-weather state, you might need half an egg to a whole egg extra. Break the egg, mix it, then add it to the dough until the dough is of the right consistency.

Cheese Puffs

L'Explorateur, Brillat-Savarin, and St. André are triple-crème cheeses, which are great American favorites. Along with blue cheese, Brie, and Camembert (but not Roquefort—it is too salty), all these cheeses mixed with butter and cream make lovely fillings for puffs, served with drinks.

Special kitchen utensil. Two 14″ x 17″ cookie sheets.

MAKES 40 PUFFS

Cream Puff Dough, page 49	*Filling*
Egg glaze	½ pound cheese
	3–7 tablespoons sweet butter
1 egg yolk	1–3 tablespoons heavy cream
1 tablespoon water	

1. Prepare the Cream Puff Dough recipe, page 49.

2. Grease 2 cookie sheets and dust them with flour. (a) Fit a ½″ tube into a large pastry bag, twist the bag over the top of the tube, and (b) push the twisted part of the bag inside the tube to prevent the dough from slipping out of the tube while filling the bag. (c) Fill the bag with half the dough. Untwist the bag. Push the dough down to the tube, closing the top of the pastry bag by twisting it. Squeeze from the top of the bag with one hand while holding the bag with the other hand perpendicular to and 1″ away from the cookie sheet. (d) Cut off every 1½ inches to make each puff, allowing room between them for expansion. Dip a fork in cold water and with the back of the fork gently flatten the top of each puff. Combine the egg yolk and water, and brush this glaze on the puffs.

Preheat oven to 400°F.

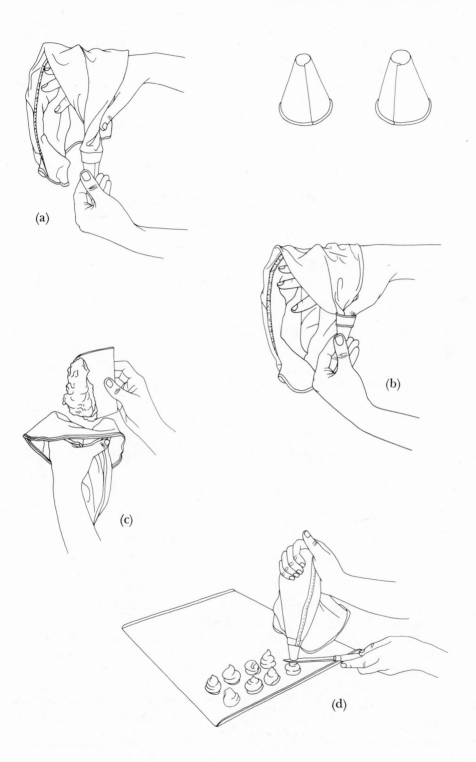

(a)

(b)

(c)

(d)

3. Bake in the middle shelf of the oven for about 20–25 minutes. Remove one puff from the oven and slice it open to check the inside. It should be a little moist, not completely dried out.

4. Remove puffs from the oven. Cool slightly, then cut a hole in each puff to fill with the cheese filling.

Note. You may freeze the puffs in aluminum foil if you are making them several days ahead of time.

5. Discard the rind of the cheese. Place the cheese in the bowl of the processor fitted with the metal blade. Add 3 tablespoons butter and 1 tablespoon cream and process for 1 minute. Check the consistency of the cheese; it must not be too stiff or too runny in order to fill the puffs. Add more butter and cream according to the thickness of the cheese filling.

6. For the blue cheese, add all 7 tablespoons butter and 3 tablespoons cream.

7. Using the same technique as for the shaping of the puffs, fill a pastry bag fitted with a tube to fill the puffs. Fill the puffs an hour before dinner.

Note. Heat frozen baked puffs for 5 minutes or so in a 400°F. preheated oven.

Crudités:

Celery Root Rémoulade
Grated Carrots in a Vinaigrette
Grated Red Cabbage in a Vinaigrette

The French counterpart of American coleslaw, these crudités (meaning raw vegetables) can be served separately or together. Together celery root, carrots, and red cabbage make a particularly beautiful presentation with their colors—orange, purple, and ivory. Served with crusty country bread and a dry white wine, you can make a whole lunch with them.

I serve these three vegetables together in the autumn and winter because celery root is available only then. In the summer, I serve the carrots mixed with tuna fish, capers, and olives.

The crudités should be prepared ahead of time, so their flavor will mingle with the vinaigrette sauce, in the case of the carrots and red cabbage, and with the rémoulade (a flavored mayonnaise) for the celery root. The seasoning and the color combination are of prime importance.

Special kitchen utensil. Shredding in the food processor takes no time at all, but when I have the time I cut the cabbage with a knife to get very fine shreds and I use a mouli-julienne for the celery root and carrots for a more even, firm cut.

SERVES 6

1 pound celery root	1 pound red cabbage
1 teaspoon lemon juice	1 cup vinaigrette, page 11
1 pound carrots	⅔ cup rémoulade

1. Peel the celery root, quarter it, and shred in a food processor (julienne blade) or mouli-julienne (blade number 2). Toss shredded celery root with 1 teaspoon lemon juice to prevent discoloration. Makes about 4 cups. Peel the carrots and shred in a food processor (julienne blade) or mouli-julienne (blade number 3). Makes about 4 cups. Discard the outer dark leaves of the cabbage (a whole cabbage is generally bigger than 1 pound). Sometimes it is possible to buy just what you need; otherwise, wrap the extra cabbage in plastic wrap. It keeps well in the refrigerator. Using a stainless steel knife, cut the cabbage into 2" thick wedges (be sure to use a stainless steel knife; a carbon steel blade will darken the cabbage). Shred the cabbage in the food processor or with a knife. Keep the shredded vegetables in separate mixing bowls.

2. Prepare the vinaigrette as directed, page 11, doubling the recipe. Pour half the vinaigrette over the carrots and half over the red cabbage and mix very well. Taste to correct seasoning with salt and pepper. The red cabbage needs more salt in general, perhaps ½ teaspoon more. Cover with plastic wrap and refrigerate.

3. The rémoulade is a mayonnaise with mustard, capers, small tart gherkins (cornichons), minced fresh parsley, fresh chervil, and fresh tarragon. I use only parsley if fresh chervil and fresh tarragon are not available. If cornichons are not available, omit them. Do not substitute sweet gherkins.

Rémoulade (mayonnaise with herbs)

MAKES ⅔ CUP

⅔ cup oil (⅓ cup vegetable oil, ⅓ cup olive oil)	1 tablespoon minced fresh parsley or a mixture of minced fresh parsley, fresh chervil, and fresh tarragon
1 egg yolk	
1 teaspoon Dijon-type prepared mustard	
1 tablespoon minced capers	½ tablespoon minced gherkins (cornichons)
1 teaspoon vinegar from the capers	½ teaspoon salt
	Freshly ground black pepper

1. *Making the mayonnaise by hand.* The egg yolk and the oil must be at room temperature to emulsify. Pour almost boiling water in a 2-cup mixing bowl (a cereal bowl is perfect) and let stand for 5 minutes. (The warm bowl will help to thicken the mayonnaise.) Drain and wipe dry. Wet a potholder and place it under the bowl to keep the bowl from moving and to have both hands free so you can whisk with one hand and pour with the other. I prefer a hand whisk, but an electric hand beater is fine as long as you beat slowly. Measure ⅔ cup oil in a glass measuring cup with a spout. Put the egg yolk in the bowl and beat it with the whisk for 10 seconds. Dribble in the oil, drop by drop, while whisking constantly. Once the egg yolk and oil start to thicken, you can add oil faster. If the mayonnaise does not thicken after using ¼ cup oil, reserve it. Start over with another egg yolk in a warm bowl and gradually dribble the "failed" mayonnaise into the egg yolk; then continue with the rest of the oil.

   Using an electric beater. Warm the bowl by pouring boiling water in it. Drain, wipe dry, and proceed as in the hand method, beating at medium speed.

2. *To turn the finished mayonnaise into a rémoulade.* Mix in 1 teaspoon mustard, 1 tablespoon minced capers, 1 teaspoon vinegar from the capers, 1 tablespoon minced fresh parsley or a mixture of parsley, chervil, and tarragon, ½ tablespoon minced gherkins (cornichons), ½ teaspoon salt, and freshly ground pepper.

   Mix the rémoulade and the celery root together. Taste to correct seasoning with salt. Cover. Refrigerate.

The presentation

One hour before serving, remove the crudités from the refrigerator. Toss each salad to fluff it up. Then decorate a round platter, about 12″ in diameter, with the celery root in the center, then the carrots around the celery root, and finish with the red cabbage.

Optional. Decorate with small black olives. Eat the salad with country bread, smeared with butter.

Grated Carrots and Tuna Salad

In the summer, grated carrots with tuna fish, capers, and black olives make a substantial meal. Eaten with homemade bread and accompanied by lots of dry white wine, the salad of grated carrots becomes a feast.

SERVES 4

1 pound carrots, grated
6½-ounce can of chunk tuna,
    oil or water packed, drained
1 tablespoon capers

½ cup vinaigrette, page 11
Lettuce
2 hard-boiled eggs
About a dozen small black olives

Mix together the grated carrots, tuna, capers, and vinaigrette. Serve on lettuce and garnish with hard-boiled eggs and olives.

Braised Spareribs with Winter Vegetables

There are times when the cooking utensil is of prime importance for the success of a dish. Such a dish is this one. It is a hearty, succulent concoction of my Aunt Tatane, and very simple to prepare. Spareribs are broiled, then baked in layers with the usual winter vegetables: potatoes, carrots, onions, and white turnips. The juices and fats of the ribs seep through the vegetables, flavoring them. At the end of the slow-oven cooking in a covered Dutch oven, the vegetables are moist and intact and the ribs are golden brown.

My aunt uses a 2-quart Pyrex dish with a lid, but to make it in quantity, say for 6 people, you need a much larger pan. Cast-iron Dutch ovens (cocottes) like Le Creuset are perfect, but the lids need to be sealed; otherwise, the vegetables will dry out and burn. In France, to seal a cooking utensil, we make a paste of flour and water, then coat a strip of cloth (using discarded sheets) with the paste. It might seem strange to you, but this technique is used for most slow cooking in the oven. The paste bakes into a hard shell and prevents quick evaporation. An American friend calls it "The Rag-Dish Spareribs" and loves it.

Experiment with whatever pan you own, remembering that the end result must have vegetables and meat moist and full of flavor.

Special kitchen utensils. A 6½-quart Dutch oven.

SERVES 4–6

5 pounds spareribs*	3 medium-size white turnips
⅔ cup water	2 cloves garlic
3 medium-size carrots	2 teaspoons salt
3 medium-size yellow onions	Freshly ground black pepper
1½ pounds medium-size	1 tablespoon butter
Russet potatoes	½ cup water and ½ cup flour
	to seal the Dutch oven

* I like to use country spareribs when they are available, remembering that they must not be too lean; otherwise, the vegetables will taste bland.

1. Have the ribs cut in pairs, or do it yourself. Broil them in two batches, if necessary, 4″ below the broiler for 10 minutes on one side. Turn and broil on the other side for 5 minutes or until brown. Reserve. Discard the fat in the broiler pan. Over high heat, pour in ⅔ cup water and scrape (deglaze) the pan with a wooden spoon. Bring to a boil and reserve.

2. Peel the vegetables. You need 8 cups of vegetables. Cut the carrots into ½″ slices (about 1½ cups). The onions, potatoes, and turnips are cut in ½″ cubes: cut them in half lengthwise, then with each half flat side on the counter, slice lengthwise in 3 even strips, then cut crosswise into ½″ cubes for approximately 2 cups of onions, 2½ cups of potatoes, and 1½ cups of turnips. Peel and quarter the garlic cloves. Toss the vegetables in a 4-quart mixing bowl with 1 teaspoon salt and freshly ground pepper. Use your hands to mix them thoroughly with the seasonings.

Technique: To seal a pot

Cut a strip of cloth about 3 feet long and 2 inches wide. Mix ½ cup flour with a little more than ½ cup water. Dunk the strip of cloth in the flour paste and then with your fingers smear the paste on both sides of the cloth. (It's child's play and real messy.) Then, seal the lid and pot together. Be sure it is sealed around the handles.

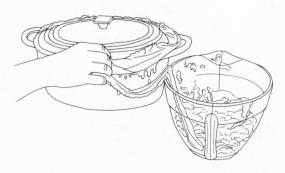

3. Grease a 6½-quart cast-iron Dutch oven with 1 tablespoon butter. Spread half the vegetables at the bottom of the pan, then a layer of spareribs. Season with ½ teaspoon salt and freshly ground pepper. Cover them with the rest of the vegetables and finish with a layer of spareribs. Sprinkle with ½ teaspoon salt and freshly ground pepper. Cover and seal.

Preheat oven to 400°F.

4. Bake on the middle rack of the oven for 2 hours—the first 30 minutes at 400°F., then drop the temperature to 300°F. and continue baking for 1½ hours.

5. Break the seal off with a pair of scissors. Remove the lid, holding it toward you, letting the steam escape away from you. Serve as is.

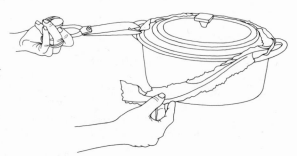

Braised Beef with Vegetables

This French-style pot roast is prepared in the same manner as the preceding Spareribs with Winter Vegetables. A 6½-quart Dutch oven (a cocotte) is perfect. The best cuts of beef for braising are bottom round and beef neck. I prefer them to brisket because they have more flavor.

Special kitchen utensil. A 6½-quart Dutch oven.

SERVES 4–6

2 tablespoons butter
1 tablespoon oil
3 pounds bottom round or
  beef neck
1 cup water
5 medium-size carrots
3 medium-size onions
5 medium-size Russet
  potatoes
8 cloves garlic, *unpeeled*
  (optional)
About 5 sprigs parsley

1 bay leaf
Pinch of thyme
2 teaspoons salt
Freshly ground black pepper
½ cup water and ½ cup flour to
  seal the Dutch oven
1 bunch watercress

For the binding of the sauce

1 tablespoon flour
1 tablespoon butter, at room
  temperature

1. Heat 2 tablespoons butter and 1 tablespoon oil in a 9″ cast-iron skillet. When the skillet is quite hot, add the meat and sear it on all sides.

2. Remove the meat and transfer it to a 6½-quart Dutch oven (cocotte) and add 1 cup water to the skillet. Bring the water to a boil, scraping all the while for 1 minute, then pour over the meat.

3. Peel the carrots and cut them into ½″ pieces. Peel the onions and potatoes, then cut in ½″ cubes (to make 8 cups) and add them to the cocotte. Add the garlic (if you wish), parsley, bay leaf, thyme, salt, and pepper.

4. Cover the Dutch oven and seal it according to the instructions on page 56.

    Preheat oven to 325°F.

5. Bake at 325°F. for 2½ hours.

6. Prepare a binding (flour and butter paste) to thicken the sauce: Mix 1 tablespoon flour with 1 tablespoon butter at room temperature. Mash the butter and flour together with a fork and work them into a smooth paste. Reserve.

7. When the meat is done, break the seal off with a pair of scissors and remove the lid, holding it toward you, letting the steam escape away from you. Remove the meat and vegetables and reserve on a hot serving platter. Bring the liquids to a *rolling boil.* Over high heat, whisk in the flour and butter paste until the sauce thickens slightly. This takes about 1 minute.

8. Slice the meat into very thin slices, surround with the vegetables and garlic cloves, and garnish with watercress. Serve the sauce in a heated sauceboat.

9. Mash the garlic (the peel will slip off easily) and spread it over the bread like butter.

For a cold beef sandwich. This leftover beef makes the best sandwiches. Spread mustard or horseradish on slices of bread; add slices of meat, a salad green leaf, and 1–2 tablespoons of vinaigrette.

Braised Curried Veal Shoulder

The veal is braised slowly in the oven without any liquid other than the juices from the braising vegetables: carrots, onion, and celery with 4 tablespoons butter. Sealing the pot with a flour and water paste keeps the veal moist and renders enough natural juices to keep the roast from drying out. The curry enhances the flavor of the veal, but it does not overpower it.

Special kitchen utensil. A 6½-quart Dutch oven.

SERVES 6

For the garnish

1 pound baby carrots
1 medium-size onion
1 celery rib
1 teaspoon salt
¼ teaspoon freshly ground black pepper
1 teaspoon dried tarragon, or 1 tablespoon fresh tarragon
4 tablespoons butter

For the roast

3 pounds center cut of veal shoulder, wrapped with beef fat
2 teaspoons curry powder
6 tablespoons butter
1 tablespoon vegetable oil
1 bay leaf
1 teaspoon thyme
Several sprigs of parsley
½ teaspoon salt
Freshly ground black pepper
½ cup flour, ½ cup water to seal the Dutch oven

1. First prepare the vegetable garnish: Peel the carrots and slice the onion and celery into 2″ cubes. Place all the vegetables along with the salt, pepper, and tarragon in a 6½-quart Dutch oven with 4 tablespoons butter. Braise, covered, over low heat for 30 minutes. Meanwhile:

2. Coat the roast with 2 teaspoons curry powder, rubbing it well into the surface with your fingers.

3. In a 12″ cast-iron skillet, heat 2 tablespoons butter and 1 tablespoon vegetable oil until hot but not smoking, and brown the roast all over for about 10 minutes.

Preheat oven to 325°F.

4. Put the roast into the Dutch oven with the vegetables; add the bay leaf, thyme, and parsley. Sprinkle ½ teaspoon salt over the roast, and freshly ground black pepper. Cover the Dutch oven and seal it, see page 56. Bake at 325°F. for 1½ hours.

5. Remove the roast and vegetables and reserve. Degrease the liquids in the pot and discard the fats.

6. Cut off the strings from the roast and remove the fat; then carve the roast into 1/8″ thick slices. It will still be pink. Don't worry because the meat will change color immediately after cutting. Gather the juices that drain out of the roast. Add to the juices in the pot.

7. Bring the juices to a boil and reduce to about 1/2 cup, stirring constantly. Turn off the heat and whisk in 4 tablespoons butter, 1 tablespoon at a time. Overlap the meat on a preheated platter, and garnish with the vegetables. Pour some of the sauce over it, and pour the rest of the sauce into a preheated sauceboat.

Note. For a richer sauce over the veal, see Curry Sauce, page 126.

Braised Fresh Pork Picnic Shoulder "Hollandaise"

The "Hollandaise" in the name has nothing to do with the Netherlands, nor the sauce. I made up this dish one evening for an actress friend, Holland Taylor, following the technique of oven-braised beef pot roast. Serve this with a tossed green salad and bread.

Special kitchen utensil. A 6½-quart Dutch oven.

SERVES 4

8 big cloves garlic	3 pounds fresh pork shoulder
5 tablespoons olive oil	picnic
4 Russet potatoes	2 teaspoons salt
2 yellow onions	Pinch of dried thyme
3 Winesap or McIntosh apples	Freshly ground black pepper
3 turnips	½ cup water and ½ cup flour
4 tomatoes	to seal the Dutch oven

1. Boil the unpeeled garlic cloves for 15 minutes in 2 quarts of water to soften them. Drain.

2. Use a 6½-quart pot with a lid (clay or cast iron). Put in 5 tablespoons olive oil. Peel the potatoes and cut into 1″ cubes. Peel onions, apples, and turnips and quarter them. Quarter and seed the tomatoes. Add the parboiled cloves of garlic. Mix everything well with the olive oil in the pot.

Preheat oven to 325°F.

3. Bury the meat in the vegetables. Sprinkle the salt, thyme, and freshly ground pepper over everything. Mix well with hands to disperse spices and salt. Cover tightly. Seal, following the illustrated directions, page 56. Bake at 325°F. for 2 hours.

4. Serve on a platter with the pan juices. Each guest peels the garlic cloves and spreads them on bread with butter.

Braised Chicken with Vegetables

This easy recipe is one I use for unexpected guests; it requires very little preparation and no watching-over during cooking. It's a standard recipe in the southwestern part of the Rhône Valley. For best results, do as the people there do, and use a covered clay pot (like the Römertopf) in place of metal or Pyrex. It can also be done in a 6½-quart cast-iron Dutch oven (cocotte) or in a club-aluminum roaster, with a tight-fitting lid. In the clay or cast-iron pan, the chicken will lightly brown, whereas in a stainless steel or Pyrex dish, the chicken will stew. The best result is a cross between stewing and roasting. Serve this chicken with country bread and a green salad.

Special instruction. You can prepare the chicken through step 4 ahead of time if you wish and cook it when needed.

Special kitchen utensil. A 6½-quart Dutch oven or a clay pot (soak the clay pot in cold water for 30 minutes before using it).

SERVES 4

6 medium-size Russet potatoes, peeled and quartered	4 cloves garlic, peeled and chopped coarsely
3 medium-size carrots, peeled and sliced 1″ thick	2 teaspoons salt
3 yellow onions, peeled and quartered	Freshly ground black pepper
	½ teaspoon dried thyme
Several tablespoons olive oil	3-pound roasting chicken
	Several sprigs of parsley
	1 small bay leaf

1. Wash the peeled and quartered potatoes and drain for a few minutes, then use your hands to mix all the vegetables, 2 tablespoons olive oil, and garlic together in a large bowl with 1½ teaspoons salt, a few twists of the pepper mill, and ½ teaspoon thyme. Reserve.

2. Remove the fat from the cavity of the chicken, cut it into small cubes, and mix it with the vegetables. (If there is no fat, add 1 more tablespoon olive oil to the vegetables instead.)

3. Sprinkle the cavity of the chicken with ½ teaspoon salt and freshly ground pepper. Add the parsley and the bay leaf.

4. Grease the clay pot or the Dutch oven with 1 tablespoon olive oil. Put the chicken in it, and surround it with the vegetables. Dribble 1 more tablespoon olive oil over the chicken. Cover. (Can be prepared up to this point ahead of time.)

   Preheat oven to 325°–350°F.

5. Cook the chicken on the middle shelf of the oven for 1½ hours without basting it. If using an aluminum, stainless steel, or Pyrex roaster, remove the lid about 20 minutes before the end of cooking and raise the oven temperature to 400°F. to lightly brown the chicken.

6. Transfer the chicken to a wooden platter with a juice-catcher. Scoop out the vegetables with a perforated spoon onto a preheated platter. There will be fat remaining in the pan. Pour it into a preheated bowl. The chicken should be very juicy. After carving, transfer the juices from the chicken over the vegetables. Serve the fat in a bowl—it is very good along with coarse salt, which I always pass, too. Each guest can spoon a bit of fat over the chicken if he or she pleases and sprinkle coarse salt over the chicken.

Caramel Custard

When I was a child, caramel custard was my favorite dessert. It was a feast for me. I grew up during World War II when eggs and milk were very scarce. It is the kind of recipe that has many variations. The classic recipe uses both whole eggs and additional egg yolks. I like my aunt's version, which is to use only whole eggs. With additional caramel poured over the unmolded baked custard which hardens as it cools, it resembles crème brulée.

Special instruction. The baking and the unmolding are the tricky steps in this recipe. The custard should cook enough so that it will unmold and not collapse, and it should not overcook; otherwise, the custard will be full of holes. Be sure your oven thermostat works correctly. The timing I give (30–35 minutes) is for an oven with the door closed during the baking. Every time the oven door is opened, heat is lost and this should be considered in the timing.

Special kitchen utensil. A 4-cup ring mold.

Caramel for the mold

½ cup superfine sugar
4 tablespoons water

Caramel for a crunchy glaze like crème brulée

⅓ cup superfine sugar
1 tablespoon water

The custard

3 cups milk
⅔ cup sugar
¼ teaspoon vanilla extract or
  2 tablespoons coffee liqueur
1½ cups eggs (6–7 large eggs)

1. *Prepare the caramel.* In a heavy-bottomed saucepan over medium heat, stir ½ cup sugar and 4 tablespoons water until the sugar is dissolved. Stop stirring. Cook the syrup for about 5–10 minutes until it colors to an amber shade. Using potholders, tip the mold or pan to even out the color. (It generally starts to color where it is cooking the fastest on one side.) Pour the caramel in the mold and quickly swirl the caramel all around the sides and bottom of the mold. Reserve mold right side up (see Special Instruction, page 25).

2. *Prepare the custard.* Bring the milk to a boil, then quickly whisk in the sugar and keep cooking until the sugar is dissolved (1 minute). Turn off the heat. Add ¼ teaspoon vanilla extract or 2 tablespoons coffee liqueur. Cover and cool for 15 minutes.

3. Measure about 1½ cups eggs in a glass measuring cup. It is important to have the proper volume of eggs. Sometimes eggs are of different sizes even in the same box. Beat the eggs for 1 minute in a 3-quart mixing bowl and pour the milk over them, whisking constantly. Strain the eggs-milk mixture through a fine-mesh sieve into a bowl, then transfer to the prepared caramelized mold.

Preheat oven to 400°F.

4. Place the mold in a water bath (a cake pan is fine). Pour boiling water in the water bath until it reaches halfway up the sides of the ring mold.

5. Bake on the middle shelf of the oven for 30–35 minutes. If the top browns slightly during the cooking, cover loosely with foil. To test for doneness, plunge a knife in the center of the custard. It should come out clean.

6. Remove from the water bath. Cool at room temperature for 30 minutes, then turn the mold upside down on a serving dish and unmold. Refrigerate. Can be eaten as is or as a crème brulée.

7. Prepare a caramel just before serving with ⅓ cup sugar and 1 tablespoon water. Cook the syrup until it caramelizes to an amber color (about 10 minutes). Pour over the top of the custard. As it cools, the caramel quickly hardens. Crack the caramel on top with the point of a knife and serve. Do not refrigerate the custard after pouring the extra caramel over it; refrigeration will soften it.

Baked Apples on Toast

Every country with apples has its version of baked apples. This is my mother's recipe, which is the classic recipe in French cooking. I especially liked the bread under the apples. The bread used was stale and was transformed into a crunchy, buttery crouton with this dessert. Using up stale bread was, in fact, the excuse for making this dessert. The apples must not be big; otherwise, they take too long to cook and become mushy. The ideal apple size is 2″ in diameter. Use Jonathans or Macouns in October– November, Staymans in the winter, and very small Granny Smiths in the spring or summer. If you are unable to find small apples, peel medium-size apples and trim until they are 8″ big around and weigh about 3 ounces. Cook the trimmings with sugar for applesauce.

Special kitchen utensil. A 2-quart rectangular or oval baking dish.

SERVES 6

6 slices of bread	6 tablespoons sugar
1 tablespoon sweet butter for the baking dish	6 tablespoons sweet butter
6 apples, about 4 ounces each	Cream-Cheese Topping, page 27

1. Cut out a 3½″ circle in each slice of bread (use a cookie cutter or a glass for this). Dry the bread slices in the oven for 10 minutes at 325°F.

2. Butter a 2-quart baking dish.

3. Peel each apple. Core the center, using a melon-ball cutter. Core from the blossom end first and do not core through the apple. Place each apple on a slice of bread in the baking dish.

4. Stuff the center of each apple with 1 tablespoon sugar and place 1 tablespoon butter on top of each apple.

Preheat oven to 325°F.

5. Bake on the lower shelf in the oven for about 25–30 minutes. When the sugar and butter melt inside the apples, baste the apple (about 10 minutes), with the melted liquids every 3–4 minutes, using a bulb baster.

6. Serve warm with Cream-Cheese Topping.

Apple Gratin

This is the quickest apple dessert I know and I make it often, especially in October when the good Jonathan apples are in season.

Special kitchen utensil. A 1½-quart baking dish.

SERVES 4

4 apples (Jonathan, Cortland, Golden Delicious, or Granny Smith)	4 tablespoons sweet butter
	¼ cup sugar
	¼ cup heavy cream
1 teaspoon lemon juice	Cream-Cheese Topping, page 27

Preheat oven to 400°F.

1. Peel, core, and quarter the apples. Cut each quarter into ⅓″ slices and sprinkle 1 teaspoon lemon juice over them.

2. Butter generously a 1½-quart baking dish and lay overlapping slices of apples in the dish. Sprinkle with sugar and add the butter, cut into very thin slices.

3. Bake for ½ hour. Turn the oven to 500°F. Spread the cream over the apples and bake 5 minutes more or until the apples are slightly golden on top.

4. Serve hot as is or serve with Cream-Cheese Topping on the side.

TECHNIQUES AND UTENSILS INTRODUCED

How to make beef and chicken stocks

How to make onion soup, using ovenproof soup bowls

How to poach meat

How to steam vegetables in a collapsible
vegetable steamer

How to mash garlic in a mortar and pestle (or with
tines of a fork and the back of a knife)

How to make crêpes, using a 7″ steel omelet or crêpe pan
and how to flip them with a long, thin, steel spatula

How to make preserves and how to use
canning paraphernalia

Lesson 4

RECIPES

Beef Stock

Onion Soup

A Boiled Dinner of Vegetables and Meats (Pot-au-Feu)

Vinaigrette Sauce with Hard-Boiled Egg

Garlic Mayonnaise

Chicken Stock

Poached Stuffed Chicken

Leftover Beef Gratinéed

Crêpes with Fruit Preserves

Bitter Orange Preserves

Peach Preserves

Tomato Preserves with Crystallized Ginger

Plum Cake

Prune Cake

Suggested Menus for Lesson 4

3-Course Menus

Leek Salad

Poached Stuffed Chicken and Vegetables
served with Garlic Mayonnaise

Crêpes Sprinkled with Sugar

Onion Soup

Tossed Green Salad with Leftover Meats
(Lesson 1)

Prune Cake

Leftover Beef Gratinéed

Rice Pilaf (Lesson 2)

Caramel Custard (Lesson 3)

4-Course Menu

Onion Soup

A Boiled Dinner of Vegetables and Meats
(Pot au Feu)

Poached Stuffed Chicken

both served with
Vinaigrette Sauce with Herbs and Hard-Boiled Egg
and Garlic Mayonnaise

Crêpes with Preserves

Beef Stock

Good cooking needs homemade stocks. I prepare stocks in the evening, let the stock cook on the lowest simmer of an electric burner overnight, then, in the morning, I strain it, degrease it, and let it cool completely before refrigerating or freezing it. For the cook who has gas burners, it is advisable to start the stock in the morning and have it cook during the day. Be sure to order bones from the butcher ahead of time.

Special kitchen utensil. A 15-quart stockpot (10½″ in diameter and 11″ high).

MAKES 8–10 CUPS

5 pounds beef marrow bones,
  cut into pieces
1 veal knuckle
18 cups cold water
1 pound carrots
2 large onions
2 cloves
A handful of fresh parsley

1 medium-size parsnip
1 rib celery
The greens of 1 leek
1 bay leaf
1 teaspoon dried thyme
5 teaspoons salt
5 peppercorns

1. Cover the marrow bones and veal knuckle with cold water to at least 1″ above the bones (about 18 cups, if you are using the size of stockpot mentioned in the special equipment). Bring the water to a slow boil, then, when the surface of the stock is at full boil, skim off the scum and fat using a ladle (not a skimmer). Replace the amount of water removed while skimming with cold water and repeat once more or until the broth is clear.

2. Do not peel the vegetables but scrub them clean. Add the carrots, the unpeeled onions (each with a clove stuck in it), parsley, parsnip, celery, leek top, bay leaf, thyme, salt, and peppercorns.

3. Regulate the heat to the lowest simmer, cover with the lid slightly ajar, and cook overnight, if possible, or at least 7 hours. It takes that many hours for the bones to release all their nutritious values.

4. Strain the stock. Discard the bones and vegetables. Discard the fat on top of the stock. For the onion soup without the meats, boil down the stock to 8 cups. For the complete boiled dinner, do not boil down the broth. Refrigerate for no more than 2–3 days. Otherwise, freeze.

Onion Soup

The best onion soup is eaten at home and is made from the broth of a Pot-au-Feu Boiled Dinner. First a stock is prepared with meat bones and vegetables. Various cuts of meat are cooked in the broth to enrich it further. The meats are eaten as a second course with mustard, horseradish, and different sauces. If you just want to eat onion soup, boil down the stock to concentrate the flavors and do not bother to enrich the broth with the meats.

Special kitchen utensils. Eight ovenproof soup bowls.

SERVES 8

8 cups Beef Stock, page 69	1 pound Swiss cheese
1½ pounds yellow onions	½ teaspoon salt
1 tablespoon oil	8 slices French bread
2 tablespoons butter	

Preheat oven to 350°F.

1. Boil the Beef Stock down to 8 cups to concentrate the flavors.

2. Cut each onion in half, place flat side down, then cut the onion in thin slices. Heat 1 tablespoon oil and 2 tablespoons butter in a 12″ cast-iron skillet until hot but not smoking. Add the onions, sprinkle with ½ teaspoon salt, and stir continuously with a wooden spoon for 5 minutes over medium-low heat. The onions must become golden brown, but should not burn.

3. Cut the bread into eight ½″ slices. Place on a cookie sheet and toast only one side under the broiler, just enough to toast the bread lightly.

4. Grate the cheese. Sprinkle about 2 tablespoons of cheese at the bottom of 8 onion soup bowls, add the cooked onions, pour the meat broth over, cover with a slice of bread, and sprinkle cheese all over the top.

5. Bake on the middle shelf of the oven for 20–30 minutes or until the top is golden brown. Wait 10 minutes before serving to avoid burning your palate.

A Boiled Dinner of Vegetables and Meats (Pot-au-Feu)

With the preceding Onion Soup as a first course, the Pot-au-Feu is my favorite dinner party with good friends. A Poached Stuffed Chicken, page 74, served along with the meats and vegetables, makes the dinner more festive.

Special kitchen utensils. A 15-quart stockpot, a collapsible vegetable steamer.

SERVES 8

10 cups Beef Stock, page 69	8 leeks
2 pounds beef short ribs	2 cups Vinaigrette Sauce with
2 pounds veal breast	Hard-Boiled Egg, page 72
2 pounds bottom round beef or	2 cups Garlic Mayonnaise,
neck meat	page 73
8 big carrots	Dijon mustard
8 Russet potatoes	Horseradish
2 teaspoons salt	Kosher salt

1. Bring the Beef Stock to a boil. Drop the short ribs and the veal into the boiling stock. Cover with the lid slightly ajar and cook over medium heat for 1½ hours. Transfer the meats to a pan with ½ cup broth. Cover, keep warm over low heat. Add the bottom round beef in one piece to the boiling broth. Boil for ½ hour. The bottom round beef remains rare.

2. While the meats are cooking, peel the carrots; split in 2 lengthwise; and with each half flat on the counter, split once more in 2 lengthwise. Pour 3 cups water in a pan. Fit a steamer inside the pan. Add the carrots. Cover tightly and steam over medium heat until the carrots are tender, about 15 minutes.

3. Peel the potatoes, rinse and dry, and cut them in half lengthwise, then with each half flat side on the counter, split in half lengthwise. Cover with cold water, add 1 teaspoon salt, and bring to a boil. Cover and cook until tender.

4. *Preparing the leeks.* Cut off the dark greens of the leeks (and reserve for future soups), leaving the light green parts of the leaves attached to the whites. Split the leeks lengthwise to 1″ from the end. Wash very carefully under running cold water to remove any sand remaining. Put the leeks in a large kettle and pour boiling water over them to cover. Add 1 teaspoon salt, cover, and simmer for 10 minutes or until tender. Drain very well.

5. Prepare 2 cups of Vinaigrette Sauce with Hard-Boiled Egg, page 72. Pour 1 cup over the hot leeks. Reserve the remaining cup for the assembly of the Pot-au-Feu.

6. Prepare 2 cups of Garlic Mayonnaise, page 73.

7. *Assembling the Boiled Dinner.* Cut the beef into thin slices. Bone the short ribs and veal breast. Decorate a large platter with the carrots and the potatoes with the meats in the center. Serve the leeks apart. Present the mustard, horseradish, and kosher salt in individual ramekins; serve the Vinaigrette Sauce and Garlic Mayonnaise in sauceboats.

For a leek salad

Follow step 4 of the above recipe, adding 1 cup Vinaigrette Sauce with Hard-Boiled Egg. Serve cold or at room temperature.

Vinaigrette Sauce with Hard–Boiled Egg

This vinaigrette sauce with a hard-boiled egg, capers, and parsley is called gribiche in French. I like this sauce with cold boiled meats, cold roasted chicken, or fish.

MAKES 1 CUP

1 egg	2 tablespoons minced parsley, dill,
1 teaspoon Dijon mustard	or tarragon
1 clove garlic, mashed	1 tablespoon capers
2 tablespoons wine vinegar	1/4 teaspoon salt
8 tablespoons olive oil	Freshly ground black pepper

1. Boil an egg: Place in a small pot with cold water and cover it. When the first boil is reached, boil about 10 minutes. Drain and pour cold water over the egg until cool. Peel.

2. Cut the egg in half, remove the yolk, and mash it. Add the mustard and the mashed garlic. Mix in the vinegar, then dribble in the oil. Add the parsley, dill, or tarragon and the capers.

3. Dice the white of the egg. Add it to the sauce. Season to taste with 1/4 teaspoon salt and freshly ground pepper.

Garlic Mayonnaise

Aïoli (pronounced EYE-OH-LEE), as it is called in southeastern France, is a "Provençal butter"—strong garlic-based mayonnaise. It is traditionally prepared in a mortar with a pestle by grinding the garlic into a paste, then slowly rotating the pestle while adding olive oil. I like to cut down the strong flavor of olive oil by mixing it with vegetable oil. Not everyone has a mortar and pestle; a mixing bowl works very well; using an electric beater at low speed gives a respectable aïoli, see page 54, but, please, try to avoid using the food processor—it will transform the aïoli into glue instead of a lovely smooth sauce.

Special kitchen utensils. Mortar and pestle or a 1-quart mixing bowl and a whisk.

MAKES 1 CUP

1 slice French bread	2 egg yolks
2 tablespoons wine vinegar	½ cup olive oil
6 large cloves garlic	½ cup vegetable oil
About 1 teaspoon salt	

1. Soak 1 slice of bread, 1" thick, crust removed, with the 2 tablespoons vinegar in a 1-quart mixing bowl and mash it to a paste. Squeeze out excess vinegar and discard it.

2. Traditionally a whole head of garlic is used; I find it too overpowering. Mash 6 large garlic cloves to a pulp with a pinch of salt. When garlic cloves are fresh, it is very easy to mash them with a small pestle. As they dry out, it is more difficult. Then, you should rub garlic cloves against the tip of the tines of a fork first, holding the back of the fork steady against a plate, see page 11. The garlic will now be easy to pulp with either a pestle or the back of a knife.

3. Add the egg yolks and the garlic paste to the bread and mix well. Place the mixing bowl on a wet potholder, to keep your hands free to whisk and pour the oil at the same time. (Pour the oil from a glass measuring cup with a spout.) Dribble ¼ cup of oil, drop by drop, whisking all the time, then when the aïoli thickens, dribble the oil faster into the mixture. Season with salt, ¼ teaspoon at a time.

Chicken Stock

Whenever I cook chicken, I freeze the necks, sometimes the carcasses, wings, etc., until I have enough chicken parts to make a stock. The stock is not salted, in case I need to boil it down to a syrupy consistency to add flavor to a sauce like that for Veal Steak with Ginger, page 132. I salt the stock when it is prepared specifically for soups—the amount will be mentioned for each recipe.

Special kitchen utensil. A 15-quart stockpot.

MAKES 8 CUPS

4 pounds chicken parts	4 peppercorns
16 cups cold water	½ teaspoon dried thyme
1 pound carrots	1 bay leaf
1 rib celery with leaves	2 onions unpeeled
A bunch of parsley	2 cloves
1 parsnip	

1. Cover the chicken with 16 cups of cold water. Bring the water to a boil. When the surface of the stock is at full boil, skim off the scum and fat which rise to the surface, using a ladle. Replace the amount of water removed with cold water and repeat once more or until the broth is clear.

2. Wash the vegetables; do not peel. Add the carrots, celery, parsley, parsnip, peppercorns, thyme, bay leaf, onions, and cloves.

3. Cover ajar, simmer for about 4 hours with the water barely quivering. Strain through cheesecloth. Discard the vegetables. Keep the chicken for sandwiches served with a Garlic Mayonnaise.

4. Reduce the stock to 8 cups. If you wish, freeze it in small containers.

Poached Stuffed Chicken

When Henri de Navarre became King Henri IV of France in the sixteenth century, he promised a chicken in every pot. Actually he promised a "hen," an aged fowl that could feed a whole family and was more economical than a roasting chicken. The best method then of cooking a hen was to poach it for several hours to tenderize it and to produce a wonderful broth. It is difficult today to find hens that have run around for their food. Instead of a tough old bird, we generally buy a tender overaged chicken, and so we simply can't poach it for many hours. If you are lucky enough to get a homegrown hen, don't forget to cook it longer than the recipe below indicates.

Special kitchen utensil. A 6½-quart Dutch oven.

SERVES 4–6

4–5-pound stewing chicken	3 large egg yolks
6 slices bread, crusts removed (4 ounces)	½ teaspoon salt
½ cup milk	Freshly ground black pepper
4 ounces mild prosciutto-type ham	1 egg white
3 cloves garlic	2 quarts homemade chicken or beef stock
A handful of coarsely chopped parsley	Several sprigs of watercress for garnish

1. Dry the chicken and cut off all extra fat and skin, but leave enough skin to close the cavity.

2. Break up the bread into small pieces, reserving 1 slice whole; soak in the milk. Grind the bread pieces, ham, garlic, parsley, and the chicken liver through a meat grinder or a food processor. Mix in 3 egg yolks, and season with salt and pepper. Mix stuffing well with hands to make sure the ingredients are evenly distributed. Beat 1 egg white stiff and fold it into the stuffing. It makes a very loose stuffing.

3. Spoon the stuffing into the cavity of the chicken, then close the cavity with a slice of bread and truss (see illustration, page 19).

4. Add the chicken, breast side up, to a stockpot or a 6½-quart Dutch oven and cover with cold stock. If there is not enough stock to cover the chicken, add water. Poach over a gentle bubbly simmer for 2 hours.

5. Drain and serve the chicken on a preheated platter garnished with watercress. Carve at the table—gently remove the stuffing from the cavity and slice it. Serve with Garlic Mayonnaise, page 73, and Vegetables for a Boiled Dinner, page 71.

Note. Boil down the chicken broth if necessary to a concentrated flavor and freeze for another use.

To poach the chicken without the stuffing. Half an hour before the chicken comes out of the broth, add peeled onions, carrots, or turnips and cook until tender. Serve with a garlic mayonnaise. Or cook noodles in the boiling broth after removing the chicken and serve with grated Swiss cheese or Parmesan to sprinkle on top of the noodles.

Leftover Beef Gratinéed

The leftover meats of a Boiled Dinner or leftover beef roast are spiced up with onions, vinegar, capers, and cornichons (tart little gherkins), then gratinéed in the oven. This is easily prepared ahead of time and reheated when needed. It can be prepared in a cast-iron skillet and gratinéed in the oven. Serve hot with a green salad and a baked potato for each serving.

Special kitchen utensil. A 12″ cast-iron skillet.

SERVES 6

3 medium-size yellow onions	1 tablespoon capers
2 tablespoons oil	1 tablespoon cornichons (do not
1 tablespoon flour	use sweet gherkins)
1½ cups Beef Stock, page 69	1–2 pounds cooked beef
2 tablespoons red-wine vinegar	3 tablespoons homemade bread
½ teaspoon salt	crumbs
Freshly ground black pepper	3 tablespoons grated Swiss cheese
2 tablespoons minced fresh parsley	

1. Peel the onions, cut in 2, then cut each half, flat side down on the counter, into thin slices. Heat 2 tablespoons oil in a 12″ cast-iron skillet; add the onions, stirring once in a while to prevent them from burning. Cook the onions for 15 minutes over medium heat.

2. Sprinkle 1 tablespoon flour over the onions and mix well with a wooden spoon. Pour 1½ cups beef stock and 2 tablespoons vinegar over them, stirring vigorously. Bring to a boil for 30 seconds. Season with ½ teaspoon salt and freshly ground pepper. Then, over low to medium heat, cook the onions covered for 15 minutes.

3. Mince 2 tablespoons parsley, 1 tablespoon capers, and 1 tablespoon cornichons. Remove any fat left on the boiled beef and cut it into paper-thin slices.

4. Bury the meat in the onions, sprinkle parsley, capers, and cornichons over the onions, and cover with 3 tablespoons bread crumbs mixed with 3 tablespoons cheese.

Preheat oven at 350°F.

5. Bake on the middle shelf of the oven for 30 minutes, or until the top is gratinéed. Serve as is.

Crêpes with Fruit Preserves

Crêpes are my earliest culinary memory. During World War II, it was difficult to find eggs, but my mother seemed to always find them to make crêpes on Mardi Gras, the day before Ash Wednesday. How I loved that Tuesday! Crêpes in my youth took the place of cookies that American children so dearly love, but like freshly baked cookies, there is nothing better than freshly made crêpes sprinkled with lots of sugar and a smidgen of freshly squeezed lemon juice, rolled and eaten as soon as they come out of the skillet. Eaten this way, crêpes are generally consumed just after school, and mothers have two crêpe pans going at the same time to pacify children who can't wait for the next crêpe.

Crêpes make an excellent dessert. Making the batter takes no time at all, and cooking a batch of 16 crêpes takes about 20 minutes, less if you have two skillets going at the same time. Cook the crêpes before dinner and keep them on a plate covered with an inverted plate in a warm oven.

Special instruction. Make the batter an hour ahead. It needs to rest for 1 hour before cooking to relax the gluten in the flour, otherwise the batter will not spread evenly in the skillet when cooking the crêpes.

Special kitchen utensils. I use my omelet pan(s) 7″ bottom diameter. It is advisable to have 2 pans to make crêpes faster. A long thin steel blade spatula is necessary to flip the crêpes.

SERVES 6 (16–18 CRÊPES)

1 cup flour	4 tablespoons butter, melted
1 teaspoon sugar	1 pint fruit preserves (see
3 large eggs	following recipes)
½ cup beer	Sugar to sprinkle (optional)
½ cup water	4 tablespoons Cointreau liqueur
1 tablespoon brandy	(optional)

1. Pour the flour and sugar into a 2-quart mixing bowl, make a well in the middle, break 3 eggs into the well, with a fork start beating the eggs together. Continue beating the flour and eggs while pouring in the beer and the water.

2. Set the batter aside to rest for 1 hour outside the refrigerator, then beat in 1 tablespoon brandy just before making crêpes.

3. Heat 1 pan first, lightly brushed with butter. Wait until the pan is hot enough but not too hot. It is a little difficult to judge at first. If the pan is too hot, the crêpe batter will shrivel instead of covering the bottom of the pan. If the pan is not hot enough, the crêpe batter will not cook properly—it will be soggy and heavy. Dribble a drop of the batter in

the skillet first. If it sizzles gently, go ahead and start making crêpes. Pour about 2–3 tablespoons batter and quickly swirl it around so the batter covers the whole bottom of the skillet. (Don't worry if there are holes in the crêpes; it's acceptable.) Cook for about 2 minutes on 1 side, then flip the crêpe with the steel blade spatula and cook about 1 minute on the other side. The crêpe should be lightly colored on both sides. If you have 2 pans, start cooking 1 crêpe and while it's cooking, start heating another pan and make a second crêpe. This way you don't lose time.

4. Stack the crêpes on a plate and cover with an inverted plate. If they are made 2–3 hours ahead of time, keep in a warm oven.

5. Heat 1 pint of fruit preserves over low heat to warm the preserve syrup so it will spread on the crêpes.

6. Fold each crêpe in 4 to form a triangle, and overlap 3 crêpes on each plate. Decorate with the fruit preserves.

7. If you like, sprinkle sugar on the crêpes, flambé 4 tablespoons Cointreau in a ladle or a pipkin, see page 24, and pour it over the crêpes.

Bitter Orange Preserves

In the Southwest, especially in Arizona, bitter-orange trees are everywhere. In the East, we see bitter oranges on the market for a very short period—in February and March. Buy them then and make this delicious preserve.

Special kitchen utensils. Tongs to handle sterilized jars. A 5-quart stainless steel pot with a heavy bottom or, if you own a copper bowl for egg whites, use it. A candy thermometer.

FOR ABOUT 4 PINTS

2 pounds bitter oranges	5¼ cups sugar
1 lemon	1 cup water

1. *Sterilizing the jars.* Bring several quarts of water to a boil. Add 4 pint jars to the boiling water. Turn off the heat and let the jars stand for 5 minutes. With tongs, remove the jars and turn them upside down on a clean towel.

2. Cover the oranges (whole) and lemon with cold water in a 6½-quart pot. Bring to a boil, and cook with the cover ajar for 30 minutes in quivering water. Drain the fruits. Discard the water. Cool the fruits under cold running water for 10 minutes.

3. Have on hand a big cutting board and sharp knives. Now comes the tedious work: Slice off ¼″ of each end of the oranges and lemon and discard. Cut the whole oranges and lemon into 1″ thick slices. Then cut the slices into small slivers. Catch the juices in a mixing bowl. (It takes about 30 minutes to do this.)

4. In a 5-quart stainless steel bowl or a copper egg white bowl, combine the sugar, 1 cup water, and the reserved juices from the oranges, if any, and bring to a boil. Cook until the syrup reaches 220°F. Add the diced oranges and lemon. Bring the syrup back to about 200°F. on a candy thermometer (it takes about 15 minutes or so). Skim the scum off the surface and discard.

5. Remove from heat and pour into the prepared jars. Seal with paraffin, or cover with plastic wrap and reserve in the refrigerator. They will keep for 3–4 months.

Technique: To seal fruit preserves with paraffin

Special instruction. Fill the sterilized jars with preserves, leaving ½″ space free at the top to cover the preserves with paraffin. Be sure the sides and rim of the jar are cleaned and not sticky; otherwise the paraffin will not seal. Wait for the preserves to be cold before sealing the jars.

Special kitchen utensil. Buy a 1-quart foil container and keep it only to melt paraffin.

To seal 5–6 jars

½ pound paraffin

Melt the paraffin in a foil container set in a water bath. Pour ¼″ thick melted paraffin over the cold preserves.

Peach Preserves

Fruit preserves are not only for breakfast, they also make great desserts. Warm the preserves and pour them over vanilla ice cream, or mix them with fresh cottage cheese or yogurt. Freshly cooked crêpes with preserves also make a great dessert.

Special instruction. It is advisable to make small quantities of preserves at a time. It is easier to control the cooking of the syrup (fruit juices and sugar), and it is much less tiring. Try to leave at least 12 hours (overnight, if possible) to marinate the peaches. To sterilize the jars, see page 78, step 1.

Special kitchen utensils. Tongs to handle sterilized jars. A 5-quart stainless steel pot with a heavy bottom or, if you own a copper bowl for egg whites, use it. A candy thermometer.

MAKES 4 PINTS

4½ pounds peaches
2 pounds sugar

¼ cup freshly squeezed lemon
  juice
1 tablespoon brandy

1. Peel the peaches. If necessary, boil 1 quart of water, turn off the heat, and drop in several peaches for 1 minute, then remove and peel. Repeat for the remaining peaches.

2. Cut the peaches into ¼" thick slices. Work over a plate to catch the juices.

3. Put the peach slices and their pits into a 2½-quart mixing bowl, add 2 pounds sugar, and mix well. Leave overnight, or at least 12 hours; stir the peaches once or twice to dissolve the sugar.

4. Drain the peaches over a bowl for 3 hours, stirring once in a while to dissolve the sugar. This is important; the sugar must dissolve into liquid.

5. Cook the peach juices in a 5-quart stainless steel pot or a copper egg white bowl. When the liquids are boiling, start skimming the peach scum that comes to the surface. (Do not throw away the scum. It is delicious mixed with cottage cheese or cream cheese or over vanilla ice cream.) Why skim? It helps clear the sugar syrup and makes a cloudless preserve. The sugar and peach juices cook for about 45 minutes to become a syrup cooked at 220°F. on a candy thermometer.

6. When the syrup is at 220°F., add the peaches and the pits. Bring it back to a boil, stirring. Boil for just 1 minute; otherwise, the peaches will

lose some of their flavor. Remove the preserves from the heat; stir in ¼ cup freshly squeezed lemon juice and 1 tablespoon brandy.

7. Fill the jars with the preserves and the pits (they give flavor; remove them when you eat the preserves) to ½″ from the top of the jars.

8. Seal the jars with paraffin, see page 79, or cover with plastic wrap and refrigerate. Preserves will keep about 4 months in the refrigerator.

Tomato Preserves with Crystallized Ginger

A friend of mine, Sherrill Roth, made tomato preserves and gave me a jar. The idea of sweet tomatoes just did not appeal to me, so I left them on the shelf until I visited her and had tomato preserves for breakfast. I fell in love. They are especially good with cottage cheese or yogurt.

Special instructions. Make these preserves at the height of the tomato season in your area so you can get good ripe tomatoes. Be very careful when you are cooking the tomatoes in the sugar syrup. When the syrup reaches 200°F., remove the tomato preserves from the heat. Tomatoes tend to burn at a higher temperature. To sterilize the jars, see page 78, step 1.

Special kitchen utensils. Tongs to handle sterilized jars. A 5-quart stainless steel pot with a heavy bottom or, if you own a copper bowl for egg whites, use it. A candy thermometer.

MAKES ABOUT 2 PINTS

3½ pounds ripe tomatoes	½ cup strips of lemon rind
3 cups sugar	½ cup crystallized ginger
¼ cup freshly squeezed lemon juice	

1. Peel the tomatoes. If necessary, pour boiling water over the tomatoes, let stand for 1 minute, then peel. Cut the tomatoes into small cubes, without seeding them. Turn in a colander and let drain for 30 minutes.

2. Transfer the tomato pieces and 3 cups sugar to a 4-quart mixing bowl. Let stand for 1 hour, stirring occasionally.

3. Squeeze ¼ cup lemon juice. Cut enough lemon rinds into thin strips to make ½ cup. Mince the crystallized ginger and add it to the tomatoes and sugar.

4. Transfer the tomatoes and their liquids, lemon rind strips, lemon juice,

and ginger to a 5-quart stainless steel pot or a copper egg white bowl. Slowly bring to a boil and cook over medium heat, stirring frequently, for about 30 minutes. Bring the syrup to about 200°F. on a candy thermometer. Remove the preserves from the heat. Let cool *while stirring* (otherwise, the tomatoes will burn at the bottom of the pot).

5. Fill the sterilized jars and seal with paraffin, see page 79, or cover with plastic wrap and reserve in the refrigerator for 3–4 months.

Plum Cake

This cake is a *clafoutis* or crêpe-type dessert for August, September, and the first half of October (for the remaining months, substitute poached prunes; see Prune Cake). It is elegant unmolded, but can also be served in a baking dish. Be careful about the type of plums you use. If they are very juicy, the cake will be soggy and will fall apart when you unmold it. If this occurs, I suggest you do not unmold it, but serve it as is—in a baking dish as a *clafoutis*.

Special kitchen utensil. A round cake mold 8″ in diameter, 1½″ deep, or a baking dish about the same size.

SERVES 6

12 small Italian purple plums	⅓ cup flour
For the cake	⅓ cup cornstarch
	⅔ teaspoon baking powder
9 tablespoons sweet	2 tablespoons sugar for topping
butter	2 tablespoons cold butter
3 eggs (¾ cup)	Cream-Cheese Topping, see page 27
¾ cup sugar	

1. Put the plums and quarter them.

2. Cream the butter. First pound it with a rolling pin, then smear it with the heel of your hand until it is very smooth.

3. With an electric mixer on high speed, beat the eggs 1 minute, then dribble in the sugar, beat until very pale yellow (5 minutes). Then beat in the butter a tablespoon at a time with the mixer at low speed. Don't worry if the mixture looks curdled.

4. Sift the flour, cornstarch, and baking powder together. Then, with the electric mixer at low speed, gradually beat the sifted ingredients into the batter. Beat just until blended. With a rubber spatula, fold the plums into the batter.

Preheat oven to 350°F.

5. Melt 1 tablespoon butter and brush it in a round 8″ cake pan 1½″ deep. Pour the batter into it. Tap it on the counter to level the batter. Bake on the middle rack of the oven at 350°F. for 45–60 minutes, until the top of the cake is golden and starts to pull away from the sides of the pan. Cover loosely with foil if browning too fast.

6. Turn the cake upside down on a broiler-proof platter. Take the cake mold and wait about 15 minutes before unmolding. Sprinkle 2 tablespoons sugar over the top and dot with 2 tablespoons (approximately) cold butter. Pass under the broiler for 2 minutes or so until the sugar caramelizes. You must watch it closely under the broiler to be sure it doesn't burn. The sugar turns dark very quickly.

7. Cool a bit and decorate with Cream-Cheese Topping. Serve warm.

Prune Cake

Special kitchen utensil. A round cake mold 8″ in diameter, 1½″ deep, or a baking dish about the same size.

SERVES 6

6 ounces pitted prunes	1 tablespoon dark rum
1 cup water	1 batch cake for Plum Cake
¼ cup sugar	

1. Most of the year fresh plums are not available, so cook with pitted prunes for a delicious dessert. Combine the prunes, water, and sugar in a saucepan. Bring to a boil and cook for 2 minutes. Turn off the heat. Add 1 tablespoon dark rum. Cover and cool completely. Drain the prunes, but reserve the liquids. Quarter the prunes.

2. Follow the directions of the Plum Cake, steps 2–7, to prepare and bake the cake.

3. Cook the reserved prune liquid until it thickens to a syrup. When the cake is baked and unmolded, brush the syrup over the cake.

TECHNIQUES AND UTENSILS INTRODUCED

How to make an all-purpose pastry dough:
the food processor method and the hand method

How to roll out dough using a heavy rolling pin
and a dough scraper

How to bake tarts in 10"–11" quiche pans and
12-cup small cupcake pans

How to make a "Provençal" fish stock

How to cut chicken into pieces

How to poach pears

How to caramelize apples

How to line a 6-cup charlotte mold with bread

Lesson 5

Suggested Menus for Lesson 5

2-Course Brunch or Light Supper Menu

Chicken Bouillabaisse
served with Garlic Mayonnaise
(Lesson 4)

Apple Charlotte

3-Course Lunch

Country-Style Potato Pie

Tossed Green Salad
(Lesson 1)

Caramelized Apple Mousseline
(Lesson 1)

3-Course Dinner

Dried Wild Mushroom Quiche
or
Onion Quiche

Fish Stew, New York Style

Caramelized Pears with
a Ginger Custard

Shortcrust Pastry

I like to use this dough, called Pâté Brisée in French, for both savory and sweet dishes. If you are used to making pastry doughs with lard only, you will find that butter pastry doughs are more difficult to roll out. The dough tends to break very easily and gets very sticky as the butter melts quickly. It is a question of practice, but it is worth the extra work. A butter pastry dough is far superior to a lard pastry dough in taste.

Special instruction. The amount of dough made with 1½ cups of flour will make one 10″–11″ tart shell with enough leftover dough to make several individual flat dough circles or Hot Individual Apple Tarts, page 135; or the entire amount of flour can make 24 finger-size tart shells for hors d'oeuvre.

Special kitchen utensil. A 10″–11″ tart or pie mold or two 12-cup small cupcake molds.

1½ cups all-purpose flour
12 tablespoons (1½ sticks) cold sweet butter

¼ teaspoon salt
2 tablespoons ice water

The food processor method

1. Place the flour, cold butter, cut into tablespoon pieces, and salt in the bowl of the machine fitted with the steel blade. Buzz-stop long enough to say alligator aloud. Repeat alligator 15 times, then add the water. Buzz-stop again about 10 times. Stop. The dough should look like slightly sticky coarse meal (see illustration). The dough must not be allowed to become a ball in the machine. If so, the dough is then harder to roll out (the gluten in the flour in contact with the water is activated too fast and the dough is too elastic). The crust is tough instead of flaky.

2. Turn the dough on a working surface. Mash about 2 tablespoons of the mixture at a time with the heel of your hand away from you to bind the dough together. When finished, gather in a ball and repeat once more if the ball of dough is still very crumbly.

3. Shape the dough into a 6″ patty, dust with flour, and wrap in waxed paper. Refrigerate just enough to chill the butter semicold (about 15 minutes) for the ideal temperature to roll out the dough.

The hand method

1. Spread the flour on your pastry surface. Sprinkle with salt. Cut the cold butter in small pieces with a knife on top of the flour, always burying the butter in the flour. Cut the butter in very tiny pieces with a pastry cutter or 2 knives until the flour and butter mixture looks like coarse meal (it takes about 5 minutes).

2. Spread the flour-butter mixture and sprinkle it with 2 tablespoons water. Quickly gather the dough together into a pile, then start mashing 2 tablespoons of the mixture at a time with the heel of your hand, away from you to bind the dough. When finished, gather it in a ball, and repeat once more if the ball of dough is still very crumbly. Shape into a 6″ patty. Dust with flour and refrigerate no more than 15 minutes to attain the ideal temperature for rolling out the dough.

How to roll out and to bake

1. Have a dough scraper and the tart or pie pan at hand. Dust flour on pastry counter. Dust flour on rolling pin. Gently pound the dough with the rolling pin, rotating the dough all the time. Cracks may appear around the edges; just tap them gently together. (If the dough is very cold, remove from refrigerator and wait 15 minutes before rolling it out or until the dough is softer.)

2. Scrape the counter surface clean. Dust the pastry surface with flour frequently while rolling the dough. At first, roll in quick, short strokes, putting pressure on the rolling pin with the heels of your hands. Every 10 seconds or so, rotate the dough counterclockwise, and proceed with rolling out the dough. Always check the bottom of the dough for a smooth counter surface, scraping if necessary, and always dusting with flour. When the circle of dough is rolled to a 9″ diameter, rotate the dough as follows: gently roll it up on the rolling pin, picking it up with the dough scraper (see illustration). Scrape the counter, dust with flour, and check the rolling pin—it must not be sticky. Scrape it to clean it, don't just dust flour over a sticky rolling pin—it does not work. Continue to roll out the dough with much less pressure now than when you started. The edges of the circle will probably start to crack; push them back together gently with your fingers, but don't worry too much about them.

3. Roll out to a 15″ circle. Pick up the dough gently with the scraper and wrap it over your rolling pin. Place the tart pan in front of you and unroll the pastry dough into it. Fit the pastry inside the pan. Roll the

pin over the edges of the pan to cut the leftover dough (see illustration). Wrap the leftovers and refrigerate. They can be used for Hot Individual Tarts with apples, page 135, or berries, page 136, or turnovers, page 137.

4. Let's say, you have made such a mess that it is impossible to fit it into the tart mold. Gather the bits and pieces together into a ball, and clean the surface of your pastry counter. Clean your rolling pin and start over, rolling the dough out to a 15″ circle.

   Preheat oven to 400°F. For a black tin pan, lower temperature to 375°F. Bake a somewhat shorter time.

5. Prick the bottom of the dough with a fork. Line and cover the pastry with foil. Crimp tightly around the edges. The dough then will not shrink while baking (see illustration).

6. Bake for 15 minutes. Remove the foil and bake 5 more minutes, or until the bottom of the shell is dry. It is now ready for a filling and to be baked once more.

7. Bake 10 more minutes or until lightly golden for a completely cooked tart shell.

8. *Baking frozen uncooked pastry shells.* For partial baking, preheat oven to 425°F. Bake 5 minutes, then drop the temperature to 400°F. Cook for another 15 minutes or so. Remove the foil and bake 5 more minutes or until the bottom of the shell is dry. For total baking, bake for another 5–10 minutes or until the crust is slightly golden.

Finger-size tart shells for hors d'oeuvre

MAKES 24 TART SHELLS

1. Melt 2 tablespoons butter and brush the inside of two 12-cup small cupcake molds. Roll out the dough to about an 18″ circle (big enough to cut out twenty-four 2½″ circles). Fit the circles of dough into the molds. Prick the dough with a fork. Refrigerate or freeze.

2. *For refrigerated shells.* Preheat oven to 350°F. Prick the dough with a fork. Cover the inside of each cupcake mold with foil, then fill with dry beans or pellets. Bake 15 minutes on the middle shelf of the oven. Remove foil and beans or pellets. Cook 5 more minutes to finish cooking the shells.

3. *For frozen shells.* Preheat oven to 425°F. Bake 5 minutes, then drop temperature to 400°F. for 15 minutes. Remove the foil and pellets. Cook 10 more minutes to finish cooking the shells.

The shells are now ready to be filled with Broccoli Puree, page 34, for instance, or any filling you like, even fresh fruits with Whipped Cream.

Country-Style Potato Pie

A "potato pie" sliced into finger-size pieces makes an excellent hors d'oeuvre, or eaten with a tossed green salad, it becomes a lovely lunch.

Special kitchen utensils. A jelly-roll pan, 12″ x 16″ by 1½″, a Chinese-style cleaver.

SERVES 6 FOR LUNCH; 12 FOR HORS D'OEUVRE

Shortcrust Pastry, page 87	1½ teaspoons salt
4 ounces slab bacon	Freshly ground black pepper
2 small onions	1 egg yolk
1 tablespoon chopped parsley	1 tablespoon water
2 pounds Russet potatoes	½ cup heavy cream

1. Cut the pastry in two, 1 piece larger than the other—⅗ to ⅖. Roll out the big piece of pastry to a 10″ x 12″ rectangle (don't worry about the exact size). Roll the rectangle on your rolling pin and transfer it to a jelly-roll pan or any pan that size with low edges. Cover with waxed paper. Refrigerate. Roll out the smaller piece to a 9″ x 10″ rectangle. Place it on top of waxed paper. Cover with waxed paper and refrigerate.

2. Slice off the rind of the slab bacon. Cover the bacon with cold water. Bring to a boil. Boil for 5 minutes. Drain, wash under running cold water, and wipe dry. Cut the bacon into ½″ thick strips, then cut each strip into 1″ long pieces. Sauté over low to medium heat until golden; discard the fat. Drain the bacon on paper towels and reserve.

3. Cut the onions in half. With the flat side on the counter, cut the onions into thin slices, then mince (yields about ½ cup).

4. Finely chop parsley for 1 tablespoon.

5. Peel the potatoes just before baking. Do not wash but wipe dry with paper towels. Using a sharp Chinese-style cleaver, shave off a thin slice from one side of the potato, then with the potato lying on this side on the counter, cut the potatoes into thin slices starting at one end (yields 4 cups).

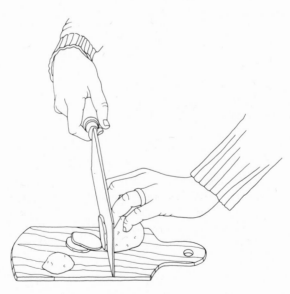

6. In a 4-quart mixing bowl, mix the potatoes, onions, bacon, and parsley together. Sprinkle in 1½ teaspoons salt and freshly ground pepper and toss once more.

7. Fill the larger rectangle of pastry with the mixture, leaving a 1″ border. Cover the mixture with the smaller rectangle of pastry. Fold up the edges of the bottom piece of pastry over the top piece.

Preheat oven to 400°F.

8. With the point of a knife, decorate the top of the pastry by drawing straight lines on the diagonal, drawing parallel lines about ¾″ apart all the way across, then draw parallel lines to make diamond-shape figures. Brush with an egg glaze (1 egg yolk beaten with 1 tablespoon water) and bake for 45 minutes. Check with a cake tester to make sure the potatoes are tender; if not, continue baking at 350°F. until the potatoes are cooked. Cover the top loosely with a piece of aluminum foil at any time the top becomes brown.

9. During the baking, the top pastry will open slightly between the slits made with the design; if not, then cut small holes to pour the cream into the pie. When baked, pour ½ cup heavy cream in a glass measuring cup and dribble it into the pie, tilting the pan once in a while so the cream spreads evenly in the potatoes. (If there are holes in the bottom part of the pastry—which can happen when you are learning to make the dough—don't panic. Stop adding cream; otherwise it will run all over the baking sheet.)

10. For a lunch, cut the pie into six pieces. For hors d'oeuvre, cut into 24 pieces.

Dried Wild Mushroom Quiche

In New York, I buy Polish or Italian dry mushrooms that remind me of the cèpes in France. In the United States, the term "quiche" is used for any kind of nonsweetened custard baked in a pastry shell. A Quiche Lorraine from the Lorraine province, next to Alsace in northeastern France, is made with eggs, milk, and ham and is baked in a crust which has not already been baked. In France, any other ingredient than the ones mentioned for Quiche Lorraine makes it a "tarte." I prefer a prebaked tart shell to one that is not baked previously. The fillings for quiche are as numerous as the imagination of the cooks who bake them. But, please, don't freeze quiches. They are awful reheated. If you don't believe me, try comparing a freshly baked quiche with a frozen one! On the other hand, you can freeze the unbaked pie shell and bake it when needed.

Special instruction. The quiche can be baked in the afternoon for dinner. Reheat at 250°F. for 15 minutes.

Special kitchen utensil. A 10″ quiche pan with removable bottom.

SERVES 6–8

1 semibaked 10″ pie shell, pages 88–90	Salt
1 ounce dried mushrooms	Freshly ground black pepper
2 cloves garlic	2 ounces boiled ham
3 tablespoons minced parsley	2 eggs
2 tablespoons olive oil	1 cup heavy cream

1. Roll out pastry dough to line a 10″ pie shell according to the instructions for Shortcrust Pastry, page 88. You may have frozen the *unbaked* pie shell; once more follow the instructions given to prebake the frozen pastry shell just before adding the filling, step 8. If the pastry is prebaked ahead of time, it becomes tough.

2. Soak the mushrooms in water for at least 1 hour, then drain. If they are large mushrooms, cut them into julienne strips.

3. Mince the garlic and parsley.

4. Heat the olive oil in a 9″ heavy-bottomed skillet and sauté the mushrooms over high heat for 2 minutes. Reduce heat to low.

5. Add garlic and parsley and sauté for 1 minute, stirring constantly so the garlic doesn't burn. Remove from heat and season with salt and freshly ground pepper.

6. Cut ham in julienne strips and lay in bottom of the semibaked pie shell. Add the mushrooms, garlic, and parsley, spreading them around evenly in the tart shell.

7. Beat the eggs lightly and mix with the cream. (Avoid ultra-pasteurized cream, if possible—check your local health-food store; they generally carry heavy cream. If you can't find just pasteurized cream, boil down 1½ cups half-and-half to 1 cup.) Season with salt and freshly ground pepper and pour over the mushrooms.

Preheat oven to 350°F.

8. Bake at 350°F. for about 40 minutes. If you are baking the quiche in a removable-bottom pan, place a piece of foil on the rack below the pan to catch any custard that might bubble over.

Onion Quiche

Alsace, the province next to the Lorraine, is also famous for its onion tart, just as Lorraine is world renowned for its quiche.

Special instruction. The quiche can be baked in the afternoon for dinner. Reheat at 250°F. for 15 minutes.

Special kitchen utensil. A 10″ quiche pan with removable bottom.

SERVES 6–8

1 semibaked 10″ pie shell,
  pages 88–90
4 medium-size yellow onions
¼ pound slab bacon (not sliced)
4 tablespoons (½ stick) butter
4 eggs

1 cup heavy cream
1 cup grated Swiss cheese
  (4 ounces)
½ teaspoon salt
Freshly ground black pepper

1. Roll out the pastry dough to line a 10″ pie shell according to the instructions for Shortcrust Pastry, page 88. You may have frozen the unbaked pie shell; follow the instructions given to prebake the frozen pastry shell. Prebake the pastry just before adding the filling, step 8. If the pastry is prebaked ahead of time, it becomes tough.

2. Peel the onions. Cut them in half, with the flat side against a cutting surface. Cut into thin slices.

3. Slice off the rind of the bacon if there is any. Slice the bacon in ¼″ thick strips, then cut each strip into 1″ long pieces.

4. Melt 3 tablespoons butter in a 12″ cast-iron skillet over medium heat. When the butter stops sizzling, add the onions, and stir constantly for 5 minutes.

5. Stir the bacon into the onions, and sauté for 5 more minutes over medium heat; then cover partially, lower the heat, and cook for 30 minutes, stirring now and again.

Preheat oven to 350°F.

6. Remove the onions and bacon to a mixing bowl with a perforated spoon in order to discard the fats remaining in the skillet. Let cool.

7. Break 4 eggs in a bowl. Add 1 cup heavy cream (or boil 1½ cups half-and-half to 1 cup if you cannot find pasteurized heavy cream). Mix in the onions, bacon, and ½ cup grated cheese. Season with ½ teaspoon salt and freshly ground pepper. Taste and correct seasonings, if necessary.

8. Pour the mixture into the prebaked pastry shell. Sprinkle on the remaining cheese and dots of butter (about 1 tablespoon).

9. If you are baking the quiche in a removable-bottom pan, place a piece of foil on the rack below the pan to catch any custard that might bubble over. Bake on the middle shelf of the oven for 30 minutes or so, or until golden brown on top. Cool before serving.

Chicken Bouillabaisse

Chicken pieces (instead of fish) and vegetables are poached in a fish broth, delicately scented with the saffron and anise that characterize Provençal fish soups. I serve it as a main course for a Sunday supper with an aïoli sauce and crusty country bread.

Special instruction. Prepare the fish stock a day ahead of time. If you wish you can substitute fish heads and bones for the whole fish, it is much cheaper but be very sure to buy 4 pounds freshly cut heads and bones. Cut the chicken into parts, and rub with Pernod (an anise-based alcohol). Season with salt and pepper and refrigerate for the next day.

Special kitchen utensil. A 6½-quart Dutch oven.

SERVES 6

The fish stock

4 pounds butterfish, whiting, or
  very fresh fish heads and bones
¼ cup olive oil
2 tablespoons Pernod
Several strands of saffron
1 medium-size onion
1 medium-size leek
1 small fennel bulb
1 clove garlic
2½ quarts water
2 teaspoons salt
Freshly ground black pepper
1 bay leaf
½ teaspoon dried thyme

The chicken

4 pounds chicken parts
2 tablespoons Pernod
1 teaspoon salt
Freshly ground black pepper
1 carrot
2 medium-size Russet potatoes
1 medium-size turnip
1 tablespoon minced fresh basil
  (in season)
Garlic Mayonnaise, page 73
Country bread

A day ahead, prepare the fish stock

1. Wash the fish under cold water and make sure that all the gills are removed. (Frequently there are still some left in the fish—they look like small bits of liver.) Dry with paper towels and lay out on a platter.

2. Make a marinade of ¼ cup olive oil, 2 tablespoons Pernod, and a pinch of saffron, and rub the fish well all over. Let stand for 30 minutes in the marinade.

3. Peel and chop the onion coarsely; cut off the green top of the leek, wash it, and chop coarsely. Split the whites. Wash and chop. Cut the bulb of fennel in half and chop coarsely. Cut a clove of garlic into several pieces.

4. Put the fish, the marinade, and all the vegetables and spices from step 3 into the 6½ quart pot. Cover with 2½ quarts water; add 2 teaspoons salt and 4 or 5 grinds of black pepper. Add bay leaf and ½ teaspoon thyme. Bring to a boil uncovered over high heat; then simmer, partially covered, for 45 minutes.

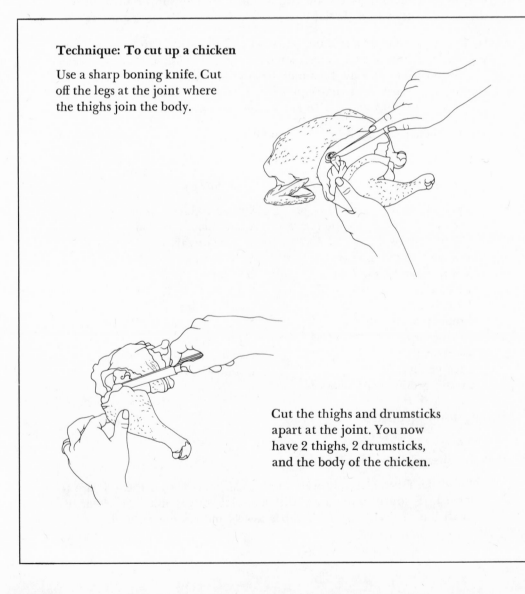

Technique: To cut up a chicken

Use a sharp boning knife. Cut off the legs at the joint where the thighs join the body.

Cut the thighs and drumsticks apart at the joint. You now have 2 thighs, 2 drumsticks, and the body of the chicken.

5. Strain the fish stock through a fine sieve lined with a triple layer of cheese-cloth. Squeeze the fish and vegetables well to extract all the broth. Discard the fish and vegetables. Reduce the stock to 6½ cups. Cool, then refrigerate.

A day ahead, marinate the chicken

6. Cut the chicken into 8 pieces.

7. Rub 2 tablespoons Pernod all over the chicken parts. Sprinkle with ½ teaspoon salt and freshly ground pepper. Cover. Refrigerate for next day.

Cut off the wings at the point where they join the body.

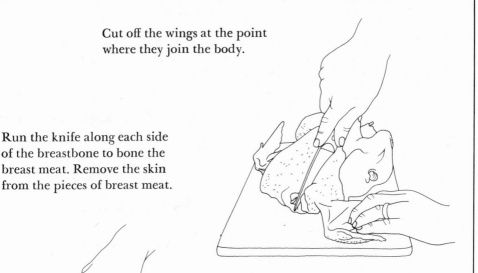

Run the knife along each side of the breastbone to bone the breast meat. Remove the skin from the pieces of breast meat.

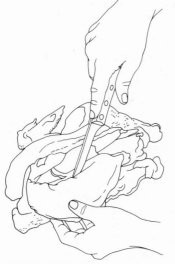

Chop the carcass into 3 pieces with a cleaver. Remove all the extra fat and skin and render the fat, see page 20. Add the skin, cut into ½″ pieces with scissors, to the fat. When the fat is melted, strain and reserve the "cracklings," the fried skin, for a tossed green salad, or an omelet. I usually use the carcass to make stock.

For supper or brunch

8. Peel and slice the carrot about ½″ thick; peel and dice the potatoes and turnips into ½″ cubes. Toss the vegetables together in a 3-quart mixing bowl. Season with ½ teaspoon salt and freshly ground pepper.

9. Reheat the fish stock, add the chicken thighs and legs, bring to a boil, cover, and simmer for 15 minutes. Add the vegetables; continue cooking for 15 minutes. Add the chicken breasts and continue simmering for 5 minutes, covered.

10. Remove the chicken breasts and thighs. Bone the chicken thighs and dice the meat into ½″ cubes. Reserve in a heated soup tureen with a cover. Remove the vegetables with a perforated spoon and put them with the chicken. Taste the broth. Correct seasonings with salt and pepper, if necessary. Pour over the chicken and vegetables.

11. Finely mince 1 tablespoon fresh basil leaves in season; sprinkle the minced basil on the soup. Cover the tureen to keep the aroma and serve in preheated soup plates or bowls.

12. Serve the Garlic Mayonnaise in a bowl. Add globs of it to the soup, and serve slices of country bread. I like to spread Garlic Mayonnaise on the bread.

Fish Stew, New York Style

This recipe is similar to the preceding Chicken Bouillabaisse, but you poach fish steaks instead of chicken in the fish broth.

Special instruction. I use cod, halibut, tile, or monkfish steaks in New York. Substitute what is available in your state. Do not use fillets; they will over-cook.

Special kitchen utensil. A 6½-quart pot such as a Dutch oven.

SERVES 6

Fish Stock, page 95	1 tablespoon, plus 1 teaspoon salt
2 tablespoons Pernod	Freshly ground black pepper
1 tablespoon olive oil	2 pounds mussels
2 pounds cod steak	Garlic Mayonnaise, page 73
1 pound halibut steak	Croutons, page 15
Several strands of saffron	

1. Prepare the Fish Stock according to the recipe, page 95.

2. Rub 2 tablespoons Pernod and 1 tablespoon olive oil all over the fish. Sprinkle with several strands of saffron, 1 teaspoon salt, and freshly ground pepper and let stand for 30 minutes in a plate.

3. *Clean the mussels.* Discard any opened mussels which do not close up again when you put them in water. Scrub them with a brush. It is time-consuming, but they need to be very clean. Soak them in cold water for 30 minutes with 1 tablespoon salt to make them disgorge sand inside the shells. Unfortunately, even with this precaution, there are times when mussels will still be gritty. Discard heavy mussels, they are full of sand.

4. Bring the fish stock back to a boil in a 6½-quart Dutch oven if you prepared it ahead of time. Drop the fish (but not the mussels), in the quivering liquids, adding the remaining Pernod and oil in the plate. Count 10 minutes time to poach the fish in quivering liquids; add the mussels for the last 5 minutes.

5. Serve as is, keeping the mussels in their shells, with a bowl of Garlic Mayonnaise and croutons on the side. Each person drops a glob of mayonnaise in the soup plate and stirs it in the broth.

Caramelized Pears with a Ginger Custard

From October to May, pears are easily found on the market, starting with the Bartlett variety in early fall, followed by the Boscs and the Anjou pears later on in the winter and early spring. Their easy availability makes them as versatile as apples.

Bartlett and Anjou pears are best for poaching, and the Bosc pear is perfect for puréeing for baked custards or sherbets. The Bosc has a stronger flavor than the other two varieties.

Special instructions. The Caramelized Pears with a Ginger Custard can be prepared in several stages. The custard is better prepared a day ahead of time. The pears can be poached several hours before dinnertime, but not earlier; otherwise, they lose their flavor. Coat the pears with the caramelized syrup just before the dessert course, to have the caramel crackling under the teeth. They can be coated with the caramel ahead of time and refrigerated; however, the caramel will soften in contact with the humidity of the refrigerator. It is still very good; just not the same.

Most pear recipes indicate 1 pear per person. I prefer ½ pear; with custard and cookies on the side, it is enough. But if you want to double the recipe, make two batches, especially for the custard. It is difficult for a beginner to properly whisk a greater volume of custard.

Special kitchen utensils. Two 9″ skillets to poach the pears. A cake rack. A 12″ serving platter, 2″ deep, to serve the pears and the custard. Do not use a deep serving dish; otherwise, the pears will sink to the bottom of the dish.

SERVES 8

Pastry Cream, page 44	½ lemon
2 tablespoons crystallized ginger	1 cup sugar
2 tablespoons pear brandy	1 cup water
4 Bartlett or Anjou pears	

1. Prepare the Pastry Cream a day ahead of time. Mince 2 tablespoons crystallized ginger and add it to the Pastry Cream. Add 2 tablespoons pear brandy. Refrigerate overnight.

2. Remove the core of the pears, but not the stem. Peel them and cut in half lengthwise, using a stainless steel paring knife. Cut out the center core. Rub half a lemon on the pears to keep them from darkening.

3. Combine ½ cup sugar and ½ cup water and bring to a boil in each of two 9″ skillets, stirring to dissolve the sugar. Put 4 pear halves in each skillet, flat side down, and cook over medium-high heat for 5 minutes, ladling syrup on top of the pears every few seconds; then turn the pears upside down (core side up), cover, and cook for 5 more minutes over medium heat. Test the pears with a cake tester; they should be tender but not mushy.

4. Have ready a cake rack on top of a platter to catch the juices. Remove the pears with a skimmer and turn them flat side down on the cake rack. Let cool completely. Pour the Pastry Cream in the serving dish.

5. Combine the cooking syrup in 1 skillet. Cook until it caramelizes to an amber color (about 5 minutes) over high heat. Ladle the hot caramel over each pear half. With a thin spatula, break the caramel drippings loose from the rack and scoop up the pears. Decorate the center of the cold Pastry Cream with 1 half pear and place the other halves around the center like flower petals. Break loose all the caramel drippings and add them to the pears and custard. Serve the dessert in pretty bowls, plates, or champagne coupes. Refrigerate. Serve cookies on the side.

Poires Charpini

At the Tour d'Argent restaurant in Paris, I had a dessert very similar to the one above called Poires Charpini. The individual presentation of the dessert was glorious, and if you happen to have the glasses and goblets and help in the kitchen, go ahead: Poach the pears and dice in ½" cubes. Reserve the syrup. Put pear cubes in glasses and fill the glasses with the Pastry Cream over the pears. Refrigerate. Cook the syrup until it caramelizes and pour it over the custard to make a hard surface. Set the glasses in cracked ice inside silver goblets and serve.

Apple Charlotte

Any dessert with apples will be my favorite dessert, so don't be surprised to read again that this is my favorite dessert.

One of the most famous French desserts, the Charlotte aux Pommes, can be made all year around with the availability of Granny Smith apples in the spring and summer. I mention Granny Smith especially because they cook into a thick, dry purée. The all-purpose Golden Delicious will do, when there are no other better apples available on the market. In the autumn, Jonathans and Macoun apples are good for this dessert.

Apple Charlotte is reminiscent of American Brown Betty. The caramelized apple purée with the crunchiness of toasted bread, served with a light custard, makes a delicious dessert for every kind of dinner, home-style or more elegant as it may be.

The presentation of a dessert is always important. This Apple Charlotte is unmolded to look very pretty with golden bread crumbs on top and toasted rectangle sticks of bread all around the sides. With the bread crumbs on top, instead of bread triangles (the classic method), it is easier to cut into the charlotte without collapsing it. The portions are then neater. I again emphasize the importance of drying out the apple purée (that is why I go to the caramelized stage) so the dessert will not collapse when it is unmolded.

Special instructions. The amount of apples will vary depending on how much liquid they will spew out while they cook. If there is leftover apple purée, serve it with a Pork Roast with Apples, page 111. The assembly of the Apple Charlotte can be done a day ahead of time. Bring it back to room temperature, then bake it in the early evening for a late dinner to allow it to be lukewarm when served. The custard can also be prepared a day ahead of time, but bring it back to room temperature. Whisk it once for a smooth texture before serving.

Special kitchen utensil. A 6-cup charlotte mold; substitute a 6-cup soufflé mold if necessary.

SERVES 8

4 pounds apples	Freshly ground black pepper
18 tablespoons (or more) sweet	1-pound loaf bread, sliced
butter	Pastry Cream, page 44,
1½ cups sugar	flavored with Calvados
1 teaspoon vanilla extract	or Crème Anglaise, page 360
3 tablespoons Calvados, apple-	
jack, or dark rum	

1. Peel, quarter, and core the apples. Cut them in thick slices, then cross-wise in cubes.

2. Melt 5 tablespoons butter in each of two 9″ cast-iron skillets. Divide the apples between the two skillets. (I use two skillets to cook the apples in shorter time and with less volume; the apples caramelize more evenly.) Add to each skillet of apples ¾ cup sugar and ½ teaspoon vanilla extract. Cook over medium-high heat, stirring often, until the apples disintegrate into a purée and caramelize a deep amber color. (It takes 20–30 minutes; the timing depends on the quality of the apples, on how much liquid they need to evaporate.) Then sprinkle 1 tablespoon Calvados (applejack) or rum in each skillet. Mash the apples into a coarse purée. Be sure the purée is dry.

3. Butter and sugar a 6-cup charlotte mold (number 16) or a 6-cup soufflé mold. Cut a piece of waxed paper to fit the bottom; butter and sugar it too, and fit it at the bottom of the pan.

4. Spread 15 slices of bread on a cookie sheet and toast it in the preheated oven for about 15 minutes, turning the bread over once.

5. Reserve 10 pieces of toast, and crumble the other 5 pieces into medium-thick crumbs.

6. Trim off the crust on the slices of toasted bread. Cut them in rectangles 2″ wide—the length should measure the depth of the mold (3½″ in the case of the 6-cup charlotte mold).

7. Melt 8 tablespoons butter (more, if needed); brush both sides of each bread rectangle with butter.

8. *To line the mold with the bread and bread crumbs.* Cover the inside bottom of the mold with bread crumbs, sprinkling about 1 tablespoon melted butter over them. Line the inside of the mold with each rectangle of bread standing up close together but not overlapping.

9. Pour half the apple purée into the mold. Add another layer of bread crumbs over the apples; sprinkle with 1 tablespoon melted butter. Fill the mold with the rest of the apples and finish with a layer of bread crumbs; sprinkle with 1 tablespoon butter.

Preheat oven to 400°F.

10. Bake for 15 minutes, then cover loosely with foil to keep the bread crumbs from burning and bake 15 more minutes.

11. Prepare Pastry Cream with 1 tablespoon Calvados (applejack), page 44.

12. Remove from oven and allow to cool completely. Place the mold upside down on the serving plate, but do not unmold until ready to serve. Don't forget to remove the waxed paper. The Apple Charlotte is eaten lukewarm. Ladle half the Pastry Cream over it and put the rest in a sauceboat. Substitute Crème Anglaise, a light egg custard, page 360, for Pastry Cream if you are an experienced cook.

TECHNIQUES AND UTENSILS INTRODUCED

How to make a very light batter for fritters

How to deep-fry

How to make mashed potatoes—without milk

How to buy pork: what cut to select
(for chops, roast, etc.)

How to bake a pastry shell for fruits in a custard

Lesson 6

RECIPES

Eggplant Fritters

Apple Fritters

Mashed Potatoes, Country Style

Pork Roast with Apples

Braised Pork Roast with Pineapple and Bananas

Pork Chops with Mustard and Cheese

Apple Custard Pie

Cherry Tart

Caramelized Bread Pudding

Suggested Menus for Lesson 6

3-Course Summer Dinner

Eggplant Fritters

Pork Chops with Mustard and Cheese

Cherry Tart

3-Course Winter Dinner

Vegetable Soup (Lesson 2)

Pork Chops with Mustard and Cheese

Apple Fritters

Caramelized Bread Pudding

Alternate Winter Dinner

Braised Pork Roast
with Pineapple and Bananas

Mashed Potatoes, Country Style

Apple Custard Pie

4-Course Summer Menu

Eggplant Fritters

Pork Roast with Apples

Mashed Potatoes, Country Style

Cherry Tart

Eggplant Fritters

Eggplant fritters are my favorite among vegetable fritters. They make a great appetizer. The average American eggplant weighs 1½ to 2 pounds, and I find the peels sometimes very bitter. Peel the skin of the eggplants in thick pieces to avoid bitterness, and slice off an inch of the stem end.

I had never heard about male and female eggplants until I started teaching cooking. Craig Claiborne, in one of his columns, was informed very explicitly by one of his readers how to distinguish between male and female eggplants. "At the large blossom end (the end opposite the stem end), there is a scar or indentation. If this scar is round, the eggplant is male. If it is oval, it is female, and the female is loaded with seeds." But there is a controversy on which is better to eat. Some like the males; some like the females!

The following deep-frying batter is excellent for fruits as well as for vegetables. The best deep-frying liquid is beef suet. Unfortunately, in today's cholesterol-conscious society, we do not dare deep-fry in this sinfully good fat. But I am still giving the technique on how to render beef suet for deep-frying for the daring ones, see page 338; otherwise, deep-fry in corn oil.

Special instructions. It is very difficult to fry the fritters ahead of time. They can last about 15 minutes in a warm oven. Some of my students deep-fry them halfway, then let them drain in a wire basket over a bowl, and, at the last minute, bring the oil back to 340°F. and deep-fry them for a minute or two, enough to crisp them.

Special kitchen utensil. A 10″ deep-fryer or wok.

MAKES ABOUT 40 FRITTERS

¾ cup all-purpose flour	1 medium-size eggplant
½ teaspoon salt	(1½ pounds)
2 egg yolks	1½ quarts corn oil for deep-
¾ cup tepid beer	frying
2 tablespoons oil	2 egg whites

1. *For the batter.* Sift the flour and salt into your mixer bowl, make a well in the center, and add 2 egg yolks. With the mixer at medium speed, beat the beer into the batter, then add 2 tablespoons oil. Do not overbeat; beat just enough to mix all the ingredients smoothly. Set the batter aside for 1 hour.

2. Make thick peels when peeling the eggplant. Slice off 1″ of the stem end and discard. Cut the eggplant lengthwise in ½″ thick slices, then lay each slice flat on the counter. Cut into ¾″ thick strips, then cut each strip in 1″ pieces. Reserve. Do not salt them. It is not necessary for this recipe.

3. Heat 1½ quarts corn oil in a deep-fryer to 325°F. Beat 2 egg whites until stiff and fold them into the beer batter.

4. Using 2 soup spoons, dip each piece of eggplant into the batter, turn it over to coat it well with batter, and lower it gently into the oil. Don't overcrowd the deep-fryer pan with the fritters; otherwise, they will not fry properly. They will soak up more oil because the oil will get cold. Remember the oil must stay around 325°F. Fry for about 6–8 minutes, turning the fritters around with a wire skimmer. Cook until golden. Drain the fritters on paper towels. Repeat with the second batch of uncooked fritters. When all the fritters are ready, sprinkle salt over them just before serving.

Technique: To deep-fry

A friend who was a chef on the French liner *Liberté* invariably called the ship's firemen when french fries were on the menu. Too often the cooks would overload the deep-fryer and cause the hot oil to overflow and catch fire. Don't let this happen to you.

- Use a deep-fry pan or a wok, or some other vessel with sloping sides. I use a deep-fryer, 12½" in diameter and 5" high.

- *Never* fill the pan to more than one-third the height of the sides with oil. The reasons for this are that: The oil expands when it is hot. When you put in the fritters or potatoes, the oil will bubble up to double the depth you started with. If it should bubble over, you will very likely have a fire.

- *Never* attempt to fry a large quantity of something; always start with a small batch first. You can add more if there is no danger of overflowing oil.

The frying. With all these precautions in mind, the rest is simple. Use a good-quality oil heated to about 325°F. If you do not have a deep-fry thermometer, test the oil with a piece of bread—it should sizzle when dropped into the oil. Be careful not to overcrowd the pan—the oil may cool too much and make whatever you are frying greasy instead of crispy.

Note. Have a lid at hand which will cover the pan tightly. In case of a fire in the pan, put the lid on quickly to smother the flame and turn off the heat. *Never, never* put water on a grease fire; it will spatter and spread the flames.

Storing used oil. Strain the used oil and refrigerate it. It can be used 6–8 times before discarding it. You will know when the time comes to throw it out: when the oil is hot, it will smell rancid (a strong, unpleasant odor).

Apple Fritters

In the East, choose Jonathan, Macoun, or Cortland apples in autumn; Northern Spies or Stayman in winter; and Granny Smiths for the spring. If you never have done deep-frying, please read the instructions opposite. I use the same fritter batter for fruits as for vegetables and sweetbreads. It is a light beer batter. The fritters are very good for an afterschool snack or as a vegetable with pork, duck, or rabbit.

Special kitchen utensil. A 10″ deep-fryer or wok.

SERVES 6 (ABOUT 24 FRITTERS)

6 apples
1 tablespoon lemon juice
¼ cup sugar
2 tablespoons Calvados, applejack, or brandy
¾ cup all-purpose flour
½ teaspoon salt
2 egg yolks

¾ cup tepid light beer
2 tablespoons oil
1½ quarts corn oil for deep-frying
2 egg whites
Powdered sugar to sprinkle on the fritters

1. Peel the apples whole. Rub each apple with lemon juice. Slice the apples in rings about ½″ thick. Remove the center with an apple corer, and marinate them in ¼ cup sugar, 2 tablespoons Calvados (French applejack—substitute brandy if necessary), and 1 tablespoon lemon juice for 1 hour.

2. *For the batter.* Sift the flour and salt into your mixer bowl. Make a well in the center and add 2 egg yolks. With the mixer at medium speed, beat the beer into the batter, then add 2 tablespoons oil. Do not overbeat, just enough to mix all the ingredients smoothly. Set the batter aside for 1 hour; this helps it stick to the apples.

3. *To make the fritters.* Drain the apples thoroughly. Pat dry with paper towels. Heat 1½ quarts of oil in a deep-fryer to 325°F. Beat 2 egg whites until stiff and fold them into the batter.

4. Dip the apple slices in the batter and drop them into the hot oil. The fritters are ready when the batter becomes puffy and golden. Remove them with a wire dipper and drain them. Remember not to deep-fry too many apples at a time; otherwise, the oil cools too much and the fritters become soggy.

5. Drain on paper towels. Then transfer them to a large platter lined with a clean towel, but do not stack them, or they will get soggy. Keep the frit-

ters in a preheated, turned-off oven until you are finished deep-frying all the apples. Sprinkle lots of powdered sugar at the last minute before serving them.

Mashed Potatoes, Country Style

The potatoes are boiled in their jackets, then peeled and mashed. The cooking water is then boiled down to concentrate the potato flavor and is used instead of milk to flavor the mashed potatoes. At the last minute, beat in several tablespoons of butter to enhance the flavor of the potatoes. Since the butter is not cooked, it is digestible, so the purée is not heavy and greasy.

Special instructions. Unfortunately, mashed potatoes lose a lot of flavor prepared too long ahead of time, so this must be one of the final preparations to do before dinner.

SERVES 8

3 pounds Russet potatoes	2 teaspoons salt
2 quarts water	5 tablespoons sweet butter

1. Scrub the potatoes clean, but do not peel. Put the potatoes in a pot with 2 quarts water and 1 teaspoon salt, cover, bring to a boil, and cook partially covered over medium heat for 30 minutes. Pierce the potatoes with a cake tester to check if they are tender.

2. Remove the potatoes with a slotted spoon. Boil the water down to 1 quart. Wash the potatoes under cold water, then peel, quarter, and mash them, with either a ricer or a food mill, but do not use the food processor, for the starch in the potatoes will make them gluey.

3. Using a beater at low speed or a wooden spoon, beat the mashed potatoes with 1⅔ cups of the boiled-down potato water, perhaps using more if necessary.

4. Reheat the mashed potatoes *covered* (otherwise, they dry out) in a water bath over medium-low heat (illustration, page 35). Beat 5 tablespoons sweet butter into the potatoes. Beat for a minute or two. The more you beat, the lighter the mashed potatoes will be. Season with 1 teaspoon salt.

Pork Roast with Apples

For a pork roast, I buy the rib end of a loin (called a blade cut) or a fresh pork butt or part of a fresh picnic shoulder. Most of the time, I find the center loin or loin end called sirloin with the tenderloin to be too dry. I know it depends on the meat, and we do not have control over the quality, but it is extremely irritating to buy the most expensive and choicest cut and have the roast turn out dry. Don't think it is your fault. It happens to all of us. But even if a pork loin roast is dry when eaten hot, cut into thin slices and eaten cold for a cold supper or a buffet, it is very good and more presentable than the other cuts. See Cold Braised Center Loin of Pork with a Bohémienne (a cousin of the ratatouille family), page 246, or Stuffed with Prunes, page 244.

Some cooks like to cook pork at 325°F. all the while. Others, like myself, cook it at a high temperature—450°F.—for 20 minutes, then lower the temperature to 375°F. for a roast. Trichinosis is killed when the temperature reaches 140°F., so to be on the safe side, cook it to an internal temperature of 160°–170°F. To be sure, cook the meat with a meat thermometer inserted vertically into the thickest part of the meat without touching the bones if the roast is not boned, or use a quick-reading thermometer. Take the meat out of the oven when you are using a quick-reading thermometer and insert it horizontally into the thickest part of the meat from the thickest part of the bottom end.

Remember that a roast with the bones in cooks faster than a boneless roast because the bones transmit heat faster to the meat. Again, do not touch the bones with a thermometer. It will give you a higher temperature reading than the meat actually is.

Special instructions. The rib end or blade cut of the loin is the end nearest to the shoulder, whereas the sirloin end is near the leg (ham). I buy the first 8 ribs and have the roast boned and tied by the butcher. The rib bones will be cooked around the roast and are delicious to nibble on. An 8-rib roast boned and lightly trimmed (5 pounds with bones in) is about 3¼ pounds, serving 4 to 6 people, depending on the length of the menu and the appetite of the guests. Buy 2 rib end roasts if you need more, instead of buying a longer roast which would include the center cut and perhaps not be as juicy. Cook the 2 pork roasts in a bigger roasting pan, use the broiler pan of the oven, big enough to allow enough air circulating around the pork roasts to avoid steaming them. Add more water and beer because the liquids will evaporate faster in a larger surface.

The best cooking apples in the East are Jonathans and Macouns in the autumn, Staymans in the winter, and Granny Smiths in the spring. Try to find small apples, about 3 ounces each, as they cook more evenly around the pork roast (or trim apples down to size, reserving the trimmings for applesauce).

Special kitchen equipment. A roasting pan about 12″ x 16″ x 2″.

SERVES 6

3¼ pounds boned rib end loin
   pork roast (or see preceding
   discussion)
1½ teaspoons salt
1 tablespoon oil

6 small apples (3 ounces each)
2 tablespoons brown sugar
3 tablespoons butter
½ cup water
1 cup light beer

Preheat oven to 450°F.

1. Have the butcher bone and tie the roast. (Ask for the bones.) Rub 1 teaspoon salt all over the roast. Grease the roasting pan with 1 tablespoon oil; roast the pork bones around the roast for 20 minutes.

2. Meanwhile, peel the apples whole. Core each apple ¾ of the way through. Put 1 teaspoon brown sugar and ½ tablespoon butter in the hole of each apple. Add the apples around the roast and the bones.

3. Reduce oven temperature to 375°F., add ½ cup water to the roasting pan, and roast for another 40 minutes. Baste frequently adding water as needed at each basting, but remember to baste with the pan juices first, then add water if necessary.

4. After the roast has cooked for an hour, pour 1 cup beer in the pan, and continue roasting for 50 minutes, basting very frequently with the pan juices, glazing the roast with the slightly syrupy pan juices.

5. Remove the roast from the oven and check to be sure its internal temperature reads at least 160°–165°F. Allow it to rest for 5 minutes to make it easier to slice. Cut the strings with scissors. Slice first from the smaller end. Cut off the crispy golden top with scissors; it will be easier to slice. The juices will still be pinkish red.

6. Degrease the pan juices, adding the juices spewing out of the roast when slicing. Bring the juices to a boil and boil until slightly syrupy, scraping all the while. Taste and correct seasonings. Serve in a hot sauceboat with the pork surrounded with apples on a hot serving platter or wooden carving board. Serve Mashed Potatoes, page 110, with the pork or Yellow Turnip Purée, page 186.

Braised Pork Roast
with Pineapple and Bananas

Read the introduction to Pork Roast with Apples, page 111, to familiarize yourself with the different cuts of pork I recommend. Don't forget to ask for the bones when the butcher bones the pork. They're wonderful to nibble on.

Special kitchen utensil. A 6½-quart Dutch oven.

SERVES 6

3½ pounds rib end pork roast, boned	9 tablespoons (or more) butter
1 teaspoon salt	1 tablespoon oil
Freshly ground black pepper	1 fresh pineapple
¼ cup dark rum	3 bananas
½ cup dry white wine	Sugar
	1 teaspoon lemon juice

1. A day before cooking the pork, rub it all over with 1 teaspoon salt and freshly ground pepper. Baste with the rum and wine. Cover it with the bones from the roast pork. Cover and refrigerate in the least cold part of the refrigerator overnight.

2. *To braise the pork.* Drain the pork for 30 minutes. Reserve the marinade liquids for later. Dry the pork with paper towels.

3. Melt 2 tablespoons butter and 1 tablespoon oil over high heat in a 12″ cast-iron skillet. The fats must be very hot to sear the meat on all sides and ends for 15 minutes or so. Lower the heat after a while so as not to burn the meat.

   Preheat oven to 350°F.

4. Transfer the pork to a 6½-quart Dutch oven. Discard the fats in the skillet, and over high heat, pour the marinade liquids into the skillet, scraping the sides and bottom of the pan while the liquids are boiling for 1 minute. Pour the liquids over the roast. Cover and braise for 30 minutes in the oven, then lower the heat to 325°F. and braise for 1 more hour.

5. *The fruits.* With a chef's knife slice off the top and bottom of the pineapple. Run a knife around the inside wall of the pineapple rind, leaving a cylindrical piece of pineapple. Cut into ½″ thick slices and remove the pithy center from each slice (there is a pineapple corer on the market if you are not adept at cutting out the center core with a knife). Cut the slices into 1″ wide wedges. Peel the bananas just before sautéing to avoid discoloring. Cut them in ½″ thick slices.

6. Just before the pork comes out of the oven, melt 3 tablespoons butter in a 9″ cast-iron skillet until it stops sizzling. Then add the pieces of pineapple without overcrowding the pan; sprinkle 1 tablespoon sugar over each batch and sauté for about 3 minutes. Repeat until the pineapple pieces are all sautéed, adding more butter if necessary. Reserve on a preheated platter. Add more butter and sauté the banana slices the same way without sprinkling sugar over them. Reserve with the pineapple.

7. Transfer the pork to a cutting board with a juice catcher. Cut the pork in ½″ thick slices and overlap them in the center of the preheated platter with the fruits surrounding the pork. Pour the juices from carving the pork back into the braising pan.

8. Degrease the pan juices, then add 1 teaspoon lemon juice. Bring the juices to a boil, scraping sides and bottom all the while with a wooden spoon. Turn off the heat and whisk 2 tablespoons butter into the sauce. Taste and correct seasonings with salt and pepper. Serve the pork and its fruits with Mashed Potatoes, page 110.

Pork Chops with Mustard and Cheese

Pork chops cut from a center pork loin are beautiful to look at, very lean, but many times they are dry and tough when cooked.

When I buy pork for a roast, I ask for the first 8 ribs starting from the shoulder; for pork chops, I ask for the same piece, cut into ½″ thick ribs. The first 2 chops from the shoulder are fatty; the next 6 chops, less so. They are the chops I use for this recipe. They give the best result—a tender and moist pork chop.

Serve with Caramelized Apple slices, page 442, a baked potato, and a Tossed Salad, page 11. It takes about 20 minutes to brown, braise, and grill the chops.

Special instructions. Ask the butcher to cut 1″ off the end bone to make it easier to fit all the chops in the skillet without overcrowding them.

Special kitchen utensils. A 12″ cast-iron skillet and a broiler pan.

SERVES 4–6

3 tablespoons butter	1½ cups grated Swiss cheese
Six ½″ thick pork chops	(6 ounces)
1 teaspoon salt	2 tablespoons Dijon mustard
Freshly ground black pepper	½ cup dry white wine

1. Melt 3 tablespoons butter in a 12″ cast-iron skillet over medium-high heat. When the butter stops sizzling, add the chops to the skillet. Don't overcrowd the skillet, or the chops will steam instead of browning slightly. If necessary, brown in 2 batches. Brown the chops 4 minutes on each side. Then sprinkle ½ teaspoon salt and freshly ground pepper over them. Discard the fat in the skillet. Then cover tightly, lower the heat to medium-low, and cook (braise) them 5 minutes on each side.

2. Meanwhile, grate 1½ cups cheese (remember to grate the cheese at the last minute; otherwise, it packs and is more difficult to sprinkle).

3. Turn the broiler on. Spread about ½ teaspoon Dijon mustard on 1 side of each chop, then sprinkle about half the grated cheese over each chop. Broil for a minute or two until the cheese starts to gratiné. Turn the chops on their other side, spread on more mustard and sprinkle on the rest of the cheese, and gratiné under the broiler.

4. Reheat the juices in the skillet and pour ½ cup white wine into the pan, scraping the sides and bottom with a wooden spatula (deglazing), bring the liquids to a boil, and reduce the liquids until slightly syrupy. There will be about 1 tablespoon of sauce for each chop.

Apple Custard Pie

Buy Granny Smith apples in the spring and summer or Jonathan apples in the autumn or substitute Golden Delicious. Jonathans are the best apples to brown in butter because they do not disintegrate into a purée. Next, bake the apples with a custard of cream and eggs and sugar; it is a very simple dessert. You can do the same with pears if you wish; see also the following recipe, Cherry Tart, which is in the same spirit.

Special kitchen utensil. A 10″ pie pan. With a removable-bottom pan, line the bottom with foil to prevent the pie from leaking while baking.

SERVES 6–8

Shortcrust Pastry, page 87	1 teaspoon Calvados or applejack
3 pounds apples	2 large eggs
6 tablespoons sweet butter	⅓ cup sugar
½ cup sugar	1 cup heavy cream
Few grinds of the pepper mill	

1. Prepare the Shortcrust Pastry, adding 2 tablespoons sugar to the ingredients. Roll out the pastry to fit a 10″ pie pan and prebake according to the instructions, pages 88–90.

2. Peel and quarter the apples. Then cut each quarter in 3 slices.

3. In two 9″ cast-iron skillets, divide the apples, add 3 tablespoons butter and, with ¼ cup sugar in each skillet over moderately high heat, cook the apples until they caramelize (about 10–15 minutes).

4. Sprinkle a pinch of freshly ground pepper over them (it brings out their flavor) and a teaspoon of Calvados or applejack, and transfer them with a skimming spoon to the prebaked pastry shell. (Reserve the butter left in the skillet for another dessert.)

5. Combine the eggs, sugar, and cream in a mixing bowl and pour it over the apples.

   Preheat oven to 375°F.

6. Bake at 375°F. until golden brown (about 35 minutes). Serve warm.

Cherry Tart

Use fresh cherries, not commercial canned ones. I have tried them. They have absolutely no flavor. This recipe must be made only when the cherries are found in the market, which is generally around the middle of June and early July. Either pie cherries or Bing cherries can be used. With the Bing cherries, do not use as much sugar as for the pie cherries.

Special kitchen utensil. A 10″ pie pan. With a removable-bottom pan, line the bottom with foil to prevent the tart from leaking while baking.

SERVES 8

Shortcrust Pastry, page 87	¾ cup heavy cream
2 cups pitted pie or Bing cherries	2 eggs
½ cup sugar for pie cherries or	
⅓ cup sugar for Bing cherries	

Preheat oven to 375°F.

1. Prepare the Shortcrust Pastry, adding 2 tablespoons sugar to the ingredients. Roll out to fit a 10″ pie pan and prebake according to the instructions, pages 88–90.

2. Pit the cherries: Split at the stem part and squeeze out pit.

3. Mix and beat the sugar, cream, and eggs together in a bowl.

4. Spread the cherries on the partially cooked pastry tart shell and pour the cream mixture over them, being careful that it doesn't run over. If you are using a pan with a removable bottom, set it on a piece of aluminum foil in the oven so that if it does bubble over, your oven won't get all dirty.

Preheat oven to 375°F.

5. Bake on the middle shelf for 30 minutes or until golden and puffy. Serve warm or cold.

Caramelized Bread Pudding

Special kitchen utensil. A 4-cup ring mold.

SERVES 8

For the caramel
½ cup superfine sugar
3 tablespoons water

½ cup almonds
1 cup milk
2 cups soft bread torn into small pieces, loosely packed

⅓ cup sugar
6 tablespoons sweet butter softened
3 eggs separated
6 pitted prunes quartered
2 tablespoons Port
2 tablespoons sugar
1 tablespoon water

1. *For the caramel.* Combine ½ cup sugar and 3 tablespoons water in a 2-quart pan. Bring to a boil and continue cooking, stirring once in a while until the sugar-water syrup turns amber color (about 8 minutes), see page 25 for more details on making caramel. Pot holders in hands, quickly pour the caramel into the mold. Tip the mold in all directions until the caramel stops running and hardens. Reserve.

2. Grind medium-coarse ½ cup almonds (shelled but not skinned) in a blender or food processor.

3. Bring 1 cup milk to a boil in a 2-quart pan. Turn off the heat and mash the crumbled bread in the milk with a fork. Add ⅓ cup sugar and mix. Continue mixing and add the butter, egg yolks, and ground almonds.

4. Combine the quartered prunes with 2 tablespoons Port, 2 tablespoons sugar, and 1 tablespoon water in a 1-quart pan and cook, stirring once in a while until the liquids become syrupy (about 5 minutes). Fold the glazed prunes into the bread mixture.

5. Beat the egg whites to the stiff peak stage. With a rubber spatula, fold the egg whites into the bread mixture. Ladle the pudding into the prepared ring mold.

Preheat oven to 350°F.

6. Place the ring mold in a water-bath pan with simmering water to immerse the mold to about two-thirds of its height. Bake on the middle shelf of the oven for 45 minutes. Cover loosely with foil after 30 minutes to avoid burning.

7. Unmold on a platter. Serve warm.

TECHNIQUES AND UTENSILS INTRODUCED

How to beat egg whites with a balloon whisk in a
12″ unlined copper bowl

How to prepare a soufflé mold

How to prepare a béchamel as a binder for a soufflé,
for a vegetable gratin, and as a sauce

How to fry croutons properly

How to determine the kind of potato to buy
for french fries

How to braise without liquids for a meat sauce

How to bind a sauce with butter

How to shape individual open tarts and turnovers

Lesson 7

RECIPES

Cheese Soufflé

Leek Soufflé

Sautéed Green Beans

Spinach Gratin

Curry Sauce

Fried Croutons

Tomatoes with Mushroom and Parsley Stuffing

French Fries, Country Style

Braised Butcher's Tenderloin

Rib Steak with a Wine Sauce

Veal Steak with Ginger

Veal Scallops and Calf's Liver with a Mushroom Sauce

Hot Individual Apple Tarts

Hot Individual Berry Tarts with Melba Sauce

Blackberry Jam Turnovers

Suggested Menus for Lesson 7

2-Course Dinners

Spinach Gratin with Bacon

Fried Croutons

Blackberry Jam Turnovers

3-Course Dinners

Veal Scallops and Calf's Liver
with a Mushroom Sauce

Rice Pilaf (Lesson 2)

Hot Individual Apple Tarts

Braised Butcher's Tenderloin

French Fries, Country Style

Baked Apples on Toast
(Lesson 3)

Braised Curried Veal Shoulder
(Lesson 3)

Leek Soufflé

Blackberry Jam Turnovers

3-Course Summer Menu

Cheese Soufflé

Veal Steak with Ginger

Sautéed Green Beans

Hot Individual Berry Tarts
with Melba Sauce

4-Course Menu

Leek Soufflé

Rib Steak with a Wine Sauce

Tomatoes with Mushroom
and Parsley Stuffing

Caramelized Apple Mousseline
(Lesson 1)

120

Cheese Soufflé

There is a certain magic about the word "soufflé." It has caught the imagination of every cook, and there is great satisfaction for the cook and the guests in contemplating a beautifully puffed-up soufflé, for truly a perfect soufflé is an ethereal creation. Cheese soufflés are the easiest to prepare of all the nondessert soufflés. They puff up the most, since cheese is one of the lightest ingredients to add to the soufflé base.

Special kitchen utensils. Of all the equipment in my kitchen, the 12″ copper soufflé bowl is my favorite. I am often asked if it is absolutely necessary to buy copper pots and pans. No, I say, there are many substitutes, but there is one utensil I cherish and that is my copper bowl. I beat the egg whites with a balloon whisk (16″ long in all) to get more air in the whites than beating them in a heavy-duty mixer. It gives more volume. Also, it is easier to know when to stop beating the egg whites. They must be stiff, but not grainy, since it is difficult to fold in the soufflé base when the egg whites are too tight and firm, and it is impossible not to deflate them. The soufflé, then, does not cook properly and will not rise as much as it should. If you do not own a copper bowl and a balloon whisk, put them on your Christmas list. But in the meantime, don't despair; beat the egg whites with a mixer or a hand beater, but remember to watch over them very carefully so as not to make them too stiff. The egg whites should cling to the whisk and be firm. Don't underbeat them either; they should hold to the whisk and not be limp.

A 6-cup soufflé (7″ in diameter) mold is perfect. It serves 6 people. A soufflé collapses faster when the mold is over 7″ in diameter. I double the recipe and cook it in two 6-cup molds for more than 6 people. Substitute a 6-cup charlotte mold if necessary. The mold needs an aluminum foil collar; otherwise, the soufflé will run over. Cut a 2-foot-long piece of aluminum foil. Fold it in half lengthwise, the shiny side out. Butter and sprinkle cheese on half the depth of the paper. Line the outside of the mold with it—be sure the paper is at least 3″ high over the rim of the mold (the part that is greased). Tie with strings. Now you are all set to prepare a soufflé.

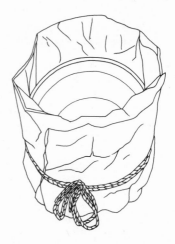

SERVES 6

1 cup milk	Pinch of nutmeg
3 tablespoons butter	½ cup grated Swiss cheese
3 tablespoons flour	(2 ounces)
4 egg yolks	½ cup grated Parmesan cheese
½ teaspoon salt	5 egg whites
Freshly ground black pepper	

1. *Soufflé base (a thick béchamel).* Bring the milk to a boil. Melt the butter in a 1½-quart heavy-bottomed saucepan, then add the flour and whisk over medium heat for 2 minutes or until the mixture bubbles. Off the flame, whisk in the boiling milk all at once. The binding (liaison) will be almost instantaneous. Continue cooking over medium heat for several minutes until the soufflé base is very thick. (It will be a very thick béchamel.)

2. Whisk the egg yolks one by one into the soufflé base. Season with ½ teaspoon salt, freshly ground pepper, and a pinch of nutmeg.

3. Grate the cheeses. Reserve a tablespoon for later and fold the rest into the soufflé base.

4. Beat the egg whites stiff. Fold a fourth of the egg whites into the soufflé base to make it lighter and to facilitate the folding of the remaining egg whites.

5. Pour the soufflé base into the remaining egg whites and, with a rubber spatula, cut through the mass in the center, bringing the mixture at the bottom of the bowl to the top, turning the bowl clockwise each time you repeat the motion of cutting into the mixture. Repeat until the whites and the soufflé base are mixed.

6. Ladle the soufflé mixture into the prepared soufflé mold.

   Preheat oven to 400°F.

7. Place it on the lower rack of the oven, then immediately drop the temperature to 375°F. Cook for 30 minutes. Remove the foil collar very gently, using a knife to help remove soufflé from the paper.

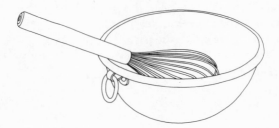

Leek Soufflé

To be served as a first course with a Tomato Cream Sauce, page 148, or as a vegetable without a sauce.

Special instructions. If you are preparing a soufflé for the first time, do not forget to read the detailed instructions for the Cheese Soufflé, page 121, beforehand. This soufflé will not rise as high as a cheese soufflé. What can be done ahead of time: Step 1 and part of step 2. Ahead of time, add the heavy cream to the soufflé base and turn off the heat until ready to finish the soufflé. When it is time to make the soufflé, cook the soufflé base for 15 minutes while you prepare steps 3 and 4. Reheat the leeks before folding them into the soufflé base. It will be easier.

Special kitchen utensils. A 12″ unlined copper bowl, a balloon whisk, a 6-cup soufflé mold.

SERVES 6

4 medium-size leeks	3 tablespoons flour
7 tablespoons butter	½ cup heavy cream
1½ teaspoons salt	⅓ cup grated Swiss cheese
Freshly ground pepper	4 eggs
1 cup milk	

1. Butter a 6-cup soufflé mold and make a collar for it as follows: Cut a 2-foot-long piece of aluminum foil. Fold in half lengthwise, shiny side out. Butter it, wrap it around the outside of the mold, and tie it with a string.

2. *Braising the leeks.* Cut off the tough green parts of the leeks and reserve to use in a stock. There should be around 9 ounces of leeks left. Split each leek lengthwise almost to the root and wash thoroughly under running cold water. Mince the leeks very fine (yields 2 cups). Melt 4 tablespoons butter in a 9″ cast-iron skillet with the minced leeks; stir with a wooden spoon for 30 seconds. Season with ½ teaspoon salt and freshly ground pepper. Cover tightly and cook (braise) over low heat for 30 minutes or until the leeks are very soft. Check once in a while to be sure they are not sticking to the bottom of the skillet. Sometimes, while braising, the leeks render a lot of liquid; when they are soft, uncover and boil down to evaporate the liquid, stirring constantly.

3. *The soufflé base.* Boil 1 cup milk. Melt 3 tablespoons butter in a 1½-quart heavy-bottomed saucepan. Add 3 tablespoons flour, and whisk briskly until the mixture is smooth and starts bubbling. Whisk in the boiling milk off the flame. Back on the heat, add ½ cup heavy cream and cook over medium heat for 15 minutes, whisking once in a while.

4. Grate ⅓ cup Swiss cheese. Separate the eggs. Fold the egg yolks into the soufflé base; add the leeks, the cheese, and about 1 teaspoon salt, tasting while sprinkling the salt, and freshly ground pepper.

5. Beat the egg whites to stiff peaks. Fold a fourth of the egg whites into the soufflé base, then transfer the soufflé base into the rest of the egg whites, folding lightly. Ladle the soufflé into the mold.

   Preheat oven to 400°F.

6. Cook for 35 minutes. Remove the foil collar very gently, using a knife to help remove soufflé from the paper.

Sautéed Green Beans

I like only freshly picked green beans, still very small, about half the diameter of a pencil. If you have a garden, pick the beans the day you plan to eat them. Serve them with a pan-broiled steak.

SERVES 4

3 quarts water	3 tablespoons butter
4 teaspoons salt	Freshly ground black pepper
1 pound very young green beans	

1. Boil 3 quarts water with 1 tablespoon salt.

2. While the water is heating, break off the stems and tips of the beans.

3. Plunge the beans into the boiling water for 3 minutes. Test 1 or 2 beans; if they are still quite crunchy, cook them for 1 more minute. Drain and rinse under cold water.

4. Melt 3 tablespoons butter in a skillet. When the butter is golden, add the beans. Shake the skillet for 1 minute; season with 1 teaspoon salt and freshly ground pepper. Sauté for 30 seconds more, shaking the skillet. Serve immediately.

Green Bean Salad

For a Green Bean Salad, heat a vinaigrette until warm. Mix in the hot drained beans and serve.

Or instead of a vinaigrette, sauté ½ cup diced bacon until crisp and mix the bacon and fat with the hot beans.

Spinach Gratin

I don't like frozen spinach. I know that spinach is a chore to clean, but it is worth it when you compare the fresh to the frozen product.

Spinach mixed with a béchamel sauce (a white sauce) is the French counterpart of American creamed spinach. Cooked with leftover meats or bacon, decorated with grated hard-boiled egg yolks, and eaten with Fried Croutons, page 127, it becomes a one-dish meal for a family dinner.

Special kitchen utensil. A 1½-quart saucepan.

SERVES 6

7 quarts water
5 teaspoons salt
5 pounds loose fresh spinach or three 10-ounce bags (spinach in bags has a lower proportion of stems)
2 tablespoons butter
Freshly ground pepper

For the béchamel

2 cups milk
2 tablespoons butter
2 tablespoons flour
½ teaspoon salt
Freshly ground pepper
Pinch of nutmeg
1 egg

1. Boil 7 quarts of water with 4 teaspoons salt. Wash the spinach leaves very well; cut off the stems with scissors and discard. Rinse the leaves several times to get rid of all the sand. Drain the spinach in a dish drainer rack. A colander is too small and doesn't drain as well.

2. Drop the spinach into the boiling water; as soon as it begins to boil again, sprinkle 1 teaspoon salt over it to keep the leaves from turning dark. Boil 2 minutes, drain, rinse in cold water, then squeeze it dry with your hands and chop very fine (yields 3½ cups). Melt 2 tablespoons butter in a 9″ skillet. When the butter is hot but not brown, add the spinach, stir, and cook for 3 minutes over medium heat. Taste and correct seasoning with salt and pepper.

3. *For a medium-thick béchamel.* Bring 2 cups milk to a boil. Melt 2 tablespoons butter in a 1½-quart saucepan, add 2 tablespoons flour, and whisk the mixture (roux) briskly while it bubbles for 1 minute. Off the flame, add the boiling milk at once and whisk fiercely for a smooth sauce. Season with ½ teaspoon salt, freshly ground pepper, and a pinch of nutmeg. Simmer over medium-low heat, whisking now and again for 15 minutes.

4. Cover 1 egg with cold water; bring to a boil and boil for 10 minutes. Drain and cool under cold water.

5. Add the spinach to the béchamel and reheat for dinner over low heat. Pour it into a preheated round serving platter and decorate as follows:

Cut the hard-boiled egg into eighths. Using a rotary-type grater like a cheese grater, grate the egg yolk over the surface of the spinach. Make a flowerlike decoration with the egg white strips, the curved side up.

Curry Sauce

This sauce is a béchamel variation. It can substitute for the plain béchamel for the Spinach Gratin, page 125. It also can be made for the Braised Curried Veal Shoulder, page 59, and mixed with the pan juices.

Special kitchen utensil. A 1½-quart saucepan.

MAKES 2 CUPS

1½ cups milk	1 medium-size onion, quartered
2 tablespoons butter	¼ teaspoon curry powder
2 tablespoons minced white bulb	¼ teaspoon salt
of scallions	Freshly ground black pepper
2 tablespoons flour	½ cup heavy cream

1. Boil the milk. Melt 2 tablespoons butter with 2 tablespoons white bulb of scallions, minced, in a 1½-quart heavy-bottomed saucepan. Add 2 tablespoons flour and mix well. When the mixture bubbles, add the boiling milk (don't worry if there is a skin on the milk). Whisk briskly for 20 seconds or so, then add the quartered onion, ¼ teaspoon curry powder, ¼ teaspoon salt, and freshly ground pepper.

2. Cook over medium-low heat, whisking once in a while. The sauce should simmer gently for 30 minutes at least. If you notice that the sauce thickens too fast or evaporates too much, add a bit of milk.

3. Dribble in ½ cup heavy cream during the next 10 minutes, so in all the sauce cooks about 40 minutes. It should have a lovely sheen on the surface.

4. Strain the sauce through a fine-mesh strainer. Taste and correct seasonings with salt and freshly ground pepper.

Fried Croutons

Any kind of bread will do as long as it is not freshly baked—a day-old bread, slightly dried out, is best—otherwise, the bread will soak up too much oil.

Special kitchen utensil. A 9″ cast-iron skillet.

SERVES 6

6 slices whole wheat bread or homemade white bread	½ cup corn oil

1. Cut the bread, if not cut already, into ¼″ thick slices. Cut each slice twice on the diagonal to get 4 triangular pieces of bread.

2. Heat ½ cup oil in a 9″ cast-iron skillet over medium-low heat for 1 minute, then add just enough bread triangles to fill the skillet without overcrowding. Fry on both sides, using a fork to turn them. Do not leave the skillet, as the bread tends to burn easily. Drain on paper towels. Continue with the next batch, adding more oil, if necessary.

3. When needed, reheat wrapped in foil, in a 250°F. oven for 10 minutes.

Tomatoes with Mushroom and Parsley Stuffing

It is best to make this recipe in the summer when ripe, fresh tomatoes are available. Choose medium-size tomatoes, about 2″ in diameter.

Special kitchen utensil. A 2-quart baking dish.

SERVES 6–8

6 ripe tomatoes, 3″ in diameter	1 tablespoon minced garlic
1 teaspoon salt	½ cup homemade bread crumbs
2 pounds mushrooms	6 tablespoons chicken fat or
4 tablespoons minced white bulbs of scallions	butter, see page 20
½ cup minced fresh parsley	Freshly ground black pepper

1. Cut the tomatoes in half horizontally and scoop out the pulp. (Save it for Vegetable Soup. Sprinkle ½ teaspoon salt in the shells of the tomatoes and set them upside down to drain.

2. Wash the mushrooms and remove the stems. (Save them for Vegetable Soup.) Mince.

3. Mince the white bulbs of scallions and mix with the minced mushrooms.

4. Mince the parsley and garlic and mix together.

5. If you do not have stale or dry bread, dry 2½″ thick slices of bread in the oven for 10–20 minutes at 250°F., then grind in a food processor or electric blender.

6. In 3 tablespoons of the fat, sauté the mushrooms and scallions at medium to high heat until the water from the mushrooms is evaporated (about 13 minutes). Reduce heat, add the parsley and garlic mixture, cover, and braise for 5 more minutes. Season with the remaining ½ teaspoon salt and freshly ground pepper.

7. Rinse the tomatoes with cold water and pat dry with paper towels. Stuff with the mushroom mixture and sprinkle bread crumbs and ½ tablespoon of the fat on top of each tomato.

Preheat oven to 400°F.

8. Bake for 25 minutes at 400°F. in a greased 2-quart baking dish or gratin pan. Serve hot (but they are good cold as leftovers, too).

Vegetable Soup

Add the tomato pulp and mushroom stems to the ingredients of Vegetable Soup, page 33.

French Fries, Country Style

At most farmhouses in Valdrôme, France, the ladies come rushing home from the fields around noon to prepare the main meal of the day. French fries eaten with a tossed green salad are invariably the first course, generally followed by a small steak, then cheese and fruits.

One day, I watched my neighbor, Marthe Corrent, prepare her fries. It took 20 minutes in all. I like the way the fries are cut; there is no need of machines. Each potato is cut in half lengthwise and then sliced on the bias. They look good and they taste great, but good fries require good potatoes. It can be an old or a new potato, but it must have certain characteristics. Choose a boiling potato and be sure when you peel it and cut it, it is waxy, moist, and easily cut. Do not use a potato that is hard to cut; otherwise, the fries will be mealy. A good fry melts in the mouth.

Wherever you live, it is by trial and error that you will find the potato you need. In the East, I generally use an eastern potato: Maine or Long Island or Russet. If the potato seems to be hard to cut, reserve it for scalloped potatoes or for a soup and buy another kind. Since you can't tell just by looking, I sometimes take a knife with me when I shop. I buy one potato, cut it, and see if it will do. I am a fanatic about good fries.

Special instruction. The fries are deep-fried twice in the same fat: once at 300°F. to cook them, then a second time at 350°F. to crisp them. Choose oval potatoes about ¼ pound each. Do not forget to read the deep-fry instructions, page 108.

Special kitchen utensil. A deep-fryer with a wire basket. For more than 4 people, either use a great big deep-fryer or two small ones, but don't try to overcrowd a small fryer with too many potatoes.

SERVES 4

2 quarts corn oil
2 pounds boiling potatoes
Salt

1. Heat 2 quarts oil to 300°F.

2. Wash and dry the potatoes. Peel them, but reserve the peels to fry. Split each potato in two, lengthwise, and cut ⅛″ thick slices on the bias.

3. Deep-fry the peels first for an appetizer. They are delicious. When they start to curl up, drain on paper towels, sprinkle them with salt, and eat with a drink.

4. Reheat the oil to 300°F. and put the french fries in the deep-fry basket. Very carefully, lower the basket in the hot oil. The oil will crackle, sputter, and augment in volume, and come almost to the top of the fryer. The essential in deep-frying the potatoes is to have all the potatoes submerged in fat and not to overcrowd the pan; otherwise, the potatoes will not cook properly. When the potatoes are cooked but not browned (about 5 minutes), lift the basket out of the oil and set on the handles of the fryer so the fries are not touching the oil. Let drain. If you are not ready to eat the fries, turn off the heat.

5. Reheat the oil to 350°F. and carefully plunge the basket once more in the hot oil. The fries will color almost at once. Cook until golden (about 2–3 minutes). Once more, lift the basket from the fat. Turn off the heat. Let drain a minute or two, then transfer the fries to a platter. Sprinkle salt over them and eat them with a tossed salad and a steak.

Braised Butcher's Tenderloin

Every beef has one piece of meat called "the butcher's tenderloin." This piece rarely appears for sale, and for a very good reason—the meat is excellent, flavorful, juicy and tender, yet just a little chewy, so the butcher keeps it for himself, says the folklore. A more practical reason is that each animal has only one "hanger," as it is called in butcherdom; it is located at the extreme end of the saddle and is not an easily marketable item. In France, where this cut of meat, called *onglet*, is prized, some enterprising butchers pass off flank steaks for butcher's tenderloin with a corresponding illegitimate profit. A scandal erupted as it developed that there were more butcher's tenderloins than animals.

Special instructions. Each piece weighs 1–2 pounds and is 1″ thick. It has a nerve running lengthwise through the middle. Ask the butcher to remove it, and you will have 2 strips of steak. Braised steak will be medium-rare, not rare.

Substitute any other cut of beef for steak, for example, filet mignon steak from the trimmings of a fillet of beef, pages 335–337.

Special kitchen utensil. A 9″ cast-iron skillet.

SERVES 2–3

4 tablespoons sweet butter	Salt
1 butcher's tenderloin	Freshly ground black pepper

1. Melt 3 tablespoons butter in a 9″ cast-iron skillet over medium heat. When the butter is not yet turning brown, add the meat and brown it for 2 minutes on each side, spooning the fat over the meat while it browns. Sprinkle on a pinch of salt and freshly ground pepper.

2. Cover the pan, decrease the heat to low, and cook (braise) for 10 minutes, 5 minutes on each side. For a 1-pound steak: braise 4 minutes on one side and 3 minutes on the other side. While braising (with the cover on the skillet over medium-low heat), the steak will create its own juices. Notice when you turn the steak over once during the cooking that steam will fall into the pan as you remove the cover, which will create liquid for the sauce.

3. Transfer the meat to a cutting board with a juice catcher. Tip the skillet and spoon out and discard the fat on top of the juices. Slice the 2 strips of meat in 1″ thick slices and transfer to warm plates.

4. Add the meat juices spewing out of the steak to the juices in the skillet. Bring to a boil and reduce for a minute or so, stirring all the while, until juices are slightly syrupy. Turn off the heat and whisk in 1 tablespoon butter. Taste and correct seasoning with salt and pepper.

Rib Steak with a Wine Sauce

I like to serve rib steaks for a small dinner party, with the meat carved into thin strips instead of having a great piece of meat with the bone taking over half the plate.

Special instruction. Each rib steak needs to be 2″ thick, weighing approximately 2–2¼ pounds. If you are serving a substantial first course, a rib steak will serve 3; otherwise, without a first course, 2. With a 2¼-pound steak, after the bone, fat, and gristle have been removed, only a pound of meat is left. Ask the butcher to saw off 4″ to 5″ of the rib bone at the end where it protrudes from the steak. Reserve that end piece for the sauce.

Special kitchen utensils. Two 9″ cast-iron skillets.

SERVES 4–6

Two 2–2¼-pound rib steaks
2 carrots
Greens of 1 leek
3 cups water
1 teaspoon salt
¼ teaspoon dried thyme

12 tablespoons (1½ sticks) sweet butter
2 tablespoons vegetable oil
Freshly ground pepper
⅔ cup red wine

1. Cut off the fat around the rib steaks.

2. Prepare a quick broth with the 2 end rib bones, 2 carrots cut into ¼″ thick slices, ½ cup chopped greens of leek, 3 cups of water, ¼ teaspoon salt, and ¼ teaspoon thyme. Bring to a boil and boil down to ⅔ cup (about 20 minutes). Strain the liquids (reserve the meat on the bone and the carrots to nibble on).

3. Melt 3 tablespoons of the butter and 1 tablespoon oil in each of two 9″ cast-iron skillets over medium heat. For medium-rare steaks, brown 10 minutes on 1 side, turn over, and brown for 7 minutes; regulate the heat during the cooking period so the fats are never burnt, but remain golden brown. With a spoon baste the meat at least twice with the fats when it is turned over. Sprinkle ½ teaspoon salt and freshly ground pepper over the 2 steaks. Transfer to a big carving board with a juice catcher.

4. Discard all the fats from the skillets and over high heat add ⅓ cup of the reserved quick broth and ⅓ cup good red table wine to each skillet. Bring it to a boil while scraping the bottom and sides of the skillet to get up the drippings. Turn off the heat.

5. With a boning knife, remove the rib bone around the steak, then with a long sharp chef's knife, slice ¼″–½″ thick strips on a slant. Do not be alarmed if the meat seems rather rare at this point; it will continue to cook while you prepare the sauce. Transfer the meat to a preheated platter, overlapping the strips, and cover with foil.

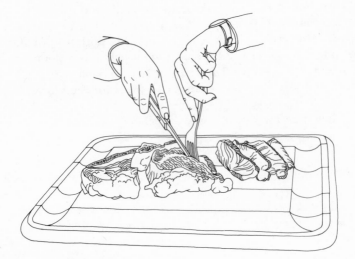

6. Pour the meat juices from the carving of the meat in the skillets and, over high heat, bring to a boil and stir with a wooden spatula until the liquids in both skillets are slightly syrupy. Turn off the heat. Whisk 3 tablespoons butter, 1 tablespoon at a time, into each skillet. Repeat with the second skillet. (It is easier to whisk in a small amount of butter in each skillet than trying to do it in one skillet.) Taste and correct seasonings with salt and pepper. Serve in a preheated sauceboat.

Veal Steak with Ginger

Quick and easy to make, and with an unexpected flavor, these veal steaks make a fine, easy main course for a small dinner party.

Special instructions. Ask the butcher for top round veal or the eye of round that runs through the leg of veal, which weighs about 2 pounds. For a less expensive cut, buy a tied rolled boned center shoulder veal roast, but for this cut, the veal must be tied so that each ¾″ slice will have a string around it.

Special kitchen utensil. A 9″ cast-iron skillet.

SERVES 4

Flour for dredging the veal
Four ¾″ thick slices of top round
  veal
8 tablespoons (1 stick) sweet
  butter
½ cup dry Madeira

⅓ cup homemade chicken or
  beef stock
1 tablespoon minced fresh ginger
½ teaspoon salt
Freshly ground black pepper

1. Have a plate filled with flour for dredging the meat. Dry the meat with paper towels, but do not dredge it yet; otherwise, the surface of the meat will become gummy.

2. Melt 4 tablespoons sweet butter in a 9″ cast-iron skillet over medium heat. Quickly dredge the veal in flour and shake each piece to remove excess flour. Sauté quickly on both sides, just long enough to brown the outside. Remove to a warm platter.

3. Discard the fat from the skillet, add the Madeira, stock, and ginger, and boil down the liquids to a deep shiny color (about 5 minutes). Reduce heat to low, add the veal and the juices that have spewed out of the meat, season with ½ teaspoon salt and freshly ground pepper, cover, and cook (braise) over a low heat, 5 minutes on each side with the liquids just quivering.

4. Transfer the veal steaks to a preheated platter. Bring the liquids back to a boil and boil down for a minute or so or until they are slightly syrupy.

5. Turn off the heat and whisk in the remaining 4 tablespoons butter, a tablespoon at a time. Correct seasonings with salt and pepper and pour the sauce over the veal just before serving. Do not reheat the sauce once you have whipped in the butter; it will separate out and make the sauce greasy.

Veal Scallops and Calf's Liver
with a Mushroom Sauce

This is a quick and easy preparation. Thin slices of top round veal and calf's liver complement each other; served with a mushroom sauce, this dish is delicious. Serve it with Rice Pilaf, page 39.

Special instructions. The mushroom stock can be prepared ahead of time, but it is not really necessary, since the whole preparation takes less than a half hour.

Ask the butcher to cut small veal scallops and slices of calf's liver, about 2 ounces each slice.

Special kitchen utensil. A 12″ cast-iron skillet.

SERVES 4

1 pound mushrooms	Four 2-ounce slices calf's liver
2 teaspoons lemon juice	Freshly ground black pepper
1½ teaspoons salt	
2½ cups water	*For the binding of the sauce*
6 tablespoons sweet butter	1 tablespoon sweet butter
Flour to dredge the meat	1 tablespoon flour
Four 2-ounce veal scallops	

1. Prepare the mushroom stock with the stems of the mushrooms. Turn the mushroom stems into a 2½-quart saucepan with 2 teaspoons freshly squeezed lemon juice and ½ teaspoon salt. Cover with 2½ cups water. Bring the water to a boil and reduce to about 1 cup (about 10 minutes). Strain through a fine-mesh sieve. Discard the stems. Reserve mushroom stock.

2. Slice the mushroom caps and reserve for later. Prepare the binding of the sauce: Mash 1 tablespoon butter in 1 tablespoon flour with the back of a fork into a paste. Reserve. Fill a plate with flour for dredging the meat.

3. Melt 3 tablespoons butter in a 12″ cast-iron skillet over medium heat (if the skillet is too hot, the scallops and the calf's liver will shrivel). Dry each slice of meat in paper towels and dredge 1 slice at a time in the flour, shaking off the excess flour (don't dredge the meat ahead of time or it will become gluey), and add to the skillet. Work quickly to cook all the slices for about the same amount of time. Cook for 2 minutes on each side, shaking the pan once in a while. Sprinkle ½ teaspoon salt and freshly ground pepper over the meat. Transfer to a preheated platter.

4. Add the mushroom slices to the skillet. Add the remaining 2 tablespoons butter and, over high heat, sauté for 2 minutes. Sprinkle ½ teaspoon salt and freshly ground pepper over them. With a perforated spoon, remove and scatter them on top of the meat.

5. Discard the fat in the skillet and pour 1 cup of reserved mushroom stock in the skillet. Bring to a boil, scraping the bottom and sides of the skillet. Boil for 1 minute to reduce the volume and quickly whisk in the butter-flour binding. Continue whisking until the sauce slightly thickens (1 minute or so). Add the juices that drain out of the meat in the platter. Bring to a boil. Turn off the heat, pour sauce over the meat, and serve.

Hot Individual Apple Tarts

These simple small apple tarts are like open turnovers. The pastry dough is rolled out into a flat circle, then decorated with apples or with pears. They can be prepared ahead of time, but must be baked at dessert time; otherwise, they become mushy.

Special kitchen utensils. A cookie cutter about 4½″ in diameter, or a small pot lid, and 2 jelly-roll pans about 16″ x 11″ x 1″.

SERVES 6 (2 TARTS PER PERSON)

Shortcrust Pastry, page 87, or
   leftover dough
6 medium-size cooking apples
½ lemon
½ cup apricot jam

8 tablespoons sugar
6 tablespoons butter
Whipped Cream, page 28,
   or Cream-Cheese Topping,
   page 27

1. Prepare the Shortcrust Pastry according to the recipe, adding 2 table-spoons sugar to the ingredients. Roll out half a batch of pastry to a 10″ circle following the instructions, pages 87–89. Cut out four 4½″ circles and transfer them to a cookie sheet. Roll out the leftover dough to a circle big enough to cut out 2 more circles. Transfer to the jelly-roll pan. Roll out the second batch of pastry in the same manner. Refrigerate covered with waxed paper at least 2 hours before adding the apples.

2. Peel the apples; rub the surfaces with lemon juice. Quarter, seed, and cut them into ¼″ thick slices, trimming them to 3″ long, if necessary. Sprinkle lemon juice over the slices.

3. Brush apricot jam over each circle of dough, then overlap about 4 or 5 slices of apples in the center of the circles, leaving a ½″ edge free. Brush the apples with apricot jam.

4. Sprinkle ½ tablespoon sugar over each apple tart and dot each tart with ½ tablespoon butter. Refrigerate until ready to bake.

5. Prepare Whipped Cream or Cream-Cheese Topping. Refrigerate.

   Preheat oven to 475°F.

6. Bake the tarts on the middle shelf of a 475°F. oven for 5 minutes, then drop the temperature to 400°F. and continue baking for about 10–15 minutes, or until the edges of the pastry become golden brown.

7. Set the broiler on high. Sprinkle 2 tablespoons sugar over the apple tarts and broil for about a minute, 4″ below the broiler.

8. Transfer each tart to an individual dessert plate. Serve the Whipped Cream or Cream-Cheese Topping in a sauceboat. Each guest scoops a dollop of cream over the tarts; the cream melts over and makes a delicious mess.

Hot Individual Berry Tarts
with Melba Sauce

These tarts are strictly for summertime when the berries are at their peak.

Special instructions. Prepare and shape the pastry tarts a day ahead of time if you wish. Refrigerate on jelly-roll pans covered with waxed paper. Decorate with the fruits several hours before baking. Be sure the fruits are very dry when you place them on top of the pastry circles.

Special kitchen utensil. A cookie cutter about 4½″ in diameter, or a small pot lid, and 2 jelly-roll pans about 16″ x 11″ x 1″.

SERVES 6 (2 TARTS PER PERSON)

Shortcrust Pastry, page 87
1 pint blueberries
½ pint raspberries
½ pint blackberries
Several tablespoons sugar

2 tablespoons butter
Two 10-ounce packages frozen
  raspberries in syrup
Cream-Cheese Topping,
  page 27

1. Prepare the pastry dough according to the recipe, page 87, adding 2 tablespoons sugar to the ingredients. Roll out half a batch of dough to a 10″ circle. Cut out four 4½″ circles and transfer them to a jelly-roll pan. Roll out the leftover dough to a circle big enough to cut out 2 more circles. Transfer to the jelly-roll pan. Roll out the second batch of dough in the same manner. Refrigerate covered with waxed paper.

2. Several hours before dinnertime, decorate the pastry with the fresh berries, being sure they are dry. First make a ring of raspberries and blackberries ¼″ from the edge of the circle, then fill the center with blueberries. Sprinkle sugar over the berries and dot each little tart with 2 shavings of butter.

3. *For the Melba Sauce.* Drain the raspberries. Boil the juice down to half. Purée the raspberries in a food mill to extract the seeds. Mix the purée with the reduced liquids. Reheat when ready to eat.

4. Prepare Cream-Cheese Topping, page 27. Refrigerate.

Preheat oven to 375°F.

5. While eating the meal, bake the tarts for 15–20 minutes, depending on your oven, but the dough should start to color slightly around the edges.

6. Transfer the tarts to individual plates. Pour 1 tablespoon hot raspberry (melba) sauce over each tart. Serve Cream-Cheese topping in a bowl.

Blackberry Jam Turnovers

Leftover Shortcrust Pastry is perfect for turnovers, but there is no reason why you can't make a fresh batch of pastry for them. I like a blackberry jam filling, but any other jam that strikes your fancy will be fine. Serve them warm, like the Hot Individual Apple Tarts, page 135.

Special kitchen utensils. A 4½″ cookie cutter, or a pot lid of the same dimension, and 2 jelly-roll pans about 11″ x 16″ x 1″.

SERVES 6 (2 TURNOVERS PER PERSON)

12 tablespoons cold blackberry jam	1 egg yolk
Shortcrust Pastry, page 87	1 tablespoon water
	Whipped Cream, page 28

1. Refrigerate the jam; it's easier to fill the turnovers.

2. Prepare Shortcrust Pastry according to the recipe, page 87, adding 2 tablespoons sugar to the ingredients. Roll out half a batch of pastry to a 12″ circle. Cut out four 4½″ circles and transfer them to a jelly-roll pan. Roll out the leftover dough once more to a circle big enough to cut out 2 more circles. Transfer to a jelly-roll pan. Refrigerate while rolling out the second batch of pastry in the same manner.

3. Bring the pastry circles back to room temperature if they have been in the refrigerator for long. It's easier to fold the dough. Brush cold water around the top of the circles. Then put 1 tablespoon cold jam in the center of each circle. Fold the dough over the jam and seal it with the bottom part of the dough to make a half-moon-shaped turnover. Crimp the edges with the back of a fork. Combine egg yolk and 1 tablespoon water and brush this glaze over each turnover.

4. Prepare the Whipped Cream, page 28. Refrigerate.

   Preheat oven to 400°F.

5. Bake on the middle shelf of the oven for about 15–20 minutes or until golden brown. The jam might spew out of the turnovers. Don't worry. When the turnovers are baked, scoop up any jam and brush it on top of the turnovers. The turnovers will flatten out but will be delicious anyway.

6. Serve them with Whipped Cream. Put a dollop of the cream on top of the turnover and a dollop of cream in your coffee if you are drinking coffee with it.

TECHNIQUES AND UTENSILS INTRODUCED

How to make vegetable pâté, to layer it, and to unmold it, using a 6-cup loaf pan; how to make individual pâtés using ½″ soufflé molds (ramekins)

How to make tomato sauce with fresh tomatoes and with canned tomatoes

How to can tomato sauce: the water bath method and the steam bath method

How to cook veal kidneys

How to cream cottage cheese

How to make Crème Fraîche with sour cream

How to make black currant liqueur

Lesson 8

Suggested Menus for Lesson 8

Winter Lunch

Vegetable Pâté

Poached Fruits with
Cream-Cheese Topping
(Lesson 1)

Summer Lunch

Vegetable Quiche

Tossed Green Salad
(Lesson 1)

Poached Peaches
with Creamed Cottage Cheese
and Crème de Cassis

2-Course Dinner

Store-bought Pasta with
Thick Tomato Sauce

Strawberries with Cream-Cheese
Topping (Lesson 1)

3-Course Dinner

Chicken with Feta Cheese

Rice Pilaf (Lesson 2)

Caramel Custard (Lesson 3)

3-Course Dinner

Molded Summer Vegetable Custard

Chicken Pie

Chocolate Fudge Cake

Vegetable Pâté

This vegetable loaf originates in the Poitou region in west central France and is called Far du Poitou there. It makes a fine vegetable course with a dinner or a main course for a brunch. It is also good cold and makes lovely sandwiches. This pâté is perhaps the most successful dish in my classes.

Special instruction. For a Layered Vegetable Pâté, follow the alternate instructions at steps 4, 6, 8, and 9. The pâté can be prepared a day ahead and baked when needed, or it can be reheated in a water-bath in a 300°F. oven for 20 minutes.

Special kitchen utensil. Bake the pâté in a 6-cup pâté mold or a loaf pan.

SERVES 8

8 quarts water
3 tablespoons salt
1 pound cabbage (about ½ small head)
3 medium leeks
3 pounds loose or two 10-ounce bags fresh spinach
½ pound slab bacon in 1 piece (or substitute 4 tablespoons roast or meat drippings or chicken, goose, or duck fat or butter)

2 medium-size onions
Freshly ground black pepper
1 pinch cayenne pepper
4 large eggs
1 cup heavy cream
1½ cups Tomato Cream Sauce, page 148
3 tablespoons grated Swiss cheese plus ⅓ cup for the layered pâté

1. In a 10-quart pot, boil 8 quarts water with 2 tablespoons salt.

2. Quarter the cabbage and discard the solid core. Cut off the tops of the leeks 2″ above the white part. (Keep the green tops for stock.) Quarter the leeks lengthwise and wash very well. Boil (blanch) the leeks and cabbage for 20 minutes. Remove the leeks and cabbage with a strainer and rinse in cold water. Squeeze very dry with your hands.

3. Wash spinach well and discard stems. Rinse several times to remove all the sand. Boil 2 minutes. Drain, rinse with cold water, and squeeze very dry with your hands.

4. Mince all vegetables together using a large knife. Squeeze out as much water as possible. Reserve.

   For a layered pâté. Mince the spinach; squeeze as much water out as possible. Mince the cabbage and leeks and squeeze out the water.

5. Boil 2 quarts water for the bacon. Cut off half the fat of the slab bacon and discard. Boil the remaining piece for 5 minutes to remove excess salt and smoky flavor. Rinse under cold water, dry, and cut into ¼″ cubes. Cook the bacon cubes slowly in a large heavy skillet until golden brown (about 10 minutes), being careful not to burn them. Remove bacon with a slotted spoon and reserve on a paper towel. Do not pour off the fat.

6. Mince the onions and add them to the skillet. Sauté in the bacon fat (or substitute other fat mentioned in ingredients list) gently until they are golden (about 5 minutes), stirring now and again to make sure they don't burn. Add the chopped vegetables and cook gently for about 5 minutes to drive off excess liquid, stirring all the while to avoid burning. Add more fat if necessary. Season with 2 teaspoons salt, 6 grinds of the pepper mill, and a pinch of cayenne.

   For a layered pâté. Mince 2 onions and sauté them until wilted. Divide the fat and onions between 2 skillets. Add the spinach in one skillet, and the leeks and cabbage in the second skillet. Cook over medium heat to drive off the excess liquid in the vegetables, stirring all the while to avoid burning. (Add more fat if necessary.) Season each vegetable mixture with 1¼ teaspoons salt, freshly ground pepper and cayenne.

7. Butter a 1½-quart loaf pan and cover the inside with waxed paper, cutting pieces to fit the sides and bottom (see illustration); grease again. It is important to do this correctly to ensure a perfect shape for the pâté.

8. Beat 4 eggs and 1 cup heavy cream together; add to the vegetables and mix well; add bacon. Taste and correct seasonings if necessary.

   For a layered pâté. Pour ½ cup cream and egg mixture in the spinach and ½ cup cream and egg mixture in the leeks and cabbage. Mix thoroughly. Grate ⅓ cup Swiss cheese into the leek and cabbage mixture to bind it (it has a looser consistency than the spinach). Taste each vegetable mixture and season with more salt if necessary; add a pinch of cayenne.

   Preheat oven to 375°F.

9. Pour the mixture into the loaf pan. Place in a water bath which is two-thirds the depth of the pan. Bake for about 1 hour at 375°F. or until the egg and cream mixture is set.

   For a layered pâté. Divide the spinach and leek cabbage mixtures in 2 piles each for 4 piles in all. First spread 1 layer of leeks and cabbage mixture in the loaf pan, then a layer of spinach. Alternate the remaining mixtures. Bake.

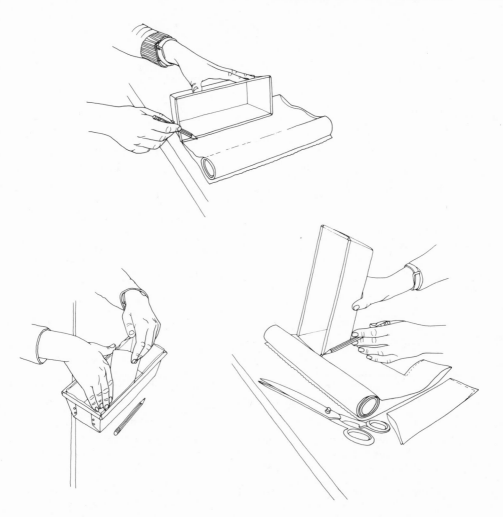

10. To unmold, run a thin knife blade between the pan and the waxed paper. Turn pan upside down on a platter but cool 30 minutes before unmolding. It will taste better; the flavors develop more as it cools. Unmold onto an ovenproof platter. If some water runs out on the platter, blot it up with a paper towel. Remove waxed paper.

11. Prepare the Tomato Cream Sauce, page 148.

12. Pour half the Tomato Cream Sauce over the vegetable loaf and sprinkle with 3 tablespoons grated cheese. Pass under the broiler for a few minutes until the cheese starts to bubble and turn golden. Present the remaining sauce in a heated sauceboat to be ladled over individual slices of the loaf. Slice the vegetable loaf in pieces about ½″ thick and serve.

Baked Spinach Loaf

This is a more elegant unmolded version of the Spinach Gratin, page 125, with a Tomato Cream Sauce, page 148, ladled over it and gratinéed. It can be served for a brunch, a buffet (excellent cold), or an appetizer. All the preparation can be done ahead of time. Without the Tomato Cream Sauce, serve it as a vegetable with a roast or fish.

Special kitchen utensil. I generally bake the dish in a 6-cup tin loaf pan, but a 6-cup (1½-quart) soufflé mold or individual molds, such as ramekins, are also fine.

SERVES 8

5 pounds loose or three
   10-ounce bags fresh spinach
   (3½ cups cooked)
8 quarts water
3 tablespoons salt
1 onion
4½ tablespoons sweet butter
1½ cups half-and-half

2 tablespoons flour
Freshly ground black pepper
4 large eggs
1½ cups Tomato Cream Sauce,
   page 148
½ cup plus 3 tablespoons grated
   Swiss cheese

1. Wash the spinach leaves very well, cut off the stems with scissors and discard them. Rinse several times to get rid of all the sand. Drain.

2. Boil 8 quarts water with 2 tablespoons salt. Drop the spinach into the boiling water; as soon as it begins to boil again, add 1 teaspoon salt. Boil for 2 minutes, drain, and rinse in cold water; then squeeze it dry with your hands and chop very fine (yields 3½ cups).

3. Mince 1 onion very fine. Melt 2 tablespoons butter in a 12" cast-iron skillet and cook the onion over low heat until it wilts (about 5–7 minutes). Add the spinach to the onion. Sprinkle 1½ teaspoons salt. Continue cooking for about 3 minutes, stirring occasionally.

4. *For a thick béchamel.* Boil 1½ cups half-and-half. In a saucepan, melt 2½ tablespoons butter. Add 2 tablespoons flour and whisk the mixture briskly while it bubbles for 1 minute. Off the flame, add the boiling half-and-half and whisk well. Simmer over medium-low heat, whisking now and again until the mixture is thick, about 5 minutes. Season with ½ teaspoon salt and freshly ground black pepper.

5. Break the eggs in a bowl and beat them well with a fork; then add spinach, eggs, and ½ cup grated cheese to the béchamel and mix well. *Taste,* then correct seasoning with salt and pepper, if necessary.

6. Butter a loaf pan that holds 6 cups. Line the mold with waxed paper, cutting a piece to fit the bottom, page 143. Grease the waxed paper.

Preheat oven to 375°F.

7. Pour the spinach mixture into the mold and bake in a hot water bath for 45–60 minutes. The water bath should be about two-thirds the depth of the mold.

8. *Unmold.* Turn the mold upside down on a preheated ovenproof platter. *Let it cool for 30 minutes before unmolding.* Can be eaten as is.

9. Ladle the 1½ cups Tomato Cream Sauce over the spinach mold. Sprinkle 3 tablespoons grated Swiss cheese on top and pass under the broiler just enough for the cheese to melt and color it a bit. Cut 1″ thick slices.

Molded Summer Vegetable Custard

Unmolded, a vegetable custard makes a pretty presentation, suitable for an hors d'oeuvre as well as for a vegetable.

Special instructions. Add 1 more onion if you have any difficulty finding leeks. To use as a vegetable course, omit the bacon, but add 2 more tablespoons of oil when the zucchini are added to the onions and leeks.

Special kitchen utensils. Bake in 8-ounce individual soufflé molds or in a 6-cup soufflé mold, then cut in wedges.

SERVES 6–8

4 tomatoes*	A pinch of cayenne pepper
2 medium-size onions	4 large eggs
1 small leek	1 cup heavy cream (not ultra-
3 small zucchini	pasteurized, if possible)
4 ounces slab bacon	1 cup grated Swiss cheese
3 tablespoons olive oil	(4 ounces)
1 teaspoon salt	

* Out of season, buy a 17-ounce can of Italian peeled plum tomatoes (not packed in tomato purée or paste). Drain the tomatoes, split in two, for one hour.

1. Peel the tomatoes. (Plunge the tomatoes in boiling water for 1 minute only, if they are difficult to peel.) Quarter, seed them, and chop into small cubes (you should have 2 cups).

2. Peel the onions and cut in half. With the flat side on the counter, cut the onions into thin slices. Cut off the outer dark green leaves of the leek and all the tough leaves. Do not discard the tender light green leaves. Slice the leek lengthwise and wash thoroughly under running cold water. Mince.

3. Wash and dry the zucchini; do not peel. Cut off the ends. Split each zucchini in half lengthwise, then split each half in two. Now you have 4 long pieces (thick julienne strips). Gather in one hand, and cut crosswise into ½" thick cubes.

4. Slice off the rind of the bacon. Cut the bacon into ½" strips, then each strip into 1" long pieces.

5. Heat 3 tablespoons olive oil in a heavy 12" cast-iron skillet. When the oil is hot but not smoking, stir in the onion slices and the leek. Cook over medium heat, stirring occasionally, for 5 minutes. Add the bacon and cook 10 more minutes, then add the zucchini cubes. Stir all the time to coat the zucchini with fat, making sure that none of the ingredients stick to the bottom of the skillet. Season with 1 teaspoon salt and a pinch of cayenne. Cook for 15 minutes. When the zucchini starts to color, add the tomatoes. Cover partially and, over low to medium heat, cook for 10 minutes; uncover and continue cooking for 10 more minutes.

6. In a 4-quart mixing bowl, break 4 eggs, beat lightly, and mix with 1 cup heavy cream.

Preheat oven to 400°F.

7. Cool the vegetables for 5 minutes, then mix them with the eggs, cream, and cheese. Taste. Correct seasonings with salt and pepper, if necessary.

8. Butter a 6-cup soufflé mold or six 8-ounce individual soufflé molds. Bake on the middle shelf of the oven for 30 minutes for the 6-cup mold, and 15 minutes for the 8-ounce molds. Turn the mold or molds upside down on a serving platter. Wait 5 minutes to unmold and serve.

Summer Vegetable Quiche

Shortcrust Pastry, page 87   Unbaked Summer Vegetable
                                              Custard, page 145

1. Prepare one batch of Shortcrust Pastry. Line a 10" tart mold with the dough and prebake according to the instructions, pages 88–90, step 8.

2. The quiche will be at its best eaten 30 minutes after coming out of the oven; if it is cooked too much ahead of time, the pastry becomes soggy. The vegetable custard can be prepared in the morning, or a day ahead, and the pastry can be rolled at that time. Refrigerate. It takes about 40 minutes to bake the quiche, and 30 minutes to let it cool, so plan to start baking 1½ hours before eating it.

Thick Tomato Sauce

If I had to tell which recipes are the favorites of my classes, this Thick Tomato Sauce and the following Tomato Cream Sauce would come first. I use a lot of tomato sauce—for pasta, for gratinéed vegetables—and I never use commercial tomato paste, but replace it with this Thick Tomato Sauce when 2 or 3 tablespoons are needed in a recipe. I can tomato sauce in September; tomatoes are good then and not expensive. Of course, I am speaking to city dwellers and nongardeners when I mention canning in September.

Special instruction. The tomato sauce freezes very well, but today with soaring electric prices, it might be just as well to learn how to can, page 148. There is a device for home canners called Squeezo Strainer sold by Garden Way, Charlotte, Vermont 05445, that will peel and purée the tomatoes.

When making tomato sauce in quantity, figure 4 pounds of tomatoes for a quart of sauce. This means that the sauce must be reduced a great deal. The advantages of this are that you don't need to use much to get the required flavor, and the storage space used is also reduced. Canned sauce keeps for two years.

MAKES 2 CUPS SAUCE

1 large onion
4 tablespoons olive oil
2 pounds fresh tomatoes*
1 tablespoon minced garlic
¼ cup minced fresh basil

1 tablespoon minced fresh parsley
½ teaspoon sugar
1 teaspoon salt
⅛ teaspoon freshly ground black pepper

* Out of season, buy a 35-ounce can of Italian peeled plum tomatoes (not packed in tomato purée or paste). Drain the tomatoes, split in two, for one hour.

1. Peel the onion. Cut it in half. With the flat side against the counter, cut the onion in very thin slices.

2. Heat 4 tablespoons olive oil in a 12″ cast-iron skillet. Add the onion and cook until soft but not brown, about 10 minutes.

3. Do not peel the tomatoes; simply cut them into small pieces, removing stem socket and blemishes. I don't peel the tomatoes when I make tomato sauce. When I make it in bulk as I do, it is too time-consuming to peel. Only when I cook with the sauce do I pass it through a fine-mesh sieve or a food mill to extract skins, seeds, and the like.

4. Add the tomatoes, minced garlic, basil, parsley, sugar, salt, and pepper to the onions. Cook over low to medium heat for 30 minutes or until the mixture of tomatoes is thick.

5. Purée the tomatoes in a food mill (medium blade) or food processor. *Be careful not to get spattered by the hot tomato sauce.*

Tomato Cream Sauce

The "aurora" is that time of day in the early morning when the sun is just about to shine through; the sky is then pale pink. Cream mixed with tomato sauce, or a béchamel with tomato sauce, justifies its name in French: Sauce Aurore. This is my standard sauce for all unmolded vegetable dishes gratinéed under the broiler. I also serve it with buttered noodles, omelets, and cheese and vegetable soufflés.

Special kitchen utensil. A 9″ cast-iron skillet.

MAKES ABOUT 1½ CUPS

1 cup heavy cream or 1½ cups
  half-and-half
1 cup Thick Tomato Sauce,
  page 147

Salt
Freshly ground black pepper

1. In a 9″ heavy-bottomed skillet, boil down the cream or half-and-half to half its original volume, stirring constantly. Notice that I use a low-sided and wide-surface pan to reduce the cream. The cream reduces much faster than in a small, high-edged pan.

2. Strain the tomato sauce. Add it to the reduced cream. Bring to a boil. Taste to correct seasonings with salt and freshly ground pepper.

Technique: To can tomato sauce

Canning is a lot of work, but how wonderful it is to have ready-made sauce during the long winter months. There is a great feeling of accomplishment looking at one's own canned jars on shelves, and using them. Here are two methods for canning: using the *water bath canner* and using the *steam bath canner.* Read the whole procedure before starting to can. This is for 6 quarts of tomato sauce. Figure 2 hours for the canning. I prefer the steam bath canner to the water bath; it goes so much faster. I give both methods for the cook who already has the equipment for the more traditional water bath method. Garden Way, Charlotte, Vermont 05445, sells the steam bath canner, or order from Ideal Harvest, Inc., P.O. Box 15481, 3272 South West Temple, Salt Lake City, Utah 84115.

Equipment required

6 quart jars (or 12 pint jars)

A steam bath canner *or* a water bath canner with rack for the jars

A 2-quart pot

Lids and rings for the jars

Canning tongs for handling the jars

A ladle

A wide-mouth canning funnel

A large kettle

3–4 clean dish towels

While the tomato sauce is simmering, sterilize the jars by submerging them completely in boiling water for 15 minutes. (This is done in your canner or another large pot if available.)

In a 2-quart pot sterilize the tongs, the lids, the ladle, and the funnel by pouring boiling water to cover over them. Let stand until ready to use. Do not boil the lids, as you may damage them. Keep a kettle of boiling water on hand to rinse implements.

After your jars are sterilized and the tomato sauce is simmering, remove each jar from the boiling water as you are ready to fill it. Try to keep the jars and sauce as hot as possible during the canning process. Uneven heat can cause the jars to fail to seal. Using the tongs, place the funnel on top of the jars and fill with tomato sauce to within ½″ of the top of the jar.

Be careful not to dribble sauce on the outside of the jar and especially not on the lip. If you dribble a bit, wipe it up with a clean towel. Whenever you set down the tongs, set them in the hot water with the lids, not on the counter top or stove.

Using the tongs, remove a lid from the hot water and place it on the filled jar. Resist the temptation to nudge it into place with your fingers. If you need another implement, sterilize a spoon or fork to work with. Still using the tongs, place a ring on top. Holding the lid with a towel, screw the ring tight. Proceed to fill your 6 jars in this manner.

Canning with a water bath canner. Place the jars on the rack of the water bath canner and gently lower them into the

boiling water. Make sure the jars are covered by at least 1″ of water. If necessary, during processing, add more boiling water from the kettle very quickly. Cover the canner and boil the jars for 35 minutes for quarts or 25 minutes for pints.

Canning with a steam bath canner.
A steam bath canner comes with
3 parts: a bottom pan, a plate with
holes, and a dome.

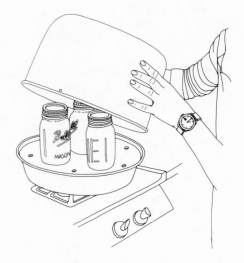

- Pour 2 quarts of water in the bottom pan. Place it on top of the stove, fit the plate on top of the pan. Place the filled jars between the holes in the plates. Cover the jars with the dome.
- Turn the heat on to medium. When the water in the bottom pan starts to boil, steam will escape from 2 small holes at the base of the dome. Begin the timing only then—30 minutes for quarts, 20 minutes for pints.

Remove the rack from the canner after the processing time is up. Using the tongs, remove the jars from the rack. *Do not touch* them until the jars are completely cooled—possibly overnight. Even though you may hear the familiar "plink" sound as the lids seal, you could break this seal if you handle them too soon.

After your jars have completely cooled, test them to see if they are well sealed.

- Push the center of the lid down; if it does not spring back, the jar is sealed.
- If the jar spontaneously gives a "plinking or pinging" sound while cooling, the jar is sealed.

If any of your jars have failed to seal, you must start over from the beginning in order to be sure you have safely canned your sauce or you can just refrigerate and eat within 2 weeks or freeze in a plastic container.

After checking your jars for a proper seal, screw the rings tight again. Store in a cool, dry, dark place; the temperature should be under 70°F. This sauce will keep over a year, but for best flavor, I would use it within the year.

Chicken Pie

My Aunt Tatane, a truly accomplished and inventive cook, devised this elaborate version of an English-style pot pie years ago in France. The key to this recipe is to brown all the ingredients in the same pan so that none of the flavor is lost. All the work can be done several hours ahead of time, including rolling the pastry for the top. Refrigerate it, and bake when needed.

Special instruction. Learn to cut a whole chicken into serving pieces—it is more economical than buying chicken pieces, see pages 96–97.

Special kitchen utensils. A 3-quart round baking dish.

SERVES 10

Two 3½-pound chickens
2 tablespoons butter and
  1 tablespoon oil, or
  3 tablespoons fat from
  roast or chicken
2½ teaspoons salt
Freshly ground black pepper
1 veal kidney
1 pound breakfast sausages
2 medium-size yellow onions
2 medium-size carrots
2 tablespoons butter
½ pound mushrooms

3 large eggs
10 green olives
Shortcrust Pastry, page 87

For the glaze

1 egg yolk
1 tablespoon water

For the sauce

2 cups heavy cream
½ teaspoon dried tarragon or
  1 tablespoon minced fresh
  tarragon

1. Cut each chicken into 8 pieces, following the technique on pages 96–97. Cut the carcasses into pieces.

2. Melt 2 tablespoons butter mixed with 1 tablespoon oil, or 3 tablespoons fat from a roast or chicken, in two 12″ cast-iron skillets. When the fat is hot but not smoking, sauté the chicken breasts for only 30 seconds on each side. Reserve on a plate. Continue to sauté the remaining pieces of chicken over medium heat for about 30 minutes. The chicken pieces must be golden brown. Season with 1 teaspoon salt and freshly ground pepper. Reserve on a plate. Brown the carcasses the same way for 10 minutes. If at any point in the recipe more fat is required for sautéing, add it.

3. Remove any fat remaining on the veal kidney. Split it in half. Cut off any gristle at the center of the kidney, then cut into ¼″ thick slices and sauté in the skillet for 1 minute only over high heat. Season with ¼ teaspoon salt. Drain in a colander. Do not save the juice that drains out. It is very strong in flavor.

4. Remove the casings of the sausages. Cut into ½" thick slices. Still in the same skillet, cook the sausage for 15 minutes over medium heat. Reserve the sausage.

5. Peel and slice the onions in half. With the flat side on the counter, cut into thin slices. Peel the carrots and cut into ¼" slices. Sauté the onions and carrots in the same skillet. Stir frequently so the onions don't stick and burn. Season with ½ teaspoon salt and freshly ground pepper. After 5 minutes, add 2 tablespoons butter if necessary. Cover, reduce the heat to low, and braise for 15 minutes. Reserve.

6. Remove the stems from the mushrooms. Wash and dry the caps. Quarter the caps (if they are very big, quarter once more). Sauté the mushrooms in the same skillet over medium heat, adding more fat if needed. Sauté for 3 minutes. Season with ¼ teaspoon salt. Pour into the skillet 2 cups heavy cream. Bring to a boil with the tarragon and reduce to 1½ cups. Season with ½ teaspoon salt and freshly ground pepper. Reserve.

7. Bone the chicken pieces. Cut into bite sizes. Reserve the bones for a stock, and the pieces from the carcass for a sandwich. Cover 3 eggs with cold water. Bring to a boil. Cover, lower the heat, and cook 10 minutes. Drain. Cool under running cold water. Peel and quarter.

8. Mix the chicken, kidney, sausage, onions and carrots, mushrooms, eggs, and olives together, season with 1 teaspoon salt and freshly ground pepper, and place in a 3-quart round baking dish.

9. Prepare 1 batch Shortcrust Pastry dough according to recipe and refrigerate 15 minutes.

10. Roll out the pastry to fit the top of the baking dish. Cover the chickens with the dough. Moisten the edge of the baking dish all around with water and pinch the pastry to the edge of the dish to seal it to the dish. With a sharp-pointed knife, cut a small hole about 1" in diameter right in the middle of the pastry. Make a little chimney of aluminum foil and stick it through the hole, just below the level of the crust. (It can be done ahead of time to this point.)

Preheat oven to 400°F.

11. Beat 1 egg yolk with 1 tablespoon water and brush the pastry all over. Bake for 40 minutes. Cover loosely with foil if the top browns too much.

12. Remove the pie from the oven, transfer the cream and tarragon to a cup with a spout, and pour it through the chimney into the pie. Serve immediately. It is very difficult to cut the pastry neatly—it is very brittle.

Chicken with Feta Cheese

A friend from Poulithra, a small village in northeastern Greece, makes this wonderful braised chicken with onions and tomatoes, then blankets the chicken pieces with feta (goat) cheese which melts into the meat and sauce.

You have to be sure to get imported feta, moist and salty, and have only very juicy tomatoes to give plenty of liquids; that is why most of the time I use canned tomatoes and their juices, since most fresh tomatoes are good only at the peak of the season (about 2 months in the summer) and you may well want to make this dish more than once during the year.

Special kitchen utensil. Use a 9″ cast-iron skillet. Cook the chicken in the skillet and present it at the table in the skillet.

SERVES 4

3-pound chicken	2 cloves garlic, minced
3 tablespoons olive oil	½ teaspoon dried oregano
4 medium-size yellow onions	½ teaspoon salt
17-ounce can plum tomatoes or	Freshly ground black pepper
1½ pounds fresh tomatoes	½ pound feta cheese

1. Cut up the chicken into 8 pieces, following the technique on pages 96–97.

2. Heat 2 tablespoons olive oil in a 9″ cast-iron skillet. When the oil is hot but not smoking, add the 2 chicken breast pieces and cook them for 30 seconds on each side. Remove them to a plate and reserve to finish cooking later because chicken breasts cook much faster than dark meat.

3. Brown the rest of the chicken pieces until golden brown (15–20 minutes) over medium heat, turning the pieces over once in a while. Transfer the chicken pieces to a plate while browning the sliced onions in the skillet. Stir the onions constantly, add 1 more tablespoon olive oil, and cook them for 15 minutes until slightly colored.

4. Peel the tomatoes (drop them in boiling water for 30 seconds if necessary) and chop them or use a 17-ounce can of plum tomatoes with their juice. Stir the tomatoes and juice into the onions; add the minced garlic and oregano. Put the chicken pieces (minus the breast pieces) on the onions and tomatoes. Sprinkle ½ teaspoon salt and freshly ground pepper over the chicken pieces. Cover and simmer over medium-low heat for 30 minutes with the surface bubbling gently.

5. Cut ½ pound feta cheese into paper-thin slices.

6. Bury the chicken breasts in the onions after 30 minutes, and add the juices in the plate to the skillet. Totally cover the chicken pieces with the feta cheese. Cover and continue cooking 15 more minutes. The feta

will melt over the chicken and into the sauce created by the onions and tomatoes.

7. Serve as is in the black iron skillet with rice or fresh noodles on the side.

Chocolate Fudge Cake

"Gateau Fateau," as it has been baptized by friends, is a rich chocolate fudge-pudding cake. It is essential that you use a good quality eating chocolate, such as Lindt or Tobler, see Special Instructions, page 43.

Special utensil. A 4-cup ring mold.

SERVES 6–8

8 ounces extra bittersweet chocolate (Lindt or Tobler)	5 tablespoons Cointreau
16 tablespoons (2 sticks) sweet butter	6 tablespoons cornstarch
1 cup eggs (4 large eggs)	1 pint strawberries *in season*
1 cup superfine sugar	2 tablespoons sugar
	Whipped Cream, page 28, or Crème Fraîche

1. Melt the chocolate in a pan set in a water bath (improvise a water bath with a low-sided pan such as a skillet one-third full of water). Keep the water below the boiling point. This is to keep the water from splattering into the chocolate, which would make it grainy. (If that happens, whisk 1 tablespoon vegetable shortening into the chocolate to smooth it out.)

2. Remove the melted chocolate from the heat and let it cool to body temperature (about 98°F.). Test the temperature of the melted chocolate as follows: dip your finger into the chocolate and touch it to your lower lip. If it feels warm, the chocolate is not yet ready to mix with butter.

3. While the chocolate melts and cools, cream the butter. Mash and smear the butter on the counter with the heel of your hand until soft but not melted. Transfer it to the mixing bowl of your beater and beat it at medium speed for 1 minute. Beat the chocolate into the butter for 2 minutes. Reserve. At this point, the chocolate-butter must not be runny —it must be a thick mixture. If it's not, refrigerate for 20 minutes, then beat again with the electric mixer before proceeding to step 5.

4. Beat the eggs. (Be sure you have 1 cup of eggs. Eggs are of all different sizes. It is better to measure them by volume.) Start dribbling the super-

fine sugar into the eggs, still beating at high speed, until the mixture turns very pale yellow and is thick (about 7 minutes).

5. The butter-chocolate mixture and the egg-sugar mixture should be of the same consistency. Beat the chocolate mixture into the egg mixture and add 2 tablespoons Cointreau. Beat 1 more minute.

6. Sift 6 tablespoons cornstarch. Then sprinkle it through a fine-mesh sieve onto the chocolate batter. Fold the cornstarch into the batter with a rubber spatula.

7. Melt 1 tablespoon butter, and brush it inside a 4-cup ring mold.

   Preheat oven to 350°F.

8. Ladle the batter into the mold. Tap on the counter a few times to level. Cover with buttered waxed paper, cut to fit exactly the top of the cake to keep the cake from drying out. Place the mold in a water bath of near-boiling water which comes halfway up the side of the mold and bake at 350°F. for 1 hour. Check the cake after 45 minutes. It should have risen ½"–1" above the mold.

9. Remove the ring mold from the water bath. Let the cake cool for 10 minutes. It will collapse a bit and the top might crack. Turn it upside down on a serving platter, *but do not unmold.* Wait at least 30 minutes, then remove the mold. It should come off easily. Unmolding the cake can be tricky. Sometimes the mold is at fault—it sticks. Never use detergent to clean it; always use a scrubbing brush and hot water. Dry the mold immediately. Let the cake cool completely at room temperature.

10. If the cake was made a day ahead of time, remove it from the refrigerator 2 or 3 hours before dessert time.

11. *The decoration.* Marinate the strawberries in 3 tablespoons Cointreau and 2 tablespoons sugar. Fill the center of the cake with Whipped Cream and place strawberries on top.

Crème Fraîche

The most common method for making an American version of *crème fraîche,* which in France is simply fresh, thick, slightly tart cream, is to mix some butter-milk with heavy cream. If you don't use buttermilk for anything else, you can make crème fraîche with sour cream. Mix 1 cup heavy cream with 1 cup sour cream and cover with plastic wrap. Let stand at room temperature for several hours or until the mixture is very thick. Serve as is, or beat in 1 tablespoon sugar and 1 tablespoon liqueur or brandy of your choice. Refrigerated, it will last for over a week.

Poached Peaches
with Creamed Cottage Cheese
and Crème de Cassis

Special instruction. Substitute pears or plums if the peaches are not ripe enough.

SERVES 6

6 peaches
⅓ cup sugar, plus 2–3 tablespoons, optional

⅓ cup water
1½ pounds cottage cheese
Crème de cassis

1. Boil 1 quart water. Drop 2 peaches at a time in the boiling water for 30 seconds and peel. Slice the peaches over a plate to catch any juices.

2. In a 12″ cast-iron skillet or sauté pan, combine ⅓ cup sugar, ⅓ cup water, and the juices that drained from the peaches while peeling them. Bring to a boil to dissolve the sugar, add the peaches, and poach for 3–4 minutes or until tender over low-medium heat. Remove the peaches with a skimmer to a fine-mesh sieve over a bowl. Let drip for 30 minutes.

3. Over high heat, boil down the liquids in the skillet until they are slightly syrupy. Cool. The syrup, when cold, should have the consistency of light honey.

4. Cream the cottage cheese in a blender or food processor with the peach syrup for 2 minutes or so, until the cottage cheese is very smooth. Taste for sweetness. If you care for a sweeter cheese, add 2–3 tablespoons sugar and whirl once more in the machine.

5. Serve the peaches in individual bowls or glasses and the creamed cheese in a serving bowl.

6. Pour ½ tablespoon crème de cassis over each serving of peaches and cheese.

Crème de Cassis

Cassis is a variety of currant. However, in English it is not the variety that most people know and use for fruit cakes and mincemeat. Cassis is a black currant, an acidic fruit, very similar in shape and size to red currants. It grows on a vinelike shrub. When the currants are picked, there is still a thin delicate-looking stem which is discarded before making crème de cassis, a black currant liqueur.

There are very good store-bought brands of crème de cassis, but buy it in reliable wine shops with big turnover, for cassis keeps only about a year. The best producers date their cassis as wine is dated. Afterward, the fruit changes color from a ruby-red to a dark, muddy, brownish red and loses most of its flavor.

Special instruction. The currants need to macerate in red wine for 8 days. Buy a moderately priced table wine. Avoid jug wines and avoid overly tannic wines. Since the fruit is already tart, choose a Zinfandel, Chianti, Beaujolais, or Côtes du Rhône.

Special kitchen utensils. A 5-quart stainless steel pot or an unlined copper bowl such as an egg white bowl. A food mill fitted with a fine blade or a cotton cloth dish towel.

TO FILL 2 WINE BOTTLES

2 pounds black currants (cassis) 4½ cups superfine sugar
1 bottle red wine 1¼ cups unflavored vodka

1. Remove the small stems from the currants. Turn the fruit in a 2-quart mixing bowl. Pour in 1 bottle of wine. Cover the bowl with a plate. Do not refrigerate. Let stand for 8 days, stirring the fruit in the wine with a wooden spoon every other day.

2. Drain the fruit through a fine-mesh sieve, catching the juice in a mixing bowl.

3. Pass 1 cup of fruit at a time through the fine disk of a food mill to extract the fruit juice. (Do not use the food processor. It will leave all the skins and seeds in the juice.) Discard the skins. If you don't have a food mill, squeeze ½ cup of fruit at a time in a cotton cloth dish towel. Add the extracted juices to the liquid in the mixing bowl.

4. Measure the number of cups of liquid. For 4 cups of liquid, combine 3½ cups of sugar in a 5-quart stainless steel pan or an unlined egg white copper bowl. For more or less liquid, adjust the sugar proportionately. Over medium heat, bring the mixture slowly to a boil (about 20 minutes), stirring occasionally with a wooden spoon. When the boil is reached, count about 3 minutes of boiling time or test the temperature of the syrup with a candy thermometer. It needs to reach to 205°–210°F. Turn off the heat.

5. For 4 cups of juice, add 1¼ cups of unflavored vodka. Cool completely, then bottle and cork it. Serve on ice cream, or with cottage cheese, or make kirs.

TECHNIQUES AND UTENSILS INTRODUCED

Introduction to yeast doughs: what kind of yeast to buy;
how to proof yeast; how to use the food processor

How to roll pasta by hand or by machine

How to cook fresh pasta

How to make a creamy sherbet and ice cream
in an ice cream machine

Lesson 9

Suggested Menus for Lesson 9

Sunday Lunch or Supper

Pizza with Deep-Fried
Eggplant and Tomatoes
or
Pizza Bohémienne

Tossed Green Salad (Lesson 1)

Apples and Cheese

2-Course Summer Dinner

Sautéed Zucchini with
Tomatoes and Onions over
Homemade Fresh Pasta
or Store-bought Pasta

Blueberry Sherbet

3-Course Dinners

Cheese Puffs (Lesson 3)

Scallops with Homemade Pasta

Raspberry Sherbet Made with
Frozen Raspberries

Broccoli Purée on Toast
(Lesson 2)

Roasted Whole Veal Shanks
(Lesson 2)
served with Bohémienne

Mango Sherbet
or
Raspberry Sherbet

Bohémienne
(Eggplant and Tomatoes)

This dish is similar to the well-known ratatouille, but it lacks zucchini and peppers and has eggs in it. It can be served as an hors d'oeuvre spread on toast, as a vegetable dish to accompany meat, or used as a filling for pizza or for a quiche, page 162.

SERVES 4–6

Special kitchen utensil. A 6½-quart Dutch oven or the equivalent pot.

2 medium-size onions	1 bay leaf
3 pounds plum tomatoes	¼ teaspoon freshly ground black
4 cloves garlic	pepper
1 medium-size eggplant	⅛ teaspoon cayenne pepper
(2 pounds)	2 egg yolks
Salt	¼ cup grated Swiss cheese
⅓ cup olive oil	¼ cup freshly grated Parmesan
1 teaspoon dried thyme	cheese
½ tablespoon sugar	

1. Slice the onions as thinly as possible; to do so, cut the onion in half, turn each half on its flat side, and slice with a sharp stainless steel knife.

2. Peel and quarter the tomatoes and mince 4 cloves of garlic.

3. Peel the eggplant. Make peelings thick. Cut the eggplant into 4 slices lengthwise. Place in colander and sprinkle with 1 tablespoon salt. Allow to stand for 30 minutes; wash salt away, dry with paper towels, and cut the eggplant slices in ¼" cubes.

4. Heat ⅓ cup olive oil in a 6½-quart Dutch oven over medium heat. When the oil is hot but not smoking, add the onions and stir with a wooden spoon. The onions must cook for 5 minutes, and they require constant stirring to get them well coated with oil and to keep them from burning.

5. After 5 minutes, add the tomatoes, the eggplant cubes, 1 teaspoon salt, thyme, sugar, bay leaf, pepper, cayenne, and minced garlic. Simmer over low heat, uncovered, stirring once in a while, for 45 minutes. Taste and correct seasonings with salt and pepper. It can be prepared ahead of time until this point. Reheat for the next step.

6. Beat 2 egg yolks in a bowl and quickly whisk them into the vegetables; then stir in a mixture of ¼ cup grated Swiss cheese and ¼ cup grated Parmesan. Serve hot with a roast or other meat dish, or at room temperature for hors d'oeuvre.

Pizza Bohémienne

Transfer the Bohémienne mixture to a bowl to cool until it becomes luke-warm. Then spread it on top of Pizza Dough, sprinkle with grated cheese, decorate with imported black olives and bake at 400°F. for 20 minutes. Allow to cool before serving.

Quiche Bohémienne

Fill a partially baked Shortcrust Pastry shell, pages 88–90. Sprinkle on the grated cheeses. Bake 30–35 minutes at 350°F. Allow to cool before serving.

Pizza Dough

The best pizza dough I ever ate was a bready-type dough made by a New York lawyer, Emanuel Popolizzio, who gave me his family recipe. I liked the crust so much that I make bread with it as well as vegetable pizzas (see Pizza Bohémienne or Pizza with Deep-Fried Eggplant and Tomatoes, page 165). I tested both hand and food processor techniques side by side; the hand technique makes a lighter dough than the food processor, but still the machine does a very good job, especially when one is in a hurry.

I bake the dough in different shapes, sometimes as a loaf. I also roll it out into a pizza shape, 12″ circle, bake it, then slice it and fill it with left-over meats and salad greens (see Steak Sandwich, page 339), and cut it in wedges for lunch.

Special instruction. For all yeast doughs, I use El Molino dry yeast or Red Star brand. El Molino is generally found in health-food stores. One table-spoon dry yeast is equal to ⅙ ounce fresh yeast. You can double the recipe easily.

Special cooking utensil. A 12″–13″ pizza pan or a 4-cup loaf pan.

MAKES ONE 12-INCH PIZZA

¾ cup tepid water
1½ teaspoons dry yeast
  (or ¼ ounce fresh yeast)

1½ cups all-purpose flour
¾ teaspoon salt
1 tablespoon olive oil

1. When you are working with yeast, prepare a "sponge" to test if the yeast is active. Do this for dry yeast as well as for fresh yeast. Never put salt in the yeast, for it will kill it. Sugar is not necessary to proof yeast. Measure ¼ cup tepid water in a glass measuring cup. Dissolve the yeast and mix in 2 tablespoons flour taken from the measured flour. Cover with plastic wrap and let stand until double in volume. If the texture

never becomes spongy and does not double in volume, start over with a new pack of yeast.

2. Add ¾ teaspoon salt to the flour.

The hand method. Mix the flour and the salt on a working surface. Make a 10″ well in the flour. Pour the sponge (yeast mixture), ½ cup tepid water, and 1 tablespoon olive oil inside the well. Incorporate 2 tablespoons flour at a time into the liquids, using a blending fork or a wooden spoon, until it is too stiff to work with the fork or the spoon. Slap the dough repeatedly against the work surface until it is very smooth, adding more flour if it is very sticky. This is in place of kneading; do it for 10 minutes. I use this method for all yeast doughs in the book, with the exception of the Croissant Dough, page 387.

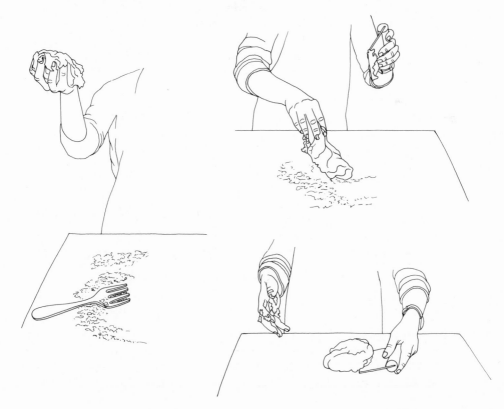

The food processor technique. Fit the bowl with the steel blade and place the flour and salt in the bowl. Process 2 seconds to mix the salt into the flour. Add the sponge (the yeast mixture), ½ cup tepid water, and 1 tablespoon olive oil to the flour. Process until the dough forms a ball. It takes about 20 seconds. Transfer the dough to a working surface and knead, slapping it against the working surface for a very smooth dough (about 2 minutes), adding more flour to the dough if it is very sticky.

3. Let dough rise in a 4-quart bowl covered tightly with plastic wrap. Keep in a 115°F. temperature. The oven of a gas range with the pilot on is fine, or warm an electric oven for 5 minutes, then turn it off, wait a minute or so before putting the bowl in the oven to cool it a bit, and place the dough in the oven until it triples in size (about 2½ hours in winter and less time in summer).

4. Punch it down, sprinkle flour over the dough, and knead for a minute or two to redistribute the yeast evenly in the dough. You can now refrigerate the dough in a covered bowl (it can last 2 days in the refrigerator; I have not been successful freezing the dough), then remove from the refrigerator and roll out when ready to bake.

5. Flour your rolling pin. Roll out the dough to a 12″ circle on a greased 12″ pizza pan. Again, let rise for 1 hour, brushing the top of the dough lightly with olive oil once or twice or give it a nice crunchy crust and to keep it from drying out too much. It is now ready for a filling such as Deep-Fried Eggplant and Tomatoes or Bohémienne, page 161. It can also be baked without filling for a Sandwich Steak, page 339.

Preheat oven to 400°F.

6. Bake at 400°F. for 20 minutes.

Pizza Bread

1. Oil a cookie sheet. Flour your hands and shape the pizza dough into a sausagelike loaf, 8″ long, or transfer into a 4-cup buttered loaf pan. With a pair of scissors, clip the surface of the bread 4 times in a straight row. Brush with oil. Let rise in a warm place (115°F.) until it has doubled in size. Brush once more with oil. Free-formed, the dough looks like pizza.

2. Bake the loaf of bread on the middle shelf of the oven for 40 minutes. Cool completely before eating. This bread freezes very well. Reheat frozen in a 400°F. oven until warm through.

Note on using a baking stone. Heat the stone to 400°F. in the oven. Sprinkle corn meal on a wooden pizza paddle, place the formed dough on it and let it rise. Then loosen the bottom of the dough with a flexible spatula, gently sliding it onto the stone. Bake for 40 minutes at 400°F.

Pizza with Deep-Fried Eggplant and Tomatoes

Special kitchen utensils. A deep-fryer, a wok, or a 12″ cast-iron skillet.

SERVES 4–6

12″ round Pizza Dough, page 162
1 medium-size eggplant
1 tablespoon coarse salt
3 medium-size onions
1½ pounds tomatoes*
4 tablespoons olive oil
1 teaspoon salt
1 clove garlic, minced

1 teaspoon minced parsley
¼ teaspoon dried thyme
½ cup freshly grated Swiss cheese
   (2 ounces)
12 small imported Niçoise black
   olives
2 cups corn oil
Flour to dredge

* Out of season buy Italian plum tomatoes (not packed in tomato purée or paste). Drain the tomatoes, split in two, for 1 hour.

1. Prepare the Pizza Dough according to the recipe, pages 162–164, steps 1–3.

2. Peel the eggplant, slice lengthwise in ¼″ slices. Sprinkle 1 tablespoon coarse salt over them and let stand 1 hour. Then wash under cold water and dry with paper towels.

3. Cut the onions into thin slices. Peel and chop the tomatoes.

4. Heat 4 tablespoons olive oil in a 12″ cast-iron skillet over medium heat. Add the onions; stir once in a while to prevent burning. Ten minutes later, add the tomatoes, 1 teaspoon salt, and minced garlic, thyme, and parsley. Cover and cook until the tomatoes are very soft (20 minutes). Stir the tomatoes once in a while. Mix in the Swiss cheese. Cool completely.

5. Heat about 2 cups corn oil in a deep-fryer, a wok, or a 12″ cast-iron skillet. When the oil is at 325°F., dredge each slice of eggplant in the flour and deep-fry until golden on each side. Don't overcrowd the pan, and dredge the slices of eggplant *just before frying.* When light golden on each side, drain on paper towels, then sprinkle a tiny bit of salt over them. Proceed frying with the remaining slices of eggplant.

6. Grease a 12″ round pizza pan, punch down the risen dough, and roll the dough on the pizza pan. Brush the dough lightly with olive oil. Let rise for 1 hour.

Preheat oven to 350°F.

7. Spread the cold tomato mixture over the risen dough, leaving a ½″ edge free, and brush olive oil on the edge. Then decorate with the slices of fried eggplant in a flower pattern. Decorate with the olives.

8. Bake at 350°F. for 25 minutes. Cool. Eat with a green salad or serve with drinks.

Homemade Fresh Pasta

This recipe originates from Aunt Chick, an Oklahoman famous for her pies and well known as a cookbook author and cooking teacher. My mother-in-law edited the recipe for her own use. It is very difficult to roll the noodle dough by hand (she had no pasta machine), so she devised a mixture of cake and all-purpose flours to lessen the elasticity of the dough. Now the dough is easy to roll.

This recipe, therefore, is especially for the cooks who do not have any machine. However, for the cook with a food processor, the dough can easily be mixed by machine. Fresh pasta can be frozen or refrigerated for 2–3 days in a plastic bag.

MAKES ⅓ POUND PASTA DOUGH

1 egg (¼ cup)	⅓ cup all-purpose flour
¼ cup heavy cream	½ teaspoon salt
⅔ cup cake flour	

Hand method

1. Measure 1 egg in a glass measuring cup. Be sure it measures ¼ cup. If not, break an egg, mix it and add enough egg to make ¼ cup.

2. Beat the egg and cream together.

3. Sift the flours together on a pastry board or a working table. Add the salt. Mix well, then make a 10″ well in the center of the flours. Pour the egg and cream mixture in the well. Use a blending fork, and start to mix 1 tablespoon flour at a time from the inside rim of the well. When it becomes difficult to use the blending fork, continue with the heel of your hand, but just enough to make the dough smooth. If the dough is sticky, add more all-purpose flour, just enough to smooth out the dough. (The more you knead, the more elastic the dough becomes and the more difficult it will be to roll.) Cut the dough into 2 pieces. Wrap each piece in waxed paper. Put it aside to let it relax for 30 minutes.

4. *To roll out the dough.* It is important to have a surface low enough so that when standing up the hands are flat on the surface and the arms are straight. For example, I am 5′ 4″ and my table is 30″ high. It gives all the leverage necessary to roll the dough. To roll out the dough on a standard height counter, I use a step stool to gain height and be comfortable. A Formica, vinyl, or marble surface is perfect to use as a pastry surface. Sprinkle flour on your pastry surface and on your rolling pin, and roll out each piece of dough into a circle about 13″ in diameter. Roll out the dough as thin as possible.

5. Lay the sheets of dough on top of a wire rack for 15–30 minutes. It will depend on how dry the kitchen is; the dough sheets must stay pliable but not sticky. Roll each sheet up like a jelly roll and cut noodles about 1/4″ wide. Uncoil each strand and dry on a pasta rack or on wire racks for about 30 minutes, or until almost brittle.

Technique: To use the pasta machine

Roll out each piece of the dough
through the roller of the machine
at the widest setting, usually No. 1.

Then sprinkle flour over the rolled-out
dough, fold the dough in thirds,
and roll it out once more through
the machine, still at setting No. 1.

Repeat one more time.

Roll out the dough through each setting
of the machine, up to setting No. 5 (to
No. 4 for whole wheat dough).
If the dough is sticky between
each setting, sprinkle flour
over the dough and fold
in thirds before rolling.

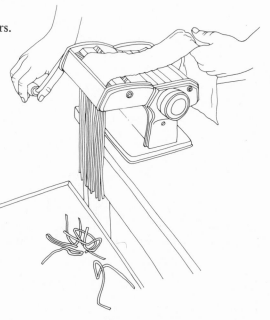

Dry the long thin sheet of dough
twenty minutes, wrapping it over
a broom handle set between 2 chairs.

Repeat with the second piece of
noodle dough.

Use the 1/4″ wide pasta cutter.
With a knife, cut the long sheet
of dough into 1½-foot-long
pieces and cut the dough
through the pasta cutter. Dry
the pasta on a rack or on a
broom handle.

Food processor method

With the machine it is easy to double the recipe. By hand, you need more practice to do it. If you have a pasta machine to roll and cut the noodles, you may use just all-purpose flour in the recipe.

MAKES ⅔ POUND PASTA DOUGH

1⅓ cups cake flour, sifted
⅔ cup all-purpose flour, sifted
1 teaspoon salt

2 eggs (½ cup)
⅓ cup heavy cream

1. In the bowl of the processor, fitted with the metal blade, add the sifted flours, salt, eggs, and cream. Process for about 20 seconds, until the dough makes a ball. If the ball is sticky, knead in more all-purpose flour, just enough to smooth out the dough.

2. Cut the dough in 4 pieces, and with a pasta machine proceed to roll the dough and cut the noodles.

Pasta Made with Fresh Basil

Hand method. Prepare Homemade Fresh Pasta, page 166, adding ¼ cup minced fresh basil leaves. Instead of fresh basil, fresh tarragon can be used, or a mixture of fresh rosemary and fresh oregano.

Food processor method. Prepare the amount of fresh noodles given for a food processor, above, adding ½ cup minced fresh basil leaves.

Pasta Made with
Whole Wheat Pastry Flour

Special Instructions. Halve the following ingredients if you are making and rolling out pasta with the hand method, page 167.

MAKES ⅔ POUND FRESH PASTA

1 cup whole wheat pastry flour, sifted
1 cup all-purpose flour, sifted

2 eggs
⅓ cup heavy cream
1 teaspoon salt

1. Proceed with the food processor instructions, opposite, to make the pasta and with the pasta machine technique, pages 168–169, to roll out and cut the pasta.

Technique: To cook fresh pasta

Fresh pasta cooks much faster than store-bought pasta; it will take from about 40 seconds or so for hand-rolled pasta made with cake flour to one minute or so for pasta made with whole wheat pastry flour.

FOR $\frac{2}{3}$ POUND FRESH PASTA

4 quarts water	4 tablespoons ($\frac{1}{2}$ stick) butter
1 tablespoon oil	Freshly ground black pepper
Salt	1 cup heavy cream

Bring 4 quarts of water with 1 tablespoon oil and 2 teaspoons salt to a boil. Drop the pasta into the boiling water. When the pasta rises back to the surface of the boiling water, cook for 30–40 seconds. Taste a strand. If tender, drain in a colander. Do not wash the pasta.

For buttered pasta. Melt 4 tablespoons butter in a 12″ cast-iron skillet and add the pasta, shaking the pan all the while for 30 seconds. Season with salt and freshly ground pepper.

For creamed pasta. Over high heat, add 1 cup cream to the noodles, stir well, and cook 1 minute or until the cream thickens slightly. Correct seasoning with salt and pepper.

Sweetbreads with Fresh Pasta

Sweetbreads are the thymus gland of a calf or lamb less than one year old. They consist of two connected sections. The throat section is an elongated, straggly piece, and the heart section is a nicely rounded lobe. Because they are readily perishable, butchers freeze them as soon as they come in. Find out from your local butcher when sweetbreads are delivered fresh and buy them then. Try to woo your butcher so he gives you the rounded lobes. Frozen sweetbreads are fine, especially for the preparation of this dish, but it is difficult to tell the sections you are buying.

Special instructions. For this dish, everything can be done ahead of time, except cooking the pasta and the final reheating of the sweetbreads and garnish of peas and carrots. Try to visualize the last stage before cooking it; as for the Scallops with Homemade Pasta, page 174, this dish needs good orchestration in its final moments.

Special kitchen utensils. A 4-quart Dutch oven and a 12″ cast-iron skillet.

SERVES 6 FOR AN ENTRÉE, 10 AS FIRST COURSE

2 pounds calf sweetbreads	½ cup shelled fresh peas
½ lemon	5 quarts water
5 medium-size yellow onions	1 tablespoon oil
6 tablespoons butter	1 cup heavy cream
Salt	3 batches (1 pound) Homemade
Freshly ground black pepper	Fresh Pasta, page 166
6 baby carrots	

1. Soak the sweetbreads in cold water for several hours with half a lemon. Squeeze a few drops of lemon juice into the water as well. Change the water when it becomes cloudy, and each time squeeze a few drops of lemon juice into the new water. The sweetbreads will become white, free of reddish spots.

2. Transfer the sweetbreads to a pan. Cover with cold water and bring slowly to a boil. Then cook for 10 minutes over medium-low heat, partly covered. Drain and rinse under cold water. Let cool.

3. Remove the pieces of gristly cartilage found on the surface of the sweetbreads and discard. Remove any of the membrane which comes loose, but do not remove the fine membrane which holds the meat together. Cut into ½″ cubes.

4. Peel the onions. Split in half, and with each half flat on the counter, slice thin. Turn the onions and 4 tablespoons butter in a 4-quart Dutch oven. Season with ¼ teaspoon salt and freshly ground pepper. Cover tightly and cook (braise) slowly for 30 minutes over medium-low heat until the onions are soft and not colored.

5. Spread the sweetbread cubes over the onions. Braise the onions and sweetbreads in a high-sided, heavy-bottomed pan with a cover, creating steam to cook and render lots of liquids. Otherwise, if you use a low-sided pan, such as a skillet, the onions burn, the juices evaporate, and the sweetbreads become rubbery. Season with ¼ teaspoon salt and again freshly ground pepper. Cover tightly and cook for 30 minutes over medium-low heat.

6. For the carrot and peas garnish: Peel and trim the carrots to olive size. (If you cannot find baby carrots, use regular ones.) Steam in a 3-quart

pan. (Pour 1½ cups water in pan, fit a steamer in it, and place the carrots in the steamer. Cover tightly and cook until tender, about 10 minutes. Be sure there is always enough water in the bottom of the pan.) Shell the peas and drop into boiling water and cook until tender, generally 10 minutes. You can substitute frozen peas, especially when the fresh ones are not in season. Buy the small baby peas, sometimes called petits pois, and cook half a package according to directions. Drain and reserve. Reserve the peas and carrots in a small skillet with 2 tablespoons butter. Sprinkle on ¼ teaspoon salt and freshly ground pepper and reserve for the final preparation.

The Last Stage (15 minutes before serving)

Read all this beforehand and have all pans and utensils ready so you can work very fast.

7. Boil 5 quarts water with 5 teaspoons salt and 1 tablespoon oil for the pasta. Measure 1 cup heavy cream and reserve outside the refrigerator.

8. Reheat the sweetbreads and onions in their juices. Reheat the carrots and peas in the skillet over high heat, shaking the pan once in a while to prevent sticking. Stir the vegetables with a wooden spoon to coat them with the butter.

9. Drain juices of the sweetbreads and onions into a 12″ cast-iron skillet.

10. Drop the pasta into the boiling water. When the water comes back to a boil and the pasta comes to the surface, count less than a minute and drain the pasta. Do not rinse it.

11. Over high heat, add the pasta to the skillet, stir it into the juices, and add 1 cup of heavy cream; continue stirring to heat the cream (about 1 minute). Correct seasonings, if necessary, with salt and freshly ground pepper.

12. Transfer the pasta to a heated platter and decorate with the sweetbreads, onions, peas, and carrots.

Scallops with Homemade Pasta

This recipe has several stages and requires that you work very fast at the end. Scallops must never be cooked ahead of time and reheated. They lose most of their subtle flavor. Read the recipe carefully. Try to visualize the last stage before cooking it. The recipe is simple, but needs good orchestration. It is one of those recipes that takes longer to read than to make.

Special instructions. The pasta and vegetable broth for the sauce can be done a day or two before the dinner. The vegetables, the sauce, and the cheese can be prepared ahead of time. Only poaching the scallops and cooking the pasta are reserved for the last minute preparation.

Special kitchen utensils. One 1½-quart saucepan; one 12″ cast-iron skillet.

First Stage (can be done day before dinner)

SERVES 6 AS A MAIN COURSE, 10 AS A FIRST COURSE

For the vegetable broth

3 carrots
1 medium-size onion
1 rib celery
3 cups water
¼ cup dry white wine
¾ teaspoon salt

1 teaspoon dried thyme
Freshly ground black pepper

For the pasta

3 batches (1 pound) Homemade
    Fresh Pasta, page 166

1. Thinly slice the carrots, onion, and celery and combine them in a saucepan with 3 cups water and ¼ cup dry white wine. Season with ¾ teaspoon salt, 1 teaspoon dried thyme, and freshly ground pepper. Bring to a boil slowly, then cover slightly ajar and simmer for 20 minutes.

2. After 20 minutes, bring the broth to a heavy boil and reduce to 2 cups. Strain. Discard the vegetables and reserve the broth for the sauce.

3. Prepare the pasta according to page 166.

Second Stage (2 or 3 hours before dinner)

For the garnish

½ cup tender fresh peas, if
    possible, or ½ package frozen
    peas

1 quart water
1 teaspoon salt
12 cherry tomatoes
4 tablespoons butter

4. Shell the peas. Boil 1 quart water with ½ teaspoon salt. Drop the peas into the boiling water and cook until tender, generally 10 minutes. Drain

and reserve. Out of season, cook frozen peas according to the directions on the package. Use only half a package. Drain and reserve.

5. Prick the tomatoes with the tines of a sharp fork to keep them from bursting during cooking. Melt 4 tablespoons butter in a 12″ cast-iron skillet. (The size of the pan is important; you will finish the dish in the same skillet.) Put in the tomatoes and ½ teaspoon salt. Cover and braise over a low flame for 15 minutes. Turn off the heat. Add the reserved peas.

Third Stage (1 hour before dinner)

For the sauce

2 cups broth from First Stage
3 tablespoons butter
3 tablespoons flour
½ cup heavy cream
Pinch of nutmeg

½ teaspoon salt
Freshly ground black pepper
2 cloves garlic, minced
½ cup finely minced fresh parsley
1 pound bay scallops

6. Reheat the broth and bring it to a boil. Melt 3 tablespoons butter in a 1½-quart saucepan, then add 3 tablespoons flour and whisk while the mixture bubbles for 1 minute. Add the boiling broth all at once, and whisk briskly. Lower the flame to a low simmer and cook for 5 minutes. Add ½ cup heavy cream, then a pinch of nutmeg, and correct seasoning with salt and pepper. Simmer very gently for another 5 minutes. Keep warm in a water bath.

7. While the sauce is cooking, mix ½ cup finely minced parsley and 2 minced garlic cloves (may be done in a food processor). Reserve.

8. Remove 1 pound bay scallops from refrigerator.

Fourth Stage (½ hour before serving)

¼ cup grated Swiss cheese   ¼ cup grated Parmesan cheese

9. Never grate Parmesan and Swiss cheeses ahead of time—especially the Parmesan, which loses its flavor. Grate them now and mix them well.

10. Boil 5 quarts water with 5 teaspoons salt for the pasta 15 minutes before serving.

The Last Stage (Just before serving—5–10 minutes)

Read all this and have all pans and utensils ready so you can work very fast.

11. Reheat the garnish of tomatoes and peas. Bring the sauce back to a boil.

12. Add the scallops to the hot sauce. Cook over medium heat about 2–3 minutes until the scallops have lost their milky appearance.

13. Drop the fresh pasta into the boiling water. Test the pasta when it comes back to the surface. Cook for 30 seconds or so.

14. Remove the tomatoes and the peas with a slotted spoon onto a hot plate and reserve. Keep the skillet on the flame.

15. Drain the pasta and pour it into the hot skillet. Shake the pan for 30 seconds. Taste pasta for seasonings. Pour the scallops and sauce over the pasta and mix well. Sprinkle in 2 tablespoons of the mixed cheeses and half the parsley and garlic. Once more stir the ingredients. Turn off the heat.

16. Decorate with the tomatoes and peas. Sprinkle the rest of the parsley and garlic over the pasta. Serve in the skillet. Serve the rest of the cheese in a bowl.

Sautéed Zucchini with Tomatoes and Onions over Fresh Pasta

This simple country dish is delicious hot or cold with fresh noodles.

Special kitchen utensil. A 12″ cast-iron skillet.

SERVES 6

2 large yellow onions	½ teaspoon dried thyme
1 pound zucchini	1 teaspoon salt
6 tomatoes*	Freshly ground black pepper
2 cloves garlic	2 batches Homemade Fresh Pasta,
4 tablespoons olive oil	page 166

* Out of season buy a 17-ounce can of Italian peeled plum tomatoes (not packed in tomato purée or paste). Drain the tomatoes, split in two, for 1 hour.

It is important to have all the vegetables ready before starting to sauté them.

1. Cut onions in half; turn each half on its flat side and thinly slice—this allows you to slice evenly and thinly and helps you avoid cutting your fingers.

2. Wash the zucchini and cut off the ends. Dry, do not peel, and slice ¼″ thick.

3. Peel the tomatoes, cut into eighths, and discard water and seeds.

4. Peel and mince the garlic.

5. In a 12″ cast-iron skillet, heat 2 tablespoons olive oil over medium heat until hot but not smoking. Add the onions and stir for 5 minutes, turning them all the while with a spatula or spoon so they don't burn. Add the zucchini and do not stop stirring. All the zucchini must be coated with oil. Add another tablespoon of olive oil now, since the zucchini will absorb a lot from the skillet; if necessary, add a bit more oil from time to time—just enough so the bottom of the skillet doesn't get dry. Stir for about 15 minutes, turning the zucchini and onions frequently with a metal spatula, using a stir-fry motion. Add the garlic after 10 minutes and mix well with the vegetables.

6. After stirring the zucchini for 15 minutes, add tomatoes, thyme, salt, and pepper and stir for 5 more minutes. Cover, reduce heat, and simmer for 15 more minutes, checking occasionally to be sure the onions and garlic are not burning. Do not cook the zucchini into a mush; the slices of zucchini should remain intact.

7. Cook the fresh pasta according to the Technique, page 171.

8. Serve the noodles in a large bowl, with the vegetables on top.

Raspberry Sherbet Made with Frozen Raspberries

Raspberry sherbet is a great dessert to have any time of the year. Thanks to the availability of frozen raspberries, it is easy to do. I prefer frozen raspberries to fresh ones when the latter are not of first quality, so I am giving two different recipes, one for sherbet made with frozen raspberries and one made with fresh fruit. See page 179.

Special kitchen utensil. A sherbet must be creamy when it is eaten, not frozen hard. For the best results, you need an ice cream machine. The non-professional ice cream machines are adequate for home-style cooking. They are not very expensive. Choose one with a 2-quart capacity and with an ice cube container that does not need to be drained all the time. Once in a while, the ice cream or the sherbet you are making will not thicken at all. Empty the ice cube container and start over again with fresh ice cubes and salt. I always buy two 5-pound bags of ice cubes for this reason. If you are great ice cream or sherbet eaters in your family and you can afford it, then splurge and buy one of the sophisticated ice cream machines on the market today.

Sherbet is never as good as when it is freshly made, but everything can be prepared in the morning and refrigerated until processed in the machine several hours before guests arrive. Keep in the freezer until ready to eat.

FOR 1½ QUARTS SHERBET

Six 10-ounce packages
   quick-thaw frozen raspberries
   medium-sweet syrup
2 teaspoons fresh lemon juice

1 teaspoon raspberry brandy or
   Kirsch
Two 5-pound bags ice
16-ounce box salt for the machine

1. Thaw and drain the raspberries, reserving the syrup.

2. Boil the raspberry syrup in 2 separate pans to reduce it faster. Reduce to about 1½ cups of concentrated syrup (215°F.). Cool completely.

3. Purée the raspberries in batches in a food mill to remove the seeds. Mix the cold concentrated syrup with the raspberry purée. Stop adding syrup if the purée of raspberry is sweet enough, but remember, it always tastes less sweet when cold. Add 2 teaspoons lemon juice and 1 teaspoon raspberry brandy or Kirsch if raspberry brandy is unavailable. Refrigerate until you are ready to make the sherbet.

4. Several hours before dinnertime or before your guests arrive, pour the sherbet in the ice cream metal bin, then fit it in the machine. Put in ice cubes nearly to the top of the metal can, then pour about ¾ pound of salt over the ice and fill with water to about three-fourths the height of the metal container. After 5 minutes, the water temperature should be 15°–20°F.; if it is not this cold, add more salt. Let the machine run for 50 minutes if it does not stop sooner. After 50 minutes, it should have the consistency of a soft purée. Unplug the machine and put the sherbet in the metal bin in the freezer. It stays soft for about 2 hours. It is at its best when soft. Remember that sherbet should be creamy like ice cream even though there is no cream in it.

Technique: To freeze fresh raspberries

To be sure that the raspberries will not discolor, add ascorbic acid (vitamin C) known under the name Fruit Fresh. You will need five 1-quart freezing containers and parchment paper.

3 cups sugar	1 teaspoon ascorbic acid
4 cups water	4 quarts fresh raspberries

Combine 3 cups sugar with 4 cups water in a 3-quart saucepan, bring the mixture to a boil and, stirring constantly to dissolve the sugar, boil for 5 minutes. Let cool until warm, then dissolve 1 teaspoon ascorbic acid in the syrup. Cool.

Fill each 1-quart container with raspberries to 1″ below the top. Wrinkle parchment paper to fit on top of the raspberries. The paper will keep the fruit from bobbing above the syrup when you pour the syrup.

Pour about 1 cup of syrup over the fruit. Remember to leave ½″ free on top, as the syrup will expand when it freezes. Cover with plastic top and freeze.

Fresh Fruit Sherbet

For fresh fruit sherbets, you need the pulp of the fruit and a syrup made with water and sugar to sweeten it. The syrup can be made several days ahead of time and kept in the refrigerator. See Raspberry Sherbet, page 178, for more detailed instructions on sherbet machines and how to use them.

MAKES 2 QUARTS SHERBET

1⅓ cups water	1 teaspoon Kirsch
1½ cups sugar	2 teaspoons lemon juice
4 cups mango purée (3½ pounds), or blackberry, blueberry, or raspberry purée (2 quarts fresh fruit)	

1. Combine in a saucepan the water and sugar and bring it to a boil. When the sugar is totally dissolved, boil for 5 more minutes (to 215°F.). Pour the syrup into a jar and cover. Refrigerate until thoroughly cold before using.

2. Peel the mangos, discard the pits, and cube the flesh. Purée the fruit (mango, blackberry, blueberry, or raspberry) in a food processor or through a food mill; then force through a fine-mesh sieve for a very smooth purée if you used the processor. Measure 4 cups.

3. Start adding syrup to the fruit purée until the purée is sweet to your taste. It is very difficult to be precise because it depends on how sweet and ripe the fruits are. Add 1 teaspoon Kirsch and 2 teaspoons lemon juice.

4. Process the sherbet following the instructions, page 178.

Lemon Ice Cream

If I make ice cream, it has to be very special with a flavor that is not easily available at the supermarket. I love lemon-flavored desserts for a dinner party—they always seem lighter than any other dessert. This lemon ice cream ends a dinner perfectly. In winter, I serve it with a raspberry (melba) sauce and in summer, I serve fresh blueberries, blackberries, or raspberries on top.

Special instructions. Ice cream is at its best when it is just made, but it can stay in the freezer for about 2 hours before it loses its creamy consistency. If you make it far ahead of time, remove from the freezer and refrigerate just enough to soften it and bring it back to a creamy consistency. To make the custard into ice cream takes about 15 minutes in a professional electric ice cream machine and about 30 minutes in an ice cream maker using ice cubes.

Special kitchen utensils. An ice cream machine, a candy thermometer.

MAKES 1½ PINTS

¾ cup sugar
1 teaspoon grated lemon rind
¾ cup freshly squeezed lemon juice
1 egg
5 egg yolks
¼ cup dry white wine
¼ cup water
½ cup heavy cream

For the melba sauce

Two 10-ounce packages frozen raspberries in sweet syrup
1 cup blackberries, blueberries, or fresh raspberries plus 3 tablespoons sugar and 1 tablespoon Kirsch or Framboise liqueur

1. Combine ¾ cup sugar, 1 teaspoon grated lemon rind with 1 egg and 5 egg yolks in a 3-quart saucepan, whisking everything together, then add ¾ cup freshly squeezed lemon juice, ¼ cup dry white wine, and ¼ cup water.

2. Cook over medium heat. Stir all the while with a flat spatula, making a figure 8 over the bottom of the pan to cook the custard evenly. Cook the custard until it reaches 180°F., but no more, on a candy thermometer.

3. Quickly transfer the custard to a mixer bowl and beat at high speed for 10 minutes; the custard will double in volume. Cover and refrigerate.

4. Beat ½ cup heavy cream until semistiff and fold it in the lemon custard with a rubber spatula.

5. Pour the custard into the ice cream maker and let churn until the custard turns into ice cream. Transfer it to the freezer until needed. If the ice cream is too hard, soften it a bit in the refrigerator before serving.

6. *Melba sauce for the winter.* Thaw out the raspberries and purée them in a food mill to discard the seeds, then boil down the purée with its syrup to two-thirds its original volume. Refrigerate. It can be done several days ahead of time. To serve, pour cold raspberry sauce on each plate, and plop two small ice cream scoops on top of the sauce.

Fresh fruit for the summer. Sprinkle sugar on fresh blackberries, blueberries, or raspberries and add 1 tablespoon Kirsch or framboise liqueur. Marinate for one hour. Sprinkle the fruits over the ice cream and serve.

TECHNIQUES AND UTENSILS INTRODUCED

How to make soups with meat stock and to enrich
them with egg yolks and cream

How to peel yellow turnips (rutabagas)

How to use overgrown zucchini from your garden

How to make a wine marinade

How to degrease, to skim, and to reduce a long-
cooking stew sauce, using a ladle

How to caramelize apples for a tart

How to keep the dough of an upside-down tart
from getting soggy

Lesson 10

Suggested Menus for Lesson 10

2-Course Winter Dinner

Short Ribs Stew

Mashed Potatoes, Country Style
(Lesson 6)

Caramel Custard
(Lesson 3)

*2-Course Menu, especially for
August and September*

Braised Butcher's Tenderloin
(Lesson 7)

Zucchini Flan

Plum Cake (Lesson 4)

3-Course Autumn Dinner

Crudités:
Celery Root Rémoulade
Grated Carrots
Grated Red Cabbage
(Lesson 3)

Oxtail Stew

Yellow Turnip Purée

Caramelized Upside-Down
Apple Tart

Other 3-Course Dinners

Cream of Celery Soup

Duck Bourguignon

Homemade Fresh Pasta
(Lesson 9)

Caramelized Upside-Down
Pear Tart

Turnip Soup

Pork Roast with Apples
(Lesson 6)

Tossed Green Salad
(Lesson 1)

Hot Individual Apple Tarts
(Lesson 7)

184

Cream of Celery Soup

For people on a diet, do not add the egg yolks and cream enrichment, but when the soup is hot, whirl just 1 tablespoon butter into the soup bowl. It won't hurt, and it makes the soup taste so much better.

Special instruction. The soup can be prepared several hours ahead of time, but add the egg yolks and cream enrichment when ready to eat; otherwise, the egg yolk will curdle when you reheat the soup if you are not very careful.

Special kitchen utensil. A 4-quart Dutch oven.

SERVES 6

1 bunch celery with leaves (1½ pounds)	Freshly ground black pepper
1 medium-size Russet potato (½ pound)	6 cups unsalted homemade Chicken Stock, page 74
4 tablespoons (½ stick) sweet butter	3 egg yolks
1½ teaspoons salt	¼ cup heavy cream
	Fried Croutons, page 127

1. Wash the celery and cut off the base. Cut the ribs into thick slices. Chop ½ cup of leaves and reserve.

2. Peel and dice the potato.

3. Melt 4 tablespoons butter in a heavy 4-quart pot. Sauté the celery and potato for about 10 minutes; sprinkle with 1½ teaspoons salt and freshly ground pepper; cover, reduce heat, and simmer for 10 more minutes.

4. Add the unsalted Chicken Stock and the reserved celery leaves, cover, and simmer with liquids quivering for 45 minutes.

5. Purée the soup through the finest blade of the food mill, or in blender or food processor. With the food processor, purée the vegetables without the liquids, because these seep through the center shaft of the processor, then mix the vegetable purée into the liquids. For a smoother result, force through a fine-mesh sieve.

6. Heat the soup again to near boiling. Beat the egg yolks well in a bowl and gradually mix into them 1 cup hot soup, whisking all the time. Pour the soup and egg mixture into the hot soup, whisking vigorously. Whisk over low to medium heat without boiling until the soup begins to thicken. This takes about 5 minutes. Correct seasonings with salt and freshly ground pepper.

7. Just before serving, bring ¼ cup heavy cream to near boiling, add to the soup, and mix well. Serve hot with croutons.

Turnip Soup

This is my November soup, when white turnips are at their best in the East. It is one of those dishes which my students eat with oh's and ah's, surprised that turnips can be so good, and promptly reproduce in their homes. Two things to note: the quality of white turnips and good chicken stock. It is less rich without the addition of egg yolks and heavy cream but still very good.

Special kitchen utensil. A 4-quart Dutch oven.

SERVES 6

1½ pounds turnips
1 medium-size onion
3 tablespoons sweet butter
1 tablespoon olive oil
1½ teaspoons salt
Freshly ground black pepper

6 cups homemade Chicken Stock, page 74
2 egg yolks
½ cup heavy cream
Fried Croutons, page 127

1. Peel turnips and slice thin. Peel onion and slice thin.

2. Melt 3 tablespoons butter and 1 tablespoon oil in a 4-quart Dutch oven. When the fats are hot but not smoking, sauté the turnips and the onion over medium heat, turning occasionally until they are golden—about 15 minutes. Season with ½ teaspoon salt and freshly ground pepper. Cover, and cook over medium-low heat for another 20 minutes.

3. Add 6 cups Chicken Stock. Season with 1 teaspoon salt if the chicken stock was not seasoned with salt. Simmer for 30 minutes, covered, over medium-low heat. The soup can be prepared ahead of time to this point. Do not purée ahead of time, or the soup will become too thick.

4. Purée the soup through a food mill or in a food processor. Then reheat, but do not boil. Beat 2 egg yolks with ½ cup heavy cream and slowly add 1 cup hot soup to the eggs and cream, whisking steadily. Then pour the mixture into the soup, which must not be boiling, whisking all the while. Heat for 5 minutes or so, stirring. Taste and correct seasoning with salt and pepper if necessary. Serve the soup in a tureen with croutons.

Yellow Turnip Purée

Called swedes by the English, rutabagas or yellow turnips by Americans, they are easily found from October to March. Because they are not an attractive vegetable, are difficult to peel, sometimes bitter to the taste, they are snubbed by most cooks. There is always a recipe that will catch the fancy of my students every year; the purée of rutabagas was the hit of the 1980 season, as the Cabbage Gratin, page 261, was the hit of the previous year.

Special instructions. When peeling a yellow turnip, slice off thick peels and then if you boil it in water first, the bitterness will disappear. Braised with onions, then puréed with cream, it becomes a delicious vegetable to serve with roasted fowls, such as turkey, page 375, or goose, page 377, or with Oxtail Stew, page 189.

Special kitchen utensil. A 4-quart Dutch oven.

SERVES 6–8

3 pounds (about 2 medium-size) yellow turnips	1 teaspoon salt
2 medium-size yellow onions	Freshly ground black pepper
7 tablespoons sweet butter	1 cup heavy cream

1. A yellow turnip is a very hard vegetable to cut raw. Slice off the waxy skin with the whitish inner layer in about 1/4″ thick peels. Cover the turnips with cold water and cook for 30 minutes with the lid on. Remove them from the water with a perforated spoon and then quarter them. Transfer them back to the water and cook until tender (about another 30 minutes).

2. Split the onions in half. With the flat surface on the cutting board, slice each half very thin. Put the onions in a 4-quart Dutch oven, and add 4 tablespoons butter and 1/2 teaspoon salt. Cover tightly and cook over low heat until the onions are soft but not colored (about 30 minutes). Check once in a while to be sure there is no coloration and that the onions are not cooking too fast.

3. Drain the yellow turnips. Cut into 1″ cubes, add them to the onions, and mix thoroughly. Add 3 tablespoons butter and 1/2 teaspoon salt and freshly ground pepper. Cover tightly and braise for 20 more minutes. Some of my students prefer to stop at this step. It's a matter of personal preference. I like the purée.

4. Purée the yellow turnips and onions in the food processor, blender, or food mill with 1 cup heavy cream. Taste and correct seasoning with salt and freshly ground pepper.

5. To reheat: Set the pan of purée in a bath of boiling water halfway up the side of the pan, see page 35.

Zucchini Flan

Les Prés is a small village near Valdrôme in the Drôme region of France. This recipe was given to me by two sisters from Les Prés, Jeanne and Suzanne Bernard. It provides a good way to use zucchini which have grown to maturity—if you have a vegetable garden. Most of the work can be done ahead of time (steps 1–6), leaving only the baking. All types of squash can be prepared in this manner.

Special kitchen utensil. A 2-quart baking pan.

SERVES 6–8

4 quarts water	4½ tablespoons butter
1 tablespoon plus 1 teaspoon salt	2½ tablespoons flour
	Freshly ground black pepper
4–5 pounds big zucchini (2 pounds each)	4 eggs
	1 cup freshly grated Swiss cheese
2 cups milk	Pinch of nutmeg

1. Boil 4 quarts water with 1 tablespoon salt.

2. Peel the zucchini, split them lengthwise, and discard the stringy fibers and seeds from the middle. Cut the remaining zucchini into large cubes and boil for about 20 minutes. Check for tenderness; then drain well in a colander for at least 15 minutes to remove as much water as possible.

3. Purée the zucchini in a food mill or food processor and drain again in a fine-mesh sieve for 1 hour.

4. *Prepare the béchamel.* Boil 2 cups milk. Melt 2½ tablespoons butter in a 2½-quart heavy-bottomed saucepan, then whisk in 2½ tablespoons flour. When the mixture bubbles, pour in the boiling milk. Season with ½ teaspoon salt and freshly ground pepper, and simmer over medium heat for 20 minutes.

5. Beat 4 eggs lightly and grate the cheese.

   Preheat oven to 400°F.

6. Mix the zucchini purée into the béchamel and, off the heat, mix in the beaten eggs, ½ cup grated cheese, and nutmeg. Taste and correct seasoning with more salt. Pour the mixture into a 2-quart baking dish, sprinkle with the remaining cheese, and dot with small pieces of butter.

7. Bake for 35 minutes or until top is golden brown.

Oxtail Stew

Oxtail meat is tender, juicy, and cheap. With the meat sauce ladled over mashed potatoes or mashed yellow turnips and onions, you have a superb meal with simple food at its best.

The oxtail meat is marinated in red wine and aromatic vegetables like carrots, onions, or leeks and cooked in the wine with water for several hours. The meat liquids are then degreased and skimmed to give a wonderful sauce full of the flavor of the vegetables and the meat. This is a Burgundy style of cooking, which is now best known in the United States in the familiar beef bourguignon.

Special instructions. Ask your butcher for oxtails cut up in 2″ long pieces, several days ahead of time. They are not always available.

Do not use jug wine for the marinade. It is generally too heavy for the sauce; buy a moderately priced red table wine in the Burgundy style, if possible; that is, a wine made with pinot noir grapes.

Pay special attention to the technique of degreasing and skimming the meat liquids. The oxtail stew can be made a day ahead of time, but keep the meat and sauce separated in different mixing bowls, covered with plastic wrap (otherwise, the meat tends to get mushy and absorb all the sauce) and remove from the refrigerator several hours before slowly reheating the meat and sauce together.

Special kitchen utensils. Because of the long, slow cooking in the oven, the liquids must not evaporate too fast. Use a 9-quart Dutch oven in cast iron or a heavy aluminum or heavy stainless steel pot. With the last two types of pot, I don't think it is necessary to seal the pot as you do for the cast-iron pot. Read the instructions on pots in the introduction of Spareribs Casserole, page 55, and the illustrations there on how to use a strip of cloth and a flour-water paste to seal a pot tightly if it is necessary.

SERVES 6–8

5 pounds oxtail, cut in 2″ long pieces

For the marinade

2 carrots
2 medium-size onions or 2 leeks
4 cloves garlic
1 teaspoon dried thyme
6 tablespoons oil
1 tablespoon red-wine vinegar
1 bottle (fifth) red wine

Flour to dredge the meat
4 cups water
2 teaspoons salt
Freshly ground black pepper

For the garnish

½ pound slab bacon
1 pound mushrooms

1. Marinate the oxtail pieces with 2 carrots, peeled and cut into ¼″ thick slices, 2 onions, peeled and quartered, or the white parts of 2 leeks (reserve the greens for a soup or a stock), split lengthwise and cut crosswise into ⅛″ thick slices, 4 whole peeled garlic cloves, 1 teaspoon thyme, 2 tablespoons oil, 1 tablespoon wine vinegar, and the bottle of wine in a 2½-quart mixing bowl, just big enough to cover the meat with the wine. Cover with a plate or with plastic wrap and marinate for 24 hours. If you have a 50°F. room, it is the perfect temperature (in the autumn, I generally keep it outside covered very tightly so no strange animals, like the neighbor's cat, can poke their noses into it), or keep in the least cold part of the refrigerator.

2. Strain the meats and vegetables over a mixing bowl to catch and reserve the liquids for later. Let drain at least 15 minutes. Dry the meat with paper towels.

3. Heat 2 tablespoons oil in each of two 12″ cast-iron skillets over medium heat. Dredge the meat with flour, shake off excess flour, and brown the meat until crusty brown (about 10–15 minutes). Sprinkle 1 teaspoon salt over the meat. Transfer the meat to a 9-quart Dutch oven.

4. In the same skillets, sauté the vegetables for 5 minutes, stirring occasionally, then spread them on top of the meat.

5. Pour 4 cups water over the meat and vegetables. Bring the water to a boil, skim the scum off the top with a perforated spoon, then pour in the reserved liquids from the marinade.

Preheat oven to 300°F.

6. If the pot you are using does not hermetically seal, cut a strip of cloth 3′ long and 2″ wide. Dunk it in a mixture of ½ cup flour with ½ cup water (illustration, page 56) and seal the lid and pot together. Bake on the middle shelf of the oven for 4 hours.

7. Break the seal off the pot. Remove the lid, holding it toward you, letting the steam escape away from you. With a perforated spoon, remove the meat and vegetables to a preheated platter. Cover with foil and keep warm in a turned-off oven, or if you are preparing the stew several hours ahead of time, let cool in a mixing bowl. Cover and refrigerate, if necessary.

8. *Degreasing and skimming.* Now you are ready to degrease and skim the liquid to make it into a sauce. First, spoon off almost all the fat that is on the surface, then set the pot over medium heat in such a way that only half the surface of the liquid is directly above the heat and bubbles gently while the other half of the liquid stands still. Spoon out the fats and skin which will converge where the surface is still. It will take

around 30 minutes or so, but you don't need to stand over the pot; just skim every now and then. The slow reduction of the liquid purifies and degreases it, finishing it into a shiny, slightly syrupy sauce. (If the pot was not sealed properly, the liquids will have reduced to a syrupy consistency; skim for 2 or 3 minutes.) Taste and correct seasonings with salt and pepper. By refrigerating the liquid, you can remove the fat after it congeals, but that does not purify or reduce the liquid into a lovely sauce which has no need of flour or butter to thicken it.

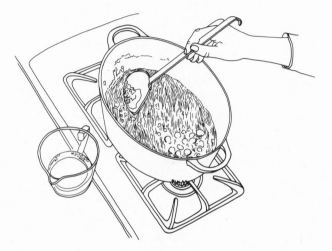

9. Prepare the bacon while you skim the sauce. Cut ½ pound slab bacon in half. Cover it with cold water, bring it to a boil, and simmer for 10 minutes to remove some of the smoky taste. Drain. Dry with paper towels. Cut the bacon into ½″ slices, then into ¼″ strips. Brown the bacon slowly in a skillet.

10. Wipe the mushrooms clean with wet paper towels. Cut off the stem ends and quarter the mushrooms. Sauté in the bacon fat over medium heat for 3 minutes or so. Sprinkle ¼ teaspoon salt and freshly ground pepper over them.

11. When the meat and sauce are reheated, at the last minute add the bacon and mushrooms. The bacon has too strong a flavor to cook with the meat—it would overpower the other flavors in the meat and vegetables—and the mushrooms are always better when cooked as little as possible.

Short Ribs Stew

Substitute short ribs for oxtail.

Special kitchen utensil. See preceding recipe.

SERVES 6–8

6 pounds short ribs   The marinade and garnish for
                                             Oxtail Stew, page 189

1. Have the butcher cut the short ribs in 3½″ long pieces.

2. Marinate the short ribs as in the recipe for Oxtail Stew, page 189, steps 1–2.

3. Brown the meat in several batches. The meat is more voluminous than the oxtail meat because the bones are bigger. Don't brown more than 4 pieces at a time; otherwise, the meat will steam instead of browning properly. Brown the short ribs on all sides and on the ends, about 2 minutes on each side to get an even golden crust.

4. Proceed with the cooking instructions in the Oxtail Stew recipe, steps 4–11. Remember that short ribs are laced with fat. Be especially careful to degrease and skim the meat liquids as long as is necessary to remove the fat.

Duck Bourguignon

The duck is cut up and marinated in wine and aromatic vegetables following the same technique as for Oxtail Stew, page 189.

Special instruction. Start a day ahead to marinate the duck. After degreasing and skimming the cooking liquids, the duck liver is puréed and added to the sauce. For the ones who do not like a liver taste, omit this step. (Sometimes the duck livers are missing from the ducks; substitute chicken livers.)

Special kitchen utensil. A 9-quart Dutch oven.

SERVES 6

Two 4-pound ducks	3 tablespoons duck fat or oil
2 carrots	Flour to dredge the ducks
2 medium-size onions	1 cup Duck Stock, page 266, or
1 teaspoon dried thyme	water
4 cloves garlic	Several sprigs of parsley
2¼ teaspoons salt	1 bay leaf
Freshly ground black pepper	2 duck or chicken livers
1 tablespoon red-wine vinegar	½ pound slab bacon
1 bottle (fifth) red wine	1 pound mushrooms

1. Cut the ducks into cooking pieces following the illustrated directions, pages 264–265.

2. Marinate the duck pieces with 2 carrots, peeled and cut in ¼″ thick slices, 2 onions, peeled and quartered, 1 teaspoon thyme, 4 whole peeled garlic cloves, 1 teaspoon salt, freshly ground black pepper, 1 tablespoon wine vinegar, and a bottle of wine in a 2½-quart mixing bowl, just big enough to cover the meat with the wine. Cover with a plate and marinate for 24 hours in a cool place or in the least cold part of the refrigerator.

3. Strain the meats and vegetables over a mixing bowl to catch and reserve the liquids for later. Let drain at least 15 minutes. Dry the ducks with paper towels.

4. Heat 2 tablespoons duck fat or oil in each of two 12″ cast-iron skillets over medium heat. Dredge the duck pieces with flour, shake off excess flour and sauté the meat until crusty brown (about 10–15 minutes). Transfer the meat to a 9-quart Dutch oven.

5. In the same skillets, sauté the vegetables for 5 minutes, stirring occasionally, then scatter them on top of the meat.

6. Pour the reserved liquids and 1 cup Duck Stock, page 266, or water in the skillets, bring to a boil, and stir for 1 minute or so while boiling,

then add the boiling liquids over the ducks and vegetables. Add 1 teaspoon salt, freshly ground pepper, several sprigs of parsley, 1 bay leaf, and the garlic cloves from the marinade. Cover with the lid slightly ajar, and simmer over low heat for at least 2 hours or until the duck pieces are tender (easily pierced with a fork).

7. *Optional step.* While the ducks are cooking, prepare the duck or chicken livers. Cut them into small pieces and grind them in a blender or food processor, then force through a fine-mesh sieve and reserve. (It is important to sieve, to separate out all bits and pieces which would tend to make the sauce lumpy or grainy.)

8. With a perforated spoon, remove the duck pieces and vegetables to a baking dish. Cover with foil and keep it in a warm oven while preparing the sauce.

9. Set the pot with the liquids over medium heat in such a way that only half the surface of the liquid is directly above the heat and bubbles gently while the other half of the liquid stands still. Spoon out the fats and skin which will converge where the surface is still (illustration, page 191). It will take around 30 minutes or so. The slow reduction of the liquids purifies and degreases them, turning them into a slightly syrupy sauce.

10. Cut ½ pound slab bacon in half. Cover it with cold water. Bring it to a boil and simmer for 10 minutes to remove the smoky flavor. Dry with paper towels. Cut the bacon in ½″ slices, then in ¼″ strips. Brown the bacon slowly in a skillet. Reserve.

11. Wipe the mushrooms clean with wet paper towels. Cut off the stem ends and quarter the mushrooms. Sauté in the bacon fat over medium heat for 3 minutes or so. Sprinkle ¼ teaspoon salt and freshly ground pepper over them. Reserve in the skillet.

12. Reheat the mushrooms. If you are adding the livers to the sauce, briskly whisk the sauce into the liver paste and reheat over medium heat. Taste and correct seasonings with salt and pepper, if necessary. Add the duck pieces, and reheat in the sauce for 5 minutes. Serve in a preheated platter with half the sauce in a sauceboat, the mushrooms and the bacon over the duck pieces.

Caramelized Upside-Down Apple Tart

According to legend, Mademoiselle Tatin put the apples into her tart tin before putting in the crust. Unwilling to undo her handiwork, so the story goes, she put the pie crust over the apples, baked the tart, inverted it before serving, and became immortalized in French cuisine for her Tarte Tatin.

Special instructions. It is difficult to reproduce this classic apple tart with complete success. The problem lies with the apples. If they are too juicy, they never caramelize but become mushy; then when the tart is unmolded, the juices trickle down and make the crust soggy. I find that the apples must be thoroughly caramelized before they are covered with the pastry dough, which then is cooked for a very short time at high temperature. This way the apples do not become soggy, nor does the crust.

For the best results, in the fall use Jonathan or Golden Delicious apples. In the spring or summer use Granny Smiths.

Special kitchen utensils. A 10″ quiche pan without a removable bottom or a 9″–10″ Pyrex plate, two 9″ cast-iron skillets.

SERVES 6–8

3 pounds apples
8½ tablespoons sweet butter
1 cup plus 1 tablespoon sugar
Shortcrust Pastry, page 87

Egg glaze: 1 egg white beaten
  with a few drops of water
½ recipe Cream-Cheese Topping,
  page 27

1. Peel, core, and slice the whole apples into ¼″ thick slices.

2. Melt 4 tablespoons butter in each of two 9″ cast-iron skillets over high heat. Divide the apples and 1 cup sugar and sauté in the pans, shaking them every so often to keep apples from scorching. Turn the apples once in a while with a pancake turner (steel spatula). Cook until the apples are heavily caramelized. The apples will render liquids which will evaporate. When the apples are caramelized, the butter should be the only liquid left in the pan (about 20 minutes).

3. Drain off and discard the excess butter; arrange the caramelized apple slices in concentric circles with the edges overlapping in the pan and allow to cool completely.

4. Prepare pastry dough, page 87, adding 2 tablespoons sugar to the ingredients. Refrigerate for 15 minutes.

5. Roll out the whole amount of dough to about 14″ in diameter on a floured surface. Roll the dough over the rolling pin and place it over

the apples. With the rolling pin, cut off the extra dough and reserve it for small individual tarts or turnovers. Prick the dough with the tines of a fork. Brush with the egg glaze.

Preheat oven to 450°F.

6. Bake on the middle shelf of the oven for about 20 minutes or until the crust is lightly browned.

7. Unmold on an ovenproof platter. Sprinkle 1 tablespoon sugar over the apples, dot with ½ tablespoon butter, and pass under the broiler for 30 seconds.

8. Serve with Cream-Cheese Topping.

Caramelized Upside-Down Pear Tart

This is a variation of the famous Tarte Tatin (see preceding recipe). I prefer Bosc pears for this because they do not disintegrate while cooking.

SERVES 6–8

6 large Bosc pears
6½ tablespoons sweet butter
½ cup plus 1 tablespoon sugar
Shortcrust Pastry, page 87

Egg glaze: 1 egg white beaten
    with a few drops of water
½ recipe Cream-Cheese Topping,
    page 27

1. Peel, core the pears, and cut them into eighths, then cut each piece twice crosswise for 1″ cubes.

2. Use two 9″ skillets (cast iron is perfect). Divide the pears, 6 tablespoons butter, and ½ cup sugar between the skillets and cook over medium-high heat until the pears caramelize (about 15–20 minutes). Turn the pears once in a while with a pancake turner (steel spatula). When they are golden brown all over, transfer them into the pan and let cool completely.

3. Prepare pastry dough, page 87, adding 2 tablespoons sugar to the ingredients. Refrigerate 15 minutes.

4. Roll out the pastry dough on a floured surface to about 14″ in diameter, then roll it over the pears. With the rolling pin, cut off the extra dough and reserve it for small individual tarts or turnovers. Prick the dough all over. Brush with the egg glaze.

Preheat oven to 450°F.

5. Bake in a 450°F. oven for 20 minutes.

6. Unmold on an ovenproof platter. Sprinkle 1 tablespoon sugar over pears, dot with ½ tablespoon butter, and pass under the broiler for 30 seconds.

7. Serve with Cream-Cheese Topping.

Upside-Down Prune and Apple Tart

This is a quick and easy substitute for the preceding upside-down apple and pear tarts. Besides prunes and apples you can use any fruit such as pineapple, peaches, or bananas.

Special kitchen utensil. An 11″ pie or tart mold.

SERVES 6

½ pound pitted prunes
1 cup tea
3 apples (Jonathan, Granny Smith, or Golden Delicious)
⅔ cup sugar
10 tablespoons soft sweet butter
1 large egg

½ cup milk
3 tablespoons dark rum
1 cup plus 2 tablespoons cake flour
1 teaspoon baking powder
Crème Fraîche, page 155, or
    Cream-Cheese Topping, page 27

1. Slice the prunes in two and soak them in tea for one hour. Peel, core and quarter the apples. Cut each quarter into ⅛″ slices.

2. Cream ⅓ cup sugar with 4 tablespoons sweet soft butter until blended. Spread the butter-sugar mixture on the bottom of the pie or tart mold, then add the apples, overlapping them in a concentric circle and alternating the rows with the drained prunes.

3. In a mixer, at medium speed beat ⅓ cup sugar with 6 tablespoons soft sweet butter for 1 minute. Continue beating while adding 1 egg, ½ cup milk, and 3 tablespoons rum.

   Preheat oven to 400°F.

4. Mix the cake flour and the baking powder together. Still at medium speed, start adding the flour to the batter, one tablespoon at a time until all the flour is incorporated. Pour the batter over the fruit.

5. Bake the tart on the middle shelf of the oven for about 35 minutes or until a cake tester comes out clean.

6. Unmold onto a serving platter. Serve warm with Crème Fraîche, page 155, on the side or a Cream-Cheese Topping, page 27.

TECHNIQUES AND UTENSILS INTRODUCED

How to make a Hollandaise Sauce and to use it as
a binder for other sauces

How to poach eggs in hot vegetables

How to bind a gratin with milk and bread

How to use salted dry cod

How to poach, bake, and sauté fish

How to make babas in small baba molds

How to make small breakfast rolls with baba dough

Lesson 11

RECIPES

Suggested Menus for Lesson 11

2-Course Summer Lunches

Red and Green Bell Pepper Salad
(Lesson 1)

Codfish Fritters

Baked Potato served with
Garlic Mayonnaise

Strawberries with Cream-Cheese
Topping (Lesson 1)

Chachouka: Poached Eggs
on Green Peppers and Tomatoes

Pizza Bread (Lesson 9)

Poached Peaches (Lesson 8)
with Creamed Cottage Cheese Topping

2-Course Winter Dinner

Roast Chicken with Vegetables
(Lesson 1)

Rum Cake or Rum Babas

3-Course Early Summer Dinner

Asparagus with Maltaise Sauce

Baked Fish Steaks with
Fresh Mint Leaves en Papillote

Baked Potato

Cherry Tart (Lesson 6)

Other 3-Course Dinners

Sautéed Trout

Steamed New Potatoes Basted
with Butter and Parsley

Tossed Green Salad
(Lesson 1)

Hot Individual Berry Tarts
(Lesson 7)

Unmolded Tomato and
Zucchini Gratin

Poached Fish Steak with Steamed New Potatoes
served with a Beurre Blanc

Blackberry Sherbet
(Lesson 9)

Hollandaise Sauce

My advice to a first-timer making Hollandaise Sauce is: "Go ahead, curdle the sauce; so what, it is not a disaster, and it is easily rectified." The egg yolks and butter will separate at 180°F., so the cook needs to be very attentive when the yolks are first cooked before adding the butter. It is advisable to have a pan of cold water next to the stove in which to dip the bottom of the pan in case it gets too hot. An ideal pan to make a hollandaise in is a 1½-quart professional copper pan with sloping sides, but it is so expensive that I recommend, as a second-best choice, the cast-iron enamel pan of Le Creuset, or any other brand.

When you become adept at making the sauce, you do not need to bother with a water bath or a double-boiler, but first, try using one. It is absolutely necessary to have a water bath if you attempt a hollandaise with a thin-bottomed stainless steel pan such as the Wearever pans. Also, the yolks will cook faster than in a heavier-bottom pan, and the sauce will thicken faster. I use a 9″ cast-iron skillet which I fill to one-third high with water to create a water bath.

There are many different versions of how to make a hollandaise. My advice to you is to stick to one version such as the following one and then, after having mastered it, try others. I cut the butter in small pieces and have it ready next to me by the stove. I whisk the egg yolks over a low to medium flame either with or without a water bath until the yolks start to thicken. I also touch the bottom of the pan with my finger occasionally; when it becomes too hot to touch, I quickly start to whisk in the butter piece by piece, taking the pan off the flame once in a while. If you see any steam coming up from the pan, dip it right away in cold water. Don't double a hollandaise recipe; make two batches—it's always easier. The finished hollandaise can stay in a warm water bath while you prepare the next one.

Special instructions. There are several questions you should ask yourself; for instance: How thick should a hollandaise be? The answer: It depends on what you are using it for. If it is a primary sauce, that is to say, to be served as is with asparagus, then the sauce should be runny enough to coat the asparagus. For this result, do not cook the egg yolks too long before starting to add the butter; in case it thickens too much, add warm water to loosen the sauce and add a bit more lemon juice. If the hollandaise serves as a base for another sauce, such as the Maltaise Sauce, then the hollandaise must be thicker, since it will thin out a bit with the orange juice and lemon juice you add.

How long can it be prepared ahead of time? It can be kept for 1 hour in a warm water bath. It will thicken while waiting, so get about ½ cup very warm water and start whisking the sauce to smooth it out while dribbling water into it until the desired consistency. Personally, I like to make it at the last minute; that is when it is at its very best. As long as the ingredients are ready, it takes no time at all to make the sauce.

How to remedy a curdled hollandaise? Break an egg yolk in a bowl and whisk it while dribbling the curdled hollandaise into it, then the sauce will regain a smooth texture. Transfer it back to the saucepan (don't bother to clean it), and over low heat whisk in 4 more tablespoons butter.

Special kitchen utensils. A 1½-quart saucepan and a 9″ cast-iron skillet.

MAKES 1½ CUPS

3 egg yolks	1 teaspoon lemon juice
12 tablespoons (1½ sticks) sweet butter	½ teaspoon salt
	Freshly ground white pepper

1. Break the egg yolks into a 1½-quart heavy-bottomed saucepan. Whisk the egg yolks over a low to medium flame until the whisk leaves traces in the egg yolks. For a first-timer, place the sauce pan in a 9″ skillet with water coming halfway up the sides of the pan.

2. Start adding 1 tablespoon butter at a time, whisking rapidly and constantly, removing the pan from the heat if necessary. If the sauce starts to thicken very rapidly, add a few drops of cool water to slow it down.

3. Season with 1 teaspoon lemon juice. Off the heat, season with salt and freshly ground white pepper. Taste and correct seasonings.

Maltaise Sauce:
An Orange-Flavored Hollandaise

This sauce can be used over steamed broccoli, asparagus, cauliflower, or carrots.

Special kitchen utensil. A 1½–2½-quart saucepan.

Special instruction. Do not double the recipe. Make 2 batches, if necessary, keeping 1 batch in a warm water bath, while preparing the second batch.

MAKES 2½ CUPS

Grated peel of 1 orange	4 egg yolks
3–4 tablespoons orange juice	½ teaspoon salt
1½ teaspoons lemon juice	Freshly ground white pepper
½ pound sweet butter	

1. Ahead of time, measure out all the ingredients for the sauce. Grate the orange. Squeeze orange and lemon juice. Squeeze more than necessary. Measure the butter and cut into tablespoons. Refrigerate until ready to use. Break the egg yolks into a 1½–2-quart heavy-bottomed saucepan and cover with plastic wrap so they do not dry out.

2. If you are serving the sauce with asparagus, after the asparagus is cooked, start the Maltaise Sauce. Gather all the measured ingredients around the stove. Start whisking the egg yolks over medium-low heat or over a water bath or double boiler. Whisk until the yolks start cooking—the whisk will leave traces in the egg yolks.

3. Start adding 1 tablespoon of butter at a time. When all the butter has been added, the sauce must be rather thick. Season with ½ teaspoon salt and freshly ground white pepper. (If it curdles, break an egg yolk in a bowl and whisk it while dribbling the curdled hollandaise into it; it will regain a smooth texture. Transfer it back to the saucepan—don't bother to clean it—and over low heat whisk in 4 more tablespoons butter.)

4. Whisk in the orange juice and the lemon juice to thin it out, then whisk in the grated orange peel. The sauce should be a little looser than the consistency of molasses. Taste and correct seasonings.

Asparagus with an
Orange-Flavored Hollandaise

Besides liking to dip asparagus spears in a vinaigrette sauce, my other favorite way to serve them is with a plain hollandaise or one flavored with orange rind and orange juice, called Sauce Maltaise. In France, blood oranges come from the island of Malta and the classic preparation is a hollandaise or mayonnaise with blood oranges that are slightly tart, but it works very well with California oranges.

Special kitchen utensil. A 6½-quart Dutch oven.

SERVES 6

36 medium-size asparagus spears (2¼ pounds)	1 tablespoon salt
4 quarts water	Maltaise Sauce, opposite

1. Snap off the ends of the asparagus stems to remove the pithy, woody part (about the last 2″). Peel off the skin of the asparagus with a very sharp

vegetable peeler, keeping each asparagus spear flat on the counter, starting from the end to expose the moist part below the skin to the head of the spear.

2. Wash the peeled spears in cold water and drain. Sort them by size and make little bundles of about 6 spears, all roughly the same size. Tie the bundles with string near each end.

3. Measure and gather all the ingredients for the Maltaise Sauce, page 202, step 1.

4. Boil water in a large kettle (not aluminum), like a 6½-quart Dutch oven, so the bundles of asparagus can lie flat. Have 4 quarts of water boiling with 1 tablespoon salt. Lay the bundles of asparagus in the boiling water. Bring the water back to a boil very quickly, then boil for 4–5 minutes. After 4–5 minutes, the aroma of the asparagus will tell you that it is about ready. Remove the bundles of small spears first. Drain well, cut the strings, and reserve on a platter. The asparagus should be warm but not hot when it reaches the table.

5. Prepare the Maltaise Sauce, see page 202. Serve in a sauceboat. The sauce is spooned over the asparagus on each plate.

Chachouka: Poached Eggs on Green Peppers and Tomatoes

Around the Mediterranean Sea, practically every country has its own version of a vegetable stew with peppers, tomatoes, eggplants, zucchini, and onions. Some of the recipes use all of these vegetables, such as the Provençal ratatouille in southeastern France. The Bohémienne, page 161, with eggs and cheese mixed at the end, and the pipérade, better known in southwestern France and Spain, use some but not all of the vegetables. Across the sea from Marseilles, there is the North African version called Chachouka, a stew including onions, green bell peppers, and tomatoes with eggs poached on top of the vegetables at the last minute; the yolks remain soft, and at the table every one mixes the yolk into the hot vegetables. It is delicious for a summer brunch, lunch, or light supper.

Special instruction. The vegetable stew can be prepared a day ahead of time and reheated to poach the eggs at the last minute. For a more elegant presentation, the eggs can be cooked sunny side up in ¼ cup oil and scooped on top of the individual egg dish filled with the vegetables. I serve it in a 12″ cast-iron skillet for a more informal brunch.

Special kitchen utensils. Two 12″ cast-iron skillets. Individual egg dishes or 1-cup porcelain ramekins for a more elegant presentation.

SERVES 6

6 green bell peppers	6 large onions
½ cup olive or vegetable oil	6 big tomatoes*
1½ teaspoons salt	8 cloves garlic
Freshly ground black pepper	6 eggs
Pinch of cumin	

* Out of season, buy a 35-ounce can of Italian peeled plum tomatoes (not packed in tomato purée or paste). Drain the tomatoes, split in two, for 1 hour.

1. Quarter the peppers and discard the seeds and white pith inside the peppers. Cut each quarter of pepper crosswise into ⅛" thick slices. Heat ¼ cup oil in a 12" cast-iron skillet. When the oil is hot but not smoking, sauté the peppers, stirring all the while to coat them evenly with the oil, for about 3 minutes. Cook uncovered over medium-low heat for about 15 minutes. Sprinkle ½ teaspoon salt, freshly ground pepper, and a pinch of cumin over them. Cover, lower the heat, and braise for another 30 minutes, checking once in a while that they are not burning.

2. Meanwhile, cut the onions in half, place each half on a cutting board, and cut into thin slices. Heat ¼ cup oil in a second 12" cast-iron skillet and add the onions, stirring continually to coat the onions with the oil, for about 3 minutes. Add ½ teaspoon salt. Cover, lower the heat to medium-low, and braise for 30 minutes.

3. Peel the tomatoes (plunge in boiling water for 30 seconds if it is necessary). Quarter and remove and discard the seeds and liquid. Peel the garlic and chop coarsely.

4. When the peppers are soft, transfer the onions to the peppers, add the tomatoes and garlic, and sprinkle with ½ teaspoon salt and freshly ground pepper. Cook over medium heat, covered, for another 30 minutes or until the tomatoes are soft.

5. Make 6 small nests in the piping hot vegetables, ½" away from the edge of the skillet. Still over medium heat, break 1 egg in each nest. With a fork, separate each egg white from its neighbors, bringing back the white toward the center of the eggs. Cook until the whites are set but do not overcook the yolks—they must stay soft. Serve as is.

Chachouka and rice. Without the eggs, the chachouka is very good over rice, served with broiled lamb chops.

Chachouka in a Pie

This onion, pepper, and tomato stew is excellent in a partially precooked pie shell, covered with an uncooked pie top, then baked for 35 minutes. Eaten warm with a green salad, it is lunch. It is equally good with drinks as an hors d'oeuvre.

Special instruction. Prepare the dough, line the pie pan with it, and refrigerate until you bake the pie, that is, the morning of the brunch, or the afternoon for an hors d'oeuvre. Roll out the top for the pie and keep it between 2 pieces of waxed paper and refrigerate until needed. You can prepare the Chachouka, without the eggs, a day ahead of time.

Special kitchen utensil. A 10″ quiche pan.

SERVES 6–8

Shortcrust Pastry, page 87   Chachouka, page 204

1. Prepare the pie dough according to the recipe. Cut the dough in 2 unequal pieces, a bigger piece to roll out for the bottom and a smaller piece for the top. Roll out the dough, following the illustrated technique, pages 88–89. Line the pan with the dough. Prick the bottom. Line the dough with foil, crimping the sides tightly. Refrigerate until needed. Roll out the remaining piece of dough to a 10″ circle. Reserve between 2 pieces of waxed paper on a cookie sheet and refrigerate.

2. Prepare the Chachouka, but do not add the eggs until the end. Cool it completely before adding to the precooked pie shell.

   Preheat oven to 400°F.

3. The day of the dinner or lunch: Anticipate the time you will eat the pie and work accordingly. Give 2 hours for baking and cooling; that is when the pie is at its best. Bake the bottom part of the dough for 15 minutes. Remove the foil, and dry the bottom in the oven for another 3–4 minutes. Meanwhile, remove the top part of the dough from the refrigerator and let it come to room temperature to soften it. It will be easier to cover the top of the Chachouka with it; the dough, when cold, is very brittle. Lower the oven to 350°F.

4. Remove most of the oil that will have come up to the top of the Chachouka. Fill the prebaked pie shell with the cold Chachouka and place the dough on top of the mixture. Brush with some of the oil removed from the Chachouka.

5. Bake on the middle shelf of the oven for 30–35 minutes. Cool before eating.

Tomato and Zucchini Gratin

Georgette, my neighbor in France, prepares a purée of zucchini and to-matoes and bakes it into a custard. It is excellent, especially if the vege-tables are sautéed first in meat drippings. It can be prepared in advance and reheated in a water bath. Or it is very good cold as an hors d'oeuvre unmolded. When the gratin is eaten cold, it is important to overseason at step 8.

Special kitchen utensil. A 6-cup soufflé mold.

SERVES 8

2 pounds zucchini	1 clove garlic
¼ cup drippings from a roast or olive oil	1 teaspoon dried thyme
	2 slices ½″ thick of French bread
1 medium onion, minced finely	1 cup milk
2 teaspoons salt	3 large eggs
Freshly ground black pepper	½ cup freshly grated Swiss cheese
1 pound ripe tomatoes*	

* Out of season, buy a 17-ounce can of Italian peeled plum tomatoes (not packed in tomato purée or paste). Drain the tomatoes, split in two, for 1 hour.

1. Wash the zucchini, cut off the stems, and cut in ¼″ thick slices.

2. Melt the drippings or oil in a 12″ cast-iron skillet and sauté the onions for 5 minutes, stirring constantly to make sure they don't burn.

3. Add the zucchini to the skillet and sauté at moderate heat until the slices start to turn golden around the edges (about 15 minutes longer). Stir the zucchini occasionally so all the pieces will be coated with fat. Season with 1 teaspoon salt and freshly ground pepper.

4. Peel tomatoes (drop in boiling water for 30 seconds), quarter, and add them to the zucchini.

5. Mince 1 garlic clove and add it with 1 teaspoon thyme and 1 teaspoon salt to the zucchini. Mix well. Cover and simmer for 25–30 minutes, stirring occasionally so it does not stick. If the mixture is swimming in liquid at the end, uncover and reduce it to a soft consistency over medium-high heat, stirring to keep the vegetables from burning.

6. While the zucchini are cooking, make a bread thickening as follows: Cut the crust off the bread and combine bread and milk in a 2½-quart saucepan. Cook over medium heat, mashing the bread into the liquid until smooth (about 3 minutes). If the bread does not absorb all the liquid, add more bread to give it the consistency of mashed potatoes.

7. Mix the bread thickening and the vegetables, and purée with a food mill (medium blade) or in a food processor.

Preheat oven to 300°F.

8. Beat 3 eggs and add to the vegetables. Mix in ½ cup Swiss cheese and taste and correct seasonings with salt and pepper. Pour into a buttered 1½-quart soufflé mold and bake at 300°F. until top is golden (about 1 hour).

Codfish Fritters

Salt codfish does not look very appetizing, but it can be transformed into lovely little fritters for a summer appetizer. They can be prepared ahead of time, as they are good hot or cold, or they can be reheated in the oven for 10 minutes before eating them. Eaten hot, they need no sauce; eaten cold, they are very good with Garlic Mayonnaise, page 73. It is one of those recipes that does not generate much enthusiasm in my cooking class until the fritters are eaten—then everyone wants to make them at home.

Special instruction. If you are not familiar with deep-frying, please read the instructions, page 108.

MAKES 60 FRITTERS

1 pound salt codfish	½ teaspoon salt
2 russet potatoes	Freshly ground black pepper
1 onion, minced	4 eggs
1 tablespoon minced parsley	1 quart corn oil

1. Soak the codfish in cold water for 24 hours. During the first hour, change the water twice, then refrigerate overnight in water.

2. Drain the fish. Cut it into chunks. Peel the potatoes and quarter. Put the potatoes and fish in a 6-quart pot; cover them with cold water. Bring the water to a boil, cover, and simmer for 40 minutes or until the fish and potatoes are tender.

3. Drain the potatoes and fish. Skin and bone the fish if necessary. Process the fish in the food processor fitted with the metal blade. The fish is stringy, so don't be upset at the aspect of the fish purée.

4. Mash the potatoes with a ricer or pass through a food mill. Do not use the processor; the potatoes become gummy.

5. Mix the minced onions and parsley and the codfish and potato purées. Season with ½ teaspoon salt and freshly ground black pepper.

6. Beat 4 eggs lightly and beat them into the codfish-potato mixture. Taste and correct seasonings with salt and pepper. Everything can be done a day ahead of time to this point.

7. If the mixture has been in the refrigerator, remove it 1 hour ahead to warm up. Pour 1 quart corn oil in a deep-fryer. Heat to 325°F. Shape little balls about a third as big as an egg, using 2 spoons to help you shape them. Drop them in the hot oil and deep-fry until golden, about 5 minutes. Do not overload the deep-fryer; if you do, the oil will not be hot enough and the fritters will soak up oil and be greasy. From time to time, check the temperature with a thermometer. Drain fritters on paper towels.

Note. To speed up the frying, you can use two 9″ cast-iron skillets with 2 cups of oil in each one and fry 2 batches simultaneously.

Baked Potatoes with
Garlic Mayonnaise or Rémoulade

Choose Idaho (Russet Burbank) potatoes, the best on the market for baking. Instead of eating the potatoes with sour cream, try them with a garlic mayonnaise or with a mustard and herb mayonnaise. They are delicious.

SERVES 4

4 potatoes	Garlic Mayonnaise, page 73, or
2 tablespoons oil	rémoulade, page 53
Coarse salt	

Preheat oven to 425°F.

1. Wash and dry the potatoes. Rub them with oil and bake in a roasting pan or on a jelly-roll pan for about 1 hour, turning them occasionally for even baking.

2. Prepare the mayonnaise of your choice: Garlic Mayonnaise, page 73, or Rémoulade, page 53.

3. When the potatoes are done, serve very hot, slicing each one lengthwise and topping it with the mayonnaise. It will melt into the potato. Serve with coarse salt.

Baked Potatoes with Tomatoes, Cheese, and Fresh Basil

This is a recipe from Colombia given to me by a friend. There, queso Amarillo is used for the cheese. It resembles our Cheddar. But you can substitute any cheese you prefer.

Special kitchen utensil. A 9″ cast-iron skillet.

SERVES 4

4 baking potatoes	½ teaspoon salt
2 medium-size onions	Freshly ground pepper
1 pound plum tomatoes	⅓ cup grated cheese, Romano,
3 tablespoons olive oil	Swiss cheese, or cheddar
1 clove garlic	Handful of fresh basil leaves
A good pinch dry thyme	½ cup sour cream

1. Wash and dry the potatoes. Rub them with oil and bake in a roasting pan or on a cookie sheet for about one hour, turning them occasionally for even baking.

2. Peel two onions. Cut each one in half; then with each half flat-side-down on the counter, cut the onions into thin slices.

3. Peel and cut the tomatoes in small pieces. (If the tomatoes are difficult to peel, place them in boiling water for 30 seconds, the skin will slip off easily.)

4. Heat 3 tablespoons olive oil in a 9″ cast-iron skillet over medium heat. Add the sliced onions and stir them in the oil. Cook for 10 minutes without burning them.

5. Meanwhile, mince one clove garlic. Mix the tomatoes and minced garlic into the onions with a wooden spoon. Add a good pinch of dry thyme, ½ teaspoon salt and freshly ground pepper. Cover and continue cooking for fifteen minutes over low to medium heat.

6. Grate ⅓ cup cheese: Romano, Swiss, or cheddar. Wash and dry several basil leaves, you need just enough basil leaves to make a handful.

7. Stir the cheese into the tomatoes, then mix ½ cup sour cream into the tomatoes. Cook with the cover on, just long enough to heat the sour cream and to melt the cheese.

8. Uncover and shred the basil leaves right over the skillet by holding the basil leaves tight in one hand and cutting them with a pair of scissors.

Stir them into the tomatoes and cheese mixture. Cover and continue cooking one more minute. Correct seasoning with salt and pepper.

9. Split open the baking potatoes, sprinkle salt over them and ladle several spoonsful of tomato-cheese mixture over each of them.

Note. This mixture could also be served over fresh pasta.

Steamed New Potatoes Basted
with Butter and Parsley

Small new potatoes, about 2″ in diameter, are perfect for steaming in their jackets. Then they are peeled and sautéed briefly in butter and fresh parsley. They make just the right accompaniment to poached, broiled, or baked fish, but my favorite way is to serve them cold along with black imported olives and eat them with a garlic mayonnaise (aïoli) for a first course in a country-style dinner or for a country-style buffet. The small Red Bliss potatoes are excellent for this recipe.

Special instruction. Cook 2 batches of potatoes separately if the recipe is doubled.

Special kitchen utensil. A collapsible steamer that fits in a 3-quart pan.

SERVES 4

12 small new potatoes	1 teaspoon salt
(1½ pounds)	Freshly ground black pepper
3 tablespoons butter	2 tablespoons minced parsley

1. Wash and dry the potatoes. Stack them in a steamer, fitted in a pan with 3 cups water at the bottom. Cover the pan tightly with foil, then a cover. Steam over medium heat for about 20 minutes. After 10 minutes, turn the potatoes around so the ones on top are at the bottom. Check with a skewer if they are cooked. Sometimes they take longer than 20 minutes to cook.

2. Peel the potatoes. Melt 3 tablespoons butter in a 9″ cast-iron skillet over medium heat. Add the potatoes and shake the pan to coat the potatoes with butter. After 3 minutes, sprinkle with 1 teaspoon salt, freshly ground pepper, and 2 tablespoons minced parsley. Continue cooking for 10 more minutes over a low flame, shaking the pan once in a while. Serve hot.

Poached Fish with
Steamed New Potatoes

Not everyone has a fish poacher and, luckily, you do not need one to eat poached fish. I like to buy a chunk of a big fish like cod, haddock, sea trout, salmon, or monkfish for poaching. Buy a center cut where the fish is at its thickest. It is equally good cold or hot. With fish just poached, a white butter sauce is perfect. With cold fish, I serve a mayonnaise with or without garlic. As a garnish, steamed new potatoes make an excellent dinner, presented with the poached fish on a bed of lettuce seasoned with a vinaigrette dressing. It is a meal for family or guests which requires little work, and because there is not much work involved, the ingredients must be superlatively fresh.

Special instructions. Prepare the poaching liquids ahead of time, in the morning, for instance. The poaching time of the fish will depend on the thickness of the fish, but remember to remove the fish from the refrigerator to bring it to room temperature before poaching. I generally get a chunk of fish about 3″ thick and 6″ long, weighing about 2¼ pounds. I poach it for 15 minutes in quivering liquids. The center bone is slightly pinkish.

Special kitchen equipment. A collapsible steamer to fit a 3-quart pan, and a 4-quart Dutch oven.

SERVES 4–6 (4 WITHOUT A FIRST COURSE; 6 IF YOU HAVE A FIRST COURSE)

4–6 medium-size yellow onions	Lettuce
A small bunch of parsley	Mayonnaise with or without
Several branches of fresh tarragon	garlic, pages 53, 73
or 1 teaspoon dried	Vinaigrette dressing, page 11
2 tablespoons salt	16 small new potatoes (2 pounds)
Freshly ground black pepper	2¼-pound piece of fish
3 quarts water	A Beurre Blanc, opposite

1. For the poaching liquids, put the unpeeled onions, herbs, salt, and freshly ground pepper in a 4-quart Dutch oven. Add the water and bring to a boil uncovered. Then cover the pan and let cool completely. This preparation can be done early in the day.

2. Wash and refrigerate the lettuce. Prepare the vinaigrette dressing for the salad.

3. Wash and dry the potatoes. Stack them in a steamer, fitted in a pan with 3 cups water at the bottom. Cover the top tightly with foil and a cover. Steam over medium heat for about 20 minutes. After 10 minutes, turn

the potatoes around, so the ones on top are at the bottom. Check with a skewer if they are cooked. Sometimes they take longer than 20 minutes to cook.

4. While the potatoes are cooking, reheat the poaching liquids. When the water is quivering, add the fish, cover the pan, and simmer with the water quivering for 15 minutes. Remove the fish and drain on a rack or in a strainer.

5. Prepare a Beurre Blanc, page 213, Garlic Mayonnaise, page 73, or plain mayonnaise, page 53.

6. Remove the fish and drain on a rack or in a strainer. Skin the fish. Serve on a bed of lettuce, seasoned with a vinaigrette dressing, surrounded by the unpeeled potatoes, and the unpeeled onions. Serve with a white butter sauce or a mayonnaise. Each guest peels the onions and potatoes.

Beurre Blanc: A Butter Sauce

French folklore will make you believe that only women know how to really make a Beurre Blanc. I have men students who are very proud of their own butter sauce and will even compare theirs with the most famous restaurants. This sauce is the epitome of all sauces. There is no thickening agent in it; it's just butter, flavored by a reduction of vinegar, water, and in this case, bulbs of scallions instead of shallots, the classic combination. I prefer scallions to shallots because they will melt into a puréelike consistency, while the shallots, even minced, stay very hard, and I find it unpleasant when I eat the sauce. To thicken, the butter must never reach a temperature higher than 110°F. It looks like creamed butter, but must be fluid enough to coat a spoon.

Special instructions. The butter must be sweet and very fresh. Since the sauce is tricky, be ready to make it into a hollandaise if the butter melts (see step 2). The reduction of vinegar and water with the scallions can be prepared ahead of time.

Special kitchen utensil. A 1½-quart heavy-bottomed saucepan.

SERVES 4–6 (MAKES 1½ CUPS)

2 tablespoons minced bulbs of scallions
4 tablespoons water
3 tablespoons tarragon wine vinegar

12 tablespoons (1½ sticks) sweet butter
About ¾ teaspoon salt
Freshly ground white pepper

1. Combine minced scallions, 3 tablespoons water, and 3 tablespoons vinegar in a 1½-quart heavy-bottomed saucepan and bring it to a boil slowly in a simmering water bath. Let the liquids evaporate slowly to ½ tablespoon while the scallions soften. This can be prepared ahead of time, keeping it in a water bath.

2. Reheat the water bath and add the remaining tablespoon of water to the saucepan. When the bottom of the saucepan is warm, start whisking in the butter briskly, tablespoon by tablespoon, always checking the bottom of the pan with a finger; it must never feel hot to the touch. Remove the pan from the water bath now and again to keep it from becoming too hot. Continue until all the butter is incorporated into the sauce. Season with salt and freshly ground white pepper to taste. (If by mischance the butter melts, it is not a tragedy. Transfer the melted butter into a smaller pan to make a hollandaise and whisk 3 egg yolks in the 1½-quart saucepan in the quivering water bath until the egg yolks start to thicken, then slowly pour in the melted butter. If the hollandaise is too thick, thin it out with lemon juice and water.

Note. Never serve a white butter sauce on top of an ingredient that is very hot; the butter sauce will disintegrate on the plate.

Baked Fish Steaks with
Fresh Mint Leaves en Papillote

"En papillote" is a French expression, now used in English as a culinary term meaning "wrapped in paper." It is an excellent way to bake fish; it's especially good for those on a diet, in which case omit the sauce in this recipe.

Special instructions. A fish steak differs from a fillet of fish. From the way the fish is cut, a steak means the fish is cut crosswise and it is a cut for a large fish, such as haddock, halibut, salmon, monkfish, tile, cod, etc.; whereas the fillet cut is for a smaller fish, such as sole, and it is cut the length of the fish.

Special kitchen utensil. A 2-quart baking dish.

SERVES 4

Four 8-ounce 1″ thick fish steaks	Four ½″ slices large tomato
2 tablespoons oil	¼ cup heavy cream
4 tablespoons minced fresh mint leaves	4 tablespoons (½ stick) sweet butter
1 teaspoon salt	Freshly ground white pepper

Preheat oven to 400°F.

1. Dry the fish steaks with paper towels. Line a 2-quart baking dish with aluminum foil, extending it up over the sides. Dribble 1 tablespoon oil over the bottom of the paper, and sprinkle 2 tablespoons of the mint over the bottom of the paper. Place the steaks next to each other on the mint; sprinkle with 1 teaspoon salt and the remaining mint. Peel 1 fresh large tomato and cut it into 4 slices; place 1 slice of tomato on each steak. Dribble the remaining tablespoon of oil over the fish and tomato. Cover with a second piece of aluminum foil and crimp the edges tightly with the bottom piece to enclose the fish.

2. Bake on the middle shelf of the oven for 15 minutes at 400°F. Open up the aluminum foil and transfer the fish to a preheated platter. Drain the liquids into a 2-quart saucepan. Bring to a boil with ¼ cup heavy cream, stir continuously until the liquids start to become syrupy. Drain any liquid on the fish platter into the sauce. Bring once more to a boil to reduce it to a syrupy consistency. Turn off the heat and whisk in the butter tablespoon by tablespoon. Taste and correct seasonings with salt and pepper. Serve in a preheated sauceboat.

Sautéed Trout, Valdrôme Style

In Valdrôme, my village in southeastern France, trout or any fish fillet is basted in vinegar instead of milk before dredging it in flour, then quickly sautéed in butter or oil. The vinegar helps to bring out the flavor of the trout.

Special instructions. Substitute any fish you like, but remember, sauté the fish about 3 minutes on each side. Substitute ⅓ cup oil for the butter if you wish, but at the end of the cooking add 2 tablespoons butter on top of the fish. Do not sauté the trout when just caught if you are fishermen. Wait until the next day; otherwise the trout will curl up and will be difficult to sauté.

Special kitchen utensil. I use a 3-quart baking dish that can go over a burner, or an oval skillet.

SERVES 4

Four ½-pound trout	8 tablespoons (1 stick) sweet
¼ cup red-wine vinegar	butter
About 1 cup flour	1 teaspoon salt
1 lemon	Freshly ground black pepper

1. Wash the trout under running cold water. Be sure the gills and caked-up blood are removed (or cut off the head, if you prefer). Dry in several thicknesses of paper towels.

2. Fill a plate with the vinegar and another one with the flour. Quarter a lemon.

3. Melt 8 tablespoons butter in an oval baking dish over medium heat. Dip each trout in vinegar, then in flour. Shake off any excess flour and sauté them for 4 minutes on each side in the sizzling butter, basting constantly with a spoon. Be sure to regulate the heat so the butter does not burn. Sprinkle on 1 teaspoon salt and freshly ground pepper and serve immediately with a quarter of a lemon for each serving.

Rum Cake

French cooks are not known for baking cakes, but Savarins, better known in this country under the shape of small cakes called Babas au Rhum, are part of the repertoire of a home cook. The Savarin has given its name to the ring mold in which it is baked. The cake must be light and airy, not heavy and soggy, which, unfortunately, has been the fate of many Savarins and Babas.

Special instructions. I give the hand method, food processor method, and electric mixer method. The three methods are equally good. The cake is very good the next day. Wrap in plastic wrap and refrigerate until needed.

Special kitchen utensil. A 4-cup ring mold called a Savarin mold.

SERVES 8

For the cake

1½ teaspoons dry yeast
¼ cup lukewarm water
About 1½ cups all-purpose flour
   plus 2 tablespoons
½ cup eggs (2 large)
2 tablespoons sugar
¼ teaspoon salt
6 tablespoons (⅔ stick) sweet
   butter
Glaze: 1 egg yolk mixed with
   1 tablespoon milk

For the rum syrup

1⅓ cups water
1 cup sugar
½ cup dark rum (Myers)

For the apricot glaze

½ cup apricot jam
2 tablespoons sugar
Toasted almond slices
Green and red candied cherries
Pastry Cream with 2 tablespoons
   rum, page 44

1. Add 1½ teaspoons dry yeast to ¼ cup lukewarm water in a 1-cup glass measuring cup; mix in 2 tablespoons flour (from 1⅓ cups measured flour. Blend the flour into the liquid until no lumps remain. Cover with plastic wrap and let stand for about 20 minutes in a warm place, until double in volume (see illustration, page 163). If the texture never becomes spongy or does not double in volume start over with a new package of yeast.

2. Measure ½ cup of eggs in a glass measuring cup; beat the eggs with a fork to mix them.

3. Cream 6 tablespoons butter, kneading it with the heel of your hand until it is soft and creamy.

4. *Hand method.* Transfer the yeast sponge to a 2-quart mixing bowl. Add the beaten eggs, the creamed butter, sugar, and salt. With a blending fork or a wooden spoon, start adding flour to the yeast-egg mixture, blending in only 2 tablespoons of flour at a time. As the dough becomes more difficult to work, add 1 tablespoon flour at a time to incorporate it smoothly in the dough before adding more flour. In very dry weather, I generally incorporate 1¼–1½ cups flour; in very humid weather, I can incorporate 1½–1¾ cups flour. Continue mixing the dough for about 3 minutes. The dough is very sticky like cake batter.

Food processor method. In the bowl fitted with the steel blade, put the flour, yeast-sponge mixture, sugar, salt, eggs, and the butter cut up in small pieces. Process for 30 seconds or so until the dough is well blended.

Electric mixer method. Combine the creamed butter, eggs, risen sponge, sugar, and salt in the mixer's bowl. With the mixer running at low-medium speed, add the flour to the mixture in the bowl, 1 tablespoon at a time. Beat well after each spoonful of flour and continue until all flour has been added. It may be necessary to stop the mixer and scrape the dough off the whisk of the beater with a spatula from time to time. After the flour is all mixed in, continue mixing at low-medium speed for another 4–5 minutes until the dough is sticky like cake batter.

5. Cover with plastic wrap and let double or triple in size in a warm place such as a turned-off gas oven (or heat up an electric oven to barely warm for 5 minutes; turn off heat and place the dough in the oven). About 2–3 hours in the winter, less in the summer.

6. Gently push down the dough with a spoon. The dough is very sticky. Grease generously a 4-cup Savarin mold and pour the batter evenly in the pan; or shape like little golf balls next to each other in the mold. The dough will be very sticky. Tap the mold against the counter to

even out the dough. Cover tightly with plastic wrap and let rise to the top of the mold (about 1 hour). However, remove the plastic wrap before the dough touches it; otherwise, it's messy to unstick the plastic wrap. I like to use plastic wrap to cover yeast dough, to create humidity to activate the yeast.

Preheat oven to 400°F.

7. Brush the top of the cake with the egg glaze.

8. Bake on the middle shelf of the oven for 25–30 minutes. Cover loosely with foil if the top browns too fast. (It can be refrigerated at this point in plastic wrap. To freeze the cake: Do not add the rum syrup. Reheat the frozen cake in a 400°F. oven for 10–15 minutes, then proceed with step 9.)

9. *The rum syrup.* Just before the cake comes out of the oven, boil the water and sugar to dissolve the sugar completely. Cool 5 minutes and add the dark rum.

10. Unmold the cake immediately so it doesn't stick to the pan, then put it back into the mold as it was, prick the flat surface with a fork, and dribble 3–4 tablespoons of rum syrup over it. Unmold again onto a rack with a plate under the rack. Prick all over with a fork and dribble the very warm rum syrup over the cake until the cake is moist. This will use about half the remaining syrup. Reserve the rest of the syrup for later.

11. *The apricot glaze.* Boil ½ cup apricot jam with 2 tablespoons sugar until melted. Strain through a sieve to smooth out.

12. Prepare the Pastry Cream, page 44, with 2 tablespoons rum. Refrigerate.

13. *To decorate the cake.* Brush the apricot glaze all over. Transfer the cake to a cake plate. Make small flowers with a slice of red or green candied cherry for the center of the flower and slices of toasted almonds for the petals of the flower.

14. Serve the cake with the remaining rum syrup and the Pastry Cream in a sauceboat. Pour a tablespoon of rum syrup over each serving, then pour the Pastry Cream over each.

Rum Babas

The dough for babas can be prepared a day ahead of time and refrigerated overnight. I mention this because babas without a rum sauce make wonderful breakfast rolls, eaten warm with butter and jam.

Special kitchen utensil. For babas, you need special fourteen ⅓-cup molds called darioles that can be bought in specialty cookware stores.

MAKES 14 BABAS IN ⅓-CUP MOLDS

Same as for the Rum Cake, page 216.

1. Follow the recipe for Rum Cake through step 5.

2. After the first rise, spoon out enough sticky dough to fill each mold to about half full. Let the dough rise again in a warm place until the molds are full (about 1 hour). Brush with egg glaze.

   Preheat oven to 400°F.

3. Bake at 400°F. for 10–15 minutes. Let the cakes cool in the molds on a cake rack, then unmold them. Prick the cakes all over and roll them in the warm rum syrup to moisten them. Then brush on the apricot glaze, lay them on their sides, and decorate with a flower pattern made with almonds and candied cherries.

Babas as breakfast rolls

After the first rise, refrigerate covered with plastic wrap in the least cold part of your refrigerator (I like the vegetable bin). The next morning, butter each mold and spoon out enough dough to fill each about half full. Let the dough rise. Because the dough is cold, it will take about 1½ hours. *Preheat oven to 400°F.* and bake on the middle shelf for 10–15 minutes or until golden brown. Let cool and unmold. Eat with butter and jam. The rolls freeze well. Just wrap them in aluminum foil. Reheat them frozen for 10 minutes in a 400°F. oven.

TECHNIQUES AND UTENSILS INTRODUCED

How to make a blanquette: poaching meats in
vegetable stock

How to make brioche: hand method,
food processor method, electric mixer method

How to use brioche dough for a tart

How to make french toast with apple juice

How to prepare sorrel (sourgrass) and to
freeze it

Lesson 12

Suggested Menus for Lesson 12

Breakfast or Brunch

Chachouka: Poached Eggs
on Green Peppers and Tomatoes
(Lesson 11)

French Toast Made with Brioche

2-Course Summer Dinner

Eggplant Gratin with
Fresh Tomatoes and Bacon

Cheese Platter

Cherry Tart (Lesson 6)

2-Course Winter Dinner

Chicken with Garlic
(Lesson 1)

Eggplant Gratin with Tomato Sauce

Crêpes with Fruit Preserves
(Lesson 4)

3-Course Summer Dinner

Cold Eggplant Gratin with
Fresh Tomatoes

Poached Veal with Sorrel Sauce

Steamed New Potatoes Basted
with Butter and Parsley
(Lesson 11)

Caramel Custard (Lesson 3)

3-Course Winter Menu

Crudités:
Celery Root Rémoulade
Grated Carrots
Grated Red Cabbage
(Lesson 3)

Lamb Stew with Celery
Served on a Bed of Pasta Made with
Whole Wheat Pastry Flour
(Lesson 9)

Brioche Tart with
Apricot or Prune Whip

Eggplant Gratin with Fresh Tomatoes

This is the eggplant dish of the Languedoc, in the southwestern part of France. It is the counterpart of the following Provençal Eggplant Gratin with Tomato Sauce. I make it when the tomatoes are at the peak of the season, from July to October, when they are very juicy. Everything up to the baking can be done a day ahead. This dish is also quite good cold, and it makes excellent sandwiches. (It can be made in winter with canned tomatoes.)

Special kitchen utensil. A 2-quart baking dish.

SERVES 8

3 medium-size eggplants (3 pounds)	½ cup parsley minced
2 tablespoons coarse salt	4 cloves garlic minced
4 large tomatoes (2 pounds)*	1½ teaspoons salt
3 cups corn oil	Freshly ground black pepper
½ cup flour	1 bay leaf
	1 tablespoon olive oil

* Out of season, buy a 17-ounce can of Ialian peeled plum tomatoes (not packed in tomato purée or paste). Drain the tomatoes, split in two, for 1 hour.

1. Wash and dry each eggplant and cut off the stems. Peel, with thick peelings. Slice each eggplant lengthwise into 6 slices about ¼" thick. Place them in a strainer, sprinkle with 2 tablespoons coarse salt, and let stand for 1 hour. This makes the eggplants disgorge water and with it any bitterness.

2. Peel the tomatoes (first plunge them into boiling water for 30 seconds), quarter them, then cut into small pieces and reserve in a colander.

3. Rinse the eggplant under cold water and dry well with paper towels. Heat the oil to 325°F. in a deep-fryer, a wok or a 12" cast-iron skillet. Dredge each slice of eggplant in flour just before dropping into the deep-fryer. Don't forget to shake each piece to get rid of excess flour. If you dredge them in flour sooner, the slices will become gluey. Do not over-crowd the deep-fryer. Turn the slices over with tongs to fry on each side. The slices should be golden brown but not burnt and dried out (about 5 minutes). Drain on paper towels.

Preheat oven to 400°F.

4. Grease a 2-quart oval or rectangular baking dish with butter. Make a layer of eggplant, minced parsley, and minced garlic. Add some of the tomato pieces; season with ½ teaspoon salt and several grinds of black pepper. Continue with succeeding layers in the same manner. Finish with

eggplant slices. Place the bay leaf on top. Dribble 1 tablespoon olive oil over the top layer. Everything to this point can be done a day ahead. Cover with foil and refrigerate. Remove at least 2 hours before cooking.

5. Bake uncovered in a 400°F. oven for about 45 minutes.

Eggplant Gratin with Fresh Tomatoes and Bacon

If you want to use this gratin as a main dish, it is a good idea to include ½ pound bacon. Cover bacon with cold water. Bring to a boil. Cook for 10 minutes. Drain. Rinse under cold water. Dry and dice the bacon into ¼″ cubes. Sauté until the fat melts. Add the bacon at step 4. If used as a vegetable dish, it is better to leave out the bacon.

Eggplant Gratin with Tomato Sauce

This is the best version I have found of the classic Provençal eggplant gratin. The eggplants are sliced, deep-fried, baked with a tomato sauce, then covered with a béchamel. This dish is very good with any lamb or pork dish.

Special kitchen utensil. A 3-quart baking dish.

SERVES 8

3 medium-size eggplants	⅓ cup freshly grated Parmesan
Salt	cheese
2 cups milk	⅓ cup freshly grated Swiss cheese
2 tablespoons butter	1 cup Thick Tomato Sauce,
2 tablespoons flour	page 147
Freshly ground black pepper	1–2 tablespoons butter
3 cups vegetable oil	

1. Peel the eggplants (cut thick peelings) and slice them lengthwise, about 6 slices per eggplant. Sprinkle salt over the eggplant slices and allow them to drain in a colander for 1 hour.

2. While the eggplants are draining, make a béchamel: Boil the milk. In a 1½-quart heavy-bottomed saucepan, over medium heat, melt 2 tablespoons butter, add the flour, and stir briskly. When it is bubbling, add the boiling milk all at once. Whisk rapidly until well mixed and smooth. Simmer for at least 10 minutes. Season with ½ teaspoon salt and freshly ground pepper. Reserve.

3. Rinse the eggplant in cold water and dry well with paper towels. Heat the oil to 325°F. in a deep-fryer, a wok, or a 12″ cast-iron skillet. Deep-

fry the slices of eggplant until golden—about 5 minutes—and drain each slice on paper towels. Reserve.

Preheat oven to 350°F.

4. Grease a 3-quart rectangular or oval baking dish and arrange half the eggplant slices evenly on the bottom. Mix the grated Parmesan and Swiss cheeses and sprinkle half over the eggplant. Pour in all the tomato sauce, cover with the remaining slices of eggplant, pour the béchamel over them, and sprinkle with the rest of the cheese. Finally, dot with butter.

5. Bake for 1–1¼ hours. Check now and then to see if it is browning too fast. If so, cover loosely with a piece of aluminum foil. Serve hot.

Poached Veal with Sorrel Sauce

This recipe is a variation of a famous classic French dish called Blanquette de Veau and is a great success in my classes. It is unusual to poach veal in water with aromatic vegetables and expect it to taste good, but the flavor comes from the sauce made with sorrel and the reduction of the poaching liquids. The acidity of the sorrel gives an interesting flavor to this recipe, so do not eliminate the sorrel from the sauce or substitute something else— the dish will be bland.

Special instruction. For the dish, the best cut of veal is the shoulder. Have the veal tied as a roast about 4″ in diameter. For a shoulder of veal, ask for the center cut for more presentable slices. If you are using breast of veal, remove as much fat as possible and have it boned before rolling and tying it.

Special kitchen utensil. A 4-quart Dutch oven.

SERVES 6

2 carrots	½ pound sorrel (sourgrass)
2 leeks	5 tablespoons sweet butter
5 cups water	2½ tablespoons flour
1½ teaspoons salt	⅔ cup heavy cream
3 pounds boned veal roast	

1. Peel the carrots and cut each one into 3 pieces. Remove the tough green leaves of the leeks. Split the leeks in two and wash under running cold water to discard any remaining sand.

2. Combine 5 cups water, salt, carrots, and leek in a 4-quart Dutch oven. Cover and bring to a boil. Add the veal, cover, and poach in quivering water for 1 hour, turning the veal over once in a while.

3. Wash the sorrel and remove the stems, tearing out the center vein of the leaf as well. Melt 2 tablespoons butter in a 9″ cast-iron skillet and add the sorrel leaves, turning them over with a wooden spatula until they melt into a purée. Cook until all the water evaporates. Reserve.

4. Remove the roast with the carrots and the leeks from the poaching liquid. Cover with aluminum foil and reserve in a warm oven. Boil down the liquids to about 2½ cups.

5. Melt the remaining 3 tablespoons butter in a 1½-quart heavy-bottomed saucepan. When the butter is melted, whisk in 2½ tablespoons flour and mix well. Add the 2 cups of boiling liquids all at once and whisk briskly to smooth out the sauce. Add the sorrel and ⅔ cup heavy cream and cook for 15 minutes over medium-low heat, whisking once in a while.

6. Meanwhile, transfer the veal roast to a cutting board with a juice catcher. Cut off the strings and cut the veal into ¼″ thick slices. The veal should be slightly pinkish in the middle. Add the juices that run out of the meat to the sauce and reheat. It should have the consistency of heavy cream.

7. Overlap the meat slices on a preheated platter, decorate with the carrots and leeks around the meat, and pour half the sauce over the meat. Serve the remaining sauce in a preheated sauceboat.

Technique: To freeze fresh sorrel

I love sorrel (sometimes called sourgrass). When May comes, there is at least 1 sorrel recipe in each class. Its tangy flavor marries well with veal, fish, and eggs. It grows almost like a weed, and for city dwellers, sorrel is generally found from May to October in Italian groceries or specialty shops; if you have a garden, you can grow it with almost no effort.

Sorrel looks somewhat like arugula leaves. It must be cleaned like spinach, and like spinach it is voluminous before cooking but dwindles after cooking; fortunately, only a little is needed to make a wonderful sauce for Poached Veal, page 225, or for Cheese Omelets, page 274, or Onion and Sorrel Custard, page 352.

MAKES ½ CUP

1 pound sorrel   2 tablespoons butter

Wash the sorrel and remove the stems, tearing out the center vein of the leaf as well. Dry the sorrel leaves in a salad spinner.

Melt 2 tablespoons butter in a 12″ cast-iron skillet and add the sorrel leaves, turning them over in the skillet with a wooden spatula until the leaves melt into a purée. Cook until all the water evaporates from the sorrel—about 5 minutes—so the sorrel won't crystallize.

When cold, freeze the sorrel purée in 2 small containers.

Lamb Stew with Celery

I like roast lamb when spring arrives, and winter is my favorite season for stews. In this recipe, we use the same techniques as for the Poached Veal with Sorrel Sauce, page 225.

Special instruction. Lamb shoulder, or the top of a leg where the pelvic bone is, is excellent for stewing. Ask the butcher to cut the meat in 2″ cubes, with the bone in. (The bones give flavor to the broth. Before serving, you may bone the meat.) Steps 1–3 can be done a day ahead of time.

Special kitchen utensil. A 9-quart Dutch oven.

SERVES 6

4 pounds lamb with the bones in	20 small white onions
5 cups water	1 tablespoon sugar
2 teaspoons salt	3 egg yolks
4 ribs celery	1/3 cup heavy cream
7 tablespoons butter	Freshly ground black pepper
2½ tablespoons flour	

1. Turn the meat in a 9-quart Dutch oven. Cover with 5 cups of water and add 2 teaspoons salt. Bring slowly to a boil. Skim off any scum rising to the surface of the liquid and replace any liquid removed with additional water. Cover and simmer with the liquid barely quivering for 1½ hours or until the meat is tender. (If you are using the top part of the leg, it will cook faster than the shoulder.)

2. Wash the celery ribs and cut them into pencil-size thin strips about 2″ long. Make 3 bundles of the celery strips and tie each bundle with kitchen string. Bury the celery bundles in the meat for the last 20 minutes of the cooking of the meat.

3. Peel 20 small onions. Melt 4 tablespoons butter in a 9″ cast-iron skillet. When the butter starts to color, add the onions, sprinkle them with 1 tablespoon sugar, and sauté for 3 minutes or so. Pour in ½ cup lamb broth. Cover tightly and braise over low heat for 20 minutes or so or until soft. Check the onions once in a while and add more broth if necessary. Uncover and over high heat sauté the onions to glaze them.

4. With a perforated spoon, transfer the meat and the celery bundles to a mixing bowl. Boil the liquids down to 2½ cups to concentrate the flavors. Melt 3 tablespoons butter in a 1½-quart heavy-bottomed saucepan. When the butter is melted, whisk in 2½ tablespoons flour and mix well. Add all at once 2 cups of the boiling lamb broth (reserve ½ cup for braising the onions) and whisk briskly to smooth out the sauce. Simmer the sauce

for 15 minutes, skimming off any fat which rises to the surface (see illustration, page 191). Reheat the meat and the celery in the sauce. (It can be done ahead of time until this step.)

5. Transfer the meat and the celery to a preheated platter. Bone the meat if you wish. Break 3 egg yolks in a bowl and mix them with ⅓ cup heavy cream. Quickly whisk the egg-cream mixture into the hot sauce, whisking all the while to avoid curdling the eggs. Whisk the sauce for about 5 minutes over medium-low heat to heat the eggs, but don't bring the sauce to a boil or the eggs will curdle. Taste and correct seasonings with salt and freshly ground pepper.

6. Ladle half the sauce over the meat and serve the remaining sauce in a sauceboat.

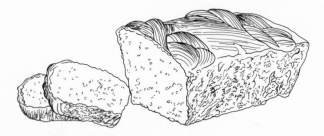

Brioche Loaf

Brioche is bread enriched with eggs and butter. Freshly baked, it is great for breakfast with jam, but if you are like me and do not eat breakfast very often, bake it, then freeze it to use when needed. Brioche makes wonderful toast with a vegetable spread like the Bohémienne, page 161, or for a dessert like French Toast Made with Brioche, page 231, or for Sausage in Brioche, page 394, or make as Brioche Tart with Apricot or Prune Whip, page 232.

Special instructions. The amount of flour used in the recipe will depend on the flour: whether it is made with soft wheat or hard wheat or a blend (for all my recipes, I use Hecker's all-purpose unbleached flour), and especially it will depend on the weather. In humid weather, the liquids will absorb more flour, and in dry weather, less flour will be absorbed.

Special kitchen utensil. A 6-cup loaf pan.

MAKES ONE 1½-POUND LOAF

2⅛ cups all-purpose unbleached
    flour
2 teaspoons dry yeast or ⅙ ounce
    (1 package) fresh yeast
¼ cup tepid water
1 tablespoon sugar
1 teaspoon salt

8 tablespoons (1 stick) sweet
    butter
3 large eggs
Glaze: 1 egg yolk mixed with
    1 tablespoon milk (and 1 table-
    spoon sugar for breakfast)

For the food processor, electric mixer, and hand methods, proceed with the first 4 steps.

1. Measure 2⅛ cups all-purpose flour and reserve in a 1-quart mixing bowl.

2. Dissolve the yeast with ¼ cup tepid water in a 1-cup glass measure, and mix it along with 2 tablespoons flour from the measured flour. With a small whisk, blend the flour into the liquid until no lumps remain. Cover with plastic wrap and let rise about 15–20 minutes in a warm place to make a sponge until double in size (see illustration, page 163). If it does not double in size, the yeast is dead. Start over again with a brand-new package of yeast. Be sure to replace the 2 tablespoons flour.

3. Mix 1 tablespoon sugar and 1 teaspoon salt into the remaining flour (don't mix the salt and sugar in beforehand; otherwise, the salt in the flour might kill the yeast when you add 2 tablespoons flour to make the sponge at step 2).

4. Knead the butter with the heel of your hand until very smooth and soft. (If the butter is very hard, pound on it first with your fist, then knead it with the heel of the hand.)

5. *Food processor method.* Secure the steel blade in the food processor bowl. Add the flour with the sugar and salt, break 3 eggs in the bowl on top of the flour, add the risen sponge of yeast, and the kneaded butter in small chunks. Process for 20 seconds or so until the dough is smooth. It will not make a ball and should not; it will remain more like a cake batter. Continue with step 6.

    Electric mixer method. Using the flat paddle or the dough hook, break 3 eggs in the mixer's bowl and beat lightly with a fork. Add the yeast sponge (doubled in size) and the butter. With the mixer at high speed, blend the eggs and sponge together. Start incorporating 1 cup of flour, ¼ cup at a time, into the dough, still at high speed. Then lower the speed to low-medium to continue incorporating more flour, 2 tablespoons at a time (it takes longer to incorporate more flour as the dough becomes slightly stiffer). Stop incorporating flour when it becomes difficult for the beater to mix the flour into the dough. Continue with step 6.

Hand method. Break the eggs into a 4-quart mixing bowl and beat them with a fork to mix them. Using a wooden spoon, mix the risen sponge of yeast into the beaten eggs, then add the very soft butter. Start incorporating flour, ¼ cup at a time, stirring with a wooden spoon. Continue adding flour. Then transfer the dough to a working surface. Sprinkle flour on your working hand and on the dough and knead the dough with the heel of your hand against the working surface until the dough is smooth and sticky (about 5 minutes). Continue with step 6.

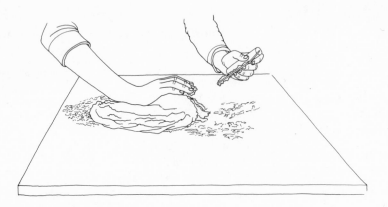

6. Transfer the dough, made either in a food processor, electric mixer, or by hand, into a 2-quart mixing bowl. Cover with plastic wrap and allow the dough to double or triple in size in a warm place (from 1 to 3 hours, depending on the weather).

7. Butter a 6-cup loaf pan. Sprinkle with flour. Gently push the dough down in its bowl and, with a rubber spatula to make it easy, transfer the dough to the loaf pan. Cover with plastic wrap, and let rise to the top of the pan.

   Preheat oven to 400°F.

8. Brush the egg glaze over the very soft dough and bake on the middle shelf of the oven for 35 minutes. Remove the brioche loaf from the pan, turning the pan upside down on a cake rack. (If the brioche sticks to the pan, wrap the pan with a damp towel for several minutes and gently dislodge the brioche with a flexible steel blade from a spatula or knife.

Note. Sometimes the brioche rises more than other times. When it bakes, part of the top will droop over. Bake it for 15 minutes, then with a serrated-edge knife trim off the part of the brioche that overflowed and continue baking the brioche.

Note on freshly baked brioche for breakfast. There are two methods:

- Instead of transferring the dough into a loaf pan and baking it, transfer the dough to a 2-quart mixing bowl, cover with plastic wrap, and refrigerate overnight in the least cold part of your refrigerator. Remove from the refrigerator, work the dough with the heel of your hand for 1 minute to soften the dough, and let rise once more in the 6-cup loaf pan. It will take longer to rise (place in a warm oven—a gas oven with the pilot light on, or turn on the electric oven to warm for 5 minutes, turn off, then wait 5 minutes before putting the brioche into the oven). Brush on egg glaze and bake at 400°F. following the above recipe.

- If your kitchen is cold enough (no more than 60°F.), let the brioche rise during the night in the loaf pan covered with a tent-like plastic cover and bake it when you get up.

French Toast Made with Brioche

Substitute brioche for bread and substitute apple juice for milk for a scrumptious breakfast or dessert.

Special instructions. It is easier to make the toast with a brioche that is several days old. If the brioche is freshly baked, the toast will be soggy. You can buy crystallized sugar from H. Roth & Son, 1577 First Avenue, New York, New York 10028, or Paprikas Weiss, 1546 Second Avenue, New York, New York 10028.

Special kitchen utensil. A 12″ cast-iron skillet.

MAKES TEN 1″ SLICES

Brioche Loaf, page 228
½ cup sugar
2 cups apple juice
2 eggs
16 tablespoons (2 sticks) sweet
    butter

Granulated sugar or crystallized
    sugar
Whipped Cream, page 28
    (optional)

1. Bake Brioche Loaf according to the recipe, page 228. Let cool completely. Slice into ten 1″ thick pieces before freezing or refrigerating in foil.

2. Dry the slices of Brioche Loaf in the oven at 300°F. for 10 minutes, or longer for the frozen slices.

3. Combine ½ cup sugar with 2 cups of apple juice in a 2-quart saucepan and dissolve the sugar in the apple juice over medium-low heat. Cool.

4. Break 2 eggs in a 2-quart mixing bowl, beat with a fork, and blend with the apple juice.

5. Melt 6–8 tablespoons butter in a 12″ cast-iron skillet. Dip the toast in the apple juice–egg mixture on both sides and sauté 4 pieces of toast at

a time in the butter. First the juice will evaporate, then the butter will darken. After 2 minutes, turn the toast on the other side with a wide steel-blade spatula to brown on both sides. Transfer to a serving plate and discard the butter in the skillet. Clean the skillet with a paper towel and proceed with the next batch of toast, adding more butter to the pan.

6. Sprinkle granulated sugar or crystallized sugar over each piece of toast and overlap them in a serving platter. Serve Whipped Cream if you wish.

Brioche Tart with
Apricot or Prune Whip

A friend of mine calls it my brioche pizza. If it is at all possible, buy the prunes or the apricots at a specialty store, where they are generally better than the supermarket variety.

Special instruction. Prepare the brioche dough and the fruits a day ahead of time.

Special kitchen utensil. A 10″–11″ quiche or tart pan, or a 1½-quart rectangular baking dish.

SERVES 6–8

For the brioche dough

1⅛ cups all-purpose flour
1 teaspoon dry yeast
¼ cup water
½ teaspoon salt
2 large eggs
6 tablespoons (¾ stick) sweet
    butter

For the prune whip

8 ounces pitted prunes
½ cup dry Madeira
½ cup water
1 cup light brown sugar

Or for the apricot whip

8 ounces dry California apricots
1 cup water
1 cup superfine sugar
2 tablespoons dark rum
Powdered sugar
Whipped Cream, page 28

1. Prepare the brioche dough according to steps 1–5, pages 228–230. Refrigerate.

2. *For the prunes.* Combine the prunes with ½ cup dry Madeira and ½ cup water in a saucepan. Bring to a boil and simmer 2 minutes. Turn off heat,

cover, and cool. Purée the prunes, liquid, and brown sugar in a food processor or an electric blender. Cover but don't refrigerate the purée; it becomes too stiff to spread later on.

For the apricots. Marinate the apricots in 1 cup water or enough to cover them and cook 20 minutes. Purée with sugar and rum. Cover but don't refrigerate or the purée becomes too stiff.

3. *Baking the tart.* Flour your pastry surface. Butter a 10″ or 11″ quiche pan or tart pan, or a 1½-quart baking dish. Remove the brioche dough from the refrigerator, flour your hands (the dough will be sticky), and transfer it to the pan. Spread it and/or roll as best as you can to fill the bottom of the pan. Brush milk over the top and let rise for 1 hour in a turned-off oven.

Preheat oven to 400°F.

4. Spread the apricot or prune whip over the top of the risen dough. Bake for 20 minutes or so on the middle shelf of the oven.

5. Let cool for 30 minutes before eating. Sprinkle powdered sugar very liberally over the top and serve with Whipped Cream.

Brioche Tart with
Apricot and Prune Whip

You can use both the apricot whip and the prune whip to decorate a single tart.

1. Prepare only half a recipe each of prune and apricot whip.

2. Cut out a piece of parchment paper the size of the tart pan or baking dish; fold the paper in half, then in quarters, then in eighths. Unfold the paper; there will be 8 wedgelike creases. With a pair of scissors, cut out every other wedge, leaving the remaining 4 wedges joined at the middle.

3. Place the paper on top of the dough, spread the apricot whip where the cut-out wedges are, remove the paper, and spread the prune whip in the empty spaces.

4. *Baking the tart.* Follow the instructions in the basic recipe, above, step 3.

TECHNIQUES AND UTENSILS INTRODUCED

How to steam couscous in a couscousière or in a kettle and a large sieve

How to use leftover meats in a gratin

How to cut fresh fatback for pâtés to line a 4-cup mold

How to shred meat for rillettes and to preserve them in a 2-cup glazed crock

How to test for the soft-ball stage with and without a candy thermometer

How to lighten a butter cream with pastry cream

How to cut plums for a decorative tart

Lesson 13

Suggested Menus for Lesson 13

Cold Buffet or Supper in Winter

Dried Wild Mushroom Quiche
(Lesson 5)

Cold Braised Center Loin of Pork
Stuffed with Prunes

Cold Rice Pilaf
(Lesson 2)

Caramelized Apple Mousseline
(Lesson 1)

*Alternate Cold Buffet or
Supper in Winter*

Vegetable Pâté
(Lesson 8)

Braised Center Loin of Pork
with Prunes

St. Tropez Cream Cake

Cold Buffet or Supper in Summer

Couscous Salad with Corn,
Peas, and Grapefruit

Braised Center Loin of Pork
with a Bohémienne

Home-Style Plum Tart

Summer Dinner

Country Pâté

Tomatoes Stuffed with
Salad Greens and Meat

Home-Style Strawberry Tart

Cocktail Party

Cheese Puffs (Lesson 3)

Little Cocktail Sandwiches Filled
with Prosciutto

Rillettes Spread on Bread

Tomatoes Stuffed with
Salad Greens and Meat

Tomatoes stuffed with lettuce greens and leftover meat are a specialty of my village, Valdrôme, in southeastern France. The stuffing is made of an equal volume of greens to meat. You can use almost any kind of greens you like. I use mainly salad greens, such as romaine, escarole, Boston lettuce, etc.

Special instructions. The stuffing is prepared ahead of time. To alleviate the work, prepare the meat stuffing two days ahead of time, cook the lettuce greens a day ahead, and stuff the tomatoes the day you want to eat them. They can be cooked and reheated. The stuffed tomatoes are also very good eaten cold or at room temperature.

Special kitchen utensil. A shallow oval baking dish around 8″ x 12″ (3 quarts).

SERVES 6–8

1 onion	Salt
2 cloves garlic	Freshly ground black pepper
1 pound leftover cooked meat	2½ pounds salad greens
About 8 tablespoons (1 stick) sweet	6 quarts water
butter or 4 tablespoons meat or	12 medium-size tomatoes
poultry fat plus 4 tablespoons	1 tablespoon minced fresh basil
butter	3 tablespoons olive oil

1. *The meat.* Chop 1 onion and 2 garlic cloves coarsely. Cut leftover meat (lamb, pork, beef, whatever you have) into ½″ cubes. Melt 4 tablespoons butter or fat from a roast or from a goose, chicken, or duck. Brown the meat over medium heat for about 10 minutes. After 5 minutes, add the onion and the garlic; stir occasionally to avoid burning. Sprinkle on ½ teaspoon salt and freshly ground pepper. Grind the meat, onion, and garlic through a meat grinder, and brown the ground meat once more in the same skillet for about 5 minutes, adding fat if necessary. Reserve.

2. *The greens.* If you are using romaine lettuce, remove the center stems. Boil 6 quarts water in a stockpot with 3 tablespoons salt. Wash the greens under running cold water. Drain and add to the boiling water, pushing the greens under the water with a wooden spatula. Bring the water back to a boil and cook boiling for 3 minutes. Drain the lettuce in a large colander in the sink and rinse with cold water to stop the cooking. Let drain for 30 minutes, then squeeze the greens in your hands to get rid of as much water as possible. Chop the greens very fine with a knife or a food processor. Reserve.

3. *The tomatoes.* Slice off a ½″ thick top from the stem end of each tomato and reserve. Scoop out the pulp with a spoon and let the pulp drain for 15 minutes. Lightly salt each tomato shell and reserve next to its own top. Melt 3 tablespoons butter in a 12″ cast-iron skillet and add the pulp of the tomatoes. Cook over medium heat, mashing the pulp as it is cooking until it is the consistency of soft relish. Then add the minced greens, and mix together. Add the ground meat. Stir the stuffing all the while for 3–4 minutes over medium heat. Add 1 tablespoon butter, 1 teaspoon salt, freshly ground pepper, and 1 tablespoon minced basil. Taste and correct seasoning.

Preheat oven to 325°F.

4. Overstuff the tomato shells as much as ½″ above the opening. Put the tops on and bake in a greased baking dish just big enough to hold them together. Dribble 3 tablespoons olive oil over the tops and bake for 1 hour or so, basting occasionally with the pan juices.

Couscous Salad with
Corn, Peas, and Grapefruit

Couscous is made from wheat and is sold in granular form. This is my favorite recipe for couscous given to me by a friend, Paule Basiaux, who spent her childhood in Algeria; it is a lovely refreshing and filling summer salad that will remind you of a better-known salad, tabbouleh.

Special instruction. Can be made in the morning for dinner.

Special kitchen utensil. A couscousiér or a makeshift: a large stockpot and a fine-mesh sieve.

SERVES 8

1 pound precooked medium-grain couscous	Freshly ground black pepper
1 teaspoon cumin	2 grapefruit
A bouquet of fresh coriander or parsley	3 tomatoes
2 ears fresh corn	4 Tuscan salad peppers*
2 cups fresh green peas or 1 package frozen peas	2 tablespoons butter
Salt	2 tablespoons olive oil
	1½ cups vinaigrette, page 11
	2 tablespoons minced scallions

* These are found in supermarkets with vinegars and oils; buy the hot variety called pepperoncini or Tuscan peppers.

1. Pour the couscous into a large mixing bowl and sprinkle 1 cup water over it. Rub the couscous in your hands for about 5 minutes until all the grains are damp. Cover with a wet towel and let stand for about 1 hour. Rub once more to get rid of the lumps.

2. Sprinkle the couscous with ⅓ cup water and rub again for 5 minutes.

3. Boil several quarts of water in a couscousiér or a stockpot with 1 teaspoon cumin and a bouquet of fresh coriander or parsley. Wrap the couscous in cheesecloth and steam it in the top of the couscousière or in a sieve secured to the stockpot. Steam for 30 minutes.

4. While the couscous is cooking, prepare the vegetables and fruit. Drop the corn in boiling water for 8 minutes. Drain, cool, cut off the grains, and reserve. Shell the peas and drop them in boiling water and cook for 10 minutes or until tender. If you are using frozen peas, follow the directions on the package. Drain and reserve with the corn. Season the vegetables with ½ teaspoon salt and freshly ground pepper. Peel the grapefruit and remove the skin from each piece, cut in cubes. Reserve. Cut each tomato into 8 wedges. Chop 4 salad peppers.

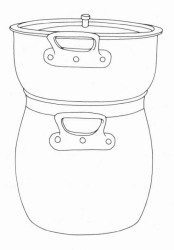

5. Remove the couscous from the cheesecloth and put it in a large salad bowl and fluff it up with the tines of two forks. Add 2 tablespoons butter and 2 tablespoons oil and mix well into the couscous, still fluffing it with the forks. Season with 1 teaspoon salt and freshly ground pepper. Taste and season some more if necessary.

6. Prepare 1½ cups vinaigrette, but use only 1 clove of garlic (otherwise it overpowers the vinaigrette) and add 2 tablespoons minced scallions.

7. Add the corn, peas, grapefruit, and salad peppers to the couscous, toss the salad with 1 cup vinaigrette (reserve ½ cup in a sauceboat for the table), and decorate the salad with the tomato wedges. Refrigerate until 1 hour before dinnertime. Sprinkle vinaigrette over the tomatoes as you are ready to eat the salad.

Country Pâté

Every cook wants to make a good pâté. But some are intimidated by the task, even though making a good pâté does not demand much technique. After all, it is just a glorified meat loaf baked wrapped in fatback to keep it moist. The secret lies in the ingredients and the serving. How do you keep a pâté from being bland?

- You must season the pâté correctly. Since a pâté is served at room temperature, it requires more salt than a hot dish.
- A pâté should mature for at least two days after cooking before serving.
- A pâté must *never* be served cold. Take it out of the refrigerator at least an hour before serving—otherwise, some of the flavors will be lost.
- Save the juices and fat from the first pâté to cook the next one. Succeeding pâtés will be better than the first one. Juices and fats freeze very well.
- Serve pâté with French bread and butter. Butter the bread and spread the pâté over it.
- A pâté is best accompanied by a crisp dry white wine.

Special instructions. Ask the butcher several days ahead of time to get pork liver and pork neck meat. If unavailable, buy pork shoulder and beef liver. Have the meats ground by the butcher or grind them with a meat grinder. Ask the butcher for fresh fatback, cut into very thin slices or sheets, or buy fresh bacon or a pork *roast* with lots of fat. Freeze it for 1 hour, and cut the fat into thin slices, enough to line a 1-quart mold.

Special kitchen utensils. A 1-quart pâté mold (terrine) with a cover. A piece of wood, the length and width to fit on the inside of the mold. A weight, such as two 1-pound cans.

SERVES 8–10

½ pound coarsely ground pork neck or picnic shoulder cut
½ pound coarsely ground veal shoulder meat
2 tablespoons brandy
1 tablespoon fresh tarragon or ½ teaspoon dried
1 tablespoon salt
½ teaspoon freshly ground black pepper
2 cloves garlic, finely minced
1 teaspoon dried thyme
2 onions

3 tablespoons fat from previous pâté or chicken fat or meat drippings
1 cup bread crumbled
½ cup jellied juice from previous pâtés or chicken or veal stock
½ pound pork or beef liver
1 egg
¾ pound fresh fatback
1 bay leaf
Boston lettuce
Capers
Vinaigrette, page 11

1. Mix the ground pork and veal with 2 tablespoons brandy and the tarragon, salt, freshly ground pepper, minced garlic, and thyme. Let stand overnight in the refrigerator.

2. Slice 2 onions thinly and sauté over low to medium heat for 10 minutes in 3 tablespoons fat from a previous pâté (use duck, chicken fat, or butter and oil if you don't have fat from a previous pâté). Reserve off the heat.

3. Cut the crusts off the bread. Tear bread into pieces and, over medium heat, mash it together with ½ cup of the juices from a previous pâté or chicken or veal stock. Reserve off the heat once the bread is thoroughly moistened and mashed.

4. Chop finely or grind in the food processor ½ pound pork or beef liver along with the sautéed onions.

5. Mix the marinated meats and spices with the liver and the bread. Use a large bowl and mix the ingredients with your hands. Add the egg, lightly beaten, and mix well again.

Preheat oven to 350°F.

6. Line a 1-quart mold (terrine) with strips of fresh fatback. First line the bottom, then the sides and end. The pieces used for the sides should be long enough to cover the top of the pâté. (Run the pieces vertically up the sides, not lengthwise.) Put the pâté meat into the mold and fold the strips of fatback over the top. Cut off the excess fatback and freeze for another use; add the bay leaf on top of the fat and cover with lid.

7. Place the pâté mold in a hot water bath to two-thirds its depth. Bake covered at 350°F. for 1½ hours.

8. Remove the pâté mold from the water bath. Allow it to cool for 30 minutes, then pour off the fats and juices and save them for the next pâté. Keep in the freezer until needed.

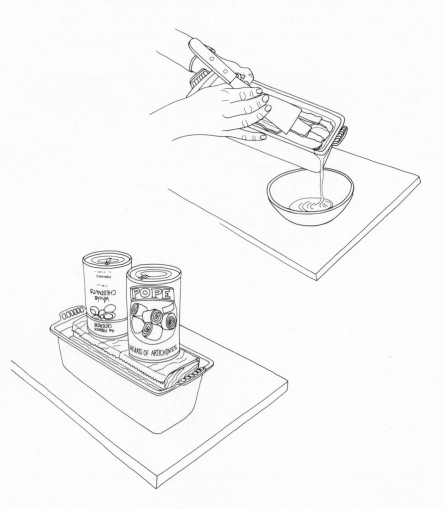

9. Place a strip of wood wrapped in foil on top of the pâté and weights on top of the wood to make the pâté more dense and easier to cut. When completely cooled, remove the weights.

10. Cover the pâté and keep it 3 days in the refrigerator so the flavors will develop. (You may keep it as long as 10 days if you wish.)

11. To serve, place the mold in warm water, then unmold the pâté on a platter lined with lettuce. Cut the pâté into ½″ thick slices and put a caper on each slice. Serve with vinaigrette on the side.

Rillettes: Shredded Pork Pâté

Shredded meat pâté, called rillettes in French (pronounced REE-YETT), differs from a country pâté in the baking technique. With Country Pâté (preceding recipe), the meat is ground raw and baked in a mold lined with fresh fatback; whereas, for rillettes, the meat is cut up in cubes and baked slowly in fat, then the meat is shredded, packed in crocks, and sealed with the cooking fat. Rillettes can be made with pork, rabbit, duck, or goose. A duck or goose preserve, for example, can be transformed into rillettes, page 271.

Spreading rillettes on a slice of bread and drinking a dry crisp white wine with it is indeed a sensual experience.

Special instructions. Ask your butcher to bone the pork shoulder. You need 2 pounds of boned meat. Order ahead of time to get fresh pork fatback. If the butcher is unwilling to sell you fresh fatback, order a cut called "sow-belly" and use it instead of the fatback. It is actually fresh bacon. Prepare rillettes several days before eating.

Special kitchen utensils. Several small-cup earthenware crocks or Mason jars, or a pâté mold.

MAKES 1 QUART SHREDDED PÂTÉ

2 pounds lean boned pork picnic
   shoulder
1 pound fresh fatback
2 large cloves garlic, minced
1 onion, minced
1 scant tablespoon salt

⅛ teaspoon freshly ground
   black pepper
½ teaspoon dried thyme
1 tablespoon Cognac
½ cup water

1. Grind the fatback through a meat grinder, and cut the pork meat into 2-inch cubes. Transfer to a 6½-quart Dutch oven then add the minced garlic, minced onions, salt, freshly ground pepper, thyme, and Cognac. Mix everything with your hands and refrigerate for 24 hours but no more, or it will become too salty.

2. Cook with ½ cup water in the same pot over low heat for 4–5 hours until the meat is very tender and the fat melted. The meat must not color during cooking, or the pâté will dry out. Every hour, check the meat and stir everything together, cutting the fat with a spatula when it is very soft, to help render it.

3. Let cool. Then strain the meat. Reserve the melted fat for later in a glass container. Do not refrigerate.

4. On a big cutting board, shred the meat into small strings about half the size of a paper match, using 2 forks. It is tedious work. For this reason, you can use the food processor, even though the machine does not do as good a job as hand shredding. Put about a quarter of the meat into the food processor, and run the machine only for 1–2 seconds; excessive chopping will reduce the meat to a mushy pulp. While cooling, the reserved fats in the glass container will have separated from the meat juices. Transfer the fat into a separate bowl.

5. Pack the shredded meat with meat juices and ¼ cup melted fat into crocks, leaving ½″ free at the top. Cover the pâté with the remaining melted fat. Refrigerate at least 3 days before eating to let the flavors develop. Pour melted lard, ½″ deep on top, to seal the rillettes if you are not going to eat them within 3 weeks. They will keep all winter in your refrigerator, sealed with lard and covered with plastic wrap; however, once you start eating the rillettes, finish them within a week.

6. Remove the rillettes from the refrigerator 1 hour before serving. To serve, scrape the fat off the top and spread the pâté on good country bread.

Note. If you have leftover fats and meat juices from previous rillettes or country pâtés, or chicken fat, use them for the next pâté, but season with less salt, perhaps ½ tablespoon salt instead of a scant tablespoon, since the fats have been salted previously.

Cold Braised Center Loin of Pork
Stuffed with Prunes

Pork and prunes are a great combination. For a cold supper or a buffet, a center cut loin of pork stuffed with prunes makes a beautiful presentation and it is delicious. I buy a center cut loin of pork when I want to serve it cold. It is easier to slice cold, and it makes slices without fat. Even though the meat is drier than a shoulder cut laced with fat, eaten cold it seems less dry (see page 111 for information on buying pork). Accompany it with a rice salad seasoned with a vinaigrette dressing and decorate the salad with some of the prunes from the roast.

Special kitchen utensils. A 12″ cast-iron skillet and a 9-quart Dutch oven.

SERVES 8

1 pound pitted prunes	1 teaspoon salt
2 cups dry white wine	Freshly ground black pepper
1 medium-size carrot	4 pounds boned pork loin roast,
2 leeks	center-cut
5 tablespoons sweet butter	Rice Pilaf, page 39
1 tablespoon oil	Vinaigrette, page 11

1. Soak the prunes for 2 hours in 2 cups wine.

2. Peel and cut the carrot in ¼″ slices. Cut off the tough green leaves of the leeks and reserve for a soup or a stock. Split the whites of leeks almost to the root and wash under cold running water to remove dirt or sand. Cut the leeks in ⅛″ thick slices.

3. Combine the leeks and carrot in a 9-quart Dutch oven with 3 tablespoons butter and ½ teaspoon salt and freshly ground pepper. Cover tightly and cook over low heat for 15 minutes, checking once in a while that the vegetables do not color.

4. Stick a long slicing knife through the center of the pork roast from one end to the other and stuff prunes in the center of the pork from both ends. Reserve prunes that will not fit in.

5. Melt 2 tablespoons butter and 1 tablespoon oil in a 12″ cast-iron skillet. When the fats are hot but not smoking, sear the roast on all sides and ends, using 2 wooden spatulas to help you hold the roast in position while searing.

Preheat oven to 325°F.

6. Scrape out the fat if it is burned; otherwise leave it. Bury the roast in the vegetables with the remaining prunes and the wine. Season with ½ teaspoon salt and freshly ground pepper. Cover.

7. Cook on the middle shelf of the oven at 325°F. for about 1½–2 hours, checking once in a while, stirring the prunes and vegetables.

8. Remove the pork from the oven, and let cool in the pot. Refrigerate until needed.

9. Discard the strings from the pork and cut into thin slices.

10. Prepare Rice Pilaf following the recipe, page 39. When still hot, mix in a vinaigrette dressing, page 11.

11. Reheat the prunes and vegetables enough to remove the chill from the refrigeration.

12. Decorate the rice salad with some of the prunes. Overlap the slices of pork on a serving platter with the prunes and vegetables around it.

Cold Braised Center Loin of Pork
with a Bohémienne (Eggplant and Tomatoes)

To change from pork and prunes, braise the pork with a Bohémienne, a cousin of ratatouille, the best-known dish of Provençal cooking.

Special instruction. Be sure to warm up the vegetables a bit when ready to slice the meat and prepare the buffet table. Warming the vegetables will take off the chill from refrigeration and will render them more flavorful.

Special kitchen utensil. A 12″ cast-iron skillet and a 9-quart Dutch oven.

SERVES 8

Bohémienne, page 161 — 4 pounds boned pork loin roast, center-cut

1. Prepare the Bohémienne in a 9-quart Dutch oven according to the recipe, but at step 5, cook the vegetables for 20 minutes or so, covered. Then uncover and continue cooking the vegetables for another 15–20 minutes. The vegetables need to be full of liquid in which to braise the pork roast. Do not add the eggs and cheese now.

2. Melt 2 tablespoons butter and 1 tablespoon oil in a 12″ cast-iron skillet. When the fats are hot but not smoking, sear the roast on all sides and ends, using 2 wooden spatulas to help you hold the roast in position while searing.

   Preheat oven to 325°F.

3. Bury the roast in the vegetables and pour in the fats from the skillet if they are not burnt. Season with ½ teaspoon salt and freshly ground pepper. Cover.

4. Cook on the middle shelf of the oven at 325°F. for about 1½–2 hours, checking once in a while, stirring the vegetables.

5. Remove the pork from the oven. Stir the egg yolks and cheese quickly into the hot vegetables. Let cool in pot, then refrigerate.

6. Refrigerate until ready to slice. Discard the strings around the pork roast and cut into thin slices.

7. Reheat the vegetables enough to remove the chill from the refrigeration.

8. Overlap slices of pork on a platter and decorate with the Bohémienne around them.

St. Tropez Cream Cake

This cake is a specialty of St. Tropez on the French Riviera. Every bakery and pastry shop has its own version; here is mine.

The cake is made with a yeast dough very much like a brioche dough. I bake it in a 12″ diameter pizza pan, because it is rather a flat cake; St. Tropezians call it a tart. I slice it in two like a sandwich and fill it with a mixture of butter cream and custard flavored with crystallized ginger.

The dough also makes wonderful breakfast rolls; see page 250.

Special instructions. The dough is prepared a day before dinnertime. The butter cream and custard can also be prepared ahead of time and refrigerated. Bake the cake about 2–3 hours before eating it. Fill it with the custard and butter cream just before eating; this is the ideal timing. The cake without the filling freezes well. Reheat frozen in a 400°F. oven for 15 minutes. Filled with fruit preserves, it is a good substitute for brioche or croissants.

Special kitchen utensil. A 12″ pizza pan.

SERVES 8–10

For the sponge

¼ cup milk
2 teaspoons dry yeast
2 tablespoons all-purpose flour

For the batter

7 tablespoons sweet butter
2¼ cups all-purpose flour
3 tablespoons sugar
1 teaspoon salt
1 egg (¼ cup)
¾ cup milk

For the filling

Butter Cream, page 252
Pastry Cream Custard
   for Filling Cakes, page 251

For the glaze

2 tablespoons sugar
1 tablespoon milk
Powdered sugar

1. *The sponge.* Heat 1 cup milk until tepid. In a glass measuring cup, pour ¼ cup milk. Add and mix 2 teaspoons yeast in the milk with 2 tablespoons flour. Cover with a plastic bag to create humidity. Let stand for about 20 minutes or until it doubles in volume. Reserve the rest of the milk for step 3.

2. Cream 8 tablespoons sweet butter with the palm of your hand until the butter is very soft.

3. *Food processor method.* Secure the steel blade in the food processor bowl. Add 2¼ cups flour, 3 tablespoons sugar, and 1 teaspoon salt. Break 1

egg into the bowl; add the sponge and the soft butter. Then pour in the remaining ¾ cup milk, being careful it does not overflow through the center shaft of the bowl. Process for 20 seconds or so until the dough is smooth; it will not make a ball; it will be more like a cake batter. Then see step 4.

Electric mixer method. Pour the sponge and the remaining ¾ cup milk in the mixer bowl. Break 1 egg into it, add the butter, and beat at medium speed until well blended. Mix 3 tablespoons sugar and 1 teaspoon salt into 2¼ cups flour. With the mixer at medium speed, using the whisk or the flat paddle, beat in ¼ cup of flour at a time. Continue until all the flour is incorporated into the dough. Continue beating for about 5 minutes. Then see step 4.

Hand method. It is identical to the electric mixer method, but instead of a whisk, use a wooden spoon and beat by hand.

4. When the dough is smooth—it is a soft cake batter—transfer it to a 2-quart mixing bowl or a 2-quart glass measuring pitcher, using a rubber spatula to scrape the dough up. Remember, it is very sticky and soft. Cover the bowl with plastic wrap to create humidity. I find the best way to let a yeast dough rise is to use a turned-off oven. Heat your gas or electric oven to warm for 5 minutes, then turn it off and wait 5 minutes. Place the dough in the oven and let rise until it triples in size, about 2 hours or so. It depends on how humid and warm the day is; the more so, the faster the yeast dough is going to rise.

5. With a rubber spatula, pour the dough into a bowl. Cover with plastic wrap. It is very messy and sticky, but don't worry—it will stiffen in the refrigerator. Refrigerate overnight in the least cold part of the refrigerator (the vegetable bin is fine).

6. That same day, or the next day, at least 3 hours before serving, prepare the Butter Cream and the Pastry Cream Custard for Filling Cakes and refrigerate.

7. The next day in late afternoon: Remove the soft dough from the refrigerator and place on a floured surface. The butter in the dough should

still be cold as you roll it out. Grease a 12″ round pizza pan and roll the dough into a 12″ circle right on the pan. Brush milk over the dough and let rise for about 1 hour in a warm place.

Preheat oven to 375°F.

8. Combine 2 tablespoons sugar and 1 tablespoon milk in a pan and bring it to a boil for 2 minutes or so until the glaze thickens slightly. Then brush this milk glaze on the dough just before baking. Bake on the middle shelf of the oven at 375°F. on top of aluminum foil (sometimes the glaze drips down in the oven) for 20–25 minutes or until golden brown. After 20 minutes, cover the top loosely with foil if necessary. Let cool completely before slicing.

9. Slice horizontally with a bread knife to make 2 layers. (It is a little tricky because the cake is flat.) Remove the butter cream and custard from the refrigerator and beat them together by hand or by electric mixer. Spread the filling on top of the bottom piece of the cake. Place the top over it. Sprinkle powdered sugar very liberally over the top. Cut into wedges and serve.

Breakfast Rolls or
Cocktail Sandwich Rolls

These small rolls, called Petits Pains au Lait in French, can also be made for cocktails, filled with salmon, prosciutto, or whatever. Just add 1 tablespoon sugar to the dough instead of the 3 tablespoons indicated in the basic recipe. These rolls can be baked ahead of time, frozen, and reheated without thawing when needed.

1. Proceed with the St. Tropez Cream Cake recipe, page 247, through step 5.

2. Remove the dough from the refrigerator. Flour your pastry surface.

   For breakfast. Sprinkle flour on the dough and cut it in 2 equal pieces. Shape each piece into a 12" long sausagelike form and cut each form into 6 equal pieces for the total of 12 pieces.

   For cocktails or buffet. You can make the rolls even smaller. Shape each piece into 18" long sausagelike forms and cut each form into 9 pieces each for a total of 18 small rolls.

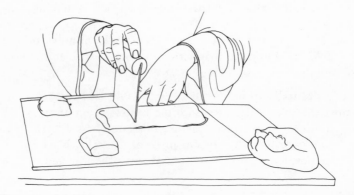

3. Place the rolls apart to let them rise on 2 greased cookie sheets. Brush on milk and let rise, using the oven technique: Heat the oven to warm, turn off, wait 5 minutes, then put them in the oven to rise until they are double in size. It will not take very long, about 30–40 minutes. Remove them from the oven.

   Preheat oven to 400°F.

4. Brush milk once more over them and bake for 15 minutes for the breakfast rolls, 12 minutes for the cocktail rolls. Interchange the cookie sheets

midway in the baking, so the ones on the top shelf, which will bake faster, are exchanged with the ones on the lower shelf.

5. Let cool completely.

Note on freezing and reheating. For a big party, freeze the rolls, wrapping them in foil. Preheat oven to 400°F. Remove the rolls from freezer, do *not* thaw them, and bake them once more just until they are soft and warm. They are still very good.

Pastry Cream Custard
for Filling Cakes

This Pastry Cream Custard requires the same technique as that for the recipe on page 44, but is much thicker. Do read the recipe clear through very carefully and try to visualize all the steps. It takes no time at all to make, but you must act quickly, because the custard will bind almost instantaneously and there is practically no cooking.

Special kitchen utensil. A 1½-quart heavy-bottomed saucepan.

MAKES ABOUT 1 CUP

1½ tablespoons all-purpose flour	2 tablespoons sweet butter
1½ tablespoons cornstarch	1 cup milk
⅓ cup sugar	1 tablespoon brandy or Cognac
2 large egg yolks	

Before making the Pastry Cream Custard, assemble and measure all the ingredients so that you have them at hand next to the stove with a pan of cold water for step 4. Once you start, allow no interruptions. It is important to work quickly.

1. Sift 1½ tablespoons flour and 1½ tablespoons cornstarch together in a 2-quart mixing bowl. Add ⅓ cup sugar and mix well.

2. In a small bowl beat the egg yolks lightly with a fork. Knead 2 tablespoons butter with the heel of your hand and reserve for step 5.

3. In a 2½-quart heavy-bottomed saucepan, bring 1 cup milk to a boil over medium heat. If you are using a stainless steel saucepan, be very careful to heat the milk slowly. Otherwise the bottom of the pan will scorch and the custard will have an unpleasant burnt taste. *Be very attentive*: When the milk is ready to boil over, that is when you quickly pour half of it in

the flour mixture and you whisk very quickly until the flour and milk mixture is smooth, then add the egg yolks and whisk until well blended.

4. Reheat the remaining milk to a boil once more. When the milk is ready to boil over, and only then, do you very quickly pour the flour-egg mixture into it. Whisk vigorously over high heat for 30 seconds or so until very thick. Take off the flame and dip the bottom of the pan into cold water to hasten the cooling process, whisking all the while, otherwise the Pastry Cream Custard will set and get lumpy at the bottom of the pan. Transfer the custard to a 2-quart mixing bowl. Cool until it is just barely warm to the touch. Add 1 tablespoon brandy or Cognac to the Pastry Cream Custard and whisk until smooth.

5. Whisk in 2 tablespoons butter in small pieces until all the butter is incorporated into the Pastry Cream Custard. Cover with plastic wrap. Refrigerate until needed.

Note on runny Pastry Cream Custard. This usually occurs because the milk was not really boiling. If it does, eat the runny custard with fresh fruits, with a chocolate cake, or as is (it's very good cold), and start over again for a custard that can be used as a filling.

Butter Cream

A butter cream filling can have different flavorings depending on the cake you are planning to fill. For the St. Tropez Cream Cake, page 247, I flavor it with crystallized ginger. For Finger-Size Chocolate Eclairs, page 447, I flavor it with chocolate. For a Paris-Brest, page 451, I flavor it with praline paste, and for the Chestnut Meringue Cake, page 381, I flavor it with chestnut purée.

Butter is the most important flavor, and it is absolutely essential that it be sweet, fresh butter. Taste the butter before using it to be sure. I am convinced that there are brands of supposedly unsalted butter with some salt in them—it happened to me once. Even a smidgen of salt will be too salty because there is a great amount of butter to be incorporated into the cream.

Special kitchen utensil. An electric mixer or an electric hand beater.

MAKES 1¾ CUPS

3 egg yolks	16 tablespoons (2 sticks) sweet butter
½ cup sugar	3 tablespoons minced crystallized
4 tablespoons water	ginger

1. In the bowl of an electric mixer, break the egg yolks and beat them at medium speed while preparing the syrup. Or, if you are using an electric hand mixer, beat the egg yolks for 1 minute and let rest while preparing the syrup.

2. Combine ½ cup sugar and 4 tablespoons water in a 2½-quart saucepan. Over medium heat, stir the sugar and water until the sugar is all dissolved. Boil to the soft-ball stage.

Technique: To test for the soft-ball stage

Without a candy thermometer. Have on hand next to your stove a 2-quart mixing bowl filled halfway with water and a soup spoon as well as water boiling in a tea kettle. Once the syrup is cooking note how the bubbles on the boiling surface get smaller and smaller as the syrup thickens. After 3 minutes, start testing the syrup: Scoop out a quarter of a spoonful of syrup

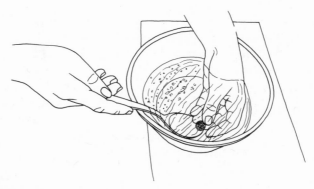

and quickly drop the spoon in the cold water. With your free hand in the water, quickly shape a small soft ball. If you can shape a soft ball, quickly turn off the heat, hold the pan with a potholder, and quickly pour the syrup into the egg yolks while the mixer is on. With a hand-held electric beater, it is more awkward, but it can be done. Pour with your right hand and beat with your left hand. Secure the mixing bowl on a wet potholder.

To remedy a soft-ball stage syrup that has reached hard-ball stage, stir ¼ cup boiling water into the syrup to thin it out, then cook it once more to the soft-ball stage.

With a candy thermometer. Tipping the pan to one side to create depth in the syrup, dip the thermometer in the syrup without touching the bottom of the pan. It should read 220°F.

3. Beat the egg yolk–syrup mixture until it is pale yellow—about 3 minutes. Remove the bowl and refrigerate the mixture for 30 minutes before adding the butter, otherwise it will melt in the syrup and it will not give the volume needed.

4. Meanwhile, cream the butter until smooth but not soft. (I smear the butter with the heel of my hand to cream it.)

5. Remove the syrup from the refrigerator and with the mixer at medium speed beat in the butter, 1 tablespoon at a time, then add the crystallized ginger. Cover with plastic wrap and refrigerate until ready to use.

Home-Style Strawberry Tart

When strawberries are in season, I could eat them every day, simply dipped in sugar, or with whipped cream, or for a more elaborate dessert, with a custard. But my favorite is this home-style tart. It is very simple to prepare. It consists of a fully baked empty pastry shell smeared with strawberry jam, then decorated with strawberries and glazed with currant jelly.

Special instructions. For this tart, I like to make a thicker dough than for a quiche or a vegetable tart baked with a filling. Thick, the pastry dough is more like a cookie and is very brittle. The unbaked pastry shell can be prepared a day ahead of time and refrigerated or frozen until ready to bake.

Special kitchen utensil. An 11″ pastry pan with removable bottom, if possible.

SERVES 6

Shortcrust Pastry, page 87
Whipped Cream, page 28
2 pints strawberries
4 tablespoons sugar

1 tablespoon raspberry liqueur
  or Kirsch
4 tablespoons strawberry jam
3 tablespoons currant jelly

1. Prepare the pastry, page 87, adding 2 tablespoons sugar to the ingredients. Roll out the whole amount of dough to about 14″ in diameter and ¼″ thick. Roll the dough on the rolling pin and line an 11″ pastry pan with it. There will be some dough left. Refrigerate and use it for turnovers, page 137, or small hot tarts, page 135.

Preheat oven to 400°F.

2. Prick the bottom of the dough. Line and cover the pastry with foil. Crimp tightly around the edges; the dough then will not shrink while baking. See illustration, page 89.

3. Bake for about 20 minutes at 350°F. Remove the foil and continue baking for 5–10 minutes or until the pastry is lightly golden and dry. Be careful not to get it too brown. Watch closely the last 5 minutes.

4. Prepare the Whipped Cream, page 28. Refrigerate.

5. Don't hull the strawberries before washing them. They keep their flavor better. Sprinkle 4 tablespoons sugar over them with 1 tablespoon raspberry liqueur (substitute Kirsch if necessary). Marinate for 1 hour.

6. Heat 4 tablespoons strawberry jam. It will be easier to spread it in the bottom of the pastry shell. Hull the strawberries. Decorate the tart with strawberries. If the strawberries are big, slice them in 3 and overlap the slices going around the tart. Leave 1 strawberry whole for the center of the tart. Heat 3 tablespoons currant jelly to brush over the strawberries.

7. *To decorate with whipped cream, using the pastry tube and bag.* Fit a serrated tube in a pastry bag, twist the bag over the top of the tube, and push the twisted part of the bag inside the tube to prevent the whipped cream from slipping out of the tube while filling the bag. Fill the bag with about 1½ cups whipped cream. Untwist the bag. Push the whipped cream down to the tube, closing the top of the pastry bag by twisting it (see illustration, page 51). Squeeze from the top of the bag with one hand while holding the bag with the other hand perpendicular to the strawberries and make small rosettes of whipped cream between each strawberry if they are small and on top of the slices of strawberries if they are cut.

Home-Style Plum Tart

From mid-August to mid-October, the little dark purple plums, sometimes called Italian plums, are in season. They make wonderful tarts either with Puff Pastry, page 320, for an elegant dinner or with Shortcrust Pastry for a home-style dinner.

Special instruction. Like the preceding Home-Style Strawberry Tart, the dough is thicker than for a quiche or a vegetable tart.

Special kitchen utensil. An 11″ pastry pan with a removable bottom, if possible.

SERVES 6

Shortcrust Pastry, page 87
36 dark purple plums
⅓ cup plus 2 tablespoons sugar

4 tablespoons coarsely ground
  almonds
Cream-Cheese Topping, page 27,
  or Whipped Cream, page 28

1. Prepare the pastry according to page 87, adding 2 tablespoons sugar to the ingredients. Roll out the whole amount of dough to about 14″ in diameter. Roll up the dough on the rolling pin and line an 11″ pan with it. There will be some dough left. Refrigerate and use it for turnovers, page 137 or small hot tarts, page 135.

2. Prick the bottom of the dough. Line and cover the pastry with foil. Crimp tightly around the edges; the dough then will not shrink while baking (see illustration, page 89).

   Preheat oven to 400°F.

3. Bake the empty shell for 20 minutes. Remove the foil and continue baking until the dough is golden all over (about 5–10 minutes).

4. Lower the temperature to 350°F.
   Wash and dry the plums,
   split open like a book
   and remove the pit,
   then with the flat sides
   of the plums on the
   counter, in each half of
   the plum cut 2 gashes about
   half the length of the plum,
   starting together at the top and
   forming a wedge which widens out
   as you go toward the bottom of the plum.

5. Sprinkle ⅓ cup sugar and 4 tablespoons coarsely ground almonds on the bottom of the precooked pastry shell. Then line the open plums standing up in a circular pattern. Sprinkle 2 tablespoons sugar over the plums and bake for 45 minutes at 350°F.

6. Serve warm with Cream-Cheese Topping or Whipped Cream.

TECHNIQUES AND UTENSILS INTRODUCED

Using a whole duck or goose: how to cut it up, how to render the fat and make cracklings, how to preserve the meat (in a confit), how to make duck or goose stock, how to use the gizzards and liver

How to season an omelet pan, how to make and stuff omelets

How to make ladyfingers

Lesson 14

RECIPES

Sautéed Apples and Potato Chips

Cabbage Gratin

Salad Greens Gratin

Duck or Goose Stock

Preserved Duck or Goose (Confit)

Tossed Green Salad with Preserved Duck or
Goose Gizzards

Stuffed Omelets with Duck or Goose Cracklings

Cheese Omelets with Sorrel Sauce

Duck or Goose Liver with Scrambled Eggs

Chocolate Mousse Charlotte

Ladyfingers

Suggested Menus for Lesson 14

A Simple Lunch

Duck Liver with Scrambled Eggs

Tossed Green Salad
(Lesson 1)

Light Chocolate Mousse

2-Course Lunch or Light Dinner

Tossed Green Salad with Preserved
Duck or Goose Gizzards

Frozen Chocolate Mousse

My Favorite Summer Luncheon

Red and Green Bell Pepper Salad
(Lesson 1)

Cheese Omelets with Sorrel Sauce

Hot Individual Berry Tarts
(Lesson 7)

My Favorite Winter Luncheon

Cream of Celery Soup
(Lesson 10)

Stuffed Omelets with Cracklings

Blackberry Jam Turnovers
(Lesson 7)

3-Course Winter Dinner

Rillettes: Pork (Lesson 13)
or
Rillettes: Duck or Goose

Onion Soup (Lesson 4)

Apple Custard Pie
(Lesson 6)

3-Course Dinner

Turnip Soup (Lesson 10)

Preserved Duck

Sautéed Apples

Cabbage Gratin

Chocolate Mousse Charlotte

Sautéed Apples and Potato Chips

Sautéed Apples and Potato Chips can be prepared and served together to accompany Preserved Duck or Goose, page 268, or a pork roast such as Braised Pork Roast with Pineapple and Bananas, page 113, or Pork Chops, page 114. Use Cortland, Jonathan, or Golden Delicious apples in autumn; Granny Smith apples in spring.

Special kitchen utensils. Two 12″ cast-iron skillets, a wok, or a deep-fat fryer.

SERVES 4–6

2 pounds Russet potatoes	2 pounds apples
Salt	4 tablespoons sugar
3¼ cups duck or goose* fat	Freshly ground black pepper

* If this recipe is made to accompany a pork roast, use bacon fat instead of duck fat to brown the apples and potatoes.

1. *Preparation of potatoes* (ahead of time). Slice the potatoes as thin as for potato chips: Shave a slice of potato lengthwise, lay flat on the counter, and cut slices with a cleaver. Salt generously.

2. Heat 3 cups duck or goose fat to 300°F. in a 12″ cast-iron skillet, a wok, or a deep-fat fryer, and deep-fry potatoes in several batches, about a quarter of them at a time. Do not overcrowd the skillet. Add more fat if necessary.

3. Drain the chips in a wire basket over a bowl. Just before serving, deep-fry the chips at 350°F. in several batches for 30 seconds.

4. *Preparation of apples* (at the last minute). Peel and core the apples. Cut them into slices 1″ thick.

5. When ready to eat, sauté the apple slices in about 2 tablespoons duck or goose fat in a 12″ cast-iron skillet over high heat. Sprinkle 4 tablespoons sugar over them and sauté 5 minutes or until slightly colored, shaking the pan once in a while. Season with salt and pepper.

Cabbage Gratin

When Cabbage Gratin is on the menu for a class, no one wants to make it, yet, many a time, the lowly cabbage turns out to outshine everything else on the menu. I generally use the plain green or white cabbage, but Savoy or Chinese cabbage can be substituted. The gratin can be baked ahead of time. It's very good reheated. Reheat for 15 minutes at 250°F.

SERVES 6–8

5 quarts water	1 cup grated Swiss cheese
1 tablespoon salt	(4 ounces)
1 medium-size cabbage	1 cup heavy cream, or 1½ cups
(3 pounds)	half-and-half reduced to 1 cup
½ pound slab bacon (not sliced)	1 tablespoon butter

1. Boil 5 quarts water in a large pot with 1 tablespoon salt. Remove any tough outer cabbage leaves. Quarter the cabbage, slice off the core, and boil for 15 minutes partially covered. Drain the cabbage and rinse in cold water, then drain and squeeze out excess water. Chop medium coarse.

2. Slice off the bacon rind, if any. Remove excess fat. Cut bacon into ½″ thick strips, then each strip into 1″ long pieces. Parboil the bacon to remove its smoky flavor. Turn the bacon into a pan with cold water to cover it. Bring to a boil and cook 5 minutes. Drain.

3. Mix the chopped cabbage and bacon cubes and separate into 3 equal piles. Grate Swiss cheese (use good-quality cheese) for 1 cup grated cheese.

Preheat oven to 400°F.

4. Butter a 2-quart baking dish. Spread a third of the cabbage over the bottom and sprinkle on ⅓ cup of the grated cheese. Make 2 more such layers. Pour the heavy cream or reduced half-and-half over the cabbage. Dot the top with 1 tablespoon butter. Bake for 30–35 minutes or until golden brown.

Salad Greens Gratin

As a variation to the Cabbage Gratin, substitute salad greens that are over-grown and too tough to eat in a tossed salad.

SERVES 6

1 head Boston lettuce	A small handful fresh parsley
1 head Romaine lettuce	minced
8 quarts water	½ cup meat juices or chicken stock
2 tablespoons salt plus 1 teaspoon	1–2 tablespoons flour
3 tablespoons meat fat (or butter	1 cup heavy cream or milk
and olive oil)	Pinch of cayenne
1 medium-size onion minced	1 tablespoon sweet butter
1 clove garlic minced	3 tablespoons Swiss cheese grated

1. Wash the lettuces. Remove and discard the cores. Boil 8 quarts water with 2 tablespoons salt. Plunge the lettuce into boiling water and boil

10 minutes. Drain and wash under cold running water. Squeeze the lettuce as much as possible to extract water. Chop very fine.

2. Mince the onion, garlic, and parsley very fine. Heat 3 tablespoons meat fat (or butter and olive oil) in a 9″ cast-iron skillet and sauté the onion, parsley, and garlic over low heat for 5 minutes, enough to just slightly color the onion.

3. Still over low heat, add the lettuce to the onion, stirring together. Sprinkle on 1 tablespoon flour (or more if using milk) and mix well, then add 1 cup cream or milk and ½ cup meat juices (or ½ cup chicken stock or ½ cup cream in lieu of the meat juices). Add ½ teaspoon salt and pinch of cayenne. Stir the mixture and taste, correcting seasonings if necessary. Turn off the heat.

Preheat oven to 350°F.

4. Butter a 2-quart baking or gratin dish, pour in the greens. Dot with butter and bake in the oven for 30 minutes at 350°F. Then sprinkle with 3 tablespoons Swiss cheese and bake for 5 more minutes or until the top is slightly golden brown.

Using the Whole Duck or Goose

There is no waste on a duck or on a goose. Everything you get is good; you just have to know how to use it. For Preserved Goose or Duck (confit), I choose the Long Island white Pekin duck because it renders a lot of fat, necessary for the confits, page 268. The fat can also be melted to use for shredded pâtés (Rillettes), page 270, or simply to brown vegetables and meat. Fat freezes perfectly.

The skin, cooked with the fat, makes wonderful cracklings, more flavorful than chicken cracklings. They freeze well and are used for stuffing omelets, page 271.

The carcass, wings, and neck make a very good stock. The meat left on the wings and on the carcass after it has cooked to make a stock can be shredded and seasoned with salt and pepper for wonderful sandwich meats.

The legs and drumsticks and breasts are used for several different recipes: Preserved Duck or Goose, page 268, or Duck Bourguignon, page 193.

This seems involved written down, but it really is not. You need to visualize the work and have time to learn how to cope with the different steps, but there are no complicated procedures and variables.

I generally prepare 2 ducks (5 pounds each) or 1 goose (10 pounds) at a time to have enough fat for the Preserved Duck or Goose and enough meat to serve from 4 to 6 people. It takes about one hour's work to get the duck or goose ready for the different recipes.

Technique: How to cut up a duck or a goose

Have on hand before you start: 3 big mixing bowls; 1 small mixing bowl; a pair of good-size scissors; a sharp boning knife; paper towels (it's messy—you need to wash your hands, the scissors, and the knife several times during the work); a cleaver; and a big cutting board.

In the cavity of the duck or goose, you should find the neck, gizzard, and liver. Unfortunately, sometimes the liver is not there. Reserve the neck for bowl number 1 and the gizzard for bowl number 3; the liver for the small bowl.

Wash the duck or goose inside and out and dry with paper towels.

Using a pair of scissors, cut off the neck skin; reserve in bowl number 2. With a sharp boning knife or the scissors, cut off the wings just at the joint where they are attached to the body. Reserve in bowl number 1. There is a V-shaped bone which corresponds roughly to a person's collarbone. Cut around it with a knife, trying to leave as little meat attached to it as possible. Reserve in bowl number 1.

With the scissors, cut off all skin, fat, and tail at the opening of the cavity. Reserve in bowl number 2.

With a knife, cut off the legs at the joint where the thigh bone is attached to the body. This joint is sometimes difficult to find. It is connected to the backbone of the duck or goose, a third of the way from the tail end. With a pair of scissors, cut off any excess fat and skin from the legs. Reserve thighs and drumsticks in bowl number 3 and fat and skin in bowl number 2.

Bone the breast as follows: With a knife, cut along each side of the breastbone and down over the carcass. With the scissors cut off all the fat. Reserve the boned breasts in bowl number 3, the fat and skin in bowl number 2.

Remove all the fat and skin from the carcass and reserve in bowl number 2. With the cleaver, chop the carcass in small pieces in bowl number 1.

Pour 2 tablespoons sherry or brandy over the duck or goose livers and add a pinch of thyme, a pinch of salt, and freshly ground pepper. Cover with plastic wrap and refrigerate until you want to make scrambled eggs with it. It lasts 2–3 days in the refrigerator. See page 275 for Duck Liver with Scrambled Eggs.

For the Duck Bourguignon, page 193, sprinkle a pinch of salt over the duck or goose meat and cover with plastic wrap. Refrigerate until needed.

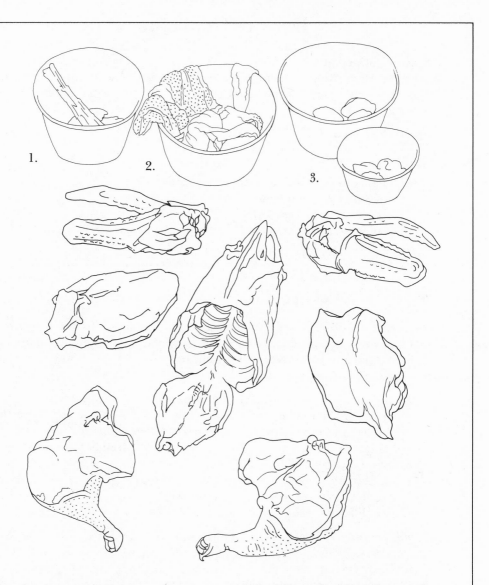

For the Preserved Duck or Goose, page 268, follow the directions and prepare it right away, as the meat must macerate in salt and herbs for 24 hours before cooking it.

Render the fat and make cracklings following the recipe, page 267. Follow the recipe, page 266, for the Duck or Goose Stock. It can be done the same day as you cut up the ducks or goose, or if you wish, prepare it the next day, then cover the bowls with plastic wrap and refrigerate, but remember to make the stock ahead of time and to render the fat before baking the Preserved Duck or Goose.

Duck or Goose Stock

Special instruction. Duck stock can be a substitute for chicken stock or be used for Duck Bourguignon, page 193, or Roast Duck with a Caramel-Vinegar Sauce, page 425. Substitute goose stock for water in the White Bean Purée, page 286, or Bean Soup, page 287.

Special kitchen utensil. A 10–15-quart stockpot.

MAKES 1–1½ QUARTS

4 tablespoons rendered duck or
  goose fat or 3 tablespoons
  butter and 1 tablespoon oil
Duck or goose carcasses, wings,
  and necks
3 carrots
2 ribs celery

3 onions
1 teaspoon salt
Freshly ground black pepper
½ teaspoon dried thyme
Several sprigs of parsley
Water to cover, about 2 quarts

1. In each of two 12″ cast-iron skillets, melt 2 tablespoons duck or goose fat or a mixture of butter and oil. When the fats are hot but not smoking, sauté the cut-up carcasses, wings, and necks until golden (about 10 minutes) over medium heat.

2. Meanwhile, peel and cut up the carrots and celery in 1″ thick slices. Peel and quarter the onions. Remove the bones to a stockpot and sauté the vegetables, stirring all the while, for 5 minutes. Add the vegetables to the bones in the stockpot, plus 1 teaspoon salt, freshly ground pepper, thyme, and parsley. Pour enough water to cover the vegetables and bones. Leave the cover ajar and simmer over medium heat for about 3 hours. Strain and degrease (reserve the fats). Reserve the duck or goose stock for the different recipes. It freezes well.

3. Remove any meat left on the bones and wings and neck. Shred it with the tines of a fork. Season with salt and pepper to taste. Place in a small bowl, cover with duck or goose fat, and refrigerate. Spread it on bread. It makes wonderful sandwiches.

Technique: To render duck and goose fat and make cracklings

Reserve the fat in a container. You should have about 4 cups of duck fat from 2 ducks, or 6 cups of fat from 1 goose. Refrigerate or freeze.

MAKES 4 CUPS OF DUCK FAT; 6 CUPS OF GOOSE FAT

Fat and skins of 2 ducks or of 1 goose
½ cup water

Cut up the duck or goose skin with a pair of scissors in 1″ pieces. Put the fat and the skins into a heavy 6½-quart pot and add ½ cup water. Cover the pot and cook for 30 minutes over medium-low heat. Uncover and keep cooking over low heat until all the fat is melted (about 2 hours). Raise the heat to medium and continue cooking until the skin is light golden brown; it will crackle in the fat. Do not wait until they are crisp to remove them from the fat; this will be done when they are used for each individual preparation. Once in a while during the cooking period, scrape the bottom of the pot with a steel spatula to loosen the pieces of skin that might stick to the pot.

Line 2 thicknesses of paper towels in a fine-mesh sieve over a medium-size bowl and strain the fat and cracklings. Remove the cracklings, drying them in more paper towels. Let cool and refrigerate in a container or freeze them for Stuffed Omelets with Duck or Goose Cracklings, page 271. Refrigerate or freeze for later uses.

Preserved Duck or Goose (Confit)

Preserved duck or goose is marinated in salt for a day, desalted, then cooked slowly in rendered fat until the meat is very tender. Packed in a crocklike container and covered with fat, it stays refrigerated at least for a month before it is eaten. While preserved in the fat, the meat develops lots of flavor. To eat it, the duck or goose pieces are nudged out of the fat and reheated gently until the skin is crisp. Even though the bird is cooked in fat and preserved in fat, when eaten no fat should remain but just a very tender meat and crisp skin. It is delicious with potatoes and apples, page 261, or in a tossed salad, page 270, or made into shredded pâté, page 270. One batch of preserved duck (two 5-pound ducks) or one 10-pound goose will serve 4–6 as a main course, 8 as a first course in a tossed salad, and will make enough shredded pâté for 8–10 people as an hors d'oeuvre.

For the first duck or goose preserve, you will need extra fat to bake the preserve. Buy goose fat in a specialty store or render chicken fat, or even use lard. From there on you can reuse the fats from the last confit. Freeze until the next confit.

2 big cloves garlic	2 gizzards
1 bay leaf	4–6 cups duck or goose fat
3 ounces coarse salt	Chicken fat or lard, if necessary
1 teaspoon dried thyme	½ cup water
2 ducks or 1 goose, cut in pieces, pages 264–265	

1. Mince the garlic cloves, crumble the bay leaf, and mix with 3 ounces salt and the thyme. Rub each piece of duck or goose and gizzards with the salt and refrigerate in a covered crock or pot for 24 hours, but not much more; otherwise, the meat gets oversalty.

2. Wash each piece of duck or goose under running cold water to discard any salt. Turn the duck or goose pieces into a pot, cover with cold water, and bring to a boil. Boil gently for 10 minutes, drain the water, and repeat once more with cold water. Or soak the pieces in cold water with a thin stream of tap water running all night long. This procedure is to get rid of all the salt in the meat.

3. Turn the duck or goose pieces into a pot just big enough so the rendered fat covers all the meat. Since it is slow cooking, the meat must be submerged in fat; otherwise, the meat outside the fat will dry out while cooking. If there is not enough duck or goose fat, add chicken fat or lard. Add ½ cup water. Cover and cook over low heat or in a 225°F. oven for 1½–2 hours for ducks and 2–3 hours for a goose or until the meat is very tender. Pierce the meat with the tip of a knife; it should

show no resistance. Check it once in a while during the cooking period to be sure the fats are not boiling but just quivering.

4. Remove the duck or goose pieces and gizzards with a perforated spoon to a crock big enough for the duck and the fat covering the meat. Cover the pieces of meat with the fat. Cover with foil and refrigerate for at least 3–4 weeks, and up to 1 month if you like, to give time for the meat to develop flavor. If you want to keep the preserve for a longer period of time, melt ½ pound lard and pour about 1″ of lard on top of the preserve. (When you are ready to eat the preserve, scrape off the lard and discard it.)

To use for a main course

SERVES 4–6

1 batch Preserved Duck or Goose

For the sauce
Duck or Goose Stock, page 266

1 tablespoon flour
4 tablespoons butter
Watercress or young spinach
  leaves

1. The day of the dinner, remove the Preserved Duck or Goose from the refrigerator. Let stand for 1 hour for the fat to soften.

2. Remove the pieces of duck or goose, nudging them gently out of the fat. Reserve the gizzards for a Tossed Green Salad with Preserved Duck or Goose Gizzards, page 270. Freeze the fat for another preserve, pâté, etc. Reserve the jelly at the bottom of the crock for the sauce later on.

Preheat oven to 300°F.

3. Turn the pieces of duck or goose into a 6½-quart Dutch oven. Cover and place on the middle shelf of the oven to reheat the meat and until all the fat clinging to the pieces of duck or goose melts (about 30 minutes).

4. Remove the meat from the Dutch oven. The skin on the meat will still look very pale, but don't worry—it will be broiled at the last minute. Wrap the protruding knuckles of the legs in foil so they won't burn while broiling. Reserve the pieces of meat on a broiler pan, skin side up. Cover them tightly with foil and keep in a 200°F. oven until you are ready to broil the meat just before eating it.

5. Combine the jellied juices found at the bottom of the preserve crock with duck or goose stock to make about 1½ cups of liquid. Mash 1 tablespoon flour with 1 tablespoon butter with the back of a fork until the mixture looks like a paste. Reserve.

6. Just before serving: Preheat the broiler. Broil the meat 4″ away from the heat to crisp the skin (about 2–3 minutes).

7. Meanwhile, bring the juices to a boil, then whisk in the butter-flour paste. Whisk for 30 seconds. Turn off the heat and whisk in the remaining 3 tablespoons of butter, 1 tablespoon at a time. Season with salt, if necessary.

8. Garnish a big serving platter with watercress or spinach leaves, then arrange the duck pieces or goose pieces, cut up in smaller pieces, on it. Serve the sauce in a sauceboat.

To use for a salad

SERVES 8–10 AS A FIRST COURSE

Bone the meat after having broiled it, then cut it in bite-size pieces. Serve it on a bed of tossed green salad, season with a warm vinaigrette, and add sautéed apple slices, page 261.

To prepare as rillettes

Instead of eating the preserved duck or goose as a main course, you can prepare it as rillettes, shredded pâté, for an hors d'oeuvre. My favorite way to eat the pâté is to spread a bit of duck or goose fat on a slice of hot toasted crusty country bread, then to put a big glob of meat over it, and to drink a dry crisp cold white wine with it.

1. Follow the instructions of the Preserved Duck or Goose through step 3.

2. Remove the duck pieces. Bone and reserve the bones to cook with beans for the White Bean Purée, page 286, for example. Then shred the meat with 2 forks. Add ½ cup fat to the shredded meat. Pack tightly in a pâté mold. Refrigerate while the fat is cooling.

3. When the fat is completely cool, but still liquid, pour it over the packed meat and refrigerate at least 3 weeks before eating.

4. Serve the pâté in its crock. Scrape off the fat and put it in a small container to serve with the pâté.

Tossed Green Salad with
Preserved Duck or Goose Gizzards

I ate a similar salad in a wonderful bistro-type restaurant called La Côte Basque on the rue du Cirque, in the eighth arrondissement of Paris. I fell in love. Gizzards are wonderful cooked in a confit.

SERVES 2

4 preserved duck gizzards or 2
   preserved goose gizzards

¼ pound arugula or spinach
   leaves
Vinaigrette, page 11

1. Reheat the gizzards covered over a low flame for about 30 minutes to warm through.

2. Cut each gizzard in several slices and toss them warm in a salad of young arugula or spinach leaves seasoned with a vinaigrette.

Note on preserving just the gizzards. Find a butcher who roasts ducks in his shop, ask him to reserve the gizzards; in general they are thrown out. When you have about 1 pound, follow the directions for the Preserved Duck or Goose, page 268. Salt the gizzards with 3 tablespoons coarse salt, sprinkle ½ teaspoon thyme and ½ tablespoon minced garlic. Refrigerate overnight. Desalt them under running cold water for several hours or overnight under a thin stream of water. Cook in duck fat for 2 hours or until tender. When cold, refrigerate them covered with fat in several small containers and refrigerate for several weeks. As long as they are covered with fat, they keep for several months refrigerated.

Stuffed Omelets with Duck
or Goose Cracklings

Omelets make a quick and simple lunch. They are my standard for unexpected lunch guests. Since I love Preserved Duck or Goose, page 268, my freezer is stocked with duck and goose cracklings. These stuffed omelets are served with crackers and a crisp, dry white wine. I serve cheese and fruits for dessert.

Special instruction. Make individual omelets. It's easier to work with 2 or 3 eggs than trying to make one big omelet.

Special kitchen utensils. Buy an omelet pan in steel, or a black pan in cast iron will do (around 7″ in diameter across the bottom of the pan). This pan must never be washed after it is seasoned and must be used only for omelets. To season the pan wash it once with hot water. Melt 2 tablespoons butter over low heat with a tablespoon of salt. Rub the salt and the melted butter all over the inside of the warm pan. Reheat slightly, then clean the pan with paper towels. You need to use the pan several times before it will be completely seasoned. For the first few times, heat the pan with a tablespoon of butter and sprinkle salt over the bottom, heat until warm, then dry with paper towels before starting an omelet. Don't wash the pan after the omelets are cooked, but quickly rub clean with paper towels while the pan is still hot—it is easier to clean. (If the omelets stick, which might happen for the first few times, then scrub the pan under hot water, dry quickly with paper towels, and lightly grease the pan until the next use.) Nonstick pans do not make as good an omelet as one made in a steel or iron pan. The texture is different; the nonstick pan makes an omelet with a shiny surface, almost rubbery, whereas the steel or iron skillet gives a rough texture (a meaty quality) to the omelet.

SERVES 4

1 cup duck or goose cracklings, page 268	½ teaspoon salt
	Freshly ground black pepper
8–12 large eggs*	2½ tablespoons butter

* 8 U.S. large eggs yield 2 cups blended eggs.

1. Reheat the cracklings in a skillet for about 10–15 minutes until they are very crisp. Drain on paper towels.

2. Break 8–12 eggs in a 2-quart glass measuring cup and beat them with a fork until well blended. Season with ½ teaspoon salt and freshly ground pepper.

3. Melt 1 tablespoon butter in the omelet pan over medium-high heat. When the butter starts to brown lightly, and only then, pour ½ cup beaten egg in the pan. The eggs should sizzle. If they don't, it means the pan was not hot enough and they are likely to stick to the pan.

4. Quickly, stir the eggs with a fork held in your right hand while you shake the pan with the other hand, sliding the pan backwards and forwards, across the burner. Stir the eggs vigorously until they coagulate into a light pancake consistency. When the eggs are set (about 30 seconds or so), add ¼ cup cracklings in a line across the middle of the omelet.

5. Still with your left hand, tip the skillet to a 45° angle on the burner and fold the omelet in thirds, by folding the top third over the cracklings, then rolling it over once more. Then take the handle of the omelet pan with your right hand, holding the handle with an undergrip instead of a regular grip, and roll the omelet onto a preheated plate.

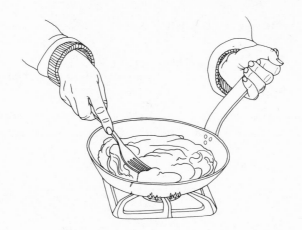

6. Continue with the other omelets, adding ½ tablespoon butter to the
   skillet each time you make an omelet.

Cheese Omelets with Sorrel Sauce

The light acidity of a sorrel (sourgrass) is a tangy complement to a cheese omelet. In the summer, I serve this omelet instead of the one with cracklings.

Special instructions and kitchen utensil. Read the instructions given for the Stuffed Omelets with Duck or Goose Cracklings, page 271, and on how to freeze sorrel, page 226.

SERVES 4

¼ pound sorrel	Freshly ground black pepper
8 tablespoons (1 stick) sweet butter	8–12 large eggs
1½ cups heavy cream	½ cup grated Swiss cheese
1 teaspoon salt	¼ cup grated Parmesan cheese

1. Wash the sorrel and rinse several times. Fold the leaves and tear off the stem clear up into the leaf. Chop coarsely.

2. Melt 2 tablespoons butter in a 9″ cast-iron skillet over medium heat. Add the sorrel and stir for about 5 minutes until the sorrel melts into a purée. Add 1 cup heavy cream and bring to a boil. Season with ½ teaspoon salt and freshly ground pepper and cook, stirring once in a while over medium-low flame, for about 10 minutes. Reserve in the skillet for later. Preheat the plates for serving the omelets.

3. Break 8–12 eggs in a 2-quart measuring cup and beat them with a fork until well blended. Season with ½ teaspoon salt and freshly ground pepper.

4. Melt 1 tablespoon butter in the omelet pan over medium-high heat. When the butter starts to brown lightly, pour ½ cup beaten eggs in the skillet.

5. Quickly, stir the eggs with your right hand while you shake the pan with the other hand, sliding the pan backwards and forwards across the burner (see illustration, page 273). When the eggs are set (about 30 seconds), add ¼ cup mixed cheeses in a line across the middle of the omelet.

6. Tip the skillet (illustration, page 273) on the burner and fold the omelet in thirds, by folding the top third over the cheese, then rolling it over once more. Take the handle of the omelet pan with your right hand, holding the handle with an undergrip instead of a regular grip (illustration, page 273) and roll the omelet onto a preheated plate.

7. Continue with the other omelets, adding ½ tablespoon butter to the skillet each time you make an omelet.

8. Reheat the sorrel sauce with ½ cup heavy cream. Bring to a boil, stirring all the while. Turn off the heat and whisk in the remaining 3½ tablespoons butter. Taste and correct seasonings with salt and pepper, if necessary. Serve in a preheated sauceboat with the omelets.

Duck or Goose Liver with Scrambled Eggs

The first great restaurant we went to in France was the Tour d'Argent in Paris, a three-star restaurant in the *Guide Michelin*. The house specialty is Pressed Duck, which means that they have lots of duck livers, and that gives them the chance to have another fine dish: Duck Liver with Scrambled Eggs. My husband liked it so much that whenever I prepare a duck I keep the liver as a special treat for him. Perhaps you will like it too.

Special kitchen utensil. A 9″ cast-iron skillet. For more than 3 eggs use a 12″ cast-iron skillet.

SERVES 1

1 duck or goose* liver	Salt
2 tablespoons Cognac	Freshly ground black pepper
3 tablespoons butter	2 eggs

* For more than 1 duck liver, add 1 more egg per duck liver, but do not add more Cognac to flambé; it would be too strong.

1. Cut the liver lengthwise in several strips. Marinate in 1 tablespoon Cognac for 1 hour.

2. Heat a 9″ cast-iron skillet over a medium flame without any fat. When hot, add 2 tablespoons butter; it will sizzle. Add the liver strips. Sauté for 30 seconds over a high flame. Turn off the heat.

3. Pour 1 tablespoon Cognac into a ladle, heat it over a gas flame, and tip it toward the flame to ignite. Pour over the duck liver, shaking the pan. Season with salt and pepper.

4. Beat 2 eggs in a bowl with 1 tablespoon melted butter. Pile the strips of liver in the center of the skillet and pour the beaten eggs around. Stir constantly with a wooden spoon (do not disturb the liver in the center) until the eggs coagulate (around 3 minutes, depending on how well done you like scrambled eggs—you must be the judge).

5. Place the liver strips on a warm plate. Spoon out the scrambled eggs to decorate around the liver. Serve immediately.

Chocolate Mousse Charlotte

This is a buttery chocolate mousse chilled in a charlotte mold lined with Ladyfingers called a Charlotte Sylvatelle in French. A charlotte mold is a versatile pan; it can be used to cook dessert custards, vegetable custards, and soufflés.

Special kitchen utensil. A 6-cup charlotte mold.

SERVES 8

6 ounces bittersweet chocolate
    (Lindt or Tobler)
8 tablespoons (1 stick) sweet butter
6 large eggs, separated
¼ cup superfine sugar

2 tablespoons Cointreau
¼ cup water
20 homemade Ladyfingers,
    page 278
Whipped Cream, page 28

1. Melt the chocolate slowly in a double boiler or water bath. Do not cover. Take care to avoid getting any water in the chocolate. This tends to make it grainy. Do not stir while melting. When melted, set aside to cool. Test the temperature of the melted chocolate as follows: Dip your finger into the chocolate and touch it to your lower lip—it must not feel warm or cold.

2. Cream the butter first by kneading it with the heel of your hand, then, using a mixer, beat for 1 minute until smooth. Then beat in the cooled chocolate.

3. Beat the egg yolks and sugar at medium speed for 8–10 minutes until the mixture is thick and very pale, then gradually beat in the chocolate-butter mixture. Add 1 tablespoon Cointreau.

4. Beat the egg whites to stiff peaks. I prefer beating egg whites in a copper bowl, 12″ in diameter, with a large balloon whisk. I get more air into the whites, which, in turn, gives more volume. It is also easier to control when to stop beating the egg whites: They must be stiff, but not grainy (that makes them hard to blend in with the chocolate mixture).

5. Fold half the egg whites into the chocolate batter, then fold the chocolate batter into the remaining egg whites. It is important to handle the egg whites and the batter gently. If you mix too hard, the batter and the egg whites will lose in volume. Refrigerate 30 minutes.

6. Butter and sprinkle sugar in a 6-cup charlotte mold (or other 6-cup mold with straight sides). Cut waxed paper to fit the bottom of the mold, and grease it on both sides. Mix ¼ cup water and 1 tablespoon Cointreau and quickly in-and-out dip one side of the Ladyfingers to soften them just a bit. Line the sides of the mold, putting the rounded side of the Ladyfingers against the mold. (You may have to trim and cut them to fit.)

7. Ladle half the mousse into the mold, tap it on the table to level it, and fit a layer of Ladyfingers on top of it. Then pour in the rest of the mousse. Trim the Ladyfingers (if necessary) to be even with the mousse. Cover with a plate and leave overnight in the refrigerator, or keep 2 hours in the freezer.

8. *To unmold.* Dip the mold in hot water for 30 seconds, turn the mold upside down on a cake plate. Wait 15 minutes before unmolding. The mousse should slip easily from the mold. If not, dip once more in water.

Frozen Chocolate Mousse

SERVES 8

Prepare the chocolate mousse, steps 1–5. Oil and sugar a 6-cup loaf pan. Turn the chocolate mousse into the mold. Cover. Freeze for at least 6 hours or overnight. *To unmold.* Remove the chocolate mousse from the freezer for 1 hour before eating it, then run the blade of a knife around the edges of the mousse. Dip the mold in hot water for 30 seconds or so. Turn the mold upside down on a serving platter. Wait until ready to eat to unmold. The mousse should slip out easily from the mold; if not, dip once more in hot water to loosen it from the mold. Serve with a Pastry Cream, page 44, or Crème Anglaise, page 360, a light egg custard.

Light Chocolate Mousse

The classic home-style chocolate mousse is without butter or cream. Follow the chocolate mousse recipe. Omit the butter in step 2. Refrigerate until cold.

Ladyfingers

A Ladyfinger is a very good cookie in its own right. Light and airy, it melts in your mouth. Serve with fresh strawberries or sherbet and champagne for a light delicious dessert.

Special kitchen utensil. The literal translation of Biscuit à la cuiller, the French term for Ladyfingers, is a biscuit shaped with a spoon. It is possible to bake perfectly shaped Ladyfingers by piping the batter with a pastry bag into a cylindrical mold called a champagne biscuit mold.

MAKES 40 LADYFINGERS (2 MOLDS)

4 large eggs	⅓ cup sifted potato starch*
¾ cup sugar	Pinch of salt
1 teaspoon vanilla extract	Powdered sugar
⅓ cup sifted cake flour	

* Health-food stores and Jewish food stores generally carry potato starch.

1. Separate the eggs, add the sugar and 1 teaspoon vanilla to the egg yolks, and beat at medium speed for 8–10 minutes, until the mixture is thick and very pale.

2. Sift together the cake flour, potato starch, and salt, and sprinkle the mixture slowly into the egg batter at low speed.

3. Beat the egg whites to stiff peaks. I prefer beating egg whites in a copper bowl, 12″ in diameter, with a large balloon whisk. I get more air into the egg whites, which, in turn, gives more volume. It also is easier to control when to stop beating the egg whites; they must be stiff, but not grainy. Gently fold the beaten egg whites into the batter.

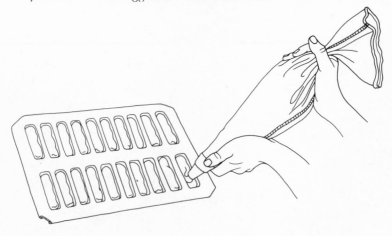

4. *To shape the Ladyfingers.* Butter 2 champagne Biscuit molds. Put half the batter into a pastry bag with a $\frac{1}{2}''$ plain nozzle and pipe the batter into the mold. Or butter 2 cookie sheets. Trace 4'' long lines with your index finger, spacing them 1'' apart. Pipe the batter over them. Sprinkle powdered sugar over the Ladyfingers.

Preheat oven to 325°F.

5. Bake for about 20–25 minutes in the middle of the oven at 325°F. When a crusty top has formed, gently remove the Ladyfingers to a cake rack to cool completely before eating. They taste better cold. Ladyfingers keep well in a tight-fitting cookie jar.

TECHNIQUES AND UTENSILS INTRODUCED

How to use cream puff dough for fritters

How to roast whole heads of garlic

How to prepare racks of lamb for roasting

How to partially bone a lamb shoulder for roasting

How to make flourless dessert soufflés

Introduction to puff pastry

How to make sugar cookies (palmiers)

Lesson 15

Suggested Menus for Lesson 15

Winter Dinner

Pine Nut Fritters

Mock Duck: Roast Shoulder of Lamb

White Bean Purée

Tossed Green Salad (Lesson 1)

Rum Cake (Lesson 11)

Spring Dinner

Asparagus with an
Orange-Flavored Hollandaise
(Lesson 11)

Rack of Lamb with Parsley

Carrot and Cauliflower Purée

Potato Fritters

Lemon Soufflé

Sugar Cookies (Palmiers)

Summer Dinner

Cold Eggplant Gratin with
Fresh Tomatoes (Lesson 12)

Mock Duck: Roast Shoulder of Lamb

Roasted Whole Heads of Fresh Garlic

Poached Peaches with Creamed
Cottage Cheese
and Crème de Cassis
(Lesson 8)

Winter Home-Style Dinner

Bean Soup

Tossed Green Salad (Lesson 1)

Cheese

Prune Cake (Lesson 4)

Pine Nut Fritters

These crusty, golden fritters are best served with a very cold, dry white wine (champagne, for example) as an hors d'oeuvre. They are made with Cream Puff Dough (pâte à choux), ham, and pine nuts. The dough mixed with the prosciutto and nuts can be made ahead of time. Refrigerate.

Special instructions. If you have never deep-fried, read the section on deep-frying, page 108.

Special kitchen utensil. A deep-fryer or wok, a deep-fry thermometer.

MAKES 30 FRITTERS

Cream Puff Dough, page 49
4 ounces prosciutto ham in 1 piece

2 ounces pine nuts
1½ quarts corn oil

1. Prepare the Cream Puff Dough, page 49.

2. Dice the prosciutto ham. It should be cut into pieces about the size of an orange seed.

   Preheat oven to 400°F.

3. Toast the pine nuts on a baking sheet in a 400°F. oven. This takes about 5 minutes, and you must be vigilant or the nuts will burn. If you smell the nuts starting to toast, get to them quickly, or they'll be burnt. When toasted, chop medium coarse.

4. Mix the ham and nuts with the Cream Puff Dough, being sure to get an even distribution throughout the dough. This can be done ahead of time. If the dough has been in the refrigerator, remove it 1 hour ahead of cooking to warm up.

5. Deep-fry the fritters in the oil at 325°F., dropping about a teaspoonful of dough into the hot oil for each fritter. Cook until golden, about 5–8 minutes. Avoid crowding the deep-fry pan, for the fritters expand while frying. Drain on paper towels and serve.

Potato Fritters

When these potatoes are done properly, they are light as air. The dough is a mixture of mashed potato, eggs, cream, and Cream Puff Dough that is deep-fried. These fritters, famous in France, are called Pommes Dauphine.

Special instruction. Read the deep-fry technique, page 108. The dough can be ready to deep-fry several hours beforehand. You can deep-fry the fritters an hour ahead of time. To reheat, deep-fry them once more before serving. Heat the oil to 350°F. Fill the deep-fryer basket with the fritters and fry for 30 seconds. Drain, sprinkle with salt, and serve.

Special kitchen utensils. Deep-fry pan and thermometer.

SERVES 8; MAKES ABOUT 50 FRITTERS, 1½″ LONG

For the Cream Puff Dough	*For the potato purée*
½ cup water	2 medium-size Russet potatoes
⅛ teaspoon salt	Salt
Scant ⅔ cup flour	2 egg yolks
2 eggs	4 tablespoons (½ stick) sweet
2½ tablespoons sweet butter	butter, at room temperature
	3 tablespoons heavy cream
	Freshly ground black pepper
	1½ quarts corn oil

1. Prepare the Cream Puff Dough with the proportions given here, following the instructions, page 49.

2. Wash the potatoes, quarter, and put them in cold salted water. Bring to a boil and cook until done (about 40 minutes).

3. Drain, peel the potatoes, and pass them through the food mill. Do not use the food processor; it makes the potatoes gummy. Transfer the purée to an electric-mixer bowl. At medium speed, beat 2 egg yolks, one at a time, and finally the heavy cream, a little at a time. The purée should have the same consistency as the cream puff dough. Correct seasoning with salt and pepper, and mix together the purée and cream puff dough thoroughly.

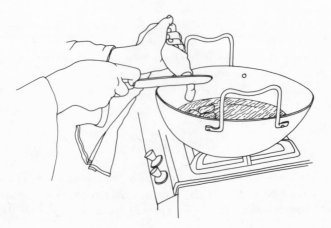

4. Heat the oil to 325°F. Fit a ½″ diameter tube in a pastry bag. Fill the pastry bag with the potato mixture. Pipe 1½″ long blobs of potato-dough mixture. Cut off with a knife and drop them into the hot oil, holding the bag as near as possible to the surface of the oil to avoid splashing hot oil. Be sure not to overfill the pan, or the fritters will not have room enough to puff up properly. They take about 7 minutes to deep-fry. Drain on paper towels. Reserve on a hot platter. Serve as soon as possible, sprinkling salt over them.

Carrot and Cauliflower Purée

Don't cheat; pass the purée through a fine-mesh sieve. This changes it from an ordinary vegetable purée to a true delicacy, silky-textured and surprisingly good.

Special instruction. Steps 1–6 can be prepared up to a day ahead of time.

Special kitchen utensil. A fine-mesh sieve.

SERVES 6

4 quarts water	1 medium-size cauliflower
1 tablespoon salt	(2 pounds)
2½ pounds medium-size carrots	4 tablespoons (½ stick) sweet butter, at room temperature

1. Boil 4 quarts water with 1 tablespoon salt.

2. Peel the carrots and cut into 1½″ thick slices. Break the cauliflower into flowerets. Discard the coarse stems. Boil the carrots until tender (about 20–25 minutes). Remove the carrots from the water with a slotted spoon. Bring the water back to a boil, and boil the cauliflower until tender (about 12 minutes).

3. Drain the vegetables and purée separately in a food mill or food processor.

4. Pass the purée through a fine-mesh sieve (see illustration, pages 36–37). Do not use the colander-sieve of the Kitchen Aid. It is made of aluminum and may discolor the vegetables.

5. Just before serving, reheat the mixture (in a water bath on the flame), and, *off the flame*, whisk in the butter at room temperature. It is important to whisk in the butter only at the last minute. If you do it beforehand and then reheat the mixture, you risk having the butter melt and separate, making the purée greasy. Correct seasoning with salt and pepper.

White Bean Purée

There is a lot of pro and con about soaking beans overnight. I find from experience that it is always preferable to soak them overnight, even if on the package of beans it mentions not to soak them. When soaked for several hours, it is easy to drain the beans and then pick out and discard the old beans amongst the good ones, and there are always a few to throw out. They don't expand during the soaking period, are hard as bullets, and their skins are all shriveled up.

It is advisable to buy beans in a store where there is a lot of turnover. Navy beans are perfect for this dish. In September and October, substitute fresh beans called cranberry beans if they are available. Do not soak the fresh beans overnight. If you have a meat bone from another preparation, bury it in the beans.

Special instruction. Can be prepared ahead of time.

SERVES 6–8

1 pound navy beans	1 scant tablespoon salt
6 cups water	Freshly ground black pepper
2 medium-size onions	½ teaspoon dried thyme
2 cloves	1 bay leaf
2 large cloves garlic	Several sprigs of parsley

1. Soak the beans overnight well covered with water in a 4-quart mixing bowl. Drain and pick out the shriveled-up beans.

2. Turn the beans into a 6½-quart Dutch oven and cover with cold water. Bring to a boil, then drain the beans and discard the shriveled beans.

3. Cover them with 6 cups water. (If you have leftover bones from meat or fowl, bury them in the beans to give more flavor.) Peel and quarter 2 onions, stick a clove in each of 2 onion pieces, and bury the onions in the beans. Peel 2 garlic cloves and bury them in the beans. Sprinkle a scant tablespoon of salt over the beans (you need a lot of salt to bring out the flavor of the beans while cooking in the water) and add freshly ground pepper, ½ teaspoon thyme, a bay leaf, and a few sprigs of parsley. Bring the beans to a boil, place the cover ajar, and continue cooking over medium heat so that the water is always quivering for about 1 hour or until the beans are tender.

4. Discard the parsley and the 2 cloves in the onions. (The beans are very good now as is.) Purée the beans, onions, and garlic in a food mill or a food processor. There should be just enough bean water left to moisten the purée.

5. Force the purée through a fine-mesh sieve (illustration, pages 36–37) to discard the skins (it is the skins that are indigestible). Transfer the purée to a 2½-quart pan, cover it tightly with foil, and keep it until dinnertime to reheat.

6. Reheat the purée in a water bath (illustration, page 35). The purée should be seasoned perfectly. There is no need to add more salt if you followed the amount to be put in at the beginning of the cooking. The only other seasoning will be the pan juices from the meat.

Bean Soup with Leftover Lamb Bones

The Bean Purée makes a lovely soup, cooked with leftover lamb bones. Double the quantity of water in the Bean Purée and add 1½ tablespoons salt.

Roasted Whole Heads of Fresh Garlic

Garlic means strength, vigor, and health. It is one of the most ancient and popular vegetables. In Egypt, the Pharaohs ordered their slaves and builders of the pyramids to eat garlic. In Greece the athletes, before the Olympic Games, traditionally ate a clove of garlic before each game. During the Middle Ages, garlic became a preventive against fevers, deafness, and consumption. Henry IV of France used it as a sexual stimulant.

Special instruction. Roasted garlic is at its best when it is freshly picked. It is planted in November for a late spring harvest. In France, garlic tresses are traditionally bought for the 29th of June, the Feast of St. Jean. California holds its Garlic Festival in late July. If you have a garden, plant garlic and roast it when freshly picked. It's delicious. Cooked garlic is not as strong-tasting as raw garlic. Do not buy supermarket garlic for this dish, and do not use overaged garlic heads; they are too strong. Buy from a good green market or better yet, plant garlic in your own garden.

SERVES 8

8 whole heads fresh garlic	Freshly ground black pepper
4 tablespoons olive oil	½ cup meat drippings, if
½ teaspoon salt	available

1. Cut off the stem and about the top one-fifth of the head of garlic, leaving a cross-section of cloves with their tops cut off. (Refrigerate the cut-off tops and use for salads.)

2. Rub each head of garlic well with olive oil and place them in a greased baking dish (or in the roasting pan with a roast, i.e., a leg of lamb, or pork, or beef roast). Dribble the remaining olive oil over and around the heads of garlic. Season with ½ teaspoon salt and freshly ground pepper. Add meat drippings to the pan, if you have some.

Preheat oven to 400°F.

3. Roast in a 400°F. oven for 20 minutes, then reduce the temperature to 375°F. Baste every 15 minutes or so with the oil and drippings in the pan. The garlic cooks in about 1 hour.

4. Present the garlic heads individually on plates. Scoop out the garlic pulp and spread it on buttered toast.

Rack of Lamb with Parsley

An untrimmed rack of lamb weighs around 4 pounds, and a little less than 3 pounds trimmed, with generally 9 ribs. With spring lamb, the racks are smaller. Be sure to have the butcher cut through the bones at the base of the ribs so you can carve the roast for serving.

How rare should the meat be is really a question of taste. I certainly don't like it so rare that the meat is not springy and is raw, but I find it perfectly cooked when the meat is completely pink. Follow with care the timing of the following recipe; it should give you that result.

Special instruction. To control the doneness of a rack, it is easier to cut it into 2 pieces, then interlace the tips of the bones to form an arch to roast it. One rack will serve 4. For 8, buy 2 racks, cut each rack in 2, and form 2 arches. A rack has 1 end with fatter ribs (about 4) than the end of the rack. So on 1 side of the arch, the chops will be rarer than on the smaller side, which should please everybody.

Special kitchen utensils. Two 9" cast-iron skillets or 1 roasting pan 9" x 16" x 2".

SERVES 8; see note at the end of the recipe for 4.

2 racks of lamb trimmed for
  roasting
4 tablespoons homemade bread
  crumbs
7 tablespoons sweet butter
1 tablespoon Dijon mustard

4 tablespoons minced parsley
Freshly ground black or green
  peppercorns
1 cup Chicken Stock, page 74
¼ teaspoon salt

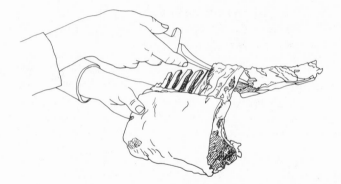

1. Remove the fat and meat between each bone with a knife down 2″ between the bones. (This is called "frenching" and may be done by the butcher.) Even if the butcher has trimmed the rack, trim it a little more, leaving just enough fat for the rack to hold together. Split each rack in 2. Interlace the ribs together to form an arch with each rack. Place the racks in two 9″ cast-iron skillets or use one 9″ x 16″ x 2″ roasting pan, leaving lots of space between each rack to cook properly.

2. Clarify 4 tablespoons of the butter: Melt the butter in a small pan (a pipkin), then wait until the whitish foam falls to the bottom of the pan. Use the clarified butter on top. Dribble half the butter on the racks.

Preheat oven to 450°F.

3. Mince the parsley very fine and mix it with the bread crumbs. (I make a big batch of bread crumbs with leftover bread in the food processor and freeze it in a plastic bag.)

4. Roast for 15 minutes in the oven on the middle rack. (I prepare this step when the guests have arrived and are having cocktails.)

5. Remove the meat from the oven and from the roasting pans onto a platter. Reduce the temperature of the oven to 400°F.

6. Brush the mustard over the racks and grind fresh black or green pepper-corns over them. Sprinkle the mixture of parsley and bread crumbs over the 2 racks and pat it with your hands.

7. Wait 15–20 minutes, but not more, before the final cooking, and that is when you must organize dinnertime. When the guests are seated, and are starting on their first course, you will need about 25 minutes from that time on before the meat will be served: 15 minutes roasting time, 5 minutes for the meat to rest, and 5 minutes to carve and serve.

8. Return the racks of lamb to the roasting pan and put back into the oven (now at 400°F.) for another 15 minutes. Remove the racks to a wooden cutting board with a catchall for the juices. Let stand for 5 minutes before cutting.

9. Discard the fat from the roasting pan or pans. Deglaze the pan or pans with the stock, stirring continually to get up the drippings, over high heat until the stock starts to shine and get syrupy. Turn off the heat. Whisk in 3 tablespoons butter. The sauce will thicken slightly. Season with ¼ teaspoon salt. Pour into a *hot* sauceboat.

10. Cut the chops and arrange, overlapping them, 2 on each hot plate. Be sure to have the plates hot for serving; there is nothing more disagree-able than eating lamb on cold plates. Each guest will salt his chops.

To serve 4 rather than the 8 for the preceding recipe, use the following:

One 5-pound rack of lamb or two 2½-pound racks of spring lamb	2 tablespoons minced parsley
	2 tablespoons bread crumbs
4 tablespoons butter	½ cup stock

The timing is the same as in preceding recipe. Split a 5-pound rack in two or use two trimmed spring lamb racks without splitting them.

Mock Duck:
Roast Shoulder of Lamb

At the turn of the century, American cookbooks referred to roast shoulder of lamb as Mock Duck because it was easy for butchers to carve a shoulder to look like a duck. The blade bone (the shoulder bone in the main part of the roast) was removed; it was then used as a tail. Berries were tucked on each side of the meatless shank for the eyes, with the bone split length-wise for a mouth. The shank and the shoulder were the neck and body.

Lemon Soufflé

To end an elegant and copious dinner, there is nothing nicer than a light, airy dessert such as a Lemon Soufflé. But a soufflé can't wait. All the ingredients can be measured and set in place beforehand. After the main course is cleared, I do the final preparations. While I am beating the egg yolks and sugar with an electric beater, my husband whisks the egg whites in the copper bowl at the dinner table; generally everyone wants to pitch in and does. Of course, everybody is impressed when my husband turns the copper bowl upside down with the egg whites clinging to the bowl. While the dessert is in the oven, I usually serve a tossed green salad, then cheeses.

Special instructions. Americans seem to prefer drier soufflés than the French, but I follow the principle of Proust's cook, Françoise, whom he called "the Michelangelo of the kitchen." A soufflé, she believed, should be dry on the outside and soft but not soupy in the center. This Lemon Soufflé is flourless, the lightest of all soufflés, therefore it needs a water bath to cook properly; otherwise, the soufflé would dry out too quickly in contact with direct heat. I have cooked this soufflé in many ovens with sometimes different results. I noticed that self-cleaning ovens 18″ in width (the standard size) are hotter than an oven without the self-cleaning feature; on the other hand, wider ovens tend to cook slower. If the soufflé is overcooked, it is dry and loses its flavor; if it is not cooked enough, it is too soupy. Always try a recipe, like this one, on your family first. Follow the timing and temperature I give, then adjust it accordingly for the next soufflé. As a rule of thumb, for a small oven that tends to overshoot its temperature, bake at 375°F. for 25 minutes, and for a big oven, 400°F. for 30–35 minutes. Steps 1–5 can be prepared ahead of time.

Special kitchen utensil. A 6-cup soufflé mold.

SERVES 6

2 tablespoons grated lemon rind	Whipped Cream, page 28
¼ cup lemon juice and pulp	¾ cup superfine sugar
6 large eggs	Pinch of salt

1. Butter and sugar a 6-cup soufflé mold. Cut out a foil collar 2 feet long, fold it in half lengthwise, butter and sugar it, and wrap the outside of the mold with it; it should extend 3″ high over the rim of the mold.

2. Grate, using the small holes of the grater, 2 tablespoons lemon rind from 1 or 2 lemons, depending on size. Squeeze fresh ¼ cup lemon juice.

3. Separate the eggs. Reserve the egg yolks in the mixing bowl to be used later. Cover with plastic wrap so the yolks won't dry out. Keep the

whites at room temperature in a covered plastic container. Measure the sugar.

4. Prepare Whipped Cream, page 28, and refrigerate. All the ingredients are now ready and set in place. These preparatory steps can all be done before dinnertime.

Preheat oven to 400°F. while you are eating the main course.

5. Beat the egg yolks and sugar in a heavy-duty mixer set at medium speed, or beat with a hand mixer until the mixture is *very thick* and very pale yellow. Then dribble the lemon juice into the mixture very slowly. It will thin out the mixture, which still must keep enough body to fold into the beaten egg whites. Add the 2 tablespoons grated lemon rind and continue beating for 3–4 minutes.

6. Beat the egg whites with a pinch of salt to firm peaks. Fold a fourth of the egg whites into the soufflé base to make it lighter and to facilitate the folding of the remaining egg whites.

7. Pour the soufflé base in the remaining egg white and, with a rubber spatula, cut through the mass in the center, bringing the mixture at the bottom of the bowl to the top, turning the bowl clockwise each time you repeat the motion of cutting into the mixture. Repeat until the whites and the soufflé base are mixed.

8. Ladle the soufflé mixture into the prepared mold. Set a pan for a water bath in the lower third of the oven. Put the soufflé mold into the pan and pour boiling water into the pan until it is two-thirds of the way up the outside of the soufflé mold.

9. Bake for 30 minutes in the lower third part of the oven. After 10 minutes of the cooking time, cover the soufflé loosely with foil.

10. Remove the soufflé from the water bath, and gently remove the foil paper from the top (the top of the soufflé might stick to the aluminum foil; remove it by gently scraping the paper with a knife). Remove the collar, using a knife to help remove the paper if it is sticking to the soufflé.

11. With 2 spoons, cut the center top of the soufflé into 6 wedges and spoon out the soufflé on the serving plates. Serve with Whipped Cream.

To serve 8. Add 1 more egg, separated, and bake for 35 minutes.

Note. If the lemon juice baked into a custard at the bottom of the soufflé, it means that you did not beat the egg yolks and sugar thick enough and the lemon juice fell to the bottom of the mold too quickly while it baked. These flourless soufflés are very fragile; sometimes they rise so high that it becomes almost impossible to remove the collar. Wrap the soufflé mold in a pretty napkin to present it at the table.

Grand Marnier Soufflé

The preparation is identical to the preceding Lemon Soufflé, but substitute ¼ cup Grand Marnier for the lemon juice. Substitute 2 tablespoons orange rind for the lemon rind and add 1 teaspoon lemon juice.

Raspberry Soufflé with Melba Sauce

Not often do I choose a frozen product over the fresh one, but in the case of raspberries, I generally prefer the frozen fruit. It tastes more like raspberries than most of the fresh raspberries of the market. This is the same technique and preparation sequence as for the Lemon Soufflés, a flourless soufflé cooked in a water bath. Please read the introduction to the Lemon Soufflé, page 293.

Special instruction. Steps 1–4 can be prepared ahead of time.

SERVES 6

3 packages (10 ounces each) quick-thaw frozen raspberries	⅓ cup superfine sugar
	6 large eggs
1 tablespoon grated rind of a lemon	1 tablespoon raspberry brandy or liqueur

1. Thaw the raspberries. Drain. Reserve the juices for the melba sauce and boil down to half the original volume. Purée the raspberries in a food mill; measure 1 cup of purée for the soufflé. If there is more than 1 cup of purée, mix it with the boiled-down raspberry liquids of the melba sauce. Reserve.

2. Butter and sugar a 6-cup soufflé mold. Cut out a foil collar 2 feet long, fold it in half lengthwise, shiny side out, butter and sugar it, and wrap the outside of the mold with it; it should extend 3″ high over the rim of the mold.

3. Grate very fine 1 tablespoon of lemon rind. Measure the sugar.

4. Separate the eggs. Reserve the egg yolks in the mixing bowl to be used later. Cover with plastic wrap so the yolks won't dry out. Keep the whites in a covered plastic container.

Preheat oven to 400°F. while you are eating the main course.

5. Beat the egg yolks and sugar in a heavy-duty mixer set at medium speed, or beat with a hand mixer until the mixture is very thick and pale yellow. Continue beating while adding the raspberry purée, grated lemon rind, and raspberry brandy or liqueur.

6. Beat the egg whites to firm peaks. Fold a quarter of the egg whites into the raspberry mixture. Pour the raspberry mixture back into the remaining egg whites and fold until just combined.

7. Ladle the mixture into the prepared mold. Set a pan for a water bath and pour boiling water into the pan until it is two-thirds of the way up the outside of the soufflé mold.

8. Bake for 40 minutes. Cover the soufflé with foil after 10 minutes.

9. Remove the foil on top of the soufflé and the collar, gently scraping with a knife if the soufflé sticks to the foil.

10. With 2 spoons, cut the center top of the soufflé into 6 wedges and spoon out the soufflé on the serving plates. Serve the cold melba sauce with it. The soufflé is also very good cold; it looks more like a mousse than a soufflé.

Puff Pastry

Think of learning puff pastry as though you were learning to make pottery. At first, it's difficult, but the more you practice, the more you succeed. First you'll make sugar cookies with the pastry, which correspond to your first ashtray in pottery; then you go on to more difficult creations. But for heaven's sake, don't attempt to make a light, puffy pastry shell, vol-au-vent, on your first try.

Follow my suggestions and you will *progressively* learn to make whatever you want. For the first stage, try sugar cookies called Palmiers (following recipe) or sometimes Elephant Ears or Pig's Ears. Do practice several times making these cookies (freeze them unbaked) before attempting stage 2, which will be the rectangular fruit tarts, in order to graduate to stage 3 with the puff pastry shells for the Orange or Onion Tart and with puffy creations like the Leek or Almond Pie. Remember puff pastry is just technique, so don't stop practicing or you will forget.

Special instructions. You need to anticipate to make puff pastry. The actual work is not long, but there are several stages to do at different times. The principle is simple enough; the dough consists of a flour-butter-water mixture and a patty of butter which needs to be refrigerated to firm up before folding into the dough. The butter is then gradually incorporated into the dough by rolling out and folding the dough several times. Use the refrigerator to firm up the dough between turns. For puff pastry with 4 turns: Start, let's say, at 11:00 A.M. to make the butter patty and the dough (flour-water-butter); at 12:00 P.M., roll out and fold the dough twice; at 2:00 P.M., repeat: roll out and fold 2 more times; at 4:00 P.M., roll out the dough to shape and bake it. Puff pastry freezes very well, but freeze it in the shape in which it will bake.

For puff pastry with 6 turns, start a day ahead of time for 4 turns, then roll out 2 more turns the next day because these 2 last turns are the hardest to roll out. If you try to do 6 turns with 2 hours between turns, the dough becomes too elastic as it is handled more.

In the summertime, keep your flour in the freezer. It is easier, especially for a beginner, to work when all the ingredients are cold. (But I don't advise a beginner to make puff pastry when it is very hot; the butter oozes out of the dough and makes a mess. If that happens anyway, sprinkle more flour on the dough, pat it, wrap it, and firm it up in the refrigerator before continuing.)

Special kitchen utensil. A flat pastry cutter, a rectangular steel blade with a wooden handle to hold onto; or a plastic cutter in the same shape minus the wooden handle.

1½ cups unsifted all-purpose flour	16 tablespoons (2 sticks) cold sweet butter
½ cup unsifted cake flour	½ cup cold water
½ teaspoon salt	

1. *Hand method.* Place both kinds of flour and salt in a pile on a pastry surface. Using a pastry cutter, mix the flour and salt together, then reserve ¼ cup of the flour mixture for later. Bury 4 tablespoons (½ stick) of cold butter in the flour and cut through the flour and butter to make a blend of flour and very small chunks of butter in a mixture resembling coarse cornmeal. This takes about 2 minutes of chopping and scraping to get a thorough blend and even distribution of butter into the flour.

2. Make a pile again of the butter-flour mixture and make a well 10″ in diameter. Pour ½ cup cold water (if it is very humid, pour a little less; if it is dry weather, pour a little more than ½ cup) into the center of the well. Flip the top of the well "dike" over the water, completely covering

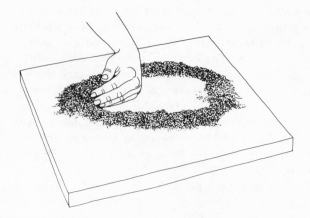

the surface of the pond. (If the dike breaks and water trickles away, don't panic; just take a bit of the remaining dry flour and sprinkle the stream to stop it from running away from you.) Then, using your fingers as if you are grasping an imaginary tennis ball, gently mix the flour and water together, starting at twelve o'clock and working around the outside of the dike, fingering the flour and water into shreds rather than into a solid ball. This way the dough does not become elastic and is not handled too much and the water is spread out evenly in the flour.

Food processor method. These first 2 steps can be done in the processor. Pour the flours and salt into the bowl of the processor fitted with the metal blade, reserving ¼ cup flour for later. Add 4 tablespoons butter. Process 10 times, with the buzz-stop method. Pour the water in the flour, then process 6 times with the buzz-stop method and stop; the dough must *not* form a ball—it should look like humid coarse meal. Pour on a pastry surface and proceed as for the hand method with the next step.

3. *For hand and processor methods.* Make a loose, crumbly pastry ball. Using the pastry cutter, cut the loose ball into 4 pieces, gather together, and turn counterclockwise. Insert the pastry cutter under the ball to help

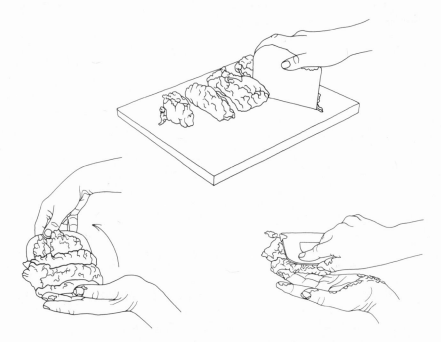

turn it, and as you remove the pastry cutter from underneath, lift the most crumbly and driest part of the ball to the top to help the mixing more evenly. Turn again ¼ turn counterclockwise and cut again into 4 pieces. When it forms a ball that stays together (about 4–8 times, depending on the humidity of the day), make a 5″ patty, wrap the dough in waxed paper, and refrigerate 1 hour to firm up.

4. On your pastry counter, hit 12 tablespoons (1½ sticks) of cold butter with a rolling pin to soften enough for handling, then blend the butter and the reserved ¼ cup flour with the heel of your hand. Blend the 2 together, using firm strokes away from yourself (if you have hot hands, keep a bowl of cold water handy to dip your hand into to cool it). The

butter must be smooth, but it must not melt; otherwise, you will have problems later on when you incorporate it into the dough. Flatten the butter into a patty about 4″ in diameter. Wrap the butter patty and refrigerate for less than 1 hour.

5. Sprinkle flour on your pastry surface and roll out the chilled dough to a 12″ circle. Place the chilled, but not too hard, butter in the middle and fold up the edges of the dough (stretching it) to cover the butter patty and to make a package. Turn the dough over with the seam side down and quickly roll out to a narrow rectangle about 8″ x 18″. Pick up the dough several times while rolling it to make sure it isn't sticking (pick it up as you would a small carpet; don't worry about it—it is not fragile). Sprinkle more flour underneath if necessary. Dust flour on your rolling pin when needed. When the dough is the desired length, turn it upside down.

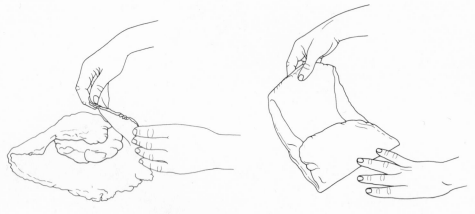

6. You are now ready to make a fold and a turn: Fold the dough in thirds like a business letter; that is to say, fold up the bottom, then fold the top down over it. Turn the dough counterclockwise ¼ of a turn. The dough now resembles a book with the binding on the left.

7. Roll out the dough again to a long rectangular strip about 8″ x 18″: First, press the rolling pin down firmly on all 3 edges of the dough to seal the flaps. Then start rolling from the center away from yourself to within ¼″ of the far edge so as not to flatten the edge too much. Roll again from the center toward yourself to within ¼″ of the bottom edges, then place the length of the rolling pin lengthwise on the dough and flatten the top and bottom edges to match the thickness of the rest of the dough. Repeat rolling out until the dough reaches about 18″ long. Fold as before and make 2 dents in the surface with your fingertips to indicate that the dough has been rolled twice (2 turns). Wrap in waxed paper then in a plastic bag to keep the butter from hardening too much; refrigerate for 2 hours.

8. Two hours later, roll out and fold again 2 turns. Never forget to start rolling the dough in "book position"—the open edge on the right—and always follow the instructions to roll out the dough as in step 7. Mark 4 finger dents; wrap and refrigerate 2 hours before shaping the dough and baking it, or refrigerate overnight for the last 2 turns if the recipe calls for 6 turns. Before rolling out the last 2 turns, beat it lightly with the rolling pin to soften the dough. Refrigerate 2 hours before shaping the dough for a recipe.

Sugar Cookies (Palmiers)

These are great cookies that everyone likes; one batch of Puff Pastry makes about 60 cookies. They can be frozen unbaked and baked whenever you want them. For a beginner in Puff Pastry, the dough can be badly made and yet, sprinkled with lots of sugar, the cookies will caramelize and be delicious. Don't worry about the shape of the cookies; if they don't look exactly as they should, the taste is still there. Do practice with these several times before attempting anything else with puff pastry.

MAKES 60 COOKIES

Puff Pastry, page 297   About ½ cup sugar

1. Halve Puff Pastry dough that has been rolled 4 times. Refrigerate 1 piece while working with the other one.

2. Sprinkle flour on a pastry surface (lightly flour the rolling pin several times during the rolling out of the dough, otherwise the dough becomes very sticky) and roll out the dough into a strip about 24″ long and 8″

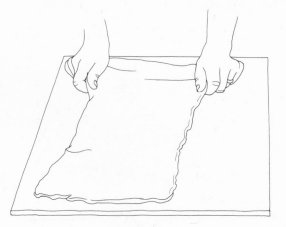

wide or whatever length and width you can do for the first time. If it is difficult to roll with a rolling pin, stretch the dough with your hands to make the dough as thin as possible. It will be easier to fold later on.

3. Sprinkle about 2–3 tablespoons sugar over the dough and fold each end to meet at the center of the dough. Sprinkle more sugar. Then fold each end toward the center once more. Sprinkle sugar and fold over 1 fold on top of the other for a strip about 8″ long and 3″ wide. Place on a cookie sheet and freeze for 30 minutes to facilitate cutting the cookies. The dough will be sticky.

4. Using a sharp thin knife, cut ⅛″ thick slices for about 30 cookies. Lay the cookies flat on an ungreased cookie sheet with 1″ space between them. Refrigerate the cookies while rolling out the other half of the dough into 30 more cookies.

Preheat oven to 400°F.

5. Sprinkle lots of sugar over the cookies and bake for about 15 minutes at 400°F., but after 8 minutes or so, peek to make sure the sugar is not burning. Flip them over when the cookies start to caramelize. Sprinkle a little more sugar over them and continue cooking for about 5 more minutes, but watch them closely to make sure they don't burn. (I can't tell you how many batches I have burnt, forgetting to look.) Cool before eating them. Wash the cookie sheets right away under hot water while they are still hot, using a spatula to scrape the burnt pieces stuck to the cookie sheets.

6. You can freeze unbaked cookies on cookie sheets. When frozen, transfer them to a freezer bag. When you want to bake them, bake at 425°F. Put the frozen cookies on a cookie sheet, sprinkle sugar over them, and put them directly into the hot oven without thawing. They won't take much longer to bake than the unfrozen cookies.

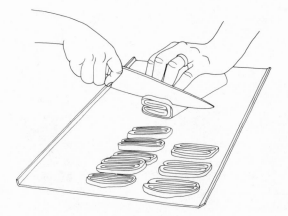

TECHNIQUES AND UTENSILS INTRODUCED

How to prepare calf's brains and sweetbreads

How to poach chicken breasts to avoid overcooking

How to make a tomato-butter sauce

How to bind a sauce with a hollandaise and with a beurre blanc

How to prepare long, narrow puff pastry rectangles for fruit tarts

How to make almond butter cream

Lesson 16

Suggested Menus for Lesson 16

Summer or Winter Luncheon

Pine Nut Fritters
(Lesson 15)

Cold Brain Salad
or
Cold Sweetbread Salad

Frozen Chocolate Mousse
(Lesson 14)
with Ladyfingers
(Lesson 14)

3-Course Winter Dinner

Country-Style Potato Pie
(Lesson 5)
as an Appetizer

Braised Chickens in Lemon Juice
with Raisins

Steamed Broccoli and Carrots

Apple and Almond Butter
Cream Tart

3-Course Summer Dinner

Eggplant Fritters
(Lesson 6)

Chicken with a Tomato-Butter Sauce

Watercress Purée

Plum Tart

One of My Favorite Dinners

Roast Chicken with Pernod
(Lesson 1)

Fennel Purée

Hot Individual Apple Tarts
(Lesson 7)

Cold Brain Salad

This recipe and the following Cold Sweetbread Salad recipe are for those who love variety meats. In this type of salad the imagination of the cook can let go, allowing the combination of vegetables, fruits, and salad greens to vary according to the seasons.

Special instruction. Most of the cooking preparations can be done ahead of time but not the assembly of the salad. If you are using pears in the salad, peel and cut them last, as they darken quickly.

SERVES 4–6

2 calf's brains
1 carrot
1 onion
¼ cup red-wine vinegar
1 tablespoon capers
4 cups water
1 teaspoon salt
¼ teaspoon dried thyme
Few sprigs of parsley
1½ cups Rémoulade, page 53
2 heads Bibb lettuce or 1 head
    red leaf lettuce or ¼ pound
    lamb's lettuce (mâche)

In autumn and winter

1 medium-size celery root
1 pineapple
4 Bartlett pears

In spring or summer

1 cucumber
1 small cantaloupe
¼ pound white or red grapes
    (avoid Concords, they are too
    strong)

The dressing

Vinaigrette, page 11

1. Soak the brains for 2 hours in cold water, changing the water once in a while.

2. Split each brain in 2 separate lobes. Remove the fine membrane that covers the surface of the lobes, gently opening up the crevices to remove the blood stains.

3. Soak the cleaned brains in cold water for another half hour while preparing a vegetable-vinegar broth to poach them in. Peel and cut 1 carrot into ¼″ thick slices. Peel and coarsely chop an onion. Combine the carrot slices, onion, ¼ cup red-wine vinegar, 1 tablespoon capers, and 4 cups water in a 3-quart pan with 1 teaspoon salt, ¼ teaspoon thyme, and several parsley sprigs. Cover, bring the liquids slowly to a boil, and simmer for 30 minutes. Slip the calf's brains into the liquids. Cover and poach with the liquid barely quivering for 25 minutes. Turn off the heat and cool for 15 more minutes. With a perforated spoon,

gently remove the brains to a plate and cool completely. Refrigerate until ready to assemble the salad.

4. Prepare 1½ cups Rémoulade, page 53. Refrigerate.

5. Wash the lettuce under running cold water. Dry in a salad dryer or pat it dry in a dish towel or paper towel. Refrigerate in a plastic bag.

6. *The celery root.* Peel the celery root (sometimes called celery knob), quarter, and shred in a food processor (julienne blade) or in a mouli-julienne (blade No. 2).

7. *The cucumber.* Peel the cucumber, and cut it into very thin slices, as thin as you can slice by hand or through a food processor fitted with an extra-thin blade. Turn into a 2-quart mixing bowl, sprinkle 1 table-spoon coarse salt over the cucumbers, and let stand for 2 hours. Wash under running cold water and dry in paper towels.

8. *The melon.* Split in 2 crosswise, scoop out the seeds, and scoop out 40 small balls with a melon baller.

9. *The pineapple.* With a chef's knife, slice off the top and bottom of the pineapple. Run a knife around the inside wall of the pineapple rind, leaving a cylindrical piece of pineapple. Cut into ½" thick slices. Remove the pithy center from each slice. Cut the slices into 1" wide wedges.

The assembly of the salad

10. Decorate each plate with several leaves of lettuce.

11. Mix the celery root or the cucumber slices with several tablespoons of rémoulade. Taste and correct seasonings with salt and pepper. Pile it in the center of the lettuce.

12. Cut each calf's brain lobe in 5 slices—but not right through, in order to keep the shape of the lobe—and place it on top of the cucumber or celery root. Open up the slices and place a caper or two between each slice.

13. Prepare a vinaigrette dressing according to the recipe, page 11, but while making it, place the mixing bowl in a water bath with simmering water over medium-low heat to warm the dressing (it will not thicken as it does when cold). Pour the dressing over the brains and arrange fruits decoratively around the brains. Peel and quarter the pears now, if using pears and add to the salad.

Cold Sweetbread Salad

If you prefer sweetbreads to brains, substitute sweetbreads in the Cold Brain Salad, page 307.

Special instruction. The sweetbreads can be prepared a day ahead of time.

SERVES 4–6

1 pound calf sweetbreads	4 tablespoons butter
½ lemon	1 teaspoon salt
2 onions	Freshly ground white pepper

1. Soak the sweetbreads in cold water for several hours with half a lemon in the water.

2. Transfer the sweetbreads to a pan, cover with cold water, and bring slowly to a boil. Cook 10 minutes over medium-low heat, partly covered. Drain and rinse under cold water. Let cool and discard the pieces of gristly cartilage.

3. Peel the onions; slice thin. Put the onions and 2 tablespoons butter in a 9″ cast-iron skillet; season with ½ teaspoon salt and freshly ground white pepper. Cook over medium-low heat, stirring the onion slices in the butter for 1 minute, then cover and cook for 20 minutes, stirring the onions once in a while.

4. Cut the sweetbreads in ½″ cubes. Uncover the onions and add the sweetbreads to the skillet with the remaining 2 tablespoons butter; sprinkle ½ teaspoon salt and freshly ground pepper over them. Cook for 1 minute, stirring the onions and sweetbreads together. Cover and cook for another 15 minutes. Uncover, turn the heat up, and sauté the sweetbreads and onions, stirring all the while until they are slightly colored. If sweetbreads are prepared ahead of time, reheat them with the onions until warm and add them to the salad, following the recipe, page 308, steps 4–12.

Steamed Broccoli and Carrots

Special instruction. Steam only the broccoli flowerets with their slender stems. Reserve the big broccoli stems for a purée, page 34.

Special kitchen utensils. A 3-quart saucepan and a collapsible vegetable steamer.

SERVES 6–8

10½-ounce bag baby carrots
2 bunches of broccoli

3 cups water

1. Peel baby carrots. (Substitute regular carrots if baby carrots are unavailable, but after peeling them, cut them into olive shapes.)

2. Cut off the broccoli flowerets from their main stem.

3. Pour 3 cups water in a 3-quart saucepan. Fit the vegetable steamer inside the saucepan. Place the carrots in the steamer. Cover the pan tightly (I use aluminum foil). Cook until the carrots are tender, about 10 minutes, but this is a question of personal taste. I don't like half-cooked carrots; I like them eaten raw or cooked. Remove the carrots to a preheated plate. Add the broccoli flowerets to the steamer. Cover tightly. Cook for barely 2 minutes or so, just enough to remove the edge of rawness of the broccoli.

Watercress Purée

SERVES 4–6

6 quarts water
Salt
6 bunches of watercress

3 tablespoons sweet butter
1 tablespoon flour
Freshly ground black pepper

1. Boil 6 quarts water with 2 tablespoons salt. Wash the watercress thoroughly in several waters, discard all the big stems, and drain. Then blanch in the boiling water for 10 minutes (to rid the watercress of its bitterness). Drain well. Purée through the food mill or in the food processor.

2. Melt 1 tablespoon butter, then add the flour. When the mixture bubbles, add the watercress purée. Season with salt and pepper to your taste. Simmer over a low flame, stirring constantly with a wooden spoon, until

the liquids evaporate (5–10 minutes). Can be done to this point ahead of time. Reheat the purée if necessary in a covered pan; set the pan in boiling water (water bath). Whisk the purée once in a while while reheating.

3. Start whisking in 2 tablespoons butter. Taste and correct seasonings with salt and pepper.

To serve Watercress Purée in individual tarts

The purée can be presented in small pastry shells, page 90. Fill the cooked pastry shells, then sprinkle grated Swiss cheese over each small tart. Gratiné for 1 minute or so. In winter, substitute Fennel Purée.

Fennel Purée

SERVES 6

4 pounds untrimmed fennel bulbs	5 tablespoons butter
3 quarts water	1 tablespoon flour
1 tablespoon lemon juice	Freshly ground black pepper
4½ teaspoons salt	

1. Discard the fennel branches, but reserve several strands for the decoration. Cut the fennel bulbs into vertical slices around ½″ thick, then chop coarsely.

2. Turn the fennel into a large pan. Cover with 3 quarts water, 1 tablespoon lemon juice, and 4 teaspoons salt, and cook, partially covered, over low to medium heat for 30–45 minutes or until the fennel is very tender. Drain the fennel in a colander for 15 minutes.

3. Purée fennel through a food mill or purée for 2 minutes in a food processor, then force the purée through a fine-mesh sieve (see illustration, pages 36–37) to discard fibers.

4. Melt 2 tablespoons butter in a 2-quart heavy-bottomed saucepan, then whisk in 1 tablespoon flour. When the mixture bubbles, stir in the fennel purée. Add ½ teaspoon salt and freshly ground pepper. Cook uncovered over low to medium heat for 2 minutes, stirring once in a while. The purée will thicken slightly. It can be prepared in early afternoon for dinner. Reheat the purée, setting the pan in a skillet with simmering water. Whisk the purée occasionally while reheating. When the fennel purée is reheated, whisk in 3 tablespoons butter, off the heat. Taste and correct seasonings, if necessary.

To serve Fennel Purée in individual tarts

Fennel purée has a much looser consistency than a potato purée. It can be served in small fully baked tart shells, decorated with several strands of fennel leaves. Serve with Roast Chicken with Pernod, page 23.

Roll out the pastry according to the instructions and line small shells and bake according to the instructions on page 90.

Braised Chicken in
Lemon Juice with Raisins

This is one of those recipes that take longer to write up than to cook. You must visualize the work and anticipate the next step as you go along. This way you establish a working rhythm. Chicken parts, browned first, then braised in lemon juice, water, and raisins, are delicious for a festive occasion. The raisins and the hollandaise sauce binding counterbalance the puckery taste of the lemon juice. Chicken breasts can be prepared that way too, see page 314.

Special instructions. What can be done ahead of time: Cutting the chicken into different parts can be done a day ahead of time. Steps 2–5, inclusive, can be prepared 1 hour before the guests arrive. From 7 to the end, organize your timing so you are set to eat the chickens when they are ready. For 1 chicken do not change the amount of liquids or the amounts for the hollandaise.

Special kitchen utensil. Two 12″ cast-iron skillets.

SERVES 6–8

Two 3-pound chickens	10 pearl onions
½ cup white raisins	½ cup chicken stock or water
3 tablespoons water	2 tablespoons butter
1 tablespoon Cognac	1 tablespoon oil
Peels from 2 lemons	About 1 teaspoon salt
⅓ cup lemon juice	Freshly ground black pepper

1. Cut the chicken into 8 parts: 2 thighs, 2 drumsticks, 2 wings, and the boned and skinned chicken breast, split in 2, see pages 96–97. Remove excess fat from one carcass and, with a cleaver, chop it into several pieces. I like to add at least the carcass pieces from 1 chicken to the braising of the chickens to add more flavor and body to the liquids. Freeze the other carcass for a chicken stock.

2. Soak the raisins in the water and Cognac for 1 hour or so. Peel the rind of 2 lemons with a vegetable peeler, and squeeze ⅓ cup lemon juice. Quarter the pearl onions. Measure ½ cup chicken stock or water.

3. Melt 2 tablespoons butter and 1 tablespoon oil in a 12″ cast-iron skillet. When the fats are hot but not smoking, sauté the chicken breasts 30 seconds on each side, remove to a plate, and sprinkle with 1 teaspoon lemon juice, ¼ teaspoon salt, and freshly ground pepper and reserve. They will be poached later because they cook very fast.

4. Continue browning the chicken pieces over a medium flame, delicately turning the pieces once in a while to brown evenly, about 20 minutes. Remove the chicken pieces to a platter.

5. Cook the onions in the same skillet for 10 minutes or so over medium-low heat, stirring occasionally to avoid burning them. Raise the heat to high, pour ½ cup chicken broth or water and ⅓ cup lemon juice into the skillet, and bring the liquids to a boil for 1 minute, scraping the sides and bottom of the skillet.

6. Lower the heat. Transfer the onions back to the skillet with the chicken pieces and add the juices gathered in the platter. Sprinkle with 1 teaspoon salt and freshly ground pepper. Add the raisins with their liquid and the lemon rind strips. Cover with foil and a lid. Cook for 30 minutes over low heat, with the liquids gently bubbling. While the chickens are braising, be careful that the liquids don't evaporate; otherwise, you will not have enough to poach the breasts and finish the sauce. (If it does happen, add ½ cup chicken stock or, at the last resort, ½ cup water after transferring the chicken pieces to a serving platter. Bring the liquids to a boil, then lower the heat and continue.)

7. Preheat a serving platter. Transfer the chicken pieces to the platter. Cover loosely with foil and keep warm in a 150°F. oven.

8. Add the chicken breasts to the liquids; don't forget the liquids gathered in the plate. Cook gently, covered, for 3 minutes on each side if the breasts are thick; if not, just 3 minutes in all, or cut into a breast to be sure it is cooked. It should be white, not pinkish.

9. Place the chicken breasts on top of the other pieces. With a skimmer, remove the raisins and decorate the top of the chicken with them. Cover and place once more in a warm oven.

10. Discard the lemon peels. Degrease the juices (about 1 cup of liquids). If you do not want to enrich the sauce with a hollandaise, boil down the liquids in the skillet, scraping the sides all the while until the juices become slightly syrupy. Turn off the heat, and whisk in 4 tablespoons butter.

The Hollandaise Sauce

1 egg yolk
4 tablespoons (½ stick) sweet
  butter

¼ teaspoon salt
Freshly ground white pepper

11. Break 1 egg yolk in a 1½-quart heavy-bottomed pan. Whisk until the yolk thickens (about 1 minute), then whisk in 1 tablespoon butter at a time. (If it curdles, put an egg yolk in a small mixing bowl, rapidly whisk the curdled hollandaise into the yolk, then transfer the smooth sauce back into the pan—don't bother to wash the pan. Add a bit more lemon juice to bring back the flavor to its original taste.)

12. Over low heat, start dribbling the chicken juices into the hollandaise to thin it so it slightly coats the spoon. The thickness of the hollandaise will determine the amount of chicken juices needed, from ½ cup to ⅔ cup. Taste and correct seasonings with salt and pepper. Serve in a preheated sauceboat.

Chicken Breasts in
Lemon Juice with Raisins

SERVES 4

Buy 3 pounds of chicken wings and backs and 4 chicken breasts, boned and skinned. Follow the recipe for Braised Chicken Breasts, page 153, step 2, browning and braising the bones and wings, instead of the chicken parts, in order to give body and flavor to the liquids to poach the breasts later on.

Chicken with a
Tomato-Butter Sauce

The sauce for this chicken recipe is made using the white butter sauce technique with tomato pulp. This chicken is at its best with fresh tomatoes.

Special instruction. Cut up the chicken ahead of time if you wish, but cook only at dinnertime. Chicken is generally never as good reheated.

Special kitchen utensils. Two 12″ cast-iron skillets; one fine-mesh sieve.

SERVES 8

Two 3½-pound roasting chickens
12 tablespoons sweet butter
2 tablespoons oil
2 tablespoons minced white bulb
 of scallions
3 tablespoons red-wine vinegar

2 pounds fresh tomatoes,
 chopped
2 cloves garlic, peeled
2 teaspoons salt
Freshly ground black pepper

1. Cut up the chicken into 8 pieces and bone the breasts as shown in the illustrated technique, pages 96–97. Freeze the carcass for a stock.

2. Melt 2 tablespoons butter and 1 tablespoon oil in each of two 12″ cast-iron skillets over medium heat. First, lightly sauté the boned chicken breast meat for just 30 seconds on each side and reserve on a plate for later. Cover with an inverted plate. Continue browning the other pieces of chicken all over, using 2 wooden spoons to turn them over delicately to avoid mangling the skins. When the skin is crisp and golden (about 15–20 minutes), remove to a plate.

3. Turn up the heat under the skillets, add the minced white bulb of scallions and 1½ tablespoons red-wine vinegar in each skillet, and bring to a boil, scraping the bottom and sides of the skillet. Add the chopped tomatoes and the garlic, and lower the heat to medium-low. Add the chicken pieces (minus the chicken breasts), placing them over the tomatoes. Sprinkle 1 teaspoon salt and freshly ground pepper over the chicken pieces in each skillet. Cover tightly and cook (braise) over medium-low heat so the liquid of the tomatoes is just barely bubbling. Cook about 30 minutes until tender.

4. Remove the chicken to a preheated platter, cover with foil, and keep warm in a turned-off oven.

5. Force the tomato pulp and juices (discard the garlic) through a fine-mesh sieve, see pages 36–37, for a smooth semithick sauce (yields about ¾ cup for each chicken). Transfer the tomato sauce to 1 skillet; add the chicken breasts. Sprinkle ¼ teaspoon salt over them. Cover tightly and cook over medium-low heat just enough to cook them through for 5 minutes.

6. Remove the chicken breasts to the chicken platter and degrease the sauce if necessary. Bring the sauce back just to a boil. Turn off the heat and whisk in the remaining 8 tablespoons butter, 1 tablespoon at a time, very quickly. The sauce must be smooth; the butter must not separate. Taste and correct seasonings with salt and pepper if necessary. Serve in a warm sauceboat.

Chicken Breasts with a
Tomato–Butter Sauce

SERVES 4

For those who eat only chicken breasts, buy pounds of wings, necks, or chicken backs, and 4 chicken breasts, boned and skinned. Follow the recipe for Chicken with a Tomato-Butter Sauce, page 314, browning and braising the wings and necks instead of the chicken parts in order to give body and flavor to the liquids to poach the breasts later on. Reserve the wings, necks, etc., for a chicken salad.

Apple and Almond Butter
Cream Tart

When you start feeling confident about puff pastry and have made lots of sugar cookies, try an apple tart with an almond butter cream filling with Jonathan, Cortland, or Golden Delicious apples during the autumn and winter months or with a caramelized apple purée filling of Granny Smith apples in the spring and summer. With a batch of puff pastry, you can make 2 long, narrow tarts.

Special instructions. For the tarts, you need only a cookie sheet. When the dough is rolled out, narrow strips of dough are cut and laid flat on top of each long end of the dough. When baked, they puff up and create the sides of the shell. The tart shells can be prepared ahead of time and frozen. When they are ready to be baked do not thaw, but bake right away in a 425°F. oven, making sure to put the frozen tart shells on a room temperature cookie sheet. If at all possible, bake the tarts just 2–3 hours before dinnertime.

Special kitchen utensils. Two cookie sheets 14″ x 17″. Order by mail if difficult to find: William Sonoma, Mail Order Department, P.O. Box 3792, San Francisco, CA 94119. I use the freezer several times during the process of shaping the tarts. A 14″ x 17″ cookie sheet will not fit into a side-by-side refrigerator-freezer. If you have a side-by-side refrigerator-freezer, at step 1 cut the pastry into 2 pieces before rolling out. Roll out each piece to a 10″ x 14″ rectangle. Place 1 rolled out piece of pastry on a jelly-roll pan, cover with waxed paper, stack the second piece of pastry on the waxed paper. Cover with waxed paper, secure the paper to the jelly-roll pan with Scotch tape and place the pan on a slant in the narrow freezer part of the side-by-side refrigerator-freezer.

MAKES 2 LONG, NARROW TARTS; SERVES 8

Puff Pastry with 4 turns, page 297

For the almond butter cream

⅔ cup shelled almonds
½ cup sugar
4 tablespoons (½ stick) sweet butter
1 egg

1 teaspoon vanilla extract
¼ teaspoon almond extract
1 tablespoon dark rum
8 large apples
1 tablespoon lemon juice
⅓ cup plus 2 tablespoons sugar
1 tablespoon sweet butter
⅔ cup apricot jam

1. Sprinkle flour on a pastry surface and rolling pin. Roll out the Puff Pastry to a 17″ x 14″ rectangle (the size of a baking sheet). It takes practice to roll it as evenly as possible. To even out the sides of the dough, don't be afraid to stretch the dough with your hands to achieve a 17″ x 14″ rectangle. Roll up the dough on a rolling pin and unroll it onto a baking sheet. Cover with waxed paper and freeze for 20 minutes to firm up the dough.

2. *Prepare the almond butter cream.* Pulverize the shelled almonds (don't bother to remove the skin; it gives more flavor to the almonds) in an electric blender or a food processor. Add ½ cup sugar, the butter, egg, vanilla and almond extracts, and rum and turn on the machine for 10 seconds or so to mix all the ingredients. Refrigerate until needed.

3. Remove the dough from the freezer. In order to make the dough bake and puff up evenly around all 4 edges, cut with a knife to a straight line, using a ruler to guide you, leaving cut edges all around the rectangle. (Save the trimmings; see Note on what to do with them.) Freeze the dough for 15 minutes once more before continuing cutting. It is always easier to shape Puff Pastry when it is very cold.

4. To make 2 long, narrow tart shells: Cut the dough lengthwise in 2 equal pieces. Working quickly, cut two ¾″ wide strips the length of

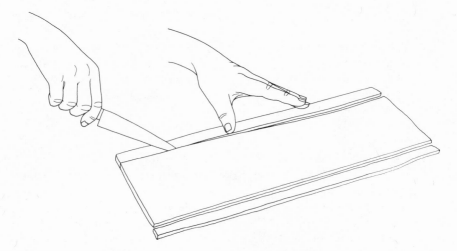

each piece. Brush water over the 2 remaining pieces and stick a ¾″ wide strip on each long side of the 2 dough pieces, leaving the short sides of the pieces free. Prick the bottom of the tart shells all over with the tines of a fork. The 2 tart shells are now ready to be baked or refrigerated or frozen for later use.

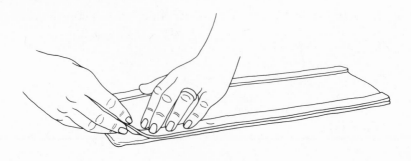

5. Peel and core the apples. With a thin Chinese cleaver or a big knife, cut ⅛″ thick apple slices. Sprinkle 1 tablespoon lemon juice and ⅓ cup sugar over them. Reserve in a mixing bowl.

Preheat oven to 425°F.

6. Remove the pastry shells from the refrigerator or freezer. Brush bottom and sides of the shell(s) with milk. Line the bottom with foil and cover the foil with dry beans or aluminum baking pellets to keep the dough from bubbling and losing its shape.

7. Bake pastry shells on the middle shelf of the oven for 20 minutes. Remove from the oven and lower the temperature to 400°F. Remove the dry beans and foil. Sometimes the foil sticks to the bottom of the dough; gently pry it loose with a knife.

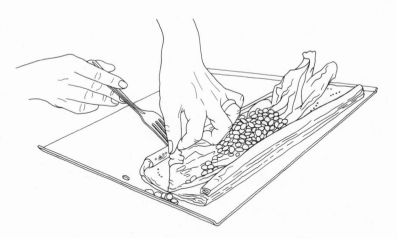

8. Spread the almond butter cream over the bottom of the pastry shell. Drain the apples, reserving the liquids for later. Line rows of overlapped apple slices *crossways* next to each other to make it easy later on to cut the tart into servings between each row of apples. If there are remaining slices, put them on top of each row. Sprinkle 2 tablespoons sugar over the apples and dot with 1 tablespoon butter in small pieces.

9. Bake for 20–25 minutes at 400°F. Check now and again to make sure the sides are not burning. If necessary, cover loosely with foil.

10. In a small saucepan combine ⅔ cup apricot jam and the liquid from the apples. Bring to a boil while stirring. Strain the hot jam into a small pan and reserve.

11. Reheat the apricot glaze, if necessary, and brush it all over the tarts, including the sides, after you have removed them from the oven.

Note on using leftover scraps and trimmings of Puff Pastry. Be careful not to roll them up into a ball. Just stick the pieces together side by side like patchwork on a piece of waxed paper before rolling it out. Overlap them a bit so you won't have holes in the dough. Refrigerate or freeze until very cold and proceed with Sugar Cookies (Palmiers), page 302.

Granny Smith Apple Tart

The difference between this tart and the Apple and Almond Butter Cream Tart, page 316, is the filling; otherwise, prepare the tarts the same way as the main recipe. Buy apples for the tarts plus 4 apples for the purée.

For the apple purée

4 Granny Smith apples
1 tablespoon lemon juice

⅓ cup sugar
2 tablespoons apricot jam
4 tablespoons (½ stick) sweet
    butter

1. Peel, core, and cube 4 apples. Combine the apple pieces, lemon juice, sugar, apricot jam, and butter in a 9″ cast-iron skillet. Cook over medium heat until the apples caramelize (about 15 minutes). Purée in a food mill or a food processor. Refrigerate until needed.

2. Proceed with the recipe of Apple and Almond Butter Cream Tart, but substitute the apple purée instead of the almond butter cream at step 8.

Plum Tart

Special instruction. Bake the tarts just before dinner time for the best results.

Special kitchen utensils. Bake the tarts in jelly-roll pans instead of cookie sheets, because the syrup may spew out of the tarts.

MAKES 2 LONG, NARROW TARTS; SERVES 6–8

Puff Pastry with 4 turns, page 297
2 pounds purple plums
½ cup plus 2 tablespoons sugar

2 tablespoons milk
Whipped Cream, page 28

1. Roll out the Puff Pastry to make 2 long, narrow tarts, following the instructions given for the Apple and Almond Butter Cream Tart, page 316, steps 1, 3, and 4. Do not prebake the shells.

2. Split the plums in two and remove their pits. Sprinkle ½ cup sugar over them and marinate for about 2 hours.

3. Combine 2 tablespoons sugar with 2 tablespoons milk. Bring to a boil and cook for 2 minutes until it becomes syrupy. Brush the bottom of the pastry with the milk glaze and the sides with cold milk. The glaze serves to keep the pastry from getting soggy when the fruit is added. If you forgot to prick the bottom of the pastry when you were making it, prick it now. Drain the plums and reserve the juice. Place the plums, skin side down, on the bottom of the dough.

Preheat oven to 425°F.

4. Bake on the middle shelf of the oven at 425°F. for 20 minutes. During the baking, check once in a while for air bubbles in the pastry. Prick them rapidly to deflate, or the plums will tip and their juices will seep into the pastry and make it soggy.

5. Boil down the reserved plum juice until it starts to become slightly syrupy. Reserve.

6. Remove the tarts from the oven, and brush them all over with the plum glaze (reheat the glaze if necessary). Reduce the oven temperature to 400°F. and bake for 15–20 more minutes. Cover the sides loosely with foil if they are browning too much.

7. Make Whipped Cream, page 28, and refrigerate.

8. Before eating the tarts, pipe Whipped Cream with a star pastry tube between each plum.

Apricot and Prune Tart with Almond Butter Filling

This is my winter dessert for special occasions. Dried apricots and prunes on top of an almond butter cream filling make a delicious as well as a very decorative tart.

Dried apricots from California are the best. I always have found excellent pitted prunes in bulk in Jewish delicatessens or in specialty stores.

I find that the big rectangular-shaped tart about 10″ x 12″ is the easiest shape to decorate.

Special instructions. The rectangular tart shell can be made ahead of time and frozen or refrigerated for a day. The almond butter cream can be prepared a day or two ahead of time.

MAKES 1 RECTANGULAR TART ABOUT 10″ X 12″; SERVES 8–10

Puff Pastry with 4 turns, page
   297

For the almond butter cream

⅔ cup shelled almonds
½ cup sugar
4 tablespoons (½ stick) sweet
   butter
1 egg
¼ teaspoon almond extract
¼ teaspoon vanilla extract
1 tablespoon dark rum

The fruits

2 cups dried apricots (11 ounces)
1 cup pitted prunes (8 ounces)
½ cup water
½ cup dry Madeira
½ cup dry white wine
¼ cup sugar
3 tablespoons sweet butter
1 tablespoon dark rum

The topping

⅔ cup apricot jam
Whipped Cream, page 28
1 tablespoon dark rum

1. Sprinkle flour on a pastry surface and rolling pin. Roll out the Puff Pastry to a 14″ x 14″ rectangle. Freeze 30 minutes on a cookie sheet.

2. *The almond butter cream.* Pulverize the almonds in an electric blender or food processor, and add ½ cup sugar, 4 tablespoons butter, egg, vanilla and almond extracts, and 1 tablespoon rum. Turn on the machine for 10 seconds or so to mix all the ingredients. Refrigerate until needed.

3. Remove the dough from the freezer and with a knife cut the edges in straight lines, using a ruler to guide you, to leave cut edges all around (illustration, page 317). Refrigerate the trimmings without bunching together to make Sugar Cookies (Palmiers), page 302. Cut a 1″ wide strip from the 4 sides of the rectangle. Brush water on the 4 sides of the remaining rectangle and first stick the long strips on each long side of the rectangle, pressing them gently into place. Be sure the strips are flush with the bottom edge of the rectangle. Then stick the shorter strips crosswise overlapping the long strips at the corners. Trim the strips to be flush with the bottom edges. Prick the bottom of the tart shell all over with the tines of a fork. The tart shell is ready to be refrigerated, frozen, or baked.

4. *The fruits.* Soak the apricots and prunes for 2 hours in separate mixing bowls, with ½ cup water and ½ cup Madeira for the apricots and ½ cup wine for the prunes.

5. Poach the apricots in their own liquid with ¼ cup sugar for 20 minutes over low-medium heat. Drain the apricots in a sieve, catching the liquid in a bowl. Reserve apricots and liquid.

6. Cook the prunes for 5 minutes in the wine over medium-low heat. Drain. Reserve fruit and juices.

7. Melt 3 tablespoons butter in a 9″ cast-iron skillet over medium heat. When the butter starts to color, sauté the fruits for a minute or two and flambé with 1 tablespoon dark rum (illustration, page 24). The fruits can be prepared the morning of the dinner.

Preheat oven to 425°F.

8. In the late afternoon remove the pastry shell from the refrigerator or freezer. Transfer it to a cookie sheet. Brush milk over the bottom and the top of the strips. Line the bottom with foil and cover the foil with dry beans or aluminum baking pellets to keep the dough from bubbling and losing its shape. Bake on the middle shelf of the oven for 20 minutes. Remove it from the oven and lower the temperature to 400°F. Remove the beans and foil. Sometimes the foil sticks to the bottom of the dough; gently pry it loose with a knife.

9. Whip the almond cream to soften it and spread it over the bottom of the prebaked pastry. Bake on the middle shelf for 15–20 minutes. After 10 minutes, cover loosely with foil to prevent burning.

10. If the prunes are very big, split them in two or even quarter them to have enough for the decoration. On a diagonal, line rows of apricots and prunes over the baked tart.

11. Combine the drained juices from the fruits with ⅔ cup apricot jam. Bring to a boil while stirring and cook until the mixture is slightly syrupy (about 10 minutes). Strain through a fine-mesh sieve and brush all over the fruits and the top of the pastry strips and the vertical sides.

12. Prepare Whipped Cream, flavoring it with 1 tablespoon rum. Just before eating the tart, pipe Whipped Cream with a star pastry tube between each row of fruits.

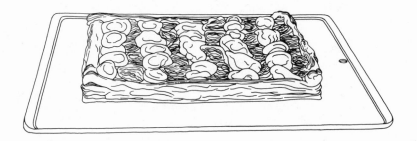

TECHNIQUES AND UTENSILS INTRODUCED

How to make cold soups

How to knead bread by hand or with an electric mixer

How to select potatoes for gratins

How to trim and cut a whole beef fillet, how to render the suet, how to use the trimmings, and how to boil it whole in a fish poacher

How to shape small finger-sized tarts

Lesson 17

Suggested Menus for Lesson 17

Quick Home-Style Dinner

Cross Rib Roast on a String

Baked Potatoes
with Garlic Mayonnaise
(Lesson 11)

Tossed Green Salad
(Lesson 1)

Strawberries with Cream-Cheese
Topping (Lesson 1)

Spring Dinner

Cold Cucumber Soup

English Muffin–Style Bread

Rack of Lamb with Parsley
(Lesson 15)

Scalloped Potatoes with Leeks

Paule's Chocolate Cake

Winter Dinner

Vegetable Pâté
(Lesson 8)

A Whole Beef Fillet Roasted
with Béarnaise Sauce

Scalloped Potatoes with Wine

Chocolate Soufflé

Sugar Cookies (Palmiers)
(Lesson 15)

Alternate Home-Style Dinner

Steak Sandwich

Cheese and Apples

Summer Luncheon

Cold Fresh Tomato Soup

English Muffin–Style Bread

Cold Sweetbread Salad
(Lesson 16)

Raspberry Tarts

Summer Dinner

Cold Fresh Tomato Soup

English Muffin–Style Bread

Boiled Beef Fillet on a String

Béarnaise Sauce

Scalloped Potatoes with Cream

Grand Marnier Soufflé
(Lesson 15)

Lemon Tarts

Fresh Tomato Soup

At the peak of summer, in August, fresh tomatoes are good and plentiful. This recipe is to be made only with ripe, juicy tomatoes. Do not use plum tomatoes, as they are too pulpy and will make the soup too thick. The success of this soup is all in the tomato. There is no cooking. It must be eaten very cold, so prepare it in the morning for dinner, but not the day before, because the tomatoes lose their flavor quickly. I serve the soup in a white tureen and white soup plates. It is very elegant.

Special kitchen utensil. A fine-mesh sieve.

SERVES 6–8

18 medium-size tomatoes (7 pounds)	1 teaspoon lemon juice (optional)
About 4 teaspoons salt	2 tablespoons minced fresh basil
Freshly ground white pepper	or fresh tarragon
	8 buttered toast, page 328

1. Peel the tomatoes. (Drop them in boiling water for 30 seconds, if necessary, but they should be very ripe and this treatment should not be necessary.) Quarter and seed them, using a spoon to discard the seeds.

2. Purée tomatoes in the food processor, fitted with the metal blade, or in a food mill, then force through a fine-mesh sieve (see illustration, pages 36–37).

3. Start seasoning with salt, a teaspoon at a time, tasting constantly until the right amount is achieved for you, and sprinkle in freshly ground white pepper. Add 1 teaspoon lemon juice if the tomatoes are very sweet. Pour in a tureen and refrigerate until very cold.

4. Just before serving, mince 2 tablespoons fresh basil or fresh tarragon. Do not substitute dry herbs; omit the herbs if you don't have fresh ones. Decorate each soup plate with the minced herb. Serve with buttered toast.

5. *Optional.* Only if you have access to fresh, thick cream, add a dollop to each plate.

Cold Cucumber Soup

My July soup—no cooking. The soup is made with raw cucumbers. So watch for the freshest cucumbers on the market. Serve fresh dill with it.

SERVES 6

6 pounds small cucumbers
2 tablespoons coarse salt
1½ cups water
1½ cups half-and-half

About 1¼ tablespoons salt
5 tablespoons lemon juice
2 tablespoons minced fresh dill

1. Peel the cucumbers. Cut off each end. Cut the cucumbers into paper-thin slices.

2. Sprinkle 2 tablespoons coarse salt over the cucumbers and let stand for 1 hour. The salt softens the cucumbers and makes them more digestible, and they won't need cooking.

3. Drain the cucumber slices; then wash them under running cold water. Put them in a colander and let drain for 15 minutes.

4. Purée in the food processor, fitted with the metal blade, for about 3 minutes, then force through a food mill to discard the seeds.

5. Add 1½ cups water and 1½ cups half-and-half, and start seasoning with salt. Then start adding fresh lemon juice, tablespoon by tablespoon, and stop when the soup is tart enough for your palate.

6. Refrigerate several hours. Half an hour before eating the soup, put it in the freezer so it will be ice cold. Mince 2 tablespoons fresh dill and decorate each plate with it.

English Muffin–Style Bread for Toast

This bread makes the most wonderful toast. It has only one rising, but two baking time periods: one in the oven, then sliced and toasted under the broiler. I use a rather unorthodox kneading process: My students call it "the walking bread" because it walks away from you during kneading. It is very much the same process as making taffy. The dough is a very sticky one because there is lots of water in it. You need a strong arm to knead it while pulling it. If you want to make it in a food processor, you must halve the recipe; otherwise, the food processor will walk away from you, and you will burn out the motor of even the best processor. It is my standard recipe for toast or croutons.

Special instruction. The dough can be prepared in an electric mixer fitted with a dough hook.

Special kitchen utensil. A standard 10-cup loaf pan 9″ x 5″ x 3″, or a baking pan 13″ x 9″ x 2″ for croutons.

1½ teaspoons salt	1 tablespoon dry yeast
2⅔–3½ cups all-purpose flour	2 tablespoons flour
1¾ cups lukewarm water	

1. Prepare a sponge with ¼ cup lukewarm water in a glass measuring cup mixed with 1 tablespoon yeast and 2 tablespoons flour; cover with plastic wrap. Let stand until double in volume and tiny bubbles form like a sponge within the mixture. It will become thick like very soft whipped cream (about 10–15 minutes) (illustration, page 163).

2. Mix the salt and flour together.

3. Transfer the sponge to a very large mixing bowl, add 1½ cups lukewarm water, and stir thoroughly.

4. Using a wooden spoon, start adding flour to the water, mixing all the while with the spoon. Blend in 3 cups of flour, then continue adding flour if the dough is still very, very wet, about ⅓ cup, but remember it must stick to the spoon.

5. *Hand method.* Now it is ready to knead in its own unique way. Transfer the dough to a table and proceed as follows: Grab the center of the dough mass and pull straight up on it, stretching the dough 8″–10″ above the work surface. Then let your hand follow it down. Grab another handful and continue stretching the dough as though playing with a yoyo until the mass cleans itself from the tabletop for just an instant. The dough will walk around on the counter top. Knead it in this fashion for 10 minutes.

The dough will get smoother and smoother. Just imagine you are making taffy and keep working the dough in this manner until it forms a mass that is very elastic and will stick to your open hand, then release itself from your hand when raised about 4″ above the table surface. The dough will spread some on the table but will contain itself in a cohesive mass.

Electric mixer method. In wintertime, first wash the mixer's bowl in hot water to warm it up. Combine 1½ cups warm water and the risen yeast in the mixer's bowl. Beat for 2 minutes at high speed, then start adding the flour mixed with the salt, 2 big spoonfuls at a time. I generally work at something else while I add the flour gradually. If you stand there next to your machine, you have the tendency to speed up the process, then you incorporate less flour. It takes about 15–20 minutes to incorporate about 3 cups of flour. I cut down to 1 tablespoon of flour at a time toward the end as the dough gets slightly stiffer, and I also lower the speed of the machine. Stop adding more flour when the dough starts to clean itself away from the sides of the bowl. Proceed with step 5, kneading by hand for 1 minute, then go on to step 6.

6. Grease a 10-cup loaf pan or baking pan. Transfer the dough to the pan. Cover with plastic wrap to keep the surface from drying out and to create humidity. It will rise to three-quarters the depth of the pan and will rise very quickly (30 minutes) on a very hot humid day. In the wintertime, set it in a warm place (110°F.); it will take 2–3 hours to rise.

Preheat oven to 350°F.

7. This bread has only one rising and is not punched down. Bake on the middle rack of the oven for about 45 minutes. It does not become golden brown, only slightly colored.

8. Run the blade of a knife around the edges of the bread. If it is sticking to the bottom, place the pan on a damp cloth for several minutes to unmold.

9. Cool completely on a rack. Wrap bread in foil. It keeps very well in the refrigerator or freezer.

10. To eat: Cut the bread in ¼″ slices. Turn on the broiler and toast on each side. Butter each slice and serve.

Note on making croutons. Cut the bread in cubes (it is very easy, especially if it has been baked in a baking pan). Dry the cubes in the oven at 300°F. for about 15 minutes until lightly golden and brush butter on all sides.

Scalloped Potatoes with Cream

There are different varieties of potatoes on the market: the round, white potato like the Katahdin; the Russets, long and oval; the Red Bliss, a small round potato with red skin; the long, white potato from Long Island; and the White Rose of California. They are divided into two types: boiling and baking. The round and long white potatoes can be called all-purpose potatoes; they are used in both baking and boiling. On the other hand, the Red Bliss potato is exclusively for boiling or roasting. The Russet Burbank potato is the classic baking potato; the best ones come from Idaho. I use Russets almost exclusively for scalloped potato gratins; they are the most consistent in their quality. For potato gratins, you need a first-rate starchy potato. To test for starch in a potato, cut it in half and rub the two sides against each other. There should be white froth forming around the edges. The starchy potatoes, when cooked, develop a cheesy taste. It is important not to wash the potatoes. This recipe, from the Dauphiné, a province lying between the Savoie and Provence, is surely the best known of the many potato gratins in France.

Special kitchen utensil. A 3-quart baking dish about 14" x 9" x 2".

SERVES 6–8

2 medium-size cloves garlic	2 teaspoons salt
8 medium-size Russet potatoes	Freshly ground black pepper
(3 pounds)	½ cup heavy cream
3 cups milk	2 tablespoons butter

1. Butter a baking dish large enough for 3 layers of potatoes (I use a 3-quart baking dish, 14" x 9" x 2"). Rub it with a garlic clove; mince the remaining garlic and reserve.

2. Scrub the potatoes clean under running cold water, wipe dry, then peel the potatoes. Slice the potatoes about ⅛" thick (illustration, page 91).

3. Combine the sliced potatoes, minced garlic, and 3 cups milk in a pot. Toss the potatoes in the milk with your hands. Sprinkle 2 teaspoons salt and grind pepper over them, and toss them once more. Cover. Bring slowly to a boil and cook over medium heat for 15 minutes. Transfer the potatoes and milk to the baking dish.

Preheat oven to 325°F.

4. Pour ½ cup heavy cream over the potatoes to just not quite cover the top layer. Dot with butter all over. Bake in a 325°F. oven for 1–1½ hours. The top should be nicely golden when done. Test for doneness with a cake tester; if no resistance is encountered, the potatoes are done.

Scalloped Potatoes with Wine

Only in the villages of Valdrôme and Les Prés, in the Drôme region, have I eaten this kind of gratin made with wine. The local people call it (incorrectly) "gratin dauphinois" because this region is in the Dauphiné. Like all gratins, this one is best when baked in a wood-burning stove. (In Valdrôme, walnut is the wood most commonly used.)

This gratin is usually eaten on a weekday, since it uses the drippings from the roast which was served on Sunday. The *drippings* of the roast (which is cooked to death in this part of the country) give the gratin lots of flavor— stolen from the meat. Lamb drippings are generally used, but any other kind of meat drippings, or a mixture of them, will do. It will give more flavor to the potatoes than just browning them in oil and butter.

Special kitchen utensils. Two 12″ cast-iron skillets.

2 medium-size onions	½ teaspoon dried thyme
8 medium-size Russet potatoes	1½ teaspoons salt
(about 3 pounds)	Freshly ground black pepper
1 clove garlic	1 cup boiling water
¼ cup fat from roast or olive oil	2 tablespoons cold butter,
or goose fat	thinly sliced
⅔ cup dry red wine	

1. Peel and cut the onions in half; then, with each half on the counter, slice the onions very thinly (yields 2 cups).

2. Peel and slice the potatoes about ⅛″ thick (yields 5 cups). Wash the slices under running cold water. Drain and wipe dry with paper towels.

3. Mince garlic very fine (1 teaspoon, approximately).

4. Heat 2 tablespoons fat or olive oil in each of two 12″ heavy iron skillets. Add the onions and cook over medium heat for 5 minutes. (The onions and potatoes can be browned in 1 skillet, but it must be done in 2 batches.)

5. Add half the sliced potatoes to each skillet and sauté over medium heat, lifting and turning them all the while so they mix well with the onions and get all coated with fat (use a steel blade spatula to lift them). You may need to add more meat fat or oil at this stage. Stop when the potatoes start coloring around the edges (after about 15 minutes). Transfer the potatoes to 1 skillet.

6. Add ⅔ cup dry red wine to the potatoes and bring to a boil for 30 seconds.

7. Off the flame, add ½ teaspoon thyme, the minced garlic, 1½ teaspoons salt, and pepper. Mix all these ingredients well with the potatoes and onions, being careful not to break the slices of potatoes.

Preheat oven to 325°F.

8. Pour 1 cup boiling water over the potatoes and dot with thin slices of butter.

9. Bake uncovered at 325°F. for about 1½ hours, until potatoes are completely tender and liquid is absorbed (but the potatoes should stay moist—pour in more boiling water if they get dry). Serve immediately upon removing from oven.

Scalloped Potatoes with Leeks

Each region of France has its own version of scalloped potatoes. I ate this one in the home of friends from Normandy. Leeks and potatoes do marry well, but it is important to buy the right potato for this gratin (for more information, see page 331). It must have a high content of starch so, while baking, it will absorb liquids. It will then melt in your mouth. If the potatoes are soggy to begin with (you can tell a soggy potato when cut—the inside core is mushy and droplets of water appear at the surface), the water in the potatoes will dilute the chicken stock, and the flavor of the leeks is lost. In other words, the dish will be a failure, and the failure will depend solely on the choice of the potato you made. I find russet potatoes best for this dish.

Special kitchen utensil. A 3-quart baking dish.

6 small leeks*	8 Russet potatoes (3 pounds)
4 tablespoons (½ stick) butter	⅔ cup strong Chicken Stock,
2 teaspoons salt	page 74
Freshly ground black pepper	½ cup heavy cream

* Substitute 2 pounds onions if leeks are unavailable.

1. Clean the leeks: Cut off the tough dark green leaves, leaving part of the tender light green leaves. Slit the leeks almost to the root and wash very well under running cold water to remove sand. Mince. (It is easier to mince the leeks if they are held together at the end; otherwise, they fall apart and are hard to handle.)

2. Place the leeks in a 4-quart pan; add 4 tablespoons butter. Cover and cook over low heat and braise for 30 minutes. Check once in a while to be sure the leeks do not color. Season with ½ teaspoon salt and freshly ground pepper.

3. Scrub the potatoes clean, then peel them and wipe them dry. Slice about ⅛″ thick (illustration, page 91).

4. Put the potatoes and leeks in the baking dish as follows:

   • Separate the potatoes into 3 approximately equal piles, one for each layer in the baking dish.
   • Lay slices of potatoes in the bottom of the pan with edges slightly overlapping. Sprinkle with ½ teaspoon salt and freshly ground pepper.
   • Spread about half the leeks over the first layer of potatoes.
   • Lay a second layer of potatoes on top of the leeks, again salt and pepper, and cover it with the rest of the leeks.
   • Arrange the last of the potatoes neatly overlapping on top of the leeks. Sprinkle with salt and pepper.

   Preheat oven to 325°F.

5. Pour the chicken stock over the potatoes. Bake for 30 minutes, then pour ½ cup heavy cream uniformly over the surface. Continue baking for 1–1½ hours. The top should be nicely browned when done. Test for doneness with a cake tester or a skewer; if no resistance is encountered, the potatoes are done.

Béarnaise Sauce

Read carefully the technique and the recipe for Hollandaise Sauce, page 201. The technique is identical for the Béarnaise. From May to November, try to use fresh French tarragon. It is so much better than when the tarragon is dried. If you have a tarragon plant in your garden, never pick the tarragon during the day when the sun is out; all the flavor of the plant recedes into its root. The ideal time to pick it is early morning.

Special instruction. I prefer scallions to shallots because they will purée while cooking, whereas the shallots will not soften enough. Of course, if you are able to get fresh shallots out of your garden, use them. If you are afraid to curdle the Béarnaise just when you need it, prepare it one hour ahead of time. Reserve, covered, on the counter, or in a lukewarm water bath. It is perfectly acceptable to eat a room-temperature Béarnaise.

Special kitchen utensil. A 1½ quart saucepan.

MAKES 2 CUPS

<table>
<tr><td>

¼ cup tarragon vinegar
¼ cup dry white wine
1 tablespoon minced white bulb
    of scallions
1 tablespoon minced fresh
    tarragon or ½ teaspoon dried

</td><td>

½ teaspoon salt
⅛ teaspoon freshly ground black
    pepper
3 egg yolks
12 tablespoons (1½ sticks) sweet
    butter

</td></tr>
</table>

1. In a 1½-quart saucepan boil down the vinegar, wine, minced scallions, tarragon, ½ teaspoon salt, and pepper.

2. Remove pan from heat and place in a cold water bath to lower the temperature before adding the egg yolks, especially if you are using a heavy saucepan. The residual heat will evaporate the liquids if you just allow it to cool by itself off the heat. Steps 1 and 2 can be done at least 2 hours ahead of time.

3. Add the egg yolks and whisk constantly over low heat until the yolks thicken, checking the inside bottom of the pan. When it becomes too hot to touch, start whisking in the butter, piece by piece, until the béarnaise is thick and creamy. Taste and correct seasonings. (If you happen to curdle it, quickly put 1 egg yolk into a bowl and start dribbling the curdled béarnaise into it whisking constantly. Transfer it back to the pan and continue adding 3 more tablespoons butter. Taste for seasonings.)

Note. Make 2 batches of béarnaise instead of doubling the recipe.

Technique: To trim and cut a whole beef fillet

There are sometimes sales on untrimmed beef fillets. Learning to trim and cut a whole beef fillet at home familiarizes you with the different cuts of the fillet and teaches you to differentiate between a chateaubriand, a tournedo, and a filet mignon. An untrimmed fillet weighs around 8 pounds, and totally trimmed it is reduced to about half its original weight. It is shocking the first time you trim the meat to see a voluminous piece of meat reduced so much, but you can save everything. I throw nothing out. I render the fat and use it to deep-fry or sauté. It freezes very well (see page 338). I make a broth with all the scraps and use it in soups. I trim the meat to have an even-shape roast, and I will sauté the trimmings for a Steak Sandwich, page 339, or braise the meat like the Butcher's Tenderloin, page 130.

There are 5 cuts in the fillet: the head, which is the big extremity with a piece of meat held to the main part of the body by fat; next is the thickest part of the body, about 3″ long, which is the chateaubriand cut; then, adjacent to the chateaubriand, is the tournedo cut (the filet mignon to

Americans); then the tail of the fillet, which is the filet mignon (to the French). Along the side of the fillet is the chain, attached to the main part of the body by fat and gristle.

Place the fillet in front of you with the head to your left. Tear the fat off with your hand, as much as possible. Reserve to render (see page 338). Remove the fat between the head flap and the main body.

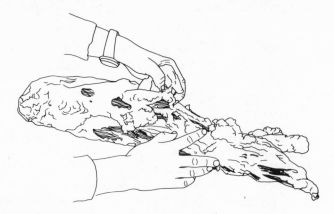

Detach the chain from the fillet. If you can't see it, poke with your fingers. If the fillet is right side up (the underside is fattier and has gristles), and the head is to your left, the chain is attached on the side of the fillet nearest you. Detach it by tearing it along the side. Reserve the chain for a Steak Sandwich, page 339.

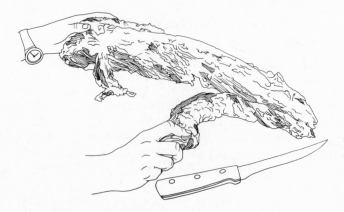

Turn the fillet underside up and, with a sharp boning knife, trim off all fat and gristle and a thinnish veil of fat.

Turn it back right side up and continue to cut off all fat and sinews on top of the fillet. The meat should be cut *à vif* (right into the red meat). If you leave a thin coat of sinews on the meat, it will cook into a tough outside crust and will make it difficult to carve the meat once it is cooked. Reserve the scraps for a stock.

Now the meat should be totally clean. To get the whole fillet ready to roast or to boil according to the 2 recipes given in this book (pages 338 and 340), slice off the flap next to the top of the fillet (reserve the meat for Steak Sandwich, page 339) so that the whole main center of the fillet is of the same diameter, and cut off a slice about ½″ thick from the head (the left end) that is slightly smaller in diameter than the rest of the fillet (reserve for Braised Butcher's Tenderloin recipe, page 130). Fold the tail of the fillet under to make the fillet about 16″ long and of the same diameter. It will weigh about 3 pounds.

Make sixteen 1-foot-long pieces of string to tie the fillet. Place the fillet underside up and start tying it every inch. When the fillet is cooked, it is easy to slice each piece where the strings were.

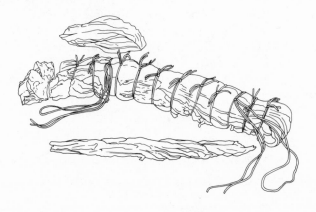

Technique: To render beef suet for deep-frying

Rendering fat means to melt solid fat into a liquid. Rendered beef suet, as every self-respecting chef knows, is the best fat for deep-frying. Unfortunately, doctors disapprove of it. But if you have low cholesterol, try it. It is cheap, has the most refined taste, and can be used several times, as long as it is taken care of properly.

MAKES 1½ QUARTS RENDERED FATS

About 4½ pounds beef suet   ⅔ cup water

Cut the suet into small pieces or ask the butcher to grind it, and melt with ⅔ cup water in your deep-fryer or any large pot. The water helps to decompose the fats of the suet. Melt on top of the stove uncovered at a very low flame. For 4½ pounds suet, it will take about 3 hours.

You will see tiny golden pieces left in the liquid. Remove with a perforated spoon and discard because they are the sinews of the meat that did not melt and are not like the skins of fowls which are delicious as cracklings.

Filter the liquids through cheesecloth. The fat is now ready to use. After using, filter it and freeze it until needed. You can usually use it 3 to 4 times. After reusing it, filter it and freeze until the next use.

A Whole Beef Fillet Roasted

Trimming the fillet of beef is the only work for this recipe, and it can be done a day ahead of time. The roasting involves no work, taking 20 minutes to cook at 500°F. (though in a self-cleaning oven, I had to drop the temperature to 475°F. when the roast started to smoke after 5 minutes of cooking). The best roasting pan is the broiler pan of your oven; on it the fillet will roast properly with enough air around it. If you are roasting two fillets, leave enough space between the fillets; to roast properly, air must pass freely between the two roasts.

Special instruction. If you buy the fillet trimmed by the butcher, be sure to ask if the "chain" has been removed. If not, roast 12 minutes on each side instead of 10.

SERVES 8–10

1 trimmed beef fillet (3½–4 pounds)	½ teaspoon salt
	Freshly ground black pepper
1 tablespoon Cognac	Watercress or parsley
3 tablespoons olive oil	Béarnaise Sauce, page 334

Preheat oven to 500°F. Drop to 475°F. if it starts smoking right away.

1. Rub the roast with 1 tablespoon Cognac, then with 2 tablespoons olive oil.

2. Grease the bottom of the roasting pan with 1 tablespoon olive oil and place the meat in the pan.

3. Roast in the 500°F. oven for 10 minutes on one side, turn over, sprinkle ½ teaspoon salt and freshly ground pepper, and roast for 10 minutes on the other side.

4. Transfer the meat to a cutting board with a juice catcher and allow to cool 10 minutes.

5. Cut the strings with a pair of scissors and discard. Carve the meat into 1″ thick pieces and serve with Béarnaise Sauce. Decorate with watercress and parsley.

To serve for a buffet. Cool the meat to room temperature. Do not refrigerate it. Cut the meat into ⅛″ thick slices just before placing on the buffet table. Do not cover it with plastic wrap, as it develops a greasy taste.

Steak Sandwich

If you have leftover meat from a boiled beef dinner, or any leftover meat from a roast, or if you have trimmed a whole fillet of beef, as I demonstrated on pages 336–337, this sandwich is great for a family lunch or with good friends.

SERVES 6

Pizza Dough, page 162	¼ cup wine vinegar
Vinaigrette, page 11	⅓ cup water
1 tomato sliced	⅓ cup dry red wine
½ pound meat (see note above)	Fresh salad greens
3 tablespoons butter	Salt
1 tablespoon Dijon-style mustard	Freshly ground black pepper

1. Roll out the Pizza Dough into a 12″ circle. Transfer it to a 12″ pizza tin. Let rise for 1 hour. Brush olive oil over it. Bake in a 400°F. oven for 20 minutes. Let cool. It can be cooked a day ahead (or use store-bought bread).

2. Prepare a vinaigrette, page 11. Slice a tomato in paper-thin slices. Reserve.

3. Cut the meat into 1/8″ thick slices. Melt 2 tablespoons butter in a 12″ cast-iron skillet over high heat. When the butter stops sizzling, brown the meat very quickly, 1 minute on each side, just enough to sear.

4. Transfer the meat to a plate. Discard the butter in the skillet, then whisk in the mustard, vinegar, water, and wine. Over high heat, stir the boiling liquids constantly until they are reduced to two-thirds. It takes about 3 minutes. Add the juices from the meat plate. Off the flame, whisk in 1 tablespoon butter.

5. Split the bread sandwichlike. Sprinkle vinaigrette over the 2 open faces of the sandwich. Decorate with some salad greens and sliced tomato on 1 top of the sandwich, then add the meat, salt, and pepper. Cover it with the mustard sauce and close the sandwich with the top. Cut it in wedges and serve.

Boiled Fillet of Beef on a String

Yes, Boiled Beef Fillet on a String. It is such a startling way to treat this venerable cut of beef. Yet for beef fillet lovers there is no better way to prepare it. It's a technique used especially around the slaughterhouses in Paris where butchers supposedly choose a choice piece and cook it for their lunches. This boiling technique seals the outside of the meat; no juice will escape because the albumin in the meat coagulates at once and forms a hermetic seal at the surface of the meat. You don't need aromatic vegetables to enhance the cooking liquid, since they won't flavor the meat. Plunging the meat into boiling water is the opposite of the technique for a stock, where meat and bones are covered with cold water and slowly brought to a boil so that they render their juices to color and to flavor the stock. Try it first with a lesser cut of meat, Cross Rib Roast on a String, page 342.

To boil a 16″ long fillet, weighing around 3 pounds, I use my fish poacher. The fillet can be cut in half and boiled in a stockpot, but remember the pots need open handles to which you can tie the strings of the meat without any difficulty. The timing of the cooking does not depend on the weight of the fillet but on its diameter. If you have trimmed the fillet yourself according to the technique given on pages 336–337, with the "chain" removed, it will cook 12 minutes after the boil has been reached again. If the butcher trimmed the meat and did not remove the "chain," boil the meat for 17 minutes.

The aspect of the meat while boiling will shock you. It is unappetizing, grayish in color, and pitiful-looking, but once sliced the transformation is completed: Glorious ruby-red slices invite you to eat. This is a perfect way to eat beef for a person who needs to watch his or her diet—just season it with salt and pepper. For the nondieters, a Béarnaise Sauce, page 334, is lovely with it.

When tying the meat for boiling, leave a foot of string at each end of the meat to tie the handles so that the meat will not touch the bottom of the pan.

Special kitchen utensil. A fish poacher or 2 pots 10″ in diameter each.

SERVES 8

1 trimmed and tied fillet of beef (3½–4 pounds)	2 teaspoons salt per quart of water Lots of boiling water

1. Take your meat out of the refrigerator at least 1 hour before cooking it if you trimmed it beforehand.

2. Choose a fish poacher long enough to fit the fillet (at least 18″), or cut the fillet in half and use 2 pots, at least 10″ in diameter. Fill each pot to three-quarters full, counting the quarts of water in order to salt the water correctly, 2 teaspoons of salt per quart of water. Cover and bring to a rolling boil.

3. Drop the meat into the boiling water and tie the long loose ends of the string to the pot's handles. Cover partially to bring the water back to a boil as quickly as possible over high heat. Uncover and count 13 minutes with water boiling, or 17 minutes for a fillet with the "chain" still attached to it.

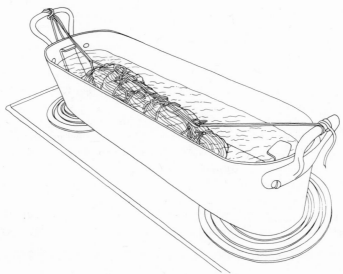

4. Cut the strings, holding the meat with one hand. Put the meat on a wooden platter with a juice catcher. Wait 5 minutes or so to relax the meat and make it easier to carve, then slice 1″ thick pieces.

Note. If some of your guests find the meat a bit too rare, you can broil a slice for 1 minute on each side for them. Do not leave the meat longer in the boiling water, as this will increase the layer of grayish boiled meat around the outside of the fillet.

Cross Rib Roast on a String

For an everyday meal, I buy cross rib, a beef cut from the shoulder. It has lots of flavor and is relatively inexpensive. Practice with this cut of meat before attempting the fillet in the preceding recipe. Leftover boiled cross rib is superb eaten cold. Whether hot or cold, serve with salt and pepper or horseradish or Rémoulade, page 53.

Special instruction. Ask the butcher to cut the meat into a 4″ wide roast, about 8″ long, weighing 2–2½ pounds. The width of the roast is important; it dictates the amount of time the roast will be in the water.

SERVES 6

2–2½-pound cross rib roast   Lots of boiling water
2 teaspoons salt per quart of water

1. Tie the roast with string, leaving a foot of string at each end of the meat so you can tie it to prevent its touching the bottom of the pan.

2. Boil lots of water in a 6-quart pot at least 10″ in diameter. Fill the pot to three-quarters full, counting the quarts of water in order to salt the water correctly, 2 teaspoons of salt per quart of water. Cover and bring to a rolling boil.

3. Drop the meat into the boiling water and tie the long loose ends of the string to the pot's handles. Cover partially to bring the water back to a boil as quickly as possible over full heat. Uncover and count 30 minutes with the water boiling.

4. Remove the meat to a wooden platter with a juice catcher. Wait 5 minutes or so to relax the meat and make it easier to carve, then slice ⅛″ thick pieces.

Paule's Chocolate Cake

Paule Basiaux, a friend of mine, makes a great cake. It is a molded loaf of chocolate mousse, half-baked and half-unbaked. It is served in slices covered with a light Pastry Cream, page 44 or Crème Anglaise, page 360, a light egg custard.

Special instructions. Can be made a day ahead of time. There are 3 mixtures to make: a chocolate-butter mixture, an egg yolk–sugar mixture, and beaten egg whites. These 3 mixtures are blended together to make a chocolate cake as light as possible.

Special kitchen utensil. A 6-cup loaf pan or charlotte pan.

SERVES 8

8 ounces bittersweet chocolate (Lindt or Tobler)	8 eggs
16 tablespoons (2 sticks) sweet butter	½ cup superfine sugar
	Pastry Cream, page 44

1. Melt the chocolate in a water bath (see page 43), then remove from the heat and let it cool. Cream the butter, smearing it on your pastry surface with the heel of your hand until the butter is soft but not melting. Transfer the butter to an electric mixer.

2. With the mixer at medium speed, dribble the cool chocolate into the butter—the melted chocolate is incorporated into the butter without melting the butter. Beat for about 3 minutes. Transfer the mixture to a regular mixing bowl.

3. Separate the eggs and reserve the whites. Beat the yolks and ½ cup super-fine sugar at medium speed in the electric mixer for about 5 minutes, then add the chocolate-butter mixture, 1 tablespoon at a time.

4. Beat the egg whites into stiff peaks. It is best to use a copper bowl and beat the egg whites by hand—they are lighter and give more volume than mixer-beaten whites. However, if you are beating the egg whites by machine, watch over them very carefully to stop when the whites look firm. Don't overbeat them—they will not fold smoothly into the chocolate mixture—but don't underbeat them either.

   Preheat oven to 400°F.

5. Fold a fourth of the whites into the chocolate batter to get a uniform mixture, then transfer this to the egg white mixture and fold the two together, trying not to deflate the batter. You must act quickly.

6. Pour half the chocolate mousse into a buttered 6-cup loaf pan or charlotte pan. Refrigerate the remaining chocolate mousse. Place the pan in a hot water bath and bake on the middle shelf at 400°F. for 45 minutes. The cake will puff up. As it cools, it will deflate; don't worry. When cold, add the remaining unbaked chocolate mousse. Cover with a plate and refrigerate overnight.

7. Prepare the Pastry Cream, page 34, add 1 tablespoon Cointreau, and refrigerate.

8. Before dinner, unmold the cake on a platter. Dip the mold in hot water and turn it upside down on the platter. Wait 15 minutes before unmolding. It should unmold easily. Keep refrigerated until 30 minutes before you serve it. Serve with the custard in a sauceboat.

Chocolate Soufflé

Paule's cake can become a delicious moist soufflé. Read all the instructions, page 293, on what can be done ahead of time for a dessert soufflé. For this specific soufflé, the chocolate-butter mixture can be mixed with the egg yolk–sugar mixture ahead of time, but at the last minute before folding the mixture in the beaten egg whites, beat the chocolate-butter mixture for 3 minutes to beat air into it.

Bake all the chocolate mousse in two 3-cup soufflé molds on the middle shelf of the oven at 400°F. for 25–30 minutes. Remove collars, sprinkle with powdered sugar, and serve immediately. The center of the soufflés must be moist. For 1 soufflé, to serve 4, prepare half the recipe.

Lemon Tarts

I first encountered these lovely little lemon tarts at the Ecole des Trois Gourmandes, the cooking school founded by Julia Child, Simone Beck, and Louisette Bertholle, authors of *Mastering the Art of French Cooking*, which should be in every cook's library. I have adapted the recipe to my own taste and cooking style, so it is somewhat different from the one I first learned.

Special kitchen utensils. Sixteen 3″ diameter tart molds.

SERVES 8 (2 PER PERSON)

1 cup sugar	Juice of 3 lemons
8 tablespoons (1 stick) sweet butter	Grated rind of 2 lemons
	Shortcrust Pastry, page 87
3 large egg yolks	Whipped Cream, page 28
3 eggs	

1. Combine sugar, butter, egg yolks and eggs, lemon juice, and lemon rind in a 1½-quart heavy-bottomed saucepan and whisk continuously over low heat for 5–6 minutes until the eggs are thoroughly blended and the custard starts to thicken. (Cooking too fast at first will cause white specks to appear in the custard.) Increase the heat to medium and continue whisking all the while for another 10 minutes (15–20 minutes cooking altogether). The custard should be the consistency of honey.

2. Remove from heat and continue whisking for 2–3 minutes to let the pan cool a bit; then cover with foil or plastic wrap and place in refrigerator for several hours. I generally do this a day ahead.

3. Prepare the pastry dough, page 87, adding 2 tablespoons sugar to the ingredients. Refrigerate for 15 minutes.

4. Cut the dough into 4 parts. Roll out each piece of dough to an 8″ circle. Assemble 4 small 3″ tart molds. Put them ¼″ apart in a nearly circular array. Roll up the dough on your rolling pin and unroll it on top of the tart molds. Now push the molds together under the dough and using a little dab of dough gently poke the dough down inside each mold. Then roll the rolling pin across the tops of molds, cutting the dough around the edge of each mold. Reserve the leftover dough. Pick up each mold, and with your thumbs, gently push the dough down into the mold so that it fits closely all around. Roll out the remaining 3 pieces of dough in the same way. Gather all the leftover dough into 1 piece. Keep for 6 Hot Individual Apple Tarts, page 135. Prick the bottom of the dough. Line and cover the pastry dough with foil, crimped tightly around the edges.

Preheat oven to 350°F.

5. Bake the little tarts for 10 minutes at 350°F. Remove the foil and dry completely in the oven, checking constantly that they do not burn.

6. Fill the tarts with lemon custard only a few hours before serving and do not refrigerate them—the butter in the pastry hardens if refrigerated. Be sure to whisk the cold lemon custard a bit before filling the tart shells.

7. Decorate each tart with a little dab of Whipped Cream, page 28, using a pastry bag with a fine star tip for decorating.

Note on making as a single tart. The filling is enough for a 10″ diameter tart. However, be sure that the filling is made a day ahead of time. It must be stiff enough to cut the tart in wedges without the filling spreading into a mess.

Raspberry Tarts

Special instruction. Prepare the custard ahead of time. Bake the small tarts in late afternoon. Fill the tarts when ready to eat.

Special kitchen utensils. Sixteen 3″ diameter tart molds.

SERVES 8 (2 PER PERSON)

Pastry Cream Custard, page 251	2 pints fresh raspberries
1 tablespoon raspberry liqueur	3 tablespoons sugar
Shortcrust Pastry, page 87	¼ cup currant jelly

1. Prepare the Pastry Cream Custard on page 251. Substitute 1 tablespoon raspberry liqueur for the Cognac.

2. Prepare the pastry dough. Add 2 tablespoons sugar to the ingredients. Refrigerate for 15 minutes.

3. Wash the raspberries; sprinkle 3 tablespoons sugar and 1 tablespoon raspberry liqueur over them. Marinate 1 hour.

4. Drain the raspberries. Combine the raspberry juices with ¼ cup currant jelly and bring to a simmer, mixing all the while. Reserve.

5. When ready to eat the raspberry tarts, whisk the custard to smooth it out, fill the small tarts with custard, and decorate with the raspberries. Brush currant jelly over them (if the jelly is too stiff, reheat barely). **Do not refrigerate. Serve.**

Orange Pound Cake

It takes no time at all to make this pound cake. I serve it sometimes for brunch, sometimes for tea time or for dessert to accompany a Chocolate Soufflé or with ice-cream. It gets better the next day if there is any left.

Special kitchen utensil. A 4-cup loaf pan.

MAKES FIFTEEN $\frac{1}{4}''$ SLICES

9 tablespoons sweet butter at room temperature
$\frac{1}{2}$ cup sugar
2 large eggs
1 cup all-purpose flour

1 teaspoon baking powder
$\frac{1}{4}$ cup freshly squeezed orange juice
2 teaspoons grated orange rind

1. Butter a 4-cup loaf pan. Cut a piece of waxed paper to fit in the bottom of the pan. Put it in place and butter it.

2. With an electric mixer or an electric hand beater, beat the softened butter and sugar together at medium speed for 2 minutes. Add 2 eggs and continue beating for 5 minutes. At this point, the mixture will look curdled, but don't worry; it will smooth out when the flour is incorporated.

3. Sift 1 cup all-purpose flour and 1 teaspoon baking powder together onto a piece of waxed paper. Reduce mixer speed to low, and add the flour, little by little, until it is all thoroughly blended.

Preheat oven to 400°F.

4. Still at low speed, beat in $\frac{1}{4}$ cup orange juice and 2 teaspoons grated orange rind.

5. Pour the batter into the pan and bake for 40 minutes at 400°F. on the middle shelf of the oven. Cover loosely with foil if the top gets too dark.

6. Remove from oven. Run a knife around the edge and turn the pan upside down on a wire rack for 15 minutes. Remove the waxed paper at the bottom of the cake, then turn it back top side up. Eat at room temperature.

TECHNIQUES AND UTENSILS INTRODUCED

How to cut up a rabbit, how to poach and sauté it

How to poach meringues

How to make a flourless custard

How to keep a caramel sauce fluid

How to form classic almond cookies and to keep
them crunchy in a cookie jar with a rubber seal and
metal clamps

Lesson 18

Menu Suggestions for Lesson 18

Luncheon Menu

Sweetbread Fritters

Sorrel and Onion Custard

Strawberries with Cream-Cheese
Topping (Lesson 1)

Almond Cookies

For a Lunchbox

Leftover Sorrel and Onion Custard
in a Sandwich

Summer Dinner

Cold Fresh Tomato Soup
(Lesson 17)

Rabbit with Mustard, Valdrôme Style

Sorrel and Onion Custard

Hot Individual Berry Tarts
(Lesson 7)

Autumn Dinner

Pine Nut Fritters

Rabbit, Portuguese Style

Pasta Made with Fresh Basil
(Lesson 9)

Floating Island

Sugar Cookies (Palmiers)
(Lesson 15)

Sweetbread Fritters

Braised sweetbreads with onions, deep-fried in a light beer batter, are a great hit with my students. Read the introduction to Sweetbreads with Fresh Pasta, page 171, to know more about sweetbreads and how to buy them. And if you have not read the instructions on deep-frying, page 108, do so before making fritters.

The sweetbreads can be prepared ahead of time, the batter 1 hour ahead of time without incorporating the beaten egg whites. Beat the egg whites while the deep-frying oil is heating. Fritters are at their best when just fried.

Special kitchen utensil. A deep-fryer or a wok.

MAKES 40 FRITTERS

2 pounds calf's sweetbreads	¾ cup all-purpose flour
½ lemon	2 eggs, separated
5 small yellow onions	¾ cup tepid beer
4 tablespoons (½ stick) butter	2 tablespoons oil
1½ teaspoons salt	1½ quarts corn oil
Freshly ground black pepper	

1. Soak the sweetbreads in cold water for several hours with half a lemon in the water. Squeeze a few drops of lemon juice into the water as well. Change the water when it clouds, and each time squeeze a few drops of lemon juice into the new water. The sweetbreads will become white, free of reddish spots.

2. Transfer the sweetbreads to a pan. Cover with cold water and bring slowly to a boil. Then cook for 10 minutes over medium-low heat partly covered. Drain and rinse under cold water. Let cool.

3. Remove the pieces of gristly cartilage found on the surface of the sweetbreads and discard. Remove any of the membrane which comes loose, but do not remove the fine membrane which holds the meat together. Cut into 1″ cubes.

4. Peel the onions; slice thin. Put the onions and 4 tablespoons butter in a 4-quart Dutch oven, and season with ¼ teaspoon salt and freshly ground pepper. Cover tightly and cook (braise) slowly for 30 minutes over medium-low heat until the onions are soft but not colored.

5. Add the sweetbread cubes on top of the onions. Season with ¼ teaspoon salt and freshly ground pepper. Cover tightly and cook for 30 minutes over medium-low heat. This can be prepared ahead of time and reheated when needed.

6. *The batter.* Sift the flour and ½ teaspoon salt into your mixer bowl, make a well in the center, and add 2 egg yolks. With the mixer at medium speed, beat the beer into the batter, then add 2 tablespoons oil. Do not overbeat, just enough to mix all the ingredients smoothly. Set the batter aside for 1 hour so it will stick to the sweetbreads.

7. *To make the fritters.* Reheat the sweetbreads just enough to warm them. Drain. (Reserve the juices for fresh pasta; see Note at end of recipe.)

8. Heat 1½ quarts corn oil in a deep-fryer to 325°F. Beat 2 egg whites until stiff and fold them into the beer batter.

9. Using 2 spoons, dip each piece of sweetbread into the batter, turn it over to coat it well, and lower it into the oil. Don't overcrowd the deep-fryer pan. Cook until golden. Drain the fritters on paper towels and sprinkle salt over them. Serve.

Note on halving the recipe. Do not halve the batter. It does not work as well as the full amount. The fritters are not as light as when they are made with the amount given.

Note on using the drained juices of the sweetbreads and onions. Cook Homemade Fresh Pasta, page 171, then add it to the skillet with the juices. Add 1 cup of cream or 3 tablespoons butter. Cook for 30 seconds and serve.

Sorrel and Onion Custard

This is my favorite summer vegetable recipe for a dinner with guests. It is equally good as a cold vegetable pâté for hors d'oeuvre or to spread on bread. It makes wonderful sandwiches, as I discovered once when I had to cancel a dinner but had already prepared it. Instead of cooking the custard in small ramekins in a water bath, I baked it in a baking dish, and for several days my husband and I ate the cold custard as a pâté.

Special instruction. Prepare the onion and sorrel purée a day ahead of time and bake for dinner.

Special kitchen utensil. Bake in one 4–5-cup ring mold or in individual molds such as eight ½-cup porcelain ramekins, or muffin cups, or sixteen ⅓-cup baba molds. Or bake in a 1½-quart dish at 325°F. for 30 minutes if you do not want to unmold.

SERVES 8

4 medium-size onions
6 tablespoons sweet butter
1½ teaspoons salt
1 pound sorrel (sourgrass)

3 eggs
1½ cups heavy cream
Freshly ground black pepper

1. Peel and slice the onions. Melt 3 tablespoons butter in a 12″ cast-iron skillet, add the onions, and stir with a wooden spoon until the onion slices are coated with butter. Sprinkle with ½ teaspoon salt. Cover tightly and cook slowly (braise) over low heat for 1 hour or until the onions are very, very soft; transfer to a bowl.

2. Wash the sorrel and remove the stems, tearing out the center vein of the leaf as well. Melt 2 tablespoons butter in the 12″ cast-iron skillet and add the sorrel leaves, turning them over with a wooden spatula until the leaves melt into a purée. Cook until all the water evaporates from the sorrel (about 5 minutes).

3. Purée the sorrel and the onions in a food mill, blender, or food processor, then force through a fine-mesh sieve.

4. Break 3 eggs in a 2-quart mixing bowl, beat very well, then add 1½ cups heavy cream, the sorrel, and the onion purée; season with 1 teaspoon salt and freshly ground pepper.

Preheat oven to 350°F.

5. Grease the mold(s) (see note on utensils above) with the remaining 1 tablespoon butter. Fill the mold(s) three-fourths full with the mixture. Place the mold(s) in a water bath with water coming halfway up the ring mold if you are using it, but be careful if you are using individual molds, especially muffin tins or baba molds; they are very light and tend to tip over if there is too much water in the water bath. Bake on the middle shelf of the oven for 20–35 minutes for individual molds, slightly longer for a single mold. Check the custard with a cake tester, but do not overcook. The custard is best when it is slightly soft, but still cooked enough to unmold.

6. Pass the blade of a knife around the edge of the mold(s) and invert on a preheated serving platter.

Note on cooking in pastry shells. Bake custard in a partially precooked pastry shell for 35 minutes at 350°F.

Technique: To cut up a rabbit

Special kitchen utensils. A cutting board, cleaver, scissors, 2–3 feet of kitchen string, and boning knife.

Place the rabbit on a cutting board and cut off the head with the cleaver. Reserve for stock.

With the rabbit on its back, bend the front legs backwards to break the shoulder joint. Then cut off the legs at the shoulder joint. If making a stock, cut off the small end of the front legs at the last joint with a cleaver and reserve for stock.

With scissors, cut open the breast of the rabbit to expose the entrails. Remove the liver and reserve in a small bowl with 2 tablespoons brandy, ¼ teaspoon salt, and freshly ground pepper; refrigerate for Duck Liver with Scrambled Eggs, page 275, substituting rabbit liver for the duck liver. Remove the remaining entrails (heart, lungs, and kidneys) and reserve for the stock. Wipe your hands.

With scissors, cut off the loose skin along both sides of the rabbit from the hind legs up to the ribs. Trim off the fat and sinew. Roll up and tie with string.

Fold hind legs outwards, breaking the hip joint. Cut off the hind legs with a knife at hip joint (around the tail bone). Trim off scraps and fat. Cut off last 2″ of each leg with the cleaver and reserve for the stock. Cut each hind leg into 3–4 approximately equal pieces with the cleaver.

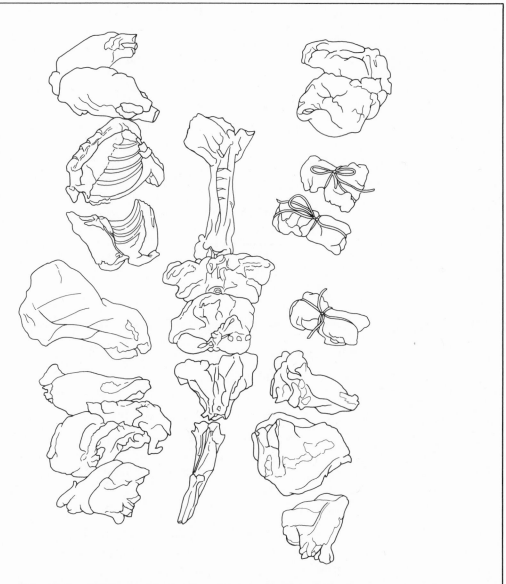

Cut off the tail bone with the cleaver to use for the stock.

Break the ribs loose at the spine by folding them backwards. Then cut off with a knife or scissors. Roll up into packages and tie.

With the cleaver, cut off the portion of the spine the ribs were attached to and use for stock.

The piece that remains is the saddle of the rabbit. Cut it into 3–4 equal pieces with the cleaver.

Rabbit, Portuguese Style

At lunchtime, on the days when my Portuguese cleaning ladies, Maria and Noellia Casthello, came to help me, I envied their lunch. Maria sautéed leftover rabbit in oil. It was absolutely delicious. They gave me the recipe, which originates from their village, Montenegro, on the south coast of Portugal in the Algarve region. Rabbit has very dense meat; it tastes more like a chicken that runs free, looking for its feed. It is a little bit chewy and full of flavors.

Special instruction. Avoid frozen rabbit. It loses most of its flavor. There are 3 stages to the preparation, but with very little work in each step. First: Cut up the rabbit and marinate for 4 hours. It can be done in the morning. Second: Cook the rabbit in its marinade in the late afternoon. And, third: Sauté the rabbit just before dinnertime. It is excellent the next day; just sauté the rabbit in 2 extra tablespoons butter.

Special kitchen utensil. A 6½-quart Dutch oven.

SERVES 4–6

5-pound fresh rabbit	3 bay leaves
8 cloves garlic	1 teaspoon salt
2½ cups dry white wine	Freshly ground black pepper
1 tablespoon red-wine vinegar	6 tablespoons sweet butter

1. Cut up the rabbit according to the illustrated technique, pages 354–355.

2. Place the rabbit and the unpeeled garlic cloves in a 6½-quart Dutch oven; cover with 2½ cups wine and the vinegar. Add 3 bay leaves, 1 teaspoon salt, and freshly ground pepper. Cover the pot. Marinate for 4 hours. Do not refrigerate.

   Preheat oven to 400°F.

3. Place the pot on the middle shelf of the oven and cook for 1 hour. Uncover and continue cooking for about another 30 minutes or until there is just about 1 cup of liquid left in the pot. Remove from the oven. This can be done ahead of time. If so, reheat slowly in the pot over medium heat before continuing with the next step.

4. Melt 3 tablespoons butter in a 12″ cast-iron skillet. When the butter stops sizzling, sauté the rabbit pieces with the garlic cloves until the rabbit is golden brown (about 5 minutes). Transfer the rabbit and the garlic to a preheated platter.

5. Pour the liquids in the skillet, turn the heat high, and scrape the sides and bottom of the pan with a wooden spatula until the liquids reduce

to about ½ cup, boiling all the while. Turn off the heat and whisk in the remaining 3 tablespoons butter, 1 tablespoon at a time. Taste and correct seasonings with salt and pepper.

Note. If all the liquid has evaporated while cooking in the oven, substitute chicken stock for the sauce. (If you don't have chicken stock on hand, add ½ cup water and 2 extra tablespoons of butter for the last step.)

Chicken, Portuguese Style

Substitute 2 chickens for the rabbit. Add 1½ cups wine at step 2. Braise for 30 minutes in the oven, then uncover and continue cooking in the oven until 1 cup liquid remains in the pot. Continue with the directions in the rabbit recipe.

Rabbit with Mustard, Valdrôme Style

A thousand miles away from Montenegro where Rabbit, Portuguese Style originates, Valdrôme, in southeastern France, has its own technique to prepare rabbit. There, the rabbit pieces are coated with mustard, minced parsley, and garlic, browned in butter, then cooked with a continual basting to finish with a tender, caramelized rabbit.

Special instruction. Cut up the rabbit ahead of time and prepare a rabbit stock or substitute unsalted chicken stock. The cooking of the rabbit needs constant watching. You need to be in the kitchen all the while.

Special kitchen utensil. A 3-quart saucepan and a 12″ cast-iron skillet.

SERVES 4–6

5-pound fresh rabbit	2 cloves garlic
4 cups water	A handful of parsley leaves
1 onion stuck with 1 clove	2 tablespoons Dijon-type mustard
Several green leaves of leek	5 tablespoons sweet butter
2 carrots, sliced	1 tablespoon oil
1 rib celery, sliced	4 tablespoons red-wine vinegar

1. Cut up the rabbit according to the illustrated technique, pages 354–355.

2. Put the rabbit head, back, and tail in a 3-quart pan with 4 cups water, 1 onion with clove, sliced carrots, leek leaves, and sliced celery. *Do not add any salt.* There will be a great reduction of the stock. It will become a glaze and would become too salty. Bring to a boil slowly, then boil down to 2 cups. (Substitute chicken stock if you wish.)

3. Mince 2 cloves of garlic with a handful of fresh parsley leaves with a knife or in the food processor. Reserve on a plate. Smear mustard over the rabbit pieces and sprinkle on the mixture of parsley and garlic. (Resist the temptation to dip the mustard-coated rabbit into the parsley. There will be too much on the first pieces and not enough for the remaining pieces.)

4. Melt 2 tablespoons butter and 1 tablespoon oil in a 12″ cast-iron skillet over medium-high heat; sauté the rabbit for about 5 minutes or until it colors slightly. Transfer the rabbit to a plate. Pour 4 tablespoons vinegar in the skillet and bring the vinegar to a boil while you scrape the sides and bottom of the skillet for 1 minute. Transfer the rabbit back to the skillet; sprinkle 1 teaspoon salt and freshly ground pepper over the rabbit. Turn the heat down to medium-low; cover the rabbit with the cover slightly ajar.

5. During the cooking period of about 1½ hours, add 2 tablespoons of stock to the skillet as soon as the liquids at the bottom of the pan become syrupy. When the liquids become syrupy, turn the rabbit pieces around to get them evenly glazed with the liquid. When the rabbit is tender, remove it to a preheated platter.

6. Pour ½ cup rabbit stock in the skillet. Bring to a boil. Turn off the heat and whisk in the remaining 3 tablespoons butter, 1 tablespoon at a time. Strain the sauce into a sauceboat. (The debris left in the sieve is very good mixed in with fresh pasta.)

Chicken with Mustard, Valdrôme Style

Substitute 2 chickens for the rabbits. Cook for 1 hour at step 5.

Floating Island

Perhaps the most famous dessert of all times in France. Airy meringues float on top of light egg custard with a caramel sauce dribbled over the meringues. It is a feast for a king and for all of us other mortals.

Special instruction. The meringues, the egg custard, and the caramel sauce can be prepared a day ahead of time and refrigerated. The given amount of Floating Island can serve 8 people.

Special kitchen utensils.
Two 12″ cast-iron skillets.

MAKES 20 MERINGUES

> 6 egg whites
> 1 cup superfine sugar
> Crème Anglaise, page 360
> Caramel Sauce, page 361

1. Beat the egg whites semifirm
   in an electric mixer, then
   continue beating, dribbling
   in 1 cup sugar. Beat until the
   meringue is stiff and shiny
   and clinging to the whisk.

2. To speed the poaching, bring 2 quarts of water in each of two 12″ cast-iron skillets to just below the boil. Regulate the heat to keep the water quivering at all times during the poaching. With a soup spoon or ice cream scoop, scoop out a mound of meringue and tap the spoon against the side of the skillet to make the meringue fall into the water. The skillet is big enough for approximately 6 meringues. Poach in barely quivering water for 8 minutes on one side, shaking the pans once in a while, then carefully turn them over with a perforated skimmer and poach for 5 more minutes. Drain them carefully on a clean dish towel and let cool. (While cooling, the meringues will deflate a bit.)

3. Remove the meringues very gently from the towel (they tend to stick a bit) and transfer them to a baking dish or dishes, placing the meringues next to each other without stacking them. Cover with plates, but not plastic wrap, which creates humidity and will soften the meringues too much. Refrigerate.

4. Prepare the Crème Anglaise, page 360, and the Caramel Sauce, page 361.

5. *To present the dessert.* In a lovely large crystal bowl, pour the egg custard, then float several meringues on top and dribble on about 3 tablespoons caramel sauce. Serve the remaining meringues in a bowl and the remaining caramel sauce in a sauceboat. Or, ladle 3–4 tablespoonfuls of egg custard in individual plates or bowls. Add 2 meringues and dribble 1–2 tablespoons caramel sauce over the meringues. Serve with cookies of your choice. I suggest Ladyfingers, page 278, or Almond Cookies, page 361.

Crème Anglaise: A Light Egg Custard

A perfectly made Crème Anglaise is the mark of an experienced cook. It must be neither too thin nor too thick; only experience is the judge. The consistency of the custard resembles that of eggnog. In fact, you can drink this custard in lieu of eggnog. Add 2 tablespoons rum instead of vanilla extract and sprinkle nutmeg over it. The custard can be flavored with any extract or liqueur. The custard is great on Chocolate Cake, page 154, or Apple Charlotte, page 101, and is a part of Floating Island.

Special instruction. Cook the custard with care, since there is no flour to stabilize the yolks. They will curdle if they are cooked too fast and reach the boiling point. The custard can be made a day ahead of time and refrigerated.

Special kitchen utensil. A mercury candy thermometer.

MAKES ABOUT 1 QUART

½ cup superfine sugar	1 tablespoon vanilla extract or
2½ cups milk	¼ vanilla bean, split in half
	6 egg yolks

1. Combine sugar and milk in a 2½-quart heavy-bottomed saucepan and bring it to a boil to dissolve the sugar. Turn off the heat and transfer the milk to a medium-size bowl. Add 1 tablespoon vanilla extract or the vanilla bean, cover, and let cool for 15 minutes.

2. Wash the saucepan and break in 6 egg yolks (reserve the whites for poached meringues if you are planning to make a Floating Island, preceding recipe). Beat the egg yolks with a hand whisk, just to mix them thoroughly. Quickly whisk in the vanilla milk (vanilla bean removed) and cook over medium-low heat, stirring all the while, making a figure 8, scraping the bottom of the pan so the custard cooks evenly. It takes about 18 minutes. After 10 minutes or so when steam starts to escape from the liquids, test the temperature of the custard with a candy thermometer; the internal temperature should be 175°F., but not more. (Be sure not to touch the bottom of the pan with the thermometer, and stir the custard while you test the temperature, because the custard might register different temperatures in the center of the pan and on its sides.)

3. Pour the custard in a mixing bowl and dip the bowl in cold water to cool the custard. When cold, cover with plastic wrap and refrigerate.

Caramel Sauce

This is a liquid caramel to pour over Floating Island, page 358, or over vanilla ice cream.

Special instruction. The sauce can be kept for a month in a container refrigerated. Read the caramel technique, page 25, if unfamiliar.

Special kitchen utensil. An enameled steel pan or unlined caramel pan.

1 cup superfine sugar	¾ cup water

1. Have boiling water ready for the end of the next step.

2. Combine 1 cup of sugar and ¼ cup water in an enameled steel pan and bring slowly to a boil, stirring occasionally to dissolve the sugar. When the sugar is dissolved, it becomes a syrup that needs to cook for about 8 minutes (it will look like a boiling paste) over medium heat to start changing color. Continue cooking for another 2–3 minutes until the syrup, now a caramel, changes to a deep amber color. (During the cooking of the syrup, there will be a coating of sugar on the sides of the pan. With a brush dipped in water, first brush the sides of the pan, but don't worry if you can't keep the sides of the pan clean.)

3. When the caramel is deep amber, quickly pour in ½ cup boiling water and mix thoroughly into the caramel. It will spatter; be careful not to get burnt. Turn off the heat. Dip the bottom of the pan in cold water. Cool completely. Check the caramel sauce. When cold, it must still be fluid enough to pour.

4. In case the caramel is still too thick to pour, reheat it in a water bath until it is soft and mix in 2 more tablespoons of boiling water. Cool. Repeat this process until you have the right consistency.

Almond Cookies

These cookies are called Tuiles in French. They are almond cookies in the shape of a Roman roof tile. The preparation of the cookie batter is simple, but it must be very fluid to make a light and crunchy cookie. When the cookies are baked, you must work fast to transfer each cookie to a mold to shape them like rounded roof tiles. They are some of the best cookies in the world and worth the practice it involves to make them.

Special instruction. The batter must be fluid. To help spread the cookie batter very thinly, warm the cookie sheets. Do not double the recipe batter for more cookies, because the batter thickens too much while waiting to be shaped in cookies.

Special kitchen utensils. Two cookie sheets 14″ x 17″. A ring mold to shape the cookie or a long rolling pin; even a broom handle resting on the back of two chairs will do. A cookie jar like an old-time candy canister, with its mouth tilted and wide enough to fit the cookies into it, with metal clamps and a rubber seal to keep the cookies fresh and crisp, is ideal.

If you don't have a cookie jar specifically like the one I mention, and if you are making them ahead of time, don't shape the cookies. Leave them flat and then at the last minute before eating them, reheat them at 250°F. for 2–3 minutes. Then quickly take them out of the oven and shape them according to the instructions. It is very important to have crisp cookies; therein lies the secret of their great taste.

FOR ABOUT 24 COOKIES, 2½″ IN DIAMETER

3 tablespoons sweet butter	1 extra-large egg white
½ cup powdered sugar	About ½ cup heavy cream
2 tablespoons all-purpose flour	About ⅓ cup almond shavings

Preheat oven to 250°F.

1. Butter 2 very clean cookie sheets. It is very important that the cookie sheets do not stick when the cookies are baking; otherwise, it will be practically impossible to scoop them up.

2. Melt 3 tablespoons butter. When melted, let stand in the saucepan. The milky particles will fall to the bottom of the pan. Use only the butter on top, which is clarified.

3. Sift ½ cup powdered sugar in a fine-mesh sieve over a medium-size mixing bowl. Sift 2 tablespoons flour on waxed paper and reserve.

4. Beat 1 egg white until frothy with a fork in a mixing bowl.

5. Heat 2 greased cookie sheets in the oven until very warm, but not burning hot. (If it is hot, the batter cooks before having time to spread out.)

6. Quickly pour the egg white into the sugar and whisk until smooth, then add half the flour. Scoop out 2 tablespoons of clarified butter, add it to the mixture, and mix quickly. Then finish mixing the batter with the remaining flour and the remaining clarified butter. Start pouring heavy cream to thin out the batter to almost a fluidlike consistency (use about half of the cream).

Turn up oven heat to 325°F.

7. Very quickly, test the cookie batter: Spread ½ tablespoon of the batter on a warm cookie sheet. It should spread to about a 2½″ in diameter circle. If it does not, add a bit more cream to the batter. Spread about 8–9 cookies per cookie sheet, leaving space between the cookies. Sprinkle

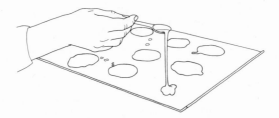

almond shavings on each cookie. Bake on the middle and middle-top racks of the oven for about 10–15 minutes. Check them once in a while; they must turn lightly golden.

8. While the cookies are baking, have on hand a ring mold or a long rolling pin or a broom handle secured to two chairs to shape the cookies, and a wide and thin steel spatula to scoop up the cookies.

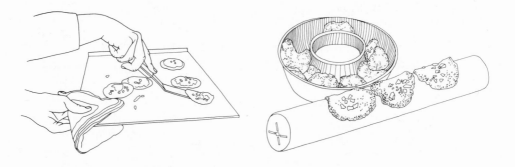

9. When baked, place 1 cookie sheet on the opened oven door to keep cookies from hardening too fast while you transfer the cookies of the second cookie sheet upside down, the almond side against the bottom of the ring mold, or place the cookies almond side up on a rolling pin or a broom handle. You must work very fast; the cookies at the contact of air will harden very quickly and become very brittle. Proceed with the next cookie sheet.

10. Scrape the cookie sheets clean and butter them again, if necessary. Thin out the batter with more cream and proceed with more cookies.

11. Serve right away or keep in a cookie jar.

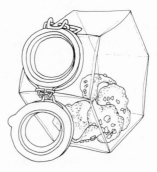

Note. Sometimes the cookies will run together on the cookie sheet. When baked, just cut them apart with the edge of the spatula and scoop them out.

TECHNIQUES AND UTENSILS INTRODUCED

How to make a basic fish stock

How to clarify stock

How to use puff pastry with 6 turns for small
pâtés en croûte

How to peel chestnuts using a chestnut knife

How to tenderize a goose and roast it for crispy skin,
and how to carve it

How to make mincemeat for immediate use

How to make pickled peach vinegar

How to make and store ladyfinger meringues

Lesson 19

RECIPES

Fish Stock

Oyster Soup

Hot Chicken Consommé

Hot Individual Pâtés en Croûte

Leek Gratin

Braised Chestnuts

Chestnut Purée

My Aunt's Turkey with Meat Stuffing

Poached and Roasted Goose

Mincemeat

Mincemeat Pie

Chestnut Meringue Cake

Suggested Menus for Lesson 19

Thanksgiving Dinner

Oyster Soup

My Aunt's Turkey with
Meat Stuffing

Braised Chestnuts

Leek Gratin

Mincemeat Pie

Alternate Thanksgiving Dinner

Hot Chicken Consommé

Hot Individual Pâtés en Croûte

Poached and Roasted Goose
without stuffing

Yellow Turnip Purée
(Lesson 10)

Hot Mincemeat

Chestnut Meringue Cake

Another Thanksgiving Menu

Cheese Soufflé
(Lesson 7)

Preserved Duck
(Lesson 14)

Mashed Potatoes, Country Style
(Lesson 6)

Apricot and Prune Tart
with Almond Butter Filling
(Lesson 16)

Fish Stock

I buy Whiting, a nonoily, soft-fleshed fish without any pronounced odor, for my fish stock, you can add leftover bones and skins from a broiled or baked fish. To make a less expensive fish stock, ask for 4 pounds of bones and heads of *very fresh-smelling* flounders, soles, or whitings. Do not use any oily fish, such as mackerel or blue fish. You must be sure that all the blood from the gills has been removed, as it gives a bitter taste. You may use the head, provided it is thoroughly cleaned out. (The coagulated blood around the gills looks about like chicken liver and is found just behind the head.)

When making fish stock, the ratio of fish to water is: 2 pounds fish or fish bones to 1 quart water.

MAKES ABOUT 6 CUPS STOCK

4 pounds whiting fish (or fish
  bones and heads)
⅔ cup peelings and stems of
  mushrooms
1 medium-size onion, thinly sliced
1 rib celery, thinly sliced
A few leaves of celery
1 teaspoon dried thyme
1 bay leaf

2 teaspoons salt
⅛ teaspoon freshly ground black
  pepper
2 quarts cold water
½ cup dry white wine
Few drops of lemon juice, freshly
  squeezed
Several stems of fresh parsley

1. Put all the ingredients in a covered pan and bring to a boil very slowly. Skim the boiling surface. Then simmer for 45 minutes with the lid slightly ajar.

2. Strain the broth through 3 layers of cheesecloth. Mash the vegetables and debris to extract all the stock and flavor. Reduce to 6 cups.

3. Grind the debris in a food processor until all the bones are completely mashed and you will have a happy cat.

Oyster Soup

Eat northern oysters in the fall and winter months; Gulf oysters are ready from December onward. It is best to buy the oysters in the shell and have them shucked while you watch; otherwise, you may get yesterday's oysters or shucked oysters sold in containers. If the natural juice is milky in color, discard. *It should be clear juice.*

Special kitchen utensil. A 4-quart saucepan or Dutch oven.

SERVES 8

6 cups Fish Stock, page 367	5 egg yolks
4 tablespoons butter	½ cup heavy cream
3 tablespoons flour	Pinch of cayenne pepper
10 medium mushroom caps	Salt
2 dozen fresh oysters	Freshly ground black pepper
The oyster liquid	Buttered toast, page 328

1. Heat 6 cups of Fish Stock, page 367.

2. Melt 4 tablespoons butter in a heavy 4-quart saucepan or Dutch oven, then add 3 tablespoons flour. Whisk rapidly until the mixture bubbles, then whisk in 6 cups of hot fish stock. Quarter the mushroom caps (if very big, quarter once more) and add them to the stock. Simmer 30 minutes over medium-low heat, stirring occasionally. Can be prepared ahead of time to this point.

3. Reheat the soup base, if prepared ahead of time, and add the oysters (quartered, if you like) and the oyster liquid. Poach them at very low heat for 10 minutes with the pan covered. Remove the oysters and mushrooms to a warm soup tureen.

4. At this point, reduce heat under the soup base so that it is *not* boiling. *The soup must not boil at this stage—that would curdle it.* Mix 5 egg yolks with ½ cup heavy cream. Add a pinch of cayenne. Carefully mix in ½ cup of the hot soup base, whisking steadily, to warm up the eggs and cream. Then add the mixture to the soup, whisking steadily. Whisk over low heat until the soup lightly coats a spoon. Again, be sure not to let the soup boil. (This takes about 5 minutes.) Taste and correct seasonings with salt and freshly ground pepper. Pour into the soup tureen.

5. Serve with buttered toast, page 328.

Hot Chicken Consommé

This consommé is a clarified chicken stock. It is a glorified chicken soup enriched with Madeira if you wish. The stock must be reduced to be rich in flavor, not watery. The clarification of the stock is tricky—a technique you need to practice to master. There are many different ways to clarify, but it is with experience you learn to do it. I have a friend who was sick with colds most of a winter, who lived on this consommé. It is a pleasure to drink it both from aesthetic and gustatory points of view. On very cold days, I like to serve a cup of consommé before a special dinner. It is very festive.

Special instructions. The consommé can be prepared a day or two before the dinner. Clarify small quantities at a time; no more than 5 cups at a time. It will be easier to control the clarification.

Special kitchen utensils. A 3-quart pot (avoid aluminum); cheesecloth.

SERVES 4–6

5 cups rich Chicken Stock, page 74	2 egg whites
2 teaspoons salt	2 cloves
¾ cup coarsely minced greens of leeks or minced parsley	2 peppercorns
	2 tablespoons dry Madeira (optional)

1. Prepare the stock according to the recipe, page 74, adding 2 teaspoons salt. Taste the stock; reduce it if necessary until rich in taste. Refrigerate it overnight. The next morning remove all the fat at the top of the stock.

2. Reheat the stock to warm in a 3-quart pot (an enameled steel pan does very well—do not use an aluminum pan; it gives a metallic taste to the consommé).

3. In a medium-size mixing bowl, mix the minced leeks or parsley with 2 egg whites, 2 cloves, and 2 peppercorns. Beat the mixture with a whisk for a minute until the egg whites are frothy.

4. Pour the mixture on top of the warm (not hot) stock, whisking briskly over medium heat until the stock is brought to a boil. The egg whites should be frothy on top of the stock all the while. Lower the heat—do not whisk—and cook for 30 minutes. The surface should barely quiver. The egg whites cook and act as a magnet for all the impurities in the stock and are caught into them until they look like a grayish blanket. (If the egg whites do not froth at the beginning of the cooking, they disintegrate in the stock; continue the cooking as if they had frothed and strain through many layers of cheesecloth. Let the consommé rest. If there are impurities left, they generally fall to the bottom of the bowl. Scoop out the clear broth or reclarify with 2 egg whites, but do not add more leeks or parsley which would give too strong a flavor to the broth.)

5. Strain the clarified broth through several layers of cheesecloth or a cotton dish towel lined in a strainer by pouring the broth very carefully with the lid over the pan to catch the blanket of egg whites (they will be discarded). Now you should have a lovely deep amber-colored consommé. Taste for seasonings, and add dry Madeira if you wish. Reheat. Serve in teacups.

Hot Individual Pâtés en Croûte

I am not generally overly fond of pâtés wrapped in a pastry dough (en croûte) and eaten cold. I always find the crust to be devoid of taste and greasy. But a pâté baked in pastry and eaten as soon as it comes out of the oven is delicious. I like to bake the pâtés either in two layers of Puff Pastry or in Shortcrust Pastry. This recipe is for pâtés in Puff Pastry. For pâtés baked in Shortcrust Pastry, see page 87.

Special instruction. The stuffing, as well as the pastry dough, is prepared ahead of time. They can be assembled and refrigerated or frozen for several hours before baking them.

Special kitchen utensil. A cookie sheet 14" x 17".

MAKES 15 INDIVIDUAL PÂTÉS

3 tablespoons minced scallions	3 tablespoons sweet butter
1 tablespoon minced parsley	or rendered chicken, goose,
1 tablespoon fresh tarragon	or duck fat
or ½ teaspoon dried	¼ teaspoon salt
½ pound mushrooms	Freshly ground black pepper
¼ pound hot Italian sausage	
¼ pound mild Italian sausage	Puff Pastry with 6 turns, page 296
¼ cup stale bread	
¼ cup chicken stock	Egg glaze: 1 egg mixed with
	1 tablespoon water

1. *The stuffing.* Mince 3 tablespoons scallions and keep in a small pile. Mince 1 tablespoon parsley and 1 tablespoon fresh tarragon or add ½ teaspoon dried tarragon and reserve in a second pile. Mince the mushrooms and reserve in a third pile. Remove the casing of the sausages, and chop coarsely. Reserve in the fourth pile. Mash ¼ cup stale bread with ¼ cup stock and reserve. Now you are ready to cook.

2. Melt 3 tablespoons butter or fat in a 12" cast-iron skillet. Stir in the scallions over low heat and cook covered for 5 minutes; avoid burning them. Uncover, raise the heat to medium-high, and add the minced mushrooms; sauté them, shaking the pan once in a while, until the liquids have evaporated (about 5 minutes). Add the sausages, mashed bread, parsley, tarragon, salt, and pepper. Mix all the ingredients and cook over medium heat for 5 more minutes. Taste and correct seasonings with salt. Cool in a fine-mesh sieve over a mixing bowl to drain the fat. Refrigerate the stuffing until very cold.

3. Sprinkle flour on a pastry surface and rolling pin. Roll out the Puff Pastry to a 17" x 14" rectangle. Freeze on a baking sheet covered with waxed paper for 20 minutes to firm up the dough.

4. Cut the edges with a knife in a straight line, using a ruler to guide you, leaving cut edges all around the rectangle (illustration, page 317). Refrigerate the trimmings for Sugar Cookies (Palmiers), page 302. Cut the dough into 30 little rectangles, cutting 6 equal strips crossways, then cutting 5 equal strips lengthwise. If the dough becomes too soft, freeze to firm up, then transfer half (15) of the small rectangles to a second baking sheet. Refrigerate half the rectangles while you work with the other half.

5. Place about 2 tablespoons pâté stuffing in the center of 15 small rectangles. Brush water around the edges on the pastry. Refrigerate 15 minutes to firm up the dough.

6. With your thumb, stretch the center of each remaining rectangle for the top to create a small concave shape to fit over the stuffing. Stick a top on each rectangle with stuffing, pressing gently all around the sides. Freeze 20 minutes, then trim the top and bottom rectangles. With the back of a knife blade, draw small lozenges.

7. Freeze for several hours before baking the pâtés. This makes them puff better.

   Preheat oven to 425°F.

8. Brush an egg, mixed with 1 tablespoon water, over the tops. Bake the pâtés on the middle shelf of the oven for 20 minutes, then drop the temperature to 400°F. and bake 10–15 minutes. If the tops brown too fast, cover loosely with foil. Serve hot.

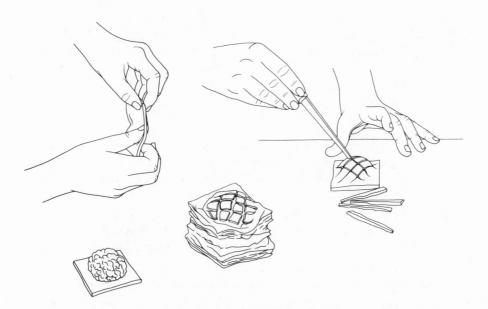

Note on extra stuffing. There will be more stuffing than necessary. Stuff omelets with it or serve the stuffing over croutons, or it is especially good over toasted Brioche.

Small Hot Pâté Turnovers

1. Prepare one batch of Shortcrust Pastry, page 87.

2. To shape and bake the turnovers, follow the recipe for Blackberry Jam Turnovers, page 137, but substitute pâté stuffing for the jam.

Leek Gratin

I love leeks. In France, there are generally two harvests, one in late spring and early summer when the leeks are small and most of the green parts can be used along with the whites; and a winter harvest with much bigger leeks whose greens are kept for stocks as an aromatic vegetable.

Special instructions. In the following recipe, I use winter leeks, puréed, then mixed with a béchamel sauce and gratinéed in the oven. It can be prepared ahead of time and baked when needed. Leeks have a very subtle flavor when cooked, so they should not be eaten too hot. They accompany steaks, veal, and pork dishes very well.

Special kitchen utensil. A 2-quart baking dish.

SERVES 6

8 big winter leeks	2 tablespoons flour
1½ teaspoons salt	Freshly ground black pepper
2 cups milk	Pinch of nutmeg
½ cup heavy cream	2 eggs
2 tablespoons sweet butter	3 tablespoons grated Swiss cheese

1. Cut off the tough green leaves of the leeks and reserve them for stocks. Keep the light green-yellow leaves with the whites and split the white of leeks lengthwise to ½″ from the end. Wash very carefully under running cold water to remove any sand remaining.

2. Put the leeks in a large kettle and pour boiling water over them to cover. Add 1 teaspoon salt. Cover and simmer for 30–40 minutes or until the leeks are tender (pierce through with a cake tester; they should be very soft). Drain the leeks.

3. Purée leeks in the food processor for 1 minute, then (optional) force through a fine-mesh strainer (see pages 36–37 if unfamiliar with this tech-

nique) to remove stringy fibers which are not eliminated by the food processor.

4. Drain the leek purée in a fine-mesh sieve over a bowl for 30 minutes. Reserve the liquids to add to the béchamel.

5. *The béchamel.* Boil 2 cups milk with ½ cup heavy cream. Melt 2 tablespoons butter in a heavy saucepan, then whisk in 2 tablespoons flour. Pour the milk and heavy cream into the mixture and whisk very hard for 30 seconds to get a smooth texture. Add ½ teaspoon salt, freshly ground pepper, and a pinch of nutmeg. Cook over a low flame for 10 minutes, whisking once in a while. Add the leek liquid to the béchamel and continue cooking for 20 more minutes, whisking once in a while.

6. Mix the leek purée into the béchamel. Break 2 eggs into the mixture and mix thoroughly. Pour into a 2-quart greased baking dish and sprinkle 3 tablespoons grated cheese over it. Can be done ahead up to this point.

Preheat oven to 350°F.

7. Bake on middle shelf for 30 minutes or until golden light brown on top. Cool 10 minutes before eating. Leeks, like onions, are better eaten warm than hot.

Braised Chestnuts

I cannot imagine a Thanksgiving dinner without having chestnuts with roast turkey. November and December are chestnut months, when they are best. Like many good things, chestnuts are a lot of work. For this reason, I tested several brands of canned whole chestnuts. I was not pleased with them; their flavor was mostly gone. Only in the canned purée of chestnuts, Faugier brand, did the flavor remain. But for special occasions, such as Thanksgiving or Christmas, it is worth the special effort to peel chestnuts, especially since they can be peeled the day before the dinner.

Special kitchen utensils. A chestnut knife or a small paring knife and a 3-quart stainless-steel pot with a tight-fitting lid.

SERVES 8

1½ pounds chestnuts, peeled	1 teaspoon salt
Water to cover	Freshly ground black pepper
5 tablespoons turkey drippings	•

1. Cover the peeled chestnuts with water in a 3-quart pot, and cover the pot tightly. Simmer over medium-low heat until tender. They take a

long time to cook, about 30–45 minutes. Drain the chestnuts and transfer them to a skillet.

2. While the turkey is roasting, remove about 5 tablespoons drippings and pour over the chestnuts. Sprinkle on 1 teaspoon salt and freshly ground pepper, and stir the chestnuts around. Cover and let cook over low heat for 15 minutes. The chestnuts will break up in small pieces. Don't worry —it makes them taste better. Add more drippings if you wish the chestnuts to take on a glazed aspect. Reheat when needed.

Technique: To peel chestnuts

How do you tell a bad chestnut? Unfortunately, too late; it is when you are ready to peel it that you discover dark spots on the meat. For this reason, always buy more than you need.

On the rounded side of each chestnut, with a small sharp paring or chestnut knife, make a long X cut deep enough to go through the outer covering and brown skin underneath.

Cover the chestnuts with water and bring to a boil slowly in about 15–20 minutes. As soon as they begin to boil, remove them from the heat. Do not pour off the hot water. Pick out one chestnut and, holding it with a potholder, try peeling the shell and the inner skin. Both should slip off easily. Keep the other chestnuts in the hot water until you have finished peeling them all. If some of the chestnuts are difficult to peel, boil them some more. You can peel the chestnuts a day before the dinner.

Chestnut Purée

SERVES 8

1½ pounds chestnuts, peeled
1 cup chicken or turkey stock

4 tablespoons (½ stick) butter

When the chestnuts are cooked, purée in a food mill or food processor with about 1 cup chicken or turkey stock, just enough to moisten the purée. Taste and correct seasonings with salt and pepper. Reheat in a water bath. When the purée is hot, whisk 4 tablespoons sweet butter into the purée and serve.

My Aunt's Turkey with Meat Stuffing

This stuffing is a kind of country pâté, delicious cooked in the cavity of a turkey or a goose. A 12-pound turkey is roasted for 3 hours—2 hours at 350°F. and 1 hour at 250°F. The turkey stays moist with the thighs slightly undercooked to keep the breast meat tender and not dry and overcooked.

Special instruction. The turkey broth and the stuffing are prepared a day ahead of time.

Special kitchen utensil. An oven broiler pan.

SERVES 10

12-pound turkey

For the turkey broth

2 tablespoons chicken, goose, or duck fat or oil
Neck and gizzard of turkey
1 onion
1 carrot
1 rib celery
4 cups water
¼ teaspoon dried thyme
1 teaspoon salt
Freshly ground black pepper

For the meat stuffing

3 tablespoons chicken, goose, or duck fat or oil
3 onions, chopped
4 large cloves garlic, chopped

1 pound pork sausage
1 pound ground beef
¼ pound slab bacon sliced
3 slices of bread plus 1 slice to seal cavity
½ cup turkey broth
Liver of the turkey
Handful of fresh parsley
¼ teaspoon dried sage
¼ teaspoon dried thyme
1 teaspoon salt
Freshly ground black pepper
2 eggs
2 tablespoons brandy
1½ cups freshly grated Swiss cheese

10 tablespoons sweet butter for roasting

1. *The broth.* Melt 2 tablespoons fat or oil in a 9″ cast-iron skillet over medium heat. When the fats are hot, sauté the neck and gizzard for 5 minutes until brown. Cut the onion, carrot, and celery in ¼″ slices, add them to the skillet, and continue browning, stirring the vegetables with the neck and gizzard. Cook for 10 minutes. Pour 4 cups of water over the meat and vegetables; add the thyme, salt, and pepper. Cover the skillet and cook over low heat for about 2 hours. Then boil the liquids down to 2 cups. Strain the broth and reserve for the stuffing and for cooking Chestnut Purée, page 374. Pick the meat from the neck and reserve for the stuffing. Reserve the gizzard.

2. *The stuffing.* Have on hand a 4-quart mixing bowl for the meats, bread, and seasonings. Melt 3 tablespoons fat in a 12″ cast-iron skillet. Sauté the chopped onions and garlic over medium heat for 15 minutes, occasionally stirring to avoid burning. When they are colored and soft like a marmalade, remove them with a large perforated spoon. Reserve in the mixing bowl.

3. In the small skillet, sauté the bacon until it browns. Transfer to the mixing bowl with a skimming spoon.

4. Remove the casings of the pork sausage and mix the sausage meat with the ground beef with a fork. Brown the meats in the skillet for 10 minutes. With a perforated spoon, transfer the meats to the mixing bowl.

5. In the same skillet, mash the 3 slices of bread and ½ cup turkey broth with a fork and cook for about a minute or two. Transfer to the mixing bowl.

6. Chop the turkey liver, but do not cook. Transfer to the mixing bowl.

7. Mince the parsley and put in the mixing bowl. Add the sage and thyme. Grind the contents of the bowl—all the meats, bread, onions, and herbs —in a grinder or in a food processor.

8. Transfer back to the mixing bowl. Add 1 teaspoon salt, freshly ground pepper, 2 eggs, 2 tablespoons brandy (or 2 tablespoons fat or butter), and the grated cheese. Refrigerate covered until the next day, or until the stuffing is totally cold.

9. Dry the cavity of the turkey and rub it well with 4 tablespoons butter. Pack the stuffing in the turkey cavity; finish with a slice of bread to cover the stuffing and the neck cavity. It can be done the eve of the dinner, if refrigerated.

Roasting the turkey

10. Remove turkey from the refrigerator to bring it back to room temperature (about 1 hour).

Preheat oven to 350°F.

11. Roast the turkey in the broiler pan of the oven. Grease the pan with 2 tablespoons butter. Place the turkey breast side up and spread the remaining 4 tablespoons butter over the breast of the turkey. Place the turkey on the middle shelf of the oven and roast 2 hours, basting with the drippings every half hour or so. Turn the pan around at least twice during this period.

12. Grease a piece of aluminum foil big enough to cover the turkey and to seal the pan with it. Lower the temperature to 250°F. Remove the pan from the oven, cover the turkey with the buttered foil, and crimp the foil tightly around the edges of the pan. Cook 1 more hour. Bring the pan juices to a boil, stirring to get up the caramelized drippings in the pan. Pour in a sauceboat.

13. *Carving the turkey.* Transfer the turkey to a big cutting board with a ridge around to catch the juices. Present at the table. Slice the breast meat crosswise on each side of the breastbone in ⅛" thick slices. Then cut the thighs and legs. Overlap the meat on a preheated platter. Remove the stuffing from the turkey and transfer to a preheated bowl.

Poached and Roasted Goose

Goose fat is gold. It is the whitest, silkiest-looking fat and it has a terrific flavor, very mild. I cherish goose fat and use it for any of my recipes wherever fat is mentioned, to brown vegetables or to enhance the flavor of country pâté. My favorite Christmas gift is to be given goose fat by neighbors or friends who cooked a goose and didn't know what to do with their goose fat.

Some specialty stores will sell goose fat around Christmastime (for instance, in New York, Schaller & Weber Pork Store, at 1654 Second Avenue, has it).

Fat freezes very well and also keeps in the refrigerator for long periods of time as long as it is hermetically closed (a plastic container is fine).

Many a time the breast of a roasted goose is dry and tough, especially with frozen goose. Poaching the goose first, then roasting it, will give a much more tender meat. This is the technique used by the Hutterites, a German Anabaptist sect, who live in South Dakota; the foremost producers of geese, they have a great reputation among poultry raisers in the United States.

Special kitchen utensils. A 15-quart stockpot with a lid; a broiler pan 16" x 16" or roasting pan 12" x 16" x 1½".

SERVES 8

12-pound goose   ½ cup stock or water
Salt   Freshly ground black pepper
Meat stuffing, page 375   1 slice of bread
7 tablespoons sweet butter

1. Put the goose in a 15-quart stockpot. Cover with boiling water; add 2 tablespoons salt. Bring back to a boil and simmer, with the water barely quivering, for 1 hour.

2. Drain the goose in a colander. The goose broth can be used to cook pasta or beans. Remove the fat at top of liquid (about 4 cups). Keep the "pristine" fat in the freezer to use for preserves like Preserved Duck or Goose, pages 268–270.

Preheat oven to 350°F.

3. Stuff goose with the meat stuffing, finish with a slice of bread, page 376, step 9 (there will be leftover stuffing; see Note at the end of recipe). Place the goose, breast side up, in a greased broiler pan, rub it with 1½ teaspoons salt, smear 4 tablespoons butter over the breast, and roast on the middle rack of the oven until the goose is golden brown (about 1½–2 hours). Prick the skin occasionally so that the fat will run out. Remove the rendered fat, leaving ¼ cup in the pan to baste the goose.

4. *To carve the goose.* Transfer the goose to a cutting board with a juice catcher. First detach the thighs from the body, cutting through the skin with a knife, then hold on to the leg and twist the leg and thigh out of the hip socket found next to the backbone above the tail. With a sharp knife, sever the legs from the thighs at the joint. Bone the breast on each side of the breastbone as for a chicken, see illustration, pages 96–97, and slice the breast meat in several pieces.

5. Remove all the fat possible from the juices in the pan and reserve in a container for storage, to brown potatoes, for example.

6. Check for and remove with a spoon the burnt particles at the bottom of the roasting pan, then reheat the remaining drippings with ½ cup stock or water, scraping the sides and bottom of the pan to get up the drippings, and bring to a boil. Boil for 1 minute, then off the flame, whisk in 3 tablespoons butter, 1 tablespoon at a time. Taste and correct seasonings with salt and pepper.

Note on the remaining meat stuffing. Make a pâté. Line a 3-cup loaf pan with fresh fatback. Fill the pan with the filling, cover with fatback, and cover the pan with foil. Place in a pan with simmering water (a water bath) and cook 1 hour in a 375°F. oven. Unmold pâté when cold. To serve, slice the pâté and remove the fat.

Mincemeat

When I got married, I had no idea what mincemeat was and tasted like. I became a fast learner with my mother-in-law's mincemeat. She is very proud of her mincemeat recipe, handed down to her by her mother, who, in turn, learned to make it from her mother. It is delicious with a roasted fowl or venison or in Mincemeat Pie. It is also delicious as soon as it is made.

Special instructions. My mother-in-law writes in a letter to me: "My dear Lydie: Since you expressed a desire for the recipe for mince meat, I have written it off in the original form which my mother used to use—the one in 'bowls.' I've watched, and helped, many times to assemble the ingredients and put it together, else I never would have been able to get it into anything like definite quantities. It is yet something of a taste process, but it usually comes out pretty good. . . .

"When the meat is purchased, have your meat cutter take out all bones and all fat. Then you know just how much meat you will have. . . . I always buy neck meat. It has a tendency to be stringy, but it does have to be ground so that makes no difference, and the flavor is very good. I never use anything but beef meat.

"*Apples*. I usually make this mince meat up in October, when the good Jonathan apples are on the market. They have a good flavor and are nice, juicy and tart. Save that juice that drips out of your grinder, and use it. You can use any good tart apple. They are to be peeled, and cored.

"I usually start assembling the ingredients about a week before I am to make the mince meat. Get the currants and raisins, wash them (I know they are supposed to be cleaned, but they are always gritty). Let them dry and you can put them in plastic bags until you are ready to use them. Get the cider and have it boiled down. It can be put in a jar and stored in the refrigerator. It is so much less work to do a little in advance. . . .

"It is a very flexible recipe at least for me, but it is fun to get a good finished product and while it is lots of work, it is very rewarding. So few people make it any more."

Special kitchen utensil. A 6½-quart Dutch oven.

Technique: To make Pickled Peach Vinegar

Drain 1 can (2½ pounds) cling peaches and combine with ¾ cup sugar, ½ cup cider vinegar, 2 sticks of cinnamon, 1 teaspoon whole cloves, and 1 teaspoon whole allspice in a 2-quart saucepan. Bring to a boil and boil for 5 minutes until the sugar is dissolved, stirring once in a while with a wooden spoon. Cool and reserve in a covered jar. Refrigerate for several weeks.

FOR 2 QUARTS MINCEMEAT

1½ pounds beef neck (boned
   and trimmed)
1 quart boiling water
¼ pound beef suet
½ tablespoon salt
1 quart apple cider
2½ pounds apples
10-ounce package dark raisins
10-ounce package currants
½ tablespoon ground nutmeg
2 teaspoons ground allspice

2 teaspoons ground cloves
2½ teaspoons ground cinnamon
1½ teaspoons ground mace
1½ cups sugar
½ cup light molasses
½ cup Pickled Peach Vinegar
   (see above)
¼ cup cider vinegar
¼ cup red table wine
½ cup dry sherry

1. Cut the meat in cubes. Pour 1 quart boiling water over the meat and the suet in a stockpot. Add ½ tablespoon salt. Bring the water to a boil. Remove any scum that may appear on the surface. With the cover ajar, simmer with the water quivering for 1½ hours or until tender. Remove the suet after 1 hour. Reserve the meat and suet covered with their own broth. Refrigerate. Can be done a day ahead of time.

2. Boil 1 quart of cider down to half its original volume (2 cups).

3. Next day: Discard the fat on the meat broth. Reserve the broth. Grind the meat and suet coarsely. Measure 3 cups.

4. Peel, core, and quarter 2½ pounds of apples. Dice the apples to ¼″ cubes. Pour a cup of water over the apple peels and cores in a kettle. Bring it to a boil. Cover and simmer gently for 20 minutes. Drain the juice and reserve for later.

5. In a 6½-quart Dutch oven, assemble meat, suet, apples, currants, raisins, and all the ground spices. With your hands, mix all the ingredients. Then add 1½ cups sugar, ½ cup molasses, 1 cup of meat broth, 2 cups reduced apple cider, ½ cup Pickled Peach Vinegar, ¼ cup cider vinegar, ¼ cup red table wine, ½ cup dry sherry, and drained apple juice from the peels.

6. Cook mincemeat covered for about 2–3 hours over medium-low heat. Every 20 minutes or so stir the mincemeat, to be sure it does not scorch.

7. *To can the mincemeat.* Read the instructions for canning tomato sauce, page 148, and proceed the same way. When the hot mincemeat is poured into the canning jars and the tops are put on, it is generally not necessary to boil the filled jars; the tops, within 24 hours at room temperature, will have sealed. To tell if a top is sealed, with your index finger push down on the center of the top. It should not spring back. If after 24 hours it should spring back, refrigerate and eat within a month.

Mincemeat Pie

Special kitchen utensil. A 10″ pie pan.

SERVES 6–8

1 quart Mincemeat
2 tablespoons rum
Shortcrust Pastry, page 87
4 apples

Glaze: 1 tablespoon milk mixed
with 1 tablespoon sugar
Whipped Cream, page 28

1. Transfer 1 quart of mincemeat to a mixing bowl and let stand overnight mixed with 1 tablespoon rum.

2. Prepare the pie dough according to the recipe, page 87. Cut the dough in 2 unequal pieces, a bigger piece to roll out for the bottom and a smaller piece for the top. Roll out the dough following the illustrated technique, page 88. Line the pan with the dough. Prick the bottom. Line the dough with foil, crimping the sides tightly. Refrigerate until needed.

3. Peel and core 4 apples and cut into ⅛″ thick slices.

Preheat oven to 350°F.

4. Bake the pie shell for 15 minutes. Remove the foil and bake 3–4 minutes more to dry out the bottom of the pie. Fill the pie with the mincemeat. Decorate the pie with apple slices, overlapping them in a coil design. Brush with 1 tablespoon milk mixed with 1 tablespoon sugar. Bake for 35 minutes or until the apples are slightly golden. Cool to warm and serve with Whipped Cream. Add 1 tablespoon rum to the Whipped Cream, but do not sweeten—the mincemeat is sweet enough.

Chestnut Meringue Cake

I make this dessert for Thanksgiving and Christmas holidays with fresh chestnuts; any other time, I use unsweetened chestnut purée from Faugier called Purée de Marrons Nature (unsweetened). It is widely available in the United States (to order by mail, if necessary, write to: Maison Glass, 52 East 58th Street, New York, NY 10022). This chestnut meringue cake is a frozen chestnut–butter cream mousse, decorated with meringues in the shape of ladyfingers and served with a chocolate sauce. It is rich, delicious, and very festive.

Special instructions. You need to anticipate for this dessert. Allocate the work to different days. For instance, bake the meringues a week or two beforehand and keep them in a glass jar with a ring top, see page 363. If you are using fresh chestnuts, cook them two days ahead of time and refrigerate. Prepare the butter cream and chestnut mousse a day ahead of time, then freeze. Finish the decoration with the meringues and the chocolate sauce the day of the dinner.

Special kitchen utensil. A 6-cup charlotte or soufflé mold.

Note on ovens. Gas ovens tend to color the meringue cookies more than an electric oven. Convection ovens are great to dry the meringues.

SERVES 8–10

6 egg whites	Butter Cream, page 252
½ teaspoon lemon juice	3 tablespoons dark rum
¾ cup superfine sugar	3 ounces bitter sweet chocolate
1 pound chestnuts or 15½-ounce	¼ cup water
unsweetened chestnut purée	4 tablespoons sweet butter
About 2 cups milk	

1. Grease 2 cookie sheets and dust them with flour. With your index finger, trace 3½″ long lines with 1″ space between the lines on the prepared cookie sheets. Fit a ½″ tube into a large pastry bag, twist the bag over the top of the tube, and push the twisted part of the bag inside the tube to eliminate the air. Now you are ready to make the meringues.

2. In a heavy-duty mixer or with a hand mixer, beat 3 egg whites with ½ teaspoon lemon juice and with 3 tablespoons sugar taken from the ¾ cup. First beat at low speed for 1 minute, then medium speed for another minute, and finally at the highest speed for about 3–5 minutes. The egg whites are ready when they cling to the whisk when the beating is over.

3. Quickly pour the rest of the sugar on top of the egg whites; then with a rubber spatula, cut into the egg white mass and mix the sugar into it while turning the bowl all the while in less than 10 seconds. Don't worry if the sugar does not seem to be totally mixed into the egg whites because the more mixing you do, the quicker the egg whites will deflate and get runny instead of staying very stiff.

Preheat oven to 200°–225°F.

4. Fill the pastry bag with the egg whites. Untwist the bag from inside the tube. Push the egg whites down to the tube, closing the top of the pastry

bag by twisting it. Squeeze from the top of the bag with one hand while holding the bag with the other hand perpendicular to the cookie sheet and, holding the bag 1″ away from the cookie sheet, pipe the meringue over the lines on the cookie sheet.

5. Bake on the middle shelf of the oven for about 1½ hours. Loosen the meringues very gently with a long steel spatula. Turn off the oven and let dry completely. The meringues might stick to your cookie sheet when totally dry. *To unstick:* Place the cookie sheet on top of the stove on very low heat, just enough for the sugar which is sticking to the bottom of the meringues to slightly melt and to be able to pry them loose with a spatula. Reserve frozen or in a cookie jar (illustration, page 363).

6. *For fresh chestnut purée.* When the chestnuts are peeled (see page 373 for technique), chop them coarsely, place in a 3-quart stainless-steel pan, and cover them with about 2 cups milk. Cover and cook over medium heat until the chestnuts are soft (about 45 minutes). Check them once in a while and add milk to the chestnuts if required. Purée the chestnuts in a food mill or a food processor. Refrigerate until needed.

   For canned chestnut purée. Transfer the purée to a mixing bowl, and beat air into it with a whisk to smooth it out.

7. *The Butter Cream.* Follow the recipe, page 252, but fold in the chestnut purée and 2 tablespoons dark rum instead of the crystallized ginger.

8. Beat 3 egg whites until stiff and fold one-third of the beaten egg whites into the chestnut–butter cream mousse. Then fold the mixture back into the remaining beaten egg whites, folding quickly but gently with a rubber spatula without deflating the mixture.

9. Grease a 6-cup charlotte or soufflé mold with corn or almond oil. Pour the mixture into the mold. Cover and freeze overnight.

10. The day of the dinner: Unmold the frozen mousse (dip the mold in hot water for 10 seconds) several hours before dinner. Cut one end of each meringue so it is flat and stick each meringue to the mousse side by side. The top of each meringue should be just flush with the top of the mousse. Put the cake back in the freezer.

11. Refrigerate the cake 1 hour before eating it to soften it.

12. *The chocolate sauce.* Melt the chocolate in a small pan set in a water bath, then add ¼ cup water and 1 tablespoon rum. Off the flame, whisk in 4 tablespoons sweet butter, 1 tablespoon at a time. Reheat to tepid in water bath when needed. Ladle 2–3 tablespoons chocolate sauce over the top of the cake and serve the remaining sauce in a sauceboat.

TECHNIQUES AND UTENSILS INTRODUCED

How to make croissants: hand method,
food processor method, electric mixer method

How to make sausage without casings

How to wrap sausage in brioche dough to bake
in a 4-cup loaf pan

How to prepare mussels

How to wrap and decorate a fish in puff pastry

How to prepare fish or chicken forcemeat

How to make coffee liqueur

How to make ice cream without a machine

How to make madeleines in a madeleine mold

Lesson 20

Suggested Menus for Lesson 20

Breakfast

Cheese Omelets
(Lesson 14)

Croissants

Homemade Preserves
(Lesson 4)

Winter Brunch

Hot Chicken Consommé
(Lesson 19)

Sole Mousse with Mussels and Spinach

Apple and Prune Tart with
Almond Butter Filling
(Lesson 16)

Home-Style Dinner

Country-Style Sausage with
Mustard Sauce

Mashed Potatoes, Country Style
(Lesson 6)

Caramel Custard (Lesson 3)

Winter Dinner

Crudités:
Celery Root Rémoulade
Grated Red Cabbage
Grated Carrots
(Lesson 3)

Mussel Stew

Chocolate Sunflower
(Lesson 2)
with Crème Anglaise
(Lesson 18)

Sunday Brunch

Sausage in Brioche with
Mustard Sauce

Chachouka: Poached Eggs
on Green Peppers and Tomatoes
(Lesson 11)

Chocolate Fudge Cake
(Lesson 8)

Summer Brunch

Cold Fresh Tomato Soup
(Lesson 17)

Baked Stuffed Sole Fillets
with a Sorrel Sauce

Steamed Broccoli and Carrots
(Lesson 16)

Plum Tart (Lesson 13)

Winter Home-Style Dinner

Mussel Soup

Roast Chicken with Vegetables
(Lesson 1)

Baked Apples on Toast
(Lesson 3)

For a Lunchbox

Mussel Salad

For Tea Time

Madeleines or
Croissant Rolls Stuffed
with Chocolate

Croissants

You can make really good croissants at home. The process is time-consuming, but not laborious. There is only about an hour and a half of work involved (no more than 30 minutes at a time), but you need a 24-hour head start.

Special instruction. This is a timetable for serving croissants for Sunday brunch at noon.

Stages	Time	Amount of work
1: Steps 1–6	Friday evening	15 minutes
2: Steps 7–9	Saturday morning	20 minutes
3: Step 10	Saturday afternoon	10 minutes
4: Steps 11–13	Sunday—9:30 A.M.	30 minutes
5: Step 14	Sunday—10:30 A.M.	2 minutes

Special kitchen utensils. Two 11″ x 16″ x 1″ jelly-roll pans.

MAKES 16 CROISSANTS

2¼ cups all-purpose unbleached
   flour plus 3 tablespoons
1 cup milk
2 teaspoons dry yeast or 0.6 ounce
   fresh yeast (1 package)
3 tablespoons sugar

1 teaspoon salt
12 tablespoons sweet butter
¼ cup milk to brush over
   croissants
Glaze: 1 egg yolk mixed with
   1 tablespoon milk

Stage 1

1. Measure 2¼ cups flour and reserve in a 1-quart mixing bowl.

2. Warm 1 cup milk to tepid. Dissolve the yeast with ¼ cup of the tepid milk in a 1-cup glass measure and mix it along with 2 tablespoons flour from the measured flour. With a small whisk blend the flour into the liquid until no lumps remain. Cover with plastic wrap and let rise until double in size in a warm place (about 15–20 minutes). If it does not double in size, the yeast is dead. Start over again with a brand-new package of yeast.

3. Keep the remaining ¾ cup milk in a warm water bath until the sponge has doubled in size.

4. Mix 3 tablespoons sugar and 1 teaspoon salt into the measured flour (don't mix the salt and sugar beforehand; otherwise, the salt in the flour might kill the yeast when you use the 2 tablespoons of flour to make the sponge at step 2).

5. *Food processor method.* Secure the steel blade in the food processor

bowl. Add the flour to the sugar and salt. Add the risen yeast sponge and the remaining milk. Process for 20 seconds or so until the dough is smooth. It will not make a ball and should not. It will stay more like a gluey cake batter (see illustration, page 248). Continue with step 6.

Electric mixer method. Use a flat paddle or a dough hook. Transfer the risen yeast sponge and the remaining warm milk to the mixer's bowl. With the mixer at high speed, start incorporating 1 cup of flour, ¼ cup at a time, into the dough, then lower the speed to low-medium, to continue incorporating flour, 2 tablespoons of flour at a time. The dough must be sticky soft. Continue with step 6.

Hand method. With a wooden spoon, blend the remaining warm milk with the risen yeast sponge in a 4-quart mixing bowl. Then start incorporating flour 2 tablespoons at a time. The dough must remain soft. Continue with step 6.

6. Transfer the soft dough made either with food processor, electric mixer, or by hand into a 2-quart mixing bowl. Cover with plastic wrap and refrigerate in the least cold part of the refrigerator for 6 hours or overnight.

Stage 2

7. Cream 12 tablespoons sweet butter with the heel of your hand to incorporate 3 tablespoons flour to make a smooth, creamy, easily spread patty of butter.

8. Sprinkle the working surface with flour, place the cold dough on it, and turn the dough over in the flour to make it easier to roll it out (it will be sticky) into a rectangle about 6″ wide, 15″ long, without using any pressure on the rolling pin while rolling the dough out. Spread the very soft butter over the upper two-thirds of the dough, leaving a ½″ border around the top and sides. Smooth out the butter to uniform thickness with a metal spatula dipped in warm water.

9. Fold the dough like a business letter. At this point the dough will be very soft. If necessary, use a wide steel-blade spatula to help you fold the dough. Fold the bottom third up, and with a soft pastry brush clean off any loose flour clinging to the dough. Fold down the top third and again brush off excess flour. Square up the edges, stretching the dough with your hand. Turn the dough counterclockwise so it resembles a book with the open flap on the right. Again flour the working surface and rolling pin. Roll out the dough as before into a 6″ x 15″ rectangle and fold as before. Transfer the dough into a baking pan bowl, cover it tightly with plastic wrap (to create humidity), and refrigerate at least 4 hours in the least cold part of the refrigerator.

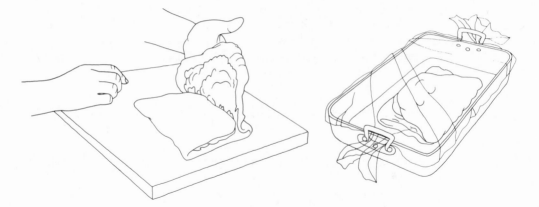

Stage 3

10. Roll out the dough 2 more times into a 6" x 15" rectangle and refrigerate at least 4 hours or overnight. Now the dough is ready to be shaped into croissants.

Stage 4

11. Remove the croissant dough from the refrigerator about 1½ hours before baking time. Butter 2 jelly-roll pans. Sprinkle flour on the working surface and with 1 of the corners of the square package of dough pointing directly at yourself, begin rolling the dough into a 16" circle. Roll a little, turn the dough ¼ turn, roll out a bit more, turn again ¼ turn, and continue until the square becomes a circle (or use your hands to stretch the dough into a circle). Work as rapidly as possible, always keeping a small amount of flour on the working surface to prevent sticking.

12. With a sharp knife, cut the circle into 4 quarters, then cut each quarter into 4 wedges. With both hands, roll each wedge into a croissant, rolling the wider piece first, finishing with the tip of the wedge. Do not curl

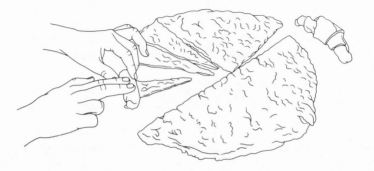

the ends in a croissant shape; if you do, the ends tend to burn while baking. Transfer the croissants on the prepared cookie sheets, leaving enough space between each croissant to rise. Be sure the pointed tip at the center of each croissant is on the bottom of the croissant; otherwise, the tip will open up the croissant while baking. Brush milk over croissants.

13. To help the croissants rise faster, turn on the oven to warm for 5 minutes. Turn it off and wait 2–3 minutes, then place the croissants in the barely warm oven to rise. Let them increase 50 percent in volume, not more; too much rising will cause them to fall during baking (about 30–45 minutes).

Stage 5

14. When ready to bake, remove the croissants from the warm oven.

    Preheat oven to 400°F.

15. Prepare the glaze with the egg yolk and milk and brush it over the croissants. Bake for about 15–20 minutes. Cover loosely with foil if they brown too fast. Transfer the croissants to a serving platter and let cool 30 minutes before eating.

Croissant Rolls Stuffed
with Chocolate

In France, children have a snack after school, around 4:00 P.M. It generally consists of bread with a piece of chocolate, or they may go to the bakery or pastry shop to buy a roll stuffed with chocolate. These rolls can be made with two different types of dough: either with the St. Tropez Cream Cake dough, page 247, or croissant dough, page 387. The croissant rolls are richer, with more butter in the dough, and I prefer them. They are called Petits Pains au Chocolat in French.

Special kitchen utensil. Two jelly-roll pans about 11″ x 16″ x 1″.

MAKES 14 ROLLS

Croissant dough, page 387	Glaze: 1 egg yolk mixed with
7½ ounces extra bittersweet	1 tablespoon milk and
chocolate (Lindt or Tobler)	2 tablespoons sugar

1. Follow the croissant recipe to the point where you are ready to shape the croissants, step 10 in the recipe, page 387.

2. Cut the chocolate in 14 pieces, each piece 3″ long.

3. Cut the croissant dough in half, lengthwise.

4. Roll out each piece to 21″ long and 6″ wide.

5. Cut the 21″ rectangle into 7 smaller rectangles each measuring 3″ x 6″.

6. Lay 1 piece of chocolate, 3″ long, crossways on the dough at one end and roll up the dough over the chocolate. The chocolate shows at both ends of the roll.

7. Transfer the rolls to 2 buttered jelly-roll pans. Brush the rolls with milk and let rise in a barely warm oven until they almost double in volume (about 30 to 45 minutes).

8. Prepare the glaze with the egg yolk, milk, and sugar and brush on the rolls just before baking.

   Preheat oven to 400°F.

9. Bake for about 15–20 minutes. Cool 30 minutes before eating.

Country-Style Sausage

You can make a very good homemade sausage using different meats and spices as long as you remember to follow these guidelines:

- The ratio of fat to meat in the sausage is 40 percent fat to 60 percent meat.
- For 2 pounds of meat mixed with fat, you need 1 tablespoon salt and (optional) a pinch of saltpeter—this preservative gives an attractive pinkish hue to the sausage. I recommend using it. Buy it in a drugstore or mail order from: Caswell-Massey Co. Ltd., 111 Eighth Avenue, New York, NY 10011. You can order 1–2-ounce bottles.

Special instructions. A sausage for poaching develops flavor while hanging for 2–3 days in a *ventilated* room, at 60°–65°F. temperature. I use a guest bedroom with cross ventilation. The ventilation is of the utmost importance in drying the sausage. Do not make sausages during the summer. It is a winter activity.

I make sausages rolled in cotton cheesecloth. With cheesecloth, you are not limited to the size of the casing; however, you must pack the meat very tightly—otherwise, when the sausage dries, it will shrink from the center and crumble when cooked. (If it does, the sausage is still very good, but not professional-looking.)

Special kitchen utensil. Cotton cheesecloth; if it is difficult to find in your area, order by mail. Write to: The Vermont Country Store, Weston, VT 05161.

MAKES 2 SAUSAGES 2½″ IN DIAMETER AND 7″ LONG, ABOUT 1¼ POUNDS EACH.

1½ pounds boned fresh pork picnic shoulder	⅛ teaspoon saltpeter (optional)
2 cloves garlic	2 cups chicken stock
½ teaspoon peppercorns	1 cup dry white wine
¾ pound fresh pork fatback	2 tablespoons minced white bulb
1 tablespoon salt	of scallions
4 tablespoons brandy	Mustard Sauce, page 396

1. Grind the meat and fat very coarsely. Chop 2 cloves of garlic medium coarse. Wrap ½ teaspoon peppercorns in waxed paper and, with a small hammer, hammer the peppercorns, crushing them coarsely. In a 2-quart mixing bowl, mix the ground meat, fat, garlic, 1 tablespoon salt, the crushed peppercorns, and 4 tablespoons brandy. Add the saltpeter if you wish. Using your clean hands, start mixing the meat and spices together until well blended. Make very tight meatballs.

2. *To shape the sausage in cheesecloth.* Use two triple-thickness pieces of cheesecloth about 12″ long and 10″ wide each. Pack the meatballs in the center of the cheesecloth, forming sausages 8″ long and about 2½″ in diameter. Wrap the sausage in the cheesecloth and tie very tightly at both ends, shaping the sausage round. Tie the body of the sausage like a rolled roast, with the string, circling the sausage about every inch or so.

3. Hang the sausage from a hook for 2 days in a ventilated cool room.

Preheat oven to 350°F.

4. In a 1-quart pan, like a pâté or loaf pan, cover the sausage with stock, wine, and minced scallions. Put the lid on and poach the sausage in the oven, still in its cheesecloth, for 30 minutes. Cool. Unwrap carefully. When removing the cheesecloth, pull gently to unstick the sausage.

5. Eat the sausage hot with a Mustard Sauce, page 396, or it can be baked in brioche, page 394.

Note on making sausages packed in pork casings. Write to Richard Kutas, The Sausage Maker, 177 Military Road, Buffalo, NY 14207, for sausage casings and sausagemaking apparatus. You must soak the casings in cold water with the tap running all night long to desalt the casings. Cut a piece of casing 16″ long. Slip one end of the casing onto the form of the sausage stuffer, tie the other end with string, and fill the horn with meatballs. Then push the plunger, filling the casing very tightly with no air bubbles until the sausage is about 8″ long. Tie the other end, being sure there are no more air bubbles left in the sausage.

Sausage in Brioche

To prepare this recipe, you must hunt for a top-quality sausage that will be moist (with enough fat in it not to dry out when baked), seasoned perfectly, and especially not too salty. Or make your own (see preceding recipe). When I try a new sausage, I first cook it according to this recipe and eat it with a potato salad to make sure that it is worth the trouble to bake it in brioche.

For the proper ratio of sausage to brioche, it is important to buy a sausage about 8″ long and 2½″ in diameter; it is wrapped in about ½ pound of brioche dough and baked in a 4-cup loaf pan.

Special instruction. Prepare the brioche dough a day ahead. Poach the sausage hours ahead so it will be room temperature when wrapped with the dough.

Special kitchen utensil. A 4-cup loaf pan about 8″ long, 2½″ deep, and 3″ wide.

SERVES 4–6

For the brioche dough	*For the sausage*
1½ cups all-purpose flour	1–1¼ pounds sausage
1½ teaspoons dry yeast	2 cups chicken stock
¼ cup water	1 cup dry white wine
½ tablespoon sugar	2 tablespoons minced white bulbs
½ teaspoon salt	of scallions
6 tablespoons sweet butter	
2 large eggs	*For the egg glaze*
	1 egg yolk
	1 teaspoon water

Mustard Sauce, page 396

1. Follow the directions of the Brioche Loaf recipe, page 228, but use the amounts of ingredients given above in this recipe. Refrigerate overnight after the first rising.

Preheat oven to 350°F.

2. That same day, poach the sausage: In a 2-quart pan, cover the sausage with stock, wine, and minced scallions. Cover the pan with a lid or aluminum foil. Bake on the middle shelf of the oven for 30 minutes. Remove the sausage. Cool; remove the cheesecloth or casing. It can now be eaten as is, served with Mustard Sauce. Or wrap in foil, and refrigerate. Reserve the liquids for the Mustard Sauce, page 396. When you wrap the sausage in the brioche, the sausage must be at room temperature, neither hot nor cold.

3. Butter a 4-cup loaf pan. Dust your pastry surface with flour. Remove the brioche dough from the bowl. It will be soft but cold enough to handle it, but you must act quickly; especially on a warm day, the butter in the dough will soften very fast. Sprinkle flour all over the dough and on a rolling pin. Gently, without pressure, roll the dough to a 10″ x 10″ more-or-less square and cut off a strip 2″ wide for the decoration. Wrap the sausage in the dough and place the bundle seam side down in the loaf pan. With a knife, cut the leftover piece of dough into 3 strips. Starting about 1″ from the end, braid the strips together. Cut the braid in two and place the 2 pieces on top of the sausage on a slant 3″ apart. Cover the top of the mold with a plastic bag, being careful to leave plenty of space for the dough to rise without touching the plastic. Let the brioche rise until it fills most of the pan in a turned-off oven (about 1–3 hours, depending on the weather).

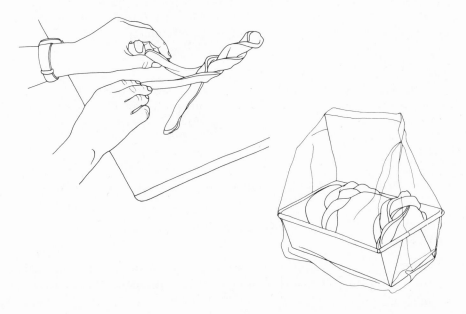

Preheat oven to 400°F.

4. Mix 1 egg yolk and 1 teaspoon water. Brush it over the brioche. Bake on the middle shelf of the oven for 30 minutes. Remove and cool 10 minutes. Then unmold on a cake rack.

5. Let cool for 30 minutes. Cut in ¼″ slices and serve with Mustard Sauce.

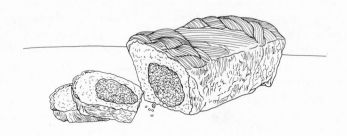

Mustard Sauce

This sauce is generally made to go with a plain poached sausage or sausage in brioche. You will have enough leftover braising liquid to make more mustard sauce. It's very good over pasta or with vegetables.

MAKES 1½ CUPS

1 tablespoon Dijon mustard
1 tablespoon sweet butter, at
  room temperature
1½ teaspoons arrowroot

1 cup sausage poaching liquid
  from preceding recipe
⅓ cup heavy cream

1. Blend the mustard, butter, and arrowroot until smooth (use the back of a fork to blend).

2. Degrease the poaching liquid reserved from braising the sausage, page 395, step 2.

3. Bring the liquid *to a boil* with heavy cream, then whisk in the mustard binding into the liquid. Whisk over high heat until the sauce thickens *slightly* (about 1 minute). Serve in a warm sauceboat.

Mussel Stew

La Mouclade (mussel stew) is a specialty of La Rochelle, a coastal city in the small region in west-central France whose best-known town is Cognac, of brandy fame. There is always a faint taste of *curry* in the stew, which is the distinguishing feature of the mouclade. In the sixteenth and seventeenth centuries, La Rochelle was an important port; trading with India brought curry powder to France.

Special instructions. Be sure the mussels are fresh; they must smell of seawater. Prepare the stew the same day you buy the mussels. The stew can be prepared a day ahead of time. Reheat slowly to just warm the mussels.

SERVES 6

6 pounds mussels

3 tablespoons minced white bulbs
  of scallions

1½ cups dry white wine

4 tablespoons (½ stick) butter

4 tablespoons flour

1½ tablespoons lemon juice

3 cloves garlic, minced

⅛ teaspoon curry powder

1 cup heavy cream

Salt

Freshly ground black pepper

1 tablespoon minced parsley

6 buttered toast, page 328

1. Discard any open mussels that do not close up again when you put them in water. Scrub them with a brush. It is the most time-consuming part of the recipe. Soak them in cold water with 1 tablespoon salt for several hours. This is to make them disgorge sand remaining inside the shells. Can be done the morning of the dinner.

2. Place the cleaned mussels, minced scallions, and white wine in a stockpot over a high flame. Cover, and shake the pot every few seconds until the mussels have opened. This normally takes about 3–5 minutes; if there are some mussels still unopened after 5 minutes, stop the cooking anyway and open them with a knife. Reserve the cooking liquid.

3. Remove the mussels. The best way to do this is to use one-half mussel shell to scoop the mussel from the other half. This way you avoid tearing the mussels. Save several mussel shells for the decoration later on. Keep the mussels covered in a warm oven.

4. Strain the liquid of the mussels through triple-layer cheesecloth, pouring carefully to avoid getting any sand that may be at the bottom.

5. Melt 4 tablespoons butter in a 3-quart saucepan and stir in 4 table-spoons flour. Cook for 1 minute, stirring with a wooden spoon, then whisk in the mussel broth and freshly squeezed lemon juice, minced

garlic, and curry powder. Simmer for about 30 minutes, whisking once in a while. Can be prepared ahead of time to this step.

6. Reheat the stew, adding the cream, the mussels, and the liquid collected in the water bath. Reheat. Correct seasonings, if necessary, with a pinch of salt and pepper.

7. Decorate with several mussel shells and sprinkle minced parsley over the stew. Serve with buttered toast or serve over fresh pasta.

To serve as Mussel Soup

Prepare the stew, but use only 3 pounds of mussels.

Mussel Salad

SERVES 6

3 pounds mussels
1½ tablespoons minced white
  bulbs of scallions

1½ cups dry white wine
1 batch of Rémoulade, page 53

1. Prepare the mussels following steps 1, 2, and 3 of the recipe for Mussel Stew, page 397.

2. Boil down the mussel broth to a concentrated flavor. Cool.

3. Prepare a Rémoulade, page 53. Add several tablespoons of mussel broth, just enough to thin the Rémoulade to a vinaigrette sauce. Mix in the hot mussels. Freeze the remaining mussel broth. Use in a Fish Stew, page 98.

Fish in Puff Pastry

Do not use an oily fish like mackerel, and try to get one which does not yield a lot of water when cooked or your puff pastry will be soggy. The best fish: striped bass, small salmon-trout, and red snapper.

This is a favorite recipe of my classes. It is an adaption of a very well-known creation of Paul Bocuse. It can be served for a buffet or a luncheon at room temperature or warm for a first course. Do not refrigerate it after baking it—the pastry loses its flavor and gets soggy.

Special instruction. May be prepared several hours ahead of time.

Special kitchen utensil. An 11″ x 16″ x 2″ jelly-roll pan.

SERVES 6 AS A FIRST COURSE, 4 AS A MAIN COURSE

3-pound striped bass (18″ long)
1 teaspoon salt
Freshly ground black pepper
1 teaspoon dried tarragon or
   1 tablespoon minced fresh
¼ cup crumbled bread

Puff Pastry with 6 turns,
   page 296
Glaze: 1 egg yolk mixed with
   1 tablespoon water
Watercress or parsley
Beurre Blanc: Butter Sauce,
   page 213

1. Have your fish market butterfly the fish, removing the backbone, gills, and entrails, but leaving the head and tail intact.

2. Wash the fish well with cold running water and dry it very well, inside and out, with paper towels. Then wrap it in several layers of paper towels and finally wrap it in newspaper. The newspapers soak up water from the paper towels, which then are able to soak up more water from the fish. Refrigerate for 1 hour in the newspaper.

3. Salt and pepper the inside of the fish and sprinkle the inside with tarragon. Fill the hole where the intestines were with crumbled bread. Measure the fish from nose to tail and make sure you have a jelly-roll pan large enough to accommodate it (perhaps diagonally if necessary). Put fish in refrigerator.

4. Cut the batch of Puff Pastry in half. Return half to the refrigerator while you roll the other half out to a rectangle big enough to accommodate the fish and still have a 1½″ border all around. Return this sheet of Puff Pastry to the refrigerator and roll out the other half the same way.

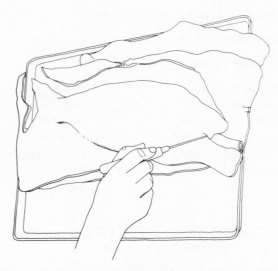

5. Place 1 sheet of Puff Pastry diagonally in the jelly-roll pan and put the fish on top of it. Generally a 3-pound bass will be 18″ long. If your fish is longer, curl up the fish slightly to fit in the jelly-roll pan. Around the outline of the fish, dab a line of cold water about ½″ wide. Drape the second sheet of Puff Pastry over the fish and stick it to the bottom piece by pressing gently all around on the line of cold water. This envelops the fish and leaves you with about 1″ double layer of Puff Pastry all around. Refrigerate 30 minutes to facilitate cutting the pastry.

6. Trim the pastry around the fish. Gently pick up the trimmed-off pastry and separate the 2 layers. Lay them flat on a baking sheet and return them to the freezer for 15–20 minutes. Put the fish in the refrigerator.

7. When the pastry trimmings are once more very cold, remove enough to make the scales. With a pastry tube, cut out ½″ circles. Make about 30 of these, cut each one in half, and freeze again. These little semicircles will make scales for the fish. Cut another piece of dough to cover the

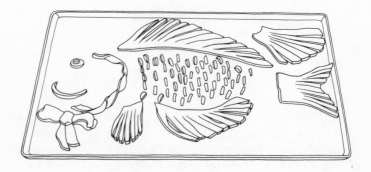

tail of the fish. (It needs a double thickness of pastry to look good.) Cut 2 pieces for fins, 1 for the belly and 1 for the back. Cut a 1″ diameter circle for the eye and a small dot for the pupil of the eye. Cut a narrow strip to make a collar for the fish. One more narrow strip is needed for the fish's mouth—it should be smiling. Some of my students go overboard at this point and make other accessories such as eyelashes, spectacles, bow ties, and the like. If you're good at this, it's a lot of fun and it looks great. Return all the cut-outs to the freezer for 10 minutes and put the fish in the refrigerator.

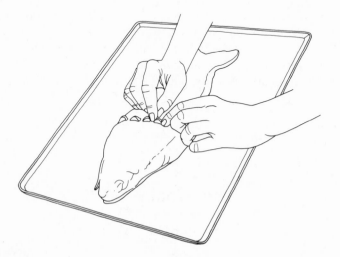

8. Remove the fish from the refrigerator and on the body of the fish cut small incisions with the back of the knife halfway through the pastry. Stick the little semicircles of dough on top of these incisions with water, placing them straight side down and leaving them projecting right straight up. (They will topple over during baking.) Decorate the rest of the fish, sticking the pieces of puff pastry on with a little cold water as before. When it is done, it should look rather like this:

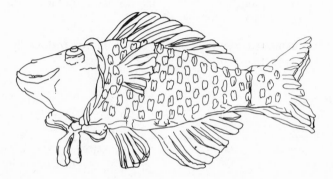

9. Make an egg glaze with 1 egg yolk and 1 tablespoon water. Brush the pastry all over with the glaze and refrigerate for 1 hour. If you want, you can prepare up to this point several hours before baking the fish.

Preheat oven to 450°F.

10. Bake for 5 minutes at 450°F. Reduce temperature to 425°F. Cover the fish loosely with a sheet of foil to keep the pastry from burning and bake for 15 minutes at 425°F. Reduce temperature to 400°F. and bake for 15 more minutes.

11. Remove from oven and allow to cool for 5 minutes before serving. It is not difficult to transfer the fish to a pretty platter, lifting and sliding it gently with 2 big spatulas. Garnish with watercress or parsley and serve with the butter sauce. Cut slices of fish and pastry crosswise, starting at the tail end of the fish. Also remove the bread from the fish when you get to it.

Note. If the underneath pastry is soggy, don't serve it.

Sole Mousse with
Mussels and Spinach

This sole mousse is served on a bed of spinach, accompanied by a sauce made with the broth of mussels. I like to make individual servings in 16 little molds holding about ⅓ cup each, or in a 4-cup ring mold. It can be presented in any form you like, but the container used for cooking must not be too large or the fish will not be cooked in the center.

Special instructions. Have the sole filleted while you are at the fish market, if possible. If the fillets stay too long on ice, the flesh absorbs water which then makes the fish forcemeat too liquid and impossible to unmold after baking. Prepare the sole mousse with mussels and spinach a day ahead of time, and refrigerate overnight.

Special kitchen utensils. Sixteen small ⅓-cup molds (called darioles) or 8 small ramekins or a 4-cup ring mold.

SERVES 8

1½ pounds fresh fillet of gray sole	Pinch of cayenne pepper
2 egg whites	4 ounces fresh salmon steak
2¼ cups cold heavy cream	2 tablespoons sweet butter
1½ teaspoons salt	2 tablespoons white wine

For the spinach bed

4 pounds fresh spinach
2 tablespoons plus 1 teaspoon salt
3 tablespoons sweet butter
2 tablespoons minced bulbs of
    scallions
½ cup heavy cream
Freshly ground black pepper

For the mussels

1½ pounds mussels
½ cup dry white wine

For the sauce

½ cup mussel liquids
½ cup heavy cream
6 tablespoons sweet butter

1. Cut the sole into small pieces and pass through the food processor (20–30 seconds) or food mill (coarse, then fine blade), then through a fine-mesh sieve (illustration, pages 36–37).

2. If you have a heavy-duty mixer with a flat paddle, it will work for this step; otherwise, mix by hand with a wooden spatula. Put the mixer bowl in the freezer for 5 minutes to get it very cold before beating heavy cream in it. Start mixing the sole purée and slowly dribble in 2 unbeaten egg whites. When they are fully mixed, slowly dribble the 2¼ cups cold heavy cream into the mixture. You must have a smooth creamy paste when done. Season with 1½ teaspoons salt and a pinch of cayenne. Reserve covered in the refrigerator.

3. Dice the salmon after skinning and deboning it. Reserve the bones for steaming the mussels. Melt 2 tablespoons butter in a small skillet and, over high heat, sauté the salmon for 2 minutes. Add 2 tablespoons white wine and stir until it evaporates completely. When cool, add the salmon to the sole purée. Taste and correct seasoning with salt and a pinch of cayenne. Refrigerate again.

4. Wash 4 pounds fresh spinach very well and remove stems and tough leaves. Boil 5 quarts of water with 2 tablespoons salt and plunge the spinach into the boiling water. Sprinkle 1 teaspoon salt on the spinach. Boil for 3 minutes after it has reached a second boil. Drain and rinse under cold water. Squeeze very dry with your hands and chop fine with a knife.

5. Melt 3 tablespoons butter in a 9″ heavy skillet over medium heat; sauté the spinach along with the 2 tablespoons of minced scallions for 3 minutes. Taste and correct seasoning with salt and pepper. Reserve, covered, in the refrigerator.

6. Scrub the mussels with a brush and discard any which are already open. Steam the mussels in a large covered kettle over high heat with ½ cup dry white wine. Add the reserved bones from the salmon steak to them. Shake the pan frequently so the shells will all have a chance to open.

It should take about 3–5 minutes. Discard the shells; reserve the mussels in a small bowl. Pass the broth through a sieve lined with several layers of cheesecloth to remove sand and grit. Reduce the mussel broth to about ½ cup, until it has a strong flavor. (The amount of reduction will depend upon how much water the mussels retained, but the reduction is on the order of a third to a half. Taste the broth once in a while. Don't overreduce it; it will become too salty, especially if you live near the ocean, where the mussels are very fresh.) Fold the mussels into the sole mixture and refrigerate.

The day of the dinner

7. One hour before dinnertime, remove the fish mousse, the spinach, and the mussel liquid from the refrigerator. Butter the mold(s).

   Preheat oven to 325°F.

8. Fill the mold (s) three-fourths full with the mousse, place in a water bath, then fill with hot water halfway up the mold(s). Cover the mold(s) with buttered parchment paper. Bake on the middle shelf of the oven until the tops are slightly springy to the touch (about 25 minutes). Check the mousse after 20 minutes. It might be ready to come out of the oven. Much depends on your oven, but don't overcook; otherwise, the sole mousse will dry out; and, of course, don't undercook it or it will collapse when you try to unmold it. If that should happen, don't panic; clean and butter the mold(s) once more, fill with the collapsed fish mousse, and bake again.

9. Reheat the spinach in a water bath (see illustration, page 35) or in a double boiler with ½ cup cream. Taste and correct seasonings with salt and freshly ground pepper.

10. Combine ½ cup mussel broth and ½ cup heavy cream in a 1½-quart heavy-bottomed saucepan and bring it to a boil over high heat until the liquids are reduced to two-thirds of their original volume. Turn off the heat and reserve for the last step.

11. Have a large plate ready and a cake rack. Remove the mold(s) from the water bath. Pass the blade of a knife around the mousse and unmold on the cake rack over the large plate to catch the liquids draining out of the mousse. Meanwhile:

12. Spread the spinach on a preheated serving platter. Place the fish mousse over the spinach. (If you baked the mousse in a ring mold, unmold the fish on a rack to drain. Replace the mold over the fish, then unmold the fish on the platter and add the spinach in the center.) Reserve in a warm oven while finishing the sauce.

13. Add the mousse liquids to the reserved mussel-cream liquids. Cut up 6 tablespoons butter into small pieces. Bring the liquids to a boil and turn off the heat. Add the butter, several pieces at a time, whisking very briskly. Pour half the sauce over the mousse and serve the remaining sauce in a preheated sauceboat.

Note. If you are unable to get mussels, prepare a thick Hollandaise Sauce, page 201, and using the fish mousse liquids, dilute it just enough to coat the spoon.

Baked Stuffed Sole Fillets

Sole fillets are stuffed with sole mousse and minced mushrooms, then baked with white wine in the oven and served in winter months with a hollandaise sauce flavored with a reduction of the fish liquids; or, in late spring, summer, and early autumn, with a sorrel sauce.

Special instruction. Sole may be stuffed a day ahead of time and kept refrigerated until time to bake it.

Special kitchen utensil. A 2-quart baking dish.

SERVES 6 AS A MAIN DISH; 12 AS AN APPETIZER

For the filling

⅔ pound fillet of gray sole
1 egg white
⅔ cup very cold heavy cream
1¼ teaspoons salt
Freshly ground white pepper
Pinch of cayenne pepper
¾ pound mushrooms
1 tablespoon minced bulbs of
    scallions
2 tablespoons butter
1 tablespoon minced fresh
    tarragon or ½ teaspoon dried

6 thin fillets of gray sole
½ cup dry white wine
Hollandaise Sauce, page 201,
    or Sorrel Sauce, page 274

1. Cube the ⅔ pound sole fillets for the stuffing and purée for 30 seconds in the food processor fitted with the metal blade, then force through a fine-mesh sieve (illustration, pages 36–37). It is very important to do this. The texture will be much finer than if you use only the food processor.

2. Put the mixer bowl in the freezer for 5 minutes to get it very cold before beating heavy cream in it. In a heavy-duty mixer, at medium speed,

beat 1 egg white into the fish purée, then slowly dribble in ⅔ cup very cold heavy cream. Season with 1 teaspoon salt, freshly ground white pepper, and a pinch of cayenne pepper. Refrigerate.

3. Mince ¾ pound mushrooms, including the stems. Melt 2 tablespoons butter in a 9″ cast-iron skillet and sauté the mushrooms and scallions over medium-high heat until all the water has evaporated from the mushrooms. Then add the tarragon. Season with ¼ teaspoon salt.

4. Cut each of the 6 fillets of sole in two lengthwise. Remove the spiny prickly cartilage in the center where the fillet is cut. On the shiny side of the fillet, make 2 small diagonal slits to help roll up the fillet. Spread a thin layer of fish mousse on each fillet, then a layer of mushrooms. Roll up the fillet to a snail-like form and secure it with a wooden toothpick. (If there is leftover fish mousse, spread on top of the rolled-up fillet.) Generously butter a 2-quart baking dish large enough to hold the fillets comfortably.

5. Pour ½ cup dry white wine over the fish and cover tightly with foil. Refrigerate until the next day if you wish.

    Preheat oven to 400°F.

6. Remove the fish from the refrigerator an hour ahead of time if it was prepared earlier. Bake on the middle shelf of the oven for 20 minutes.

7. Prepare a Hollandaise Sauce, page 201, and reserve in a warm water bath, or prepare a Sorrel Sauce, page 274.

8. From now on, you must work fast, for the fish must not get cold. Set up a cake rack over a large platter and transfer the fish, using a wide flat spatula, to the baking rack to drain. (It is important to do this; otherwise, the fillets will spew out juices and if you pour the finished sauce over them, the sauce will thin out too much and lose its concentrated flavor.)

9. Pour the fish liquids into a 9″ skillet and boil down (they will reduce faster with a large surface like a skillet). Add the liquid drippings from the fish fillets. Reduce until the boiling liquids are becoming syrupy (about ⅓ cup of syrupy liquids will remain). Whisk the syrupy liquids 1 tablespoon at a time into the hollandaise or sorrel sauce. If the sauce is getting too thin, do not add all the reduced fish liquids. Taste and correct seasonings with salt and pepper.

10. *For the presentation.* For a main course, serve 2 fillets; for an appetizer, 1 fillet is enough. Serve the sauce in a sauceboat. Do not pour the sauce over the fillets until they are served on individual plates to be sure that the fish is totally drained and will not thin out the sauce.

Sweetbreads in Puff Pastry

Special instruction. The unbaked puff pastry sticks can be prepared ahead of time and frozen. The sweetbreads can be cooked several hours ahead of time.

Special kitchen utensil. A 4-quart Dutch oven.

MAKES 8 PUFF PASTRY STICKS

Puff Pastry with 6 turns,
   page 296
1 pound sweetbreads
3 teaspoons lemon juice
3 onions
5 tablespoons butter
1 teaspoon salt

Freshly ground white pepper
1 pound mushrooms
2½ cups water
Glaze: 1 egg yolk diluted with
   ½ tablespoon water
½ cup heavy cream
1 tablespoon flour

1. Several days ahead of time, prepare the Puff Pastry, page 296, and, on a floured pastry board, roll it into a rectangle of even thickness 17″ x 14″. Freeze on a cookie sheet for 15 minutes. Trim the pastry on the cookie sheet so that there is a cut edge all the way around to ensure even baking (illustrated technique, page 317). Cut crosswise into 3 equal pieces and finally cut each piece crosswise again into 6 pieces for 18 sticks about 4½″ long and 2¼″ wide. Freeze the sticks until needed. You will have more than you need, but they can be used for other recipes.

2. Soak sweetbreads in cold water for 2 hours with 1 teaspoon lemon juice.

3. Peel and slice the onions very thin. Melt 4 tablespoons butter in a 4-quart Dutch oven and add the onions; stir with a wooden spatula to coat the onions with butter. Sprinkle ½ teaspoon salt and freshly ground pepper. Cover and cook (braise) over low heat until the onions are soft but not colored (about 30 minutes).

4. Cover the sweetbreads with cold water in a saucepan. Bring to a boil over medium heat; then simmer gently for about 10 minutes, partially covered. Drain and rinse under cold water; then remove the gristle and fat around the sweetbreads. Cut them into ½″ cubes.

5. Add the sweetbreads to the onions, season with ½ teaspoon salt and freshly ground pepper, cover, and continue braising over low heat for another 20 minutes. Again, be sure that the heat is low enough so that the onions do not color. Reserve in the pot for the final preparation.

6. Prepare a mushroom broth for the sauce. Remove the stems from 1 pound of mushrooms (reserve the mushroom caps for a salad: slice them raw and serve with a vinaigrette dressing). Put the mushroom stems in a 2-quart saucepan; cover with 2½ cups of water with a pinch of salt and 1 teaspoon lemon juice. Bring to a boil and boil down to ½ cup of mushroom broth. Discard the stems. Up to this point, everything can be prepared ahead of time.

The assembly of the Puff Pastry sticks with the sweetbreads

Preheat oven to 425°F.

7. Transfer the *frozen* Puff Pastry sticks to a room temperature cookie sheet, quickly brush an egg glaze over the top, and bake immediately on the middle shelf of the oven for about 20 minutes. Check them once in a while to be sure they are not burning; if so, lower the temperature to 375°F. and loosely cover the sticks with aluminum foil.

8. While the Puff Pastry is in the oven, reheat the sweetbreads; when warm, remove them with a slotted spoon to a preheated bowl. With a fork, mash the remaining 1 tablespoon butter and 1 tablespoon flour into a paste. Reserve on a plate.

9. Turn on the heat high, pour the mushroom broth and ½ cup of heavy cream into the sweetbread pan, stirring all the while for about 1 minute. Whisk in the butter and flour paste, and continue whisking until the sauce slightly thickens. Taste and correct seasonings with salt, pepper, and drops of lemon juice.

10. Split each piece of baked Puff Pastry in half horizontally, and bake the insides once more for 3 minutes or so to dry them out, if necessary.

11. Add the sweetbreads to the sauce to warm them. Fill the bottom half of the pastry with sweetbreads, cover with the top, and dribble some sauce over each stick.

Cheese in Puff Pastry

Blue cheese or gorgonzola or any of the cheeses mentioned in the Cheese Puffs, page 50, can be used to fill Puff Pastry sticks for an appetizer.

1. Blend the cheese with cream and butter, following step 6 of the Cheese Puffs, page 52.

2. Fill the bottom half of the baked Puff Pastry sticks. Cover with the top and heat in a 350°F. oven for 5 minutes. Serve with drinks.

Frozen Coffee Mousse
with Meringues

The coffee mousse is an egg custard, flavored with ground coffee beans and instant espresso coffee, folded into whipped cream. It is frozen in a soufflé mold unlined or lined with ladyfinger meringues. This dessert is very rich. It will serve 10 people, especially eaten after a full meal.

Special instructions. Must be prepared a day ahead of time. The meringues can be made several days ahead and kept frozen or in an old-fashioned cookie jar with a rubber ring (illustration, page 363).

Special kitchen utensil. Be sure to use a small 3-cup soufflé mold with a 3″ high collar (use parchment paper or a paper stiff enough to hold the mousse without the paper collapsing).

SERVES 10

Meringue ladyfingers, page 382	1–2 tablespoons praline cream* or
1 tablespoon coffee beans	2 tablespoons ground hazelnuts
1 cup milk	1 cup heavy cream
1 cup superfine sugar	1 tablespoon coffee liqueur
5 teaspoons instant espresso	(Kahlua, or see following
coffee powder	recipe)
6 egg yolks	Cocoa to sprinkle on mousse

* Praline cream may be ordered from Maison Glass, 52 East 58th Street, New York, NY 10022.

1. Several days ahead of time bake the meringues and freeze or store in cookie jar.

2. Grind 1 tablespoon coffee beans coarsely. Combine 1 cup milk, ½ cup superfine sugar, and the coarsely ground coffee beans in a 3-quart heavy-bottomed saucepan. Slowly bring to a boil to dissolve the sugar. Turn off the heat. Cover the pan and let stand for 30 minutes. Strain the milk through a fine-mesh sieve. Reserve. Discard the beans. Wash the saucepan and bring the milk back to a boil and pour it over the instant coffee, whisking all the while to dissolve it. If the coffee does not dissolve totally, strain it through cheesecloth and add more milk for 1 cup of milk-coffee. Reserve.

3. In a heavy mixer, beat 6 egg yolks with ½ cup sugar at high speed until the mixture is thick and pale yellow (about 5 minutes), then at low speed, gradually pour in the milk.

4. Pour the mixture back into the saucepan and cook over medium-low heat, stirring constantly with a wooden spoon, making a figure 8 gesture in the custard to scrape the sides of the bottom of the pan constantly with even strokes until the custard reaches 175°F. on a candy thermometer. It will take about 5 minutes. Dunk your finger into the custard. If it feels hot, remove the custard from the heat and test with the candy thermometer. Don't boil the custard or the egg yolks will curdle. Continue stirring off the flame to cool the custard. If you wish, dunk the bottom of the pan in cold water to cool it more rapidly.

5. In a heavy-duty mixer, at medium-high speed, beat the custard for 10 minutes to aerate it and at the same time to thicken it. Transfer the custard to another mixing bowl. Cover with plastic wrap and refrigerate.

6. Wash the mixer bowl and put it in the freezer empty for 5 minutes to get it very cold before beating heavy cream in it.

7. Meanwhile prepare the soufflé mold. Cut out a collar for the mold and wrap the outside of the mold with it, using tape to hold it together 2″ high over the rim of the mold. Cream 2 tablespoons praline paste with the heel of your hand and spread it around the sides at the bottom of the soufflé mold, reserving ½ tablespoon for later. Substitute butter if praline paste is unavailable to spread at the bottom of the pan. Cut one end off the meringues so that they are just long enough to line the mold. The cut end of the meringue will go on the bottom of the mold and the uncut end should be flush with the top. If you are using praline paste, lightly coat the side of the meringues that will be next to the custard with praline paste, then stick the meringues to the sides of the mold standing up all the way around. Reserve the ends of the meringues for later and spread more praline paste on them. (If praline paste is not available, do not use anything on them.)

8. Remove the mixing bowl from the freezer and whip 1 cup heavy cream until thick. Beat in 1 tablespoon coffee liqueur.

9. With a rubber spatula, gently fold the whipped cream into the coffee custard with 2 tablespoons ground hazelnuts if praline paste is unavailable. Ladle the mousse into the prepared soufflé mold until almost to the top of the collar. Freeze the leftover in a small ramekin. Bury the reserved pieces of meringues in the top of the mousse.

10. Freeze overnight. One hour before serving, remove the collar and refrigerate 1 hour to soften the mousse. Sprinkle the top of the mousse with cocoa. Wrap the soufflé mold in a white napkin and serve on a pretty platter lined with a lace doily.

Coffee Liqueur

It is easy to make your own coffee liqueur, and it is a great Christmas gift.

Special instruction. The liqueur is ready 30 days or so after all the ingredients are mixed. Then bottle and cork it.

Special kitchen utensils. A ½-gallon bottle or jug with a tight-fitting lid.

MAKES ABOUT 1 QUART

2 cups water
2 ounces instant espresso coffee
    powder
4 cups superfine sugar

1½ cups unflavored vodka
1 cup brandy
1 vanilla bean

1. Bring 2 cups of water to a boil. Pour over the instant espresso coffee and stir until all the coffee is dissolved. Mix well, then dribble in the sugar, stirring all the while for the sugar to dissolve. Add the vodka, brandy, and vanilla bean.

2. Store in a bottle or jug. Cover tightly and let stand at room temperature for 30 days. Stir the mixture every 5 days during the 30-day period.

3. Remove the vanilla bean. Bottle the liqueur and cork it.

Almond Brittle Ice Cream

You do not need an ice cream machine for this recipe. It is a mixture of an egg custard and whipped cream, flavored by almond brittle, ground coarsely.

Special instructions. You can prepare the almond brittle several days ahead of time and freeze. The ice cream is prepared a day ahead of time and kept in the freezer.

Special kitchen utensil. A 6-cup loaf pan; this ice cream is served in slices.

SERVES 8

For the almond brittle

1 tablespoon almond or corn oil
½ cup sugar
3 tablespoons water
½ cup shelled almonds

For the ice cream

1 cup milk
½ cup sugar
2 teaspoons vanilla extract or
    1 vanilla bean split lengthwise
6 egg yolks
1 cup heavy cream

1. Almond brittle is made with a caramel and almonds. Spread 1 tablespoon almond or corn oil on a cookie sheet. Combine ½ cup sugar and the water in a 1½-quart saucepan. Bring to a boil and cook the syrup for about 8 minutes or until the syrup is amber color. Off the flame, quickly stir ½ cup shelled almonds into the caramel and pour them on the prepared oiled cookie sheet. Spread the almonds out as much as you can. Let cool, then scrape up and grind medium-fine in the food processor, or chop with a knife. There will be much more brittle than you need for this recipe. Keep the excess brittle in a container and freeze it for the next time or decorate the top of the ice cream with it.

2. Combine 1 cup milk with ½ cup sugar in a 2-quart heavy-bottomed saucepan and bring to a boil to dissolve the sugar. Add 2 teaspoons vanilla extract or the vanilla bean. Let cool, covered, for 30 minutes.

3. Break 6 egg yolks into a 2-quart mixing bowl, pour the milk over them, and whisk until the yolks are well blended into the milk. Transfer the mixture back into the saucepan, remove the vanilla bean and discard, and cook over medium-low heat, stirring all the while, until the internal temperature reaches 175°F.

4. Transfer the custard to an electric mixer and beat at medium speed until the custard is cold and has thickened. Refrigerate the custard until cold.

5. Put a mixer bowl in the freezer for 5 minutes to get it very cold before beating heavy cream in it. Whip the cream just until the whisk leaves traces at the bottom of the bowl, then by hand fold the cold custard into the whipped cream. Fold ½ cup almond brittle into the mixture.

6. Oil a 6-cup loaf pan and pour in the ice cream. Freeze overnight.

7. *To unmold.* Quickly dip the pan in hot water, pass the blade of a knife around the edges of the ice cream, and unmold on a serving platter. Decorate with almond brittle. Cut ½″ thick slices and serve on individual plates.

Almond Meringue Cookies
Filled with Cream Cheese

These small meringue cookies are very easy to prepare and can be kept in an airtight jar with a rubber ring to keep the meringues crisp. The egg whites are beaten very stiff with 3 tablespoons sugar, then very quickly and very gently the remaining sugar and ground almond brittle are folded into the egg whites. Beating egg whites first, then folding the sugar into them, makes the meringues much lighter than if you add all the sugar to the egg whites before they are beaten stiff.

Special kitchen utensil. A pastry bag fitted with ½" wide tube is perfect, but you can shape small meringues with a coffee spoon.

For the meringues	For the cream cheese
¼ cup almond brittle, page 411	¼ pound cream cheese
3 egg whites	3 tablespoons heavy cream
¾ cup superfine sugar	2 tablespoons sugar
1 teaspoon Coffee Liqueur, page 411	½ tablespoon Kahlua

1. Prepare the almond brittle following the recipe for Almond Brittle Ice Cream, page 411.

   Preheat oven to 225°F.

2. For the meringue cookies: grease 2 cookie sheets. Prepare the meringues according to the recipe, page 381. Substitute Coffee Liqueur for the lemon juice and pipe little blobs about 1½" wide in diameter, leaving 1" space between them. Bake following the instructions, page 382. Freeze if you are not using the meringues right away.

3. If at all possible, buy fresh cream cheese. The amount of heavy cream prescribed is for fresh cream cheese. With packaged cream cheese, you will need more heavy cream (see page 27 for more details).

4. Refrigerate the mixing bowl for 5 minutes or so. Beat the cream cheese in the cold mixing bowl at medium speed to lighten it. Dribble enough heavy cream into the cheese to make it the consistency of whipped cream. Beat the sugar and the coffee liqueur. Keep refrigerated until ready to fill the meringues.

5. *Assembly of the meringue cookies.* Don't fill the meringue cookies ahead of time; the meringues become soft. It takes no time at all to do it at the last minute. Fill a pastry bag fitted with a serrated tube with the cream cheese and cover the bottom of 1 meringue with the cheese and press the bottom of another meringue against it like a small sandwich. Lay them on their sides and serve.

Madeleines: Individual Tea Cakes

There is nothing better than freshly baked madeleines, dunked in a cup of tea, when relaxing in the late afternoon with a friend. The fresh madeleine, with its crunchy exterior and fluffy, caky interior, is at its best eaten slightly warm.

Madeleines are so easy to make, taking only 10 minutes to prepare and 15 minutes to bake, that there is no reason to make them ahead of time.

Special instructions. Bake the madeleine batter as soon as it is mixed; the longer you wait, the thicker the batter becomes and the cookies are not as light.

If you need to make them ahead of time, reserve in a Mason jar with a rubber ring around the top to keep the madeleines airtight.

Special kitchen utensils. A madeleine pan that makes 12 madeleines 3″ long.

MAKES 12 MADELEINES

5½ tablespoons sweet butter	1 large egg
7 tablespoons all-purpose flour	Grated rind of 1 lemon
½ teaspoon baking powder	Scant ⅓ cup sugar
1 teaspoon cornstarch	Pinch of salt

1. Melt 4½ tablespoons sweet butter. Remove from heat and reserve.

2. Mix the flour, baking powder, and cornstarch and sift into the mixing bowl of an electric beater. Make a well in the flour.

3. Melt 1 tablespoon butter and brush it in the 12 individual forms of the madeleine pan.

4. Beat the egg lightly with a fork, add the grated lemon, sugar, and salt, and beat lightly. Pour mixture in the flour well.

5. With the electric mixer set on medium speed, beat the ingredients together, dribbling in the melted butter. Beat only long enough to mix the ingredients thoroughly, no more (less than 1 minute).

   Preheat oven to 400°F.

6. Spoon enough batter in each little madeleine shell to fill it halfway.

7. Bake at 400°F. on the middle shelf in the oven for 12–15 minutes. Remove the madeleines when the edges are brown and the top light golden. Using the point of a paring knife, gently pry them out of the mold and set them on a cake rack to cool. Eat warm.

Note. Right away, wash the madeleine pan by scrubbing under hot water with no detergent. Dry with paper towels.

Puff Pastry Cookies with Sugar Icing

These cookies are found in pastry shops everywhere in France. They are called Allumettes (matchsticks). When you know how to make Puff Pastry, they are easy to make at home and are better than the store-bought ones.

Special instructions. You can prepare the cookies and the icing a day ahead of time and bake them when needed. They must be frozen unbaked. Bake as follows: Do not thaw them. Preheat oven to 450°F., then turn it down to 400°F. when baking the cookies.

Special kitchen utensils. Two cookie sheets 14″ x 17″.

MAKES 40 COOKIES

Puff Pastry with 6 turns, page 296	1 egg white
About 1 cup confectioner's sugar	1 tablespoon lemon juice

1. Cut the Puff Pastry in 2 equal pieces. Roll out one piece at a time to 11″ x 12″. Transfer each piece to a cookie sheet. Freeze the 2 pieces of pastry for ½ hour.

2. *Prepare the sugar icing.* Sift the confectioner's sugar into a mixing bowl. With a fork, beat 1 egg white in a 3-quart mixing bowl. With a wooden spoon, start mixing 1 tablespoon of sugar at a time into the egg white (it takes about 15 minutes to incorporate most of the sugar). Halfway through, add 2 teaspoons lemon juice to the icing. The icing will become stiff toward the end. Dribble the remaining teaspoon of lemon juice into the icing. Stop incorporating the last ¼ cup of sugar if the icing becomes too stiff to stir. The icing looks and feels like a white paste stiff enough to spread on the unbaked Puff Pastry.

3. Divide the icing in two, and spread half on each piece of pastry, turning the spatula over and over while spreading. Wipe the excess off the spatula and use it to patch up the bare spots on the pastry. Refrigerate to firm up for at least 2 hours.

4. Leave the pastry on each cookie sheet and cut the edges with a knife to make straight sides, leaving cut edges all around the rectangle (illustration, page 317). Then cut crosswise into 4 equal pieces and finally cut each piece again into 5 small pieces to make 20 pieces in all on each cookie sheet. Leave on cookie sheets. Refrigerate to firm up or refrigerate overnight. Don't freeze them; the icing will crack.

   Preheat oven to 425°F.

5. Transfer 20 cookies to a large cookie sheet at room temperature, separating the cookies from one another so they won't stick together during baking. Turn the oven down to 400°F. and bake 1 batch of 20 cookies on the middle shelf of the oven for 15 minutes or until puffy and golden brown on top.

6. Turn oven heat back up to 425°F. and repeat with the second batch of cookies.

TECHNIQUES AND UTENSILS INTRODUCED

How to make a large quenelle and how to poach it

How to freeze fresh truffles

How to open sea urchins

How to select a duck for roasting and how to roast it
so skin is crispy and meat juicy

How to bind a sauce with caramel

How to shape puff pastry in a vol-au-vent

How to peel orange slices

Lesson 21

RECIPES

Poached Fish Mousse: A Large Quenelle

Quenelle with Salmon and Pistachios

Quenelle with Truffles

Sauce for Quenelles

Sea Urchin Sauce

Poached Chicken Mousse

Glazed Vegetables (Onions, Carrots, and Turnips)

Roast Duck with a Caramel-Vinegar Sauce

Caramel-Vinegar Sauce

Roast Chicken with Caramel-Vinegar Sauce

Orange Sunburst Tart

Strawberry Tart with Puff Pastry

Suggested Menus for Lesson 21

Small Elegant Luncheon

Poached Fish Mousse:
A Large Quenelle served with
Sea Urchin Sauce
or
with Truffle Sauce

English Muffin–Style Bread
for Toast (Lesson 17)

Strawberry Tart with
Puff Pastry

A Special Occasion Dinner

Fish in Puff Pastry (Lesson 20)
served with Beurre Blanc:
A Butter Sauce (Lesson 11)

Rack of Lamb (Lesson 15) served with
a Bohémienne (Lesson 4)

Raspberry Sherbet
(Lesson 9)

Almond Meringue Cookies
(Lesson 20)

Dinner for an Experienced Cook

Poached Fish Mousse:
A Large Quenelle

Roast Duck with a
Caramel-Vinegar Sauce

Homemade Fresh Pasta
(Lesson 9)

Glazed Vegetables
(Onions, Carrots, and Turnips)

Orange Sunburst Tart

Supper

Onion Soup (Lesson 4)

Poached Chicken Mousse

Leek Salad (Lesson 4)

Blackberry Turnovers
(Lesson 7)

Poached Fish Mousse:
A Large Quenelle

Quenelles are light, airy fish mousse dumplings poached in a fish stock which is then used to make a sauce to go over the quenelles. I prefer to make one big quenelle to small ones; it is less work, the final presentation is more spectacular, and the taste is not altered. I wrap the fish mousse in cheesecloth and shape it into a big sausage. When poached, I slice it into individual servings and serve it with a light sauce made with the poaching liquids. Pike, a freshwater fish, is the best fish to make the lightest fish mousse. If you like, you can substitute skinned and boned chicken breast for the fish; see page 423 for Poached Chicken Mousse.

Special instructions. You may prepare the fish stock and the quenelle a day ahead of time. When you buy the fish fillets, make sure you get fillets that are freshly cut and have not been kept on ice. If they stay on ice very long, they soak up water, which makes the flesh watery.

This quenelle can be poached ahead of time and eaten at room temperature. Cook the sauce the day of the party; otherwise, it thickens too much while waiting.

Special kitchen utensil. Be sure to buy cotton cheesecloth instead of the nylon cheesecloth found in supermarkets. A big hardware store generally sells cotton cheesecloth in bulk. If you don't want so much and can't find it anywhere, order it by mail from: The Vermont Store, Weston, VT 05161. Cheesecloth can be reused; simply wash it and dry for the next use.

SERVES 6 AS A MAIN COURSE, 10 AS A FIRST COURSE

1¼ pounds ground pike fillets	2 scant pinches of cayenne pepper
2 egg whites	1½ quarts Fish Stock, page 367
1¾ cups heavy cream	Sauce for Quenelles, page 422
1½ teaspoons salt	

1. Have the fish ground at the fish market or grind it in the food processor. Force through a fine-mesh sieve (illustration, pages 36–37). This smooths out the purée and gets rid of any bones and skin that remain (yields 2½ cups of purée). Add the fish debris to the Fish Stock.

2. Put the mixer bowl in the freezer for 5 minutes to get it very cold before beating heavy cream in it. Beat the egg whites lightly with a fork. Using the flat spatula of the mixer (Kitchen Aid has this) at low speed, slowly dribble the egg whites into the purée. (This can also be done by hand using a wooden spatula.)

3. Again with the flat paddle of the mixer (or a hand electric beater) at lowest speed, slowly dribble the chilled heavy cream into the purée. You must have a smooth creamy paste when done. Add 1½ teaspoons salt and 2 pinches of cayenne pepper.

4. Cut a piece of cotton cheesecloth and fold in triple thickness to a 20″ x 20″ square. Put the fish paste in the center and shape it into the form of a big sausage about 9″ long. Use a rubber spatula to smooth the surface. Fold the cheesecloth over the quenelle and tie both ends tightly with string. Can be done a day ahead of time and refrigerated.

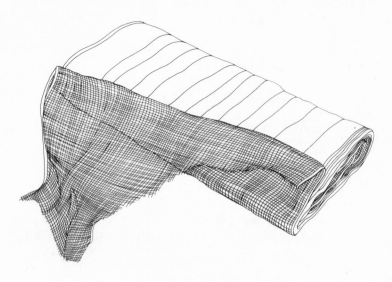

5. If your quenelle was in the refrigerator, let it warm up to room temperature before cooking. Bring the stock just under the boil in a Dutch oven or a fish poacher large enough to hold the quenelle. Poach the quenelle in quivering fish stock for 45 minutes, with the cover ajar, ladling broth over the quenelle once in a while. With a steel spatula, check the bottom of the quenelle to see that it is not sticking to the pot.

6. When the quenelle has poached for 35 minutes, dip out 1½ cups of the poaching liquid and use it to make the sauce. Continue poaching the quenelle 10 more minutes while you prepare the Sauce for Quenelles.

7. Transfer the quenelle to a draining rack set over a plate. Drain for 5 minutes, cut the strings and gently unwrap it, and transfer to a heated serving platter. Ladle half the sauce over the quenelle, pour the rest in a sauceboat, and serve.

Quenelle with Salmon and Pistachios

SERVES 6 AS A MAIN COURSE, 10 AS A FIRST COURSE

¼ pound salmon steak
1 tablespoon minced white bulbs
  of scallion
1 tablespoon butter
2 tablespoons dry white wine

2 cups water
¼ cup unsalted shelled
  pistachios
1 recipe Poached Fish Mousse,
  page 419

1. Dice ¼ pound salmon steak. Combine minced scallion with 1 tablespoon butter in a small skillet. Cover and cook for 5 minutes over low heat. Uncover, raise the heat, and sauté the salmon for 1 minute or so. Add 2 tablespoons white wine and, stirring all the while, let the wine evaporate. Cool.

2. Boil 2 cups water and parboil the pistachios for 5 minutes. Skin them and split in two.

3. Fold the pistachios and salmon into the quenelle at step 3, page 420, and complete as directed.

Quenelle with Truffles

If you want to make the Poached Fish Mousse very special, add truffles to it. You can order fresh black truffles by mail from: Mr. Paul Urbani, 130 Graf Avenue, P.O. Box 2054, Trenton, NJ 08607. Truffles freeze well, wrapped in foil. Slice frozen and cook. Do not let them thaw before cooking.
  I have had very nice results with canned truffles, which are much less expensive.

1 ounce fresh or canned black
  truffle

3 tablespoons butter
1 tablespoon Cognac

1. Cut the truffle into very thin slices. Combine 2 tablespoons butter, the sliced truffle (the truffle juice if you use canned truffle), and the Cognac in a saucepan. Cover and cook over very low heat for 15 minutes or so. Let cool. Reserve 10 truffle slices in the saucepan, covered. Mince the remaining slices and fold them into the fish paste along with the liquids at step 3 of the main recipe, page 420.

2. Reheat the reserved truffle slices with the remaining 1 tablespoon butter, covered, for several minutes. Decorate the top of the cooked quenelle with them for step 7 of the main recipe.

Sauce for Quenelles

MAKES 2 CUPS

1½ cups Fish Stock, page 367
2 tablespoons butter
2 tablespoons flour
½ cup heavy cream

2 tablespoons butter, at room
  temperature
Salt to taste
Freshly ground white pepper
A pinch of cayenne pepper

1. Bring 1½ cups Fish Stock to a boil.

2. In a heavy saucepan, melt 2 tablespoons butter. When it is hot, add 2 tablespoons flour and whisk for 1 minute over medium heat. Pour boiling stock all at once into the butter and flour mixture, whisking rapidly. Add the cream, mix, and simmer for 10 minutes. The sauce should be about as thick as heavy cream. If it is too thick, add a little fish stock to thin it.

3. Off the flame, whisk in 2 tablespoons sweet butter at room temperature, 1 tablespoon at a time.

4. Taste for seasoning. Add salt, freshly ground white pepper, and a tiny pinch of cayenne.

Note on reheating. Place the saucepan in another pan with simmering water. The sauce will not thicken too much. Don't let the sauce get too hot—it should remain lukewarm.

Sea Urchin Sauce

This is a fine rich sauce for quenelles, pâté of sole, or other delicate fish dishes. Sea urchins are at their peak in the spring from March to June. However, I have found them sometimes throughout the year. A sea urchin looks very unappetizing. Even if you have never seen them before, you may have felt them while walking barefoot on the beach. Their spikes are very sharp indeed!

When buying sea urchins, be very sure they are fresh. Their quills must be green and prickly; they should smell of strong fresh seawater, whereas overtired sea urchins have dark brown quills and a very unpleasant odor.

Have the fish market crack them open for you if you don't have the courage to do it yourself. At home, scoop out the roe and do not rinse it. To open the urchins yourself, slip a thick potholder on your left hand, grab the urchin, and with your right hand, using a pair of scissors, cut out the shell around the soft orifice until you are able to scoop out the roe. Some urchins have more roe than others, and the size has nothing to do with the amount. Sometimes a small urchin has more roe than a big one.

Substitute a small canned truffle if sea urchins are not available. Mince the truffle. Melt 1 tablespoon butter in a small saucepan and cook the truffle for 10 minutes over very low heat, tightly covered.

MAKES 2 CUPS

1½ cups Fish Stock, page 367
6 tablespoons sweet butter
2 tablespoons flour

¼–½ cup heavy cream (optional)
3 sea urchins

1. Bring 1½ cups Fish Stock to a boil. Melt 2 tablespoons butter in a heavy saucepan, add the 2 tablespoons flour, and whisk rapidly until the mixture bubbles. Immediately pour in all the boiling fish stock and whisk well for a minute or so until smooth. Simmer for 30 minutes. If necessary, thin with heavy cream (up to ½ cup). The sauce should be about as runny as heavy cream.

2. While the sauce is cooking, cut the sea urchins in half. Scoop out the coral—the soft orange part—and discard the rest. Mash the coral and 4 tablespoons butter together to make a smooth paste. Pass through a fine-mesh sieve.

3. When the sauce is ready, and just before serving, remove the sauce from the heat and whisk in the mixture of butter and sea urchin, 1 tablespoon at a time. Serve in a sauceboat that is warm but not hot.

Poached Chicken Mousse

This recipe is a variation of Poached Fish Mousse, page 419. The technique is identical. Follow the same instructions as the fish mousse for this chicken mousse. This is also very good at room temperature or slightly warm with Vinaigrette Sauce with Herbs and Hard-Boiled Egg, page 72.

SERVES 8 AS A FIRST COURSE

1¼ pounds ground chicken breast
2 egg whites
1½ cups heavy cream
1½ teaspoons salt
2 pinches of cayenne pepper
3 chicken livers

2 tablespoons butter
¼ cup unsalted shelled
  pistachios
1½ quarts Chicken Stock, page 74
Sauce for Quenelles, page 422

1. Using the first 5 ingredients above, prepare the chicken mousse following steps 1–3 for Poached Fish Mousse, page 419.

2. Remove and discard fat and sinews from the chicken livers and cut the livers into small pieces. Melt 2 tablespoons butter in a small skillet. Over high heat, add the chicken livers and sauté for 2 minutes.

3. Boil 2 cups water and parboil the pistachios for 5 minutes. Skin and split in two.

4. Fold the chicken livers and pistachios into the chicken mousse. Wrap the mousse in cheesecloth and poach it like the fish mousse (steps 4–7) for 45 minutes, using chicken stock instead of fish stock.

5. Prepare a light sauce following the Sauce for Quenelles recipe, page 422, but substitute Chicken Stock for the fish stock. Or, serve at room temperature with a Vinaigrette Sauce with Herbs and Hard-Boiled Eggs, page 72.

Glazed Vegetables
(Onions, Carrots, and Turnips)

Glazed vegetables are a wonderful garnish for roasts and fowls.

Special instructions. There are 2 parts to the preparation: steaming and glazing the vegetables. Steam them several hours ahead of time, if necessary, but glaze at the last minute.

Special kitchen utensil. A collapsible vegetable steamer that fits in a 3-quart pan.

SERVES 6–8

24 pearl onions	2 tablespoons sugar
6 small white turnips	¼ cup homemade stock or water
12-ounce bag of finger-size carrots	½ teaspoon salt
3 cups water	Freshly ground black pepper
3 tablespoons sweet butter	

1. Peel the vegetables. Quarter the turnips. If you find one that is woody or pithy inside, discard. Round off the corners of the pieces to make them look like big olives. If the small carrots are unavailable substitute medium-size ones, but quarter them lengthwise.

2. Steam each vegetable separately in a vegetable steamer fitted in a 3-quart pan with 3 cups of water at the bottom. Cover the pan tightly and steam

for about 5 minutes for the onions and turnips, and 8–10 minutes for the carrots. Reserve.

3. Melt 3 tablespoons butter in a 12" cast-iron skillet. When the butter stops sizzling, add the vegetables, shaking the skillet with one hand and turning the vegetables with a steel spatula to make sure they get coated all over with butter, then sprinkle with 2 tablespoons sugar and shake the pan once again for a minute, to coat the vegetables with the sugar. When they start caramelizing, add ¼ cup stock (or substitute water, if you do not have any stock handy), and cook over medium heat until the liquids evaporate and the vegetables are golden brown. Sprinkle ½ teaspoon salt and freshly ground pepper over them.

Roast Duck with a Caramel-Vinegar Sauce

Mallard, Muscovies, and White Pekin ducks are the varieties found in the United States, with the White Pekin duck widely available. Remember that a fresh duck might not be superior to a frozen one—it depends more on the brand. In the East, I buy the Maple Leaf Farm ducks from Milford, Indiana, and prefer it to the Long Island White Pekin ducks when I roast a duck. There is better quality control, and they are less fatty than the Long Island brands. When I make a Preserved Duck (a confit), I choose White Pekin ducks because I need as much fat as possible to preserve them.

Special instructions. Since a duck can serve only 2–3 persons, I generally roast 2 ducks for 4 people and 3 ducks for 6–8. (They may serve 8, especially with several courses.)

Special kitchen utensil. A roasting pan 12" x 16" x 1½" or a broiler pan.

SERVES 6–8

Three 3½-pound ducklings
Several parsley sprigs
¾ teaspoon salt
Freshly ground black pepper
1 tablespoon oil

About 1 cup Duck Stock, page 266
Watercress to garnish
Caramel-Vinegar Sauce, opposite

Several hours before roasting, prepare steps 1, 2, and 3.

1. Cut off the last joint of the wings of the ducks. Keep them with the necks for a stock. Reserve the livers for Duck Liver with Scrambled Eggs, page 275.

2. Feel the wishbone with your fingers under the skin at the top of the breast and remove it, using a sharp boning knife, holding it perpendicular to the bone, cracking both ends and tearing the bone loose. Wash and dry the cavities of the ducks. Stuff 1 or 2 parsley sprigs, ¼ teaspoon salt, and freshly ground pepper in each cavity.

3. Truss the ducks following the technique to truss chicken, page 19, but wrap an extra turn around the tips of the legs because duck legs are smaller than chicken legs.

   Preheat oven to 400°F.

4. Grease the bottom of the roasting pan and skillet with 1 tablespoon oil. Place the ducks on their sides in the pan and roast in the oven for 1½ hours. Every 15 minutes, turn the ducks on their opposite sides, then on their breasts, and finally on their backs. Remove the fats gathered in the pan with a basting spoon or bulb baster.

5. For the last 45 minutes roasting time, start basting the ducks with ¼ cup of duck stock every 10 minutes. There should be only about ⅔ cup of juices plus the fat at the end of the roasting time. Transfer the ducks to a carving board with a juice catcher. Stand the ducks on end to drain the juices gathered in the cavities. Remove any burnt particles in the roasting pan. If there is not enough liquid left in the roasting pan, add more duck stock. Reheat, scraping the sides. Strain the liquids, degrease, and reserve.

6. Carve each duck: legs first, then split the breast lengthwise in the center, then bone each side of the breast. Drain the juices back into the roasting pan. Keep the carved duck pieces, skin-side up, on a broiler rack. (This can be done before dinner; just cover with aluminum foil and keep in a warm oven.)

7. Prepare the Caramel-Vinegar sauce.

8. Just before eating the ducks, turn the broiler on and broil the duck pieces for 1 minute or so to crisp the skin.

9. Serve with Glazed Vegetables, page 424, and Fresh Pasta, page 166, or the Purée of Cauliflower and Carrots, page 285.

Note. The ducks are very good without the caramel sauce. Degrease and reheat the juice in the roasting pan, adding about ⅔ cup stock. Bring to a boil and boil for 1 minute. Then, off the flame, strain juices and whisk in 2 tablespoons butter. Correct seasonings with salt and pepper.

Caramel–Vinegar Sauce

MAKES ½ CUP

3 tablespoons sugar
4 tablespoons red-wine vinegar

⅔ cup duck pan juices from
  preceding recipe, page 425
2 tablespoons sweet butter

1. The first step can be prepared
   while the ducks are roasting.
   Combine the sugar and vinegar
   in a caramel pot or a 1½-quart
   stainless steel pan and stir until
   dissolved. Cook over medium
   heat until the sugar caramelizes,
   about 8 minutes. Reserve.

2. After carving the ducks (see preceding recipe), reheat the pan
   juices to a boil, scraping the
   sides of the pan with a wooden
   spoon, adding ⅔ cup duck stock.
   Boil for 1 minute or so.

3. Strain the juices through a fine-mesh sieve into the caramel. Reheat and
   whisk the sauce until smooth. Bring back to a boil. The sauce should
   be shiny in color and of a light syrupy consistency. If it is too runny,
   continue boiling it down until enough liquid evaporates to bring it to
   a syrupy consistency, about 5 minutes. Off the flame, whisk in 2 tablespoons butter.

Roast Chicken with
Caramel–Vinegar Sauce

Special kitchen utensils. A 12″ x 16″ x 1½″ roasting pan or two 9″ cast-iron
skillets.

SERVES 8

Two 3-pound chickens
1 teaspoon salt
Freshly ground black pepper
4 tablespoons butter

2 tablespoons oil
2 cups dry white wine
Caramel-Vinegar Sauce, page 427,
  using chicken juices

1. Rub each of the chicken cavities with ¼ teaspoon salt and sprinkle in freshly ground pepper.

2. Melt 2 tablespoons butter and 1 tablespoon oil in each of two 9″ cast-iron skillets. When the butter is hot but not smoking, brown the chickens evenly all over at medium-high heat. Be careful not to let the fats burn. Remove the chickens to a platter when browned (about 20 minutes).

Preheat oven to 400°F.

3. Deglaze the skillets with 1 cup dry white wine in each skillet, scraping the sides and bottom well to loosen the crusty bits. Bring the wine to a boil and turn off the heat. Return the chickens to the skillets or the roasting pan. Season each with ¼ teaspoon salt and freshly ground pepper.

4. Roast uncovered at 400°F. for 1 hour and 15 minutes, basting every 15 minutes with pan juices or ⅓ cup water if the pan juices are evaporating. At the end of the cooking you should have about ½ cup of pan juices in each skillet or 1 cup of pan juices in the roasting pan.

5. Transfer the chickens to a cutting board grooved around the edge with a juice catcher and cut each in 8 pieces (illustration, pages 96–97). Pour the chicken juices back into one skillet, bring to a boil, and reduce to ⅔ cup.

6. Prepare the Caramel-Vinegar Sauce, page 427, according to the recipe, substituting chicken juices for the duck juices.

Orange Sunburst Tart

For this orange tart, the puff pastry dough is rolled out and formed into a round pastry shell. The dough needs 6 turns for the sides to puff up quite high. The tart is baked, then caramel poured over the bottom of the tart. It is filled with an orange custard and decorated with orange slices in a sunburst design. Be sure to buy sweet California oranges. The sweeter the oranges, the better the dessert will be.

Special instructions. Most of the work can be done ahead of time. I suggest you prepare the tart shell at least 2 days ahead of time and keep it refrigerated or even frozen. Cook the orange custard a day ahead of time. Peel the oranges for the decoration and skin the wedges in the morning of the dinner. Bake the tart shell in the afternoon and make the caramel that afternoon also.

Special kitchen utensils. A 12″ lid and a 10″ lid to shape the round pastry shell.

MAKES 1 ROUND TART; SERVES 8

Puff Pastry with 6 turns,
  page 296

For the orange custard

4 egg yolks
⅓ cup sugar
2 tablespoons flour
2 tablespoons cornstarch
1 tablespoon grated orange peel
1 tablespoon grated lemon peel
1½ cups orange juice freshly
  squeezed
4 tablespoons sweet butter
1 tablespoon Cointreau

For the decoration

8 California navel oranges
1 tablespoon Cointreau
⅔ cup apricot jam

For the caramel

⅓ cup superfine sugar
2 tablespoons water

1. Roll out the Puff Pastry into a 13″ square. Roll up the square of dough
   on your rolling pin and unroll it onto a baking sheet. Freeze for 30
   minutes.

2. From now on keep the dough on the baking sheet to keep its shape
   without handling it too much. Place a 12″ in diameter pot lid over
   the dough and cut around the lid to make a circle 12″ in diameter.

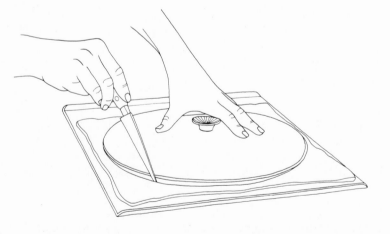

Remove the dough outside the circle; do not bunch it together, but save
the pieces flat on a baking sheet in the refrigerator to make Sugar Cookies (Palmiers), page 302.

3. Place a 10″ pot lid over the 12″ circle and cut around the lid, leaving a 1″ wide strip outside the 10″ circle. Freeze the dough for 5 minutes to firm it up before continuing.

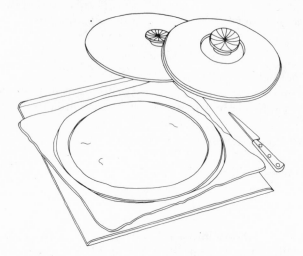

4. To shape the round Puff Pastry shell: Brush cold water 1″ wide all around the edge of the 10″ circle, and gently stick the strip of Puff Pastry on top of the circle all around; overlap the strip for 2″, cut off the remaining piece, and add it to the leftover pieces. Be sure that the strip is flush with the edge of the bottom piece. Prick the strip of dough together with the bottom part of a fork, holding the strip down with 2 open fingers while pricking between the fingers to hold the dough from moving. The tart shell is now ready to bake or freeze.

5. *The orange custard.* In a mixer at medium-high speed, beat 4 egg yolks and ⅓ cup sugar until the mixture becomes thick and pale yellow (about 5 minutes). Sift 2 tablespoons of flour and 2 tablespoons of cornstarch together. Grate 1 tablespoon of orange peel and 1 tablespoon of lemon peel. Squeeze 1½ cups of fresh orange juice. With the mixer still on, incorporate the flour and cornstarch, then add the grated orange

and lemon peels and pour in the orange juice in a continuous stream. Transfer the mixture to a 3½-quart saucepan and cook over medium heat until the mixture becomes *very thick* (about 10 minutes). Dunk the bottom of the pan in cold water to cool the mixture, still whisking for a minute or two. Transfer the custard to a mixing bowl. Cool for 20 minutes. Cream 4 tablespoons butter with the heel of your hand to soften it, then whisk 1 tablespoon of butter at a time into the orange custard. Whisk in 1 tablespoon Cointreau, but no more; otherwise, the custard will be too loose as a filling for the tart. Cover the bowl with plastic wrap and refrigerate overnight if you wish. The filling must be cold to fill the tart.

6. *How to peel the oranges for the decoration*. With a serrated knife, over a plate to catch the juices, cut off the skin and white pith of the 8 navel oranges, using a sawinglike movement; when peeled, the flesh of the orange must show. Cut each orange in half from top to bottom, not crossways. Holding half an orange in your left hand, slice off the skin that separates the wedges to the center stem but do not cut off, just fold the skin under your thumb, then with the knife, held next to the inside of the wedge, slip it under the wedge to pry it loose from the skin of the next wedge, and continue until all the wedges are free from their skins. It takes time, but can be done in the morning of the dinner. Sprinkle 1 tablespoon of Cointreau over the orange slices and reserve for the decoration at the last minute before eating the tart.

Preheat oven to 425°F.

7. *Baking the tart*. Line the inside of the pastry circle with foil and add dry beans or aluminum pellets to keep the dough from bubbling and losing its shape, but be careful not to load too many beans or pellets against the round strip; otherwise, while baking the strip (the sides of

the shell) will lose its shape and cook unevenly. Brush milk on the top of the strip. Bake on a middle shelf of the oven for 25 minutes.

8. Remove the tart shell, lower the oven temperature to 400°F. and remove the pellets and foil carefully, prying the foil loose with a knife if it sticks to the dough. The bottom of the pastry will swell up while baking; pry it loose from the sides with the tines of a fork and remove it; otherwise, the bottom all around will not be cooked enough (bake the uncooked pastry to munch on). Prick the bottom of the pastry once more with a fork. Bake 10 more minutes, or until the shell is dry. Cover loosely with foil if the edges are too brown.

9. *The caramel.* Combine ⅓ cup sugar with 2 tablespoons water in a sauce-pan and bring it to a boil. Stir to mix the sugar and water and cook over medium heat for about 8 minutes or until the syrup changes to a deep amber color. Quickly pour the caramel over the bottom of the pastry shell; spread it around with a wooden spatula, if necessary, to cover the whole bottom of the tart shell.

10. Drain the orange slices. Combine ⅔ cup apricot jam with the orange juice in a saucepan and bring it to a boil. Cook it until the mixture (glaze) is slightly syrupy (it will take several minutes). Strain through a fine-mesh sieve and reserve in a saucepan.

11. *The assembly of the tart.* Fill the tart shell with the orange custard, then, just before serving, arrange the orange wedges on top in concentric circles to make a "sunburst" design. Brush the glaze over the oranges and the top and sides of the pastry. (Reheat the glaze if necessary.) You must do this at the last minute; otherwise, the orange slices will still give more juice and will thin out the glaze on the tart. Serve.

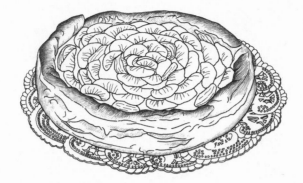

Strawberry Tart with Puff Pastry

The strawberry tart is a variation of the preceding Orange Sunburst Tart. Read carefully the instructions given on page 428 to shape the round pastry shell.

SERVES 8

Puff Pastry with 6 turns, page 296
Pastry Cream for Filling Cakes,
    page 251
2 tablespoons strawberry or
    raspberry liqueur

½ pound strawberries
½ cup superfine sugar
⅔ cup apricot jam
Cream-Cheese Topping,
    page 27

1. Follow the instructions, page 429, to make the pastry shell and to bake it.

2. Prepare the Pastry Cream according to the recipe, page 251, but substitute 1 tablespoon of strawberry or raspberry liqueur for the Cognac in the recipe.

3. Don't remove the stems when washing the strawberries; otherwise, water will penetrate. Drain well. Then sprinkle them with ½ cup sugar and the remaining tablespoon of liqueur. Marinate for 1 hour.

4. Drain the strawberries. Combine the juices with ⅔ cup apricot jam in a saucepan and boil it down to a syrupy consistency. Strain through a fine-mesh sieve and reserve in a saucepan.

5. Prepare the Cream-Cheese Topping, page 27. Serve in a sauceboat.

6. *The assembly of the tart.* Fill the tart shell with the cold custard, then decorate with the strawberries, hulling them at the last minute. Reheat the glaze, if necessary, and brush it over the strawberries and the top and sides of the pastry.

TECHNIQUES AND UTENSILS INTRODUCED

How to roast and carve a saddle of lamb or venison

How to shape éclairs

How to prepare and bake savory and sweet filled
rounds of puff pastry

How to use butter cream, pastry cream, and Italian
meringue together in a Paris-Brest

Lesson 22

RECITES

RECIPES

Onion Custard Tart

Leeks in Puff Pastry

Almond Butter Cake (Pithiviers)

Lentil Purée

Celery Root Purée

Caramelized Apples and Pears

Roasted Saddle of Lamb

Roasted Saddle of Venison

Morels Sauce for Roasted Saddle of Lamb or Venison

Finger-size Chocolate Eclairs

Chocolate Truffles

Paris-Brest: A Triple-Filling Cream Puff Cake

Suggested Menus for Lesson 22

Christmas Menus

Vegetable Pâté
(Lesson 8)

Roasted Saddle of Lamb

Scalloped Potatoes with Wine
(Lesson 17)

Lemon Soufflé (Lesson 15)
with Sugar Cookies (Palmiers)
(Lesson 15)

Leeks in Puff Pastry

Roasted Saddle of Venison

Caramelized Apples and Pears

Split Pea Purée
(Lesson 2)

Chestnut Meringue Cake
(Lesson 19)

Sweetbread Salad
(Lesson 16)

Roast Duck with
Caramel-Vinegar Sauce
(Lesson 21)

Celery Root Purée

Raspberry Sherbet
(Lesson 9)

Chocolate Fudge Cake
(Lesson 8)

Oyster Soup (Lesson 19)

Poached and Roasted Goose
(Lesson 19)

Caramelized Apples and Pears

Lentil Purée

Paris-Brest

Chocolate Truffles

Buffet for New Year's Eve

Layered Vegetable Pâté
(Lesson 8)

Onion Custard Tart

Cold Beef Fillet (Lesson 17)

Béarnaise Sauce (Lesson 17)

Steamed Broccoli and Carrots
(Lesson 16)

St. Tropez Cream Cake
(Lesson 13) or
Rum Cake (Lesson 11)

Finger-size Chocolate Eclairs

Onion Custard Tart

I serve this Onion Tart as an hors d'oeuvre. It is the Rolls Royce of all the quiches. An onion custard baked in a round puff pastry tart shell, it has a very delicate flavor and is very rich. A small wedge per person is enough, I believe, as an hors d'oeuvre. It also makes a lovely brunch or light supper served with a tossed green salad.

Special instructions. Prepare the tart shell a day or two ahead of time, refrigerate or freeze, and prepare the onion custard a day ahead of time. Bake the tart about 2 hours before eating it.

Special kitchen utensil. A jelly-roll pan about 11" x 16" x 1".

SERVES 8

Puff Pastry with 6 turns, page 296
6 medium-size yellow onions
3 tablespoons sweet butter
1½ teaspoons salt
4 large eggs

1½ cups heavy cream
½ teaspoon salt
¼ teaspoon freshly ground black
  pepper

1. Prepare the Puff Pastry dough and shape it in a round tart shell as for the Orange Sunburst Tart, page 428, steps 2–4. Freeze until needed.

2. Peel and split the onions in half. With the flat side down, cut very thin slices. Melt 3 tablespoons butter in a 12" cast-iron skillet, add the onions, and stir them for about 2 minutes, making sure that all the onions get coated with butter. Sprinkle 1 teaspoon salt over them. Cover tightly and cook over medium-low heat for 45 minutes, checking every so often to make sure the onions are not sticking or burning. Purée the cooked onions through a food mill or in a food processor, then pass through a fine-mesh sieve (illustration, pages 36–37) to make about 1 cup of very smooth liquidish purée.

3. Beat 4 eggs lightly in a 2-quart mixing bowl. Stir in the onion purée and 1½ cups heavy cream. Season with ½ teaspoon salt and ¼ teaspoon freshly ground pepper. Taste and correct seasonings if need be.

   Preheat oven to 425°F.

4. Remove the unbaked tart shell from the refrigerator or freezer. Transfer it to a jelly-roll pan. Line the inside of the circle with foil, add dry beans or aluminum pellets, but don't overload against the round strip; otherwise, while baking, the sides of the shell will bake unevenly. Brush milk on the top of the strip. Bake on the middle shelf of the oven for 20 minutes. Remove the pellets and foil, unsticking the foil, if necessary, with a knife. With a fork, prick the bottom of the pastry and bake 10 more minutes to dry out the bottom.

5. Lower the temperature to 400°F. Now you must check the sides of the pastry for holes; if you find any, plug them up with extra uncooked dough (or foil if you have no scraps of Puff Pastry). Ladle the onion-cream mixture into the tart shell, checking for leaks on the sides. If there is a leak, plug it up right away as you pour in the mixture. Bake on the middle shelf for 45 minutes or until the top of the custard is lightly golden. Cool. Serve warm. The onions develop more flavor while cooling.

An Onion Custard

You can bake the onion custard in a greased 1-quart baking dish at 350°F. for 30 minutes and serve as a vegetable with a roast. Or bake the onion custard in a precooked shell of Shortcrust Pastry, page 90, for 35 minutes in a 350°F. oven.

Leeks in Puff Pastry

A filling made with leeks is baked between two unbaked Puff Pastry circles brushed with an egg glaze. The leek pie puffs up to a beautiful-looking golden cake. It is a very versatile recipe; you can serve wedges for an hors d'oeuvre, for a vegetable course, or for a light supper with a tossed green salad.

Special instruction. Leeks in Puff Pastry can be done ahead of time and frozen. Bake when needed.

Special kitchen utensils. A 10″ pot lid and a jelly-roll pan 11″ x 16″ x 1″.

SERVES 6–8

4 medium-size leeks*	¼ cup heavy cream
3 tablespoons sweet butter	¼ cup freshly grated Swiss cheese
½ teaspoon salt	Puff Pastry with 6 turns, page 296
Freshly ground black pepper	Glaze: 1 egg yolk mixed with
Pinch of nutmeg	½ tablespoon water

* Substitute 6 yellow onions if leeks are not available.

1. *Prepare the stuffing.* Cut off the tops of the leeks at the point where they are very light green (save the dark green tops for a soup). Split the white of the leeks lengthwise to about ½″ from the root. Wash well under running cold water to remove any sand. Mince by hand (yields 2½ cups).

2. Melt 3 tablespoons butter in a 4-quart Dutch oven. When the butter stops sizzling, add the minced leeks and stir well to coat them all with butter.

Season with ½ teaspoon salt, freshly ground pepper, and a pinch of nutmeg. Cover tightly and cook for 10 minutes over low heat, checking frequently to make sure the leeks are not burning, which happens easily. Pour in ¼ cup heavy cream and cook, covered, for 15 minutes or until the mixture thickens to a purée-like consistency. Cool while you grate ¼ cup Swiss cheese. Mix the cheese with the leeks. Taste and correct seasonings with salt and pepper, if necessary. Refrigerate until very cold.

3. Cut Puff Pastry in half; refrigerate 1 piece. Flour a pastry surface and a rolling pin and roll out the remaining piece of Puff Pastry into a 10″ square of uniform thickness. Use your hands to stretch the dough, if necessary. Freeze on a baking sheet, covered with waxed paper, for 15 minutes. Repeat with the other piece of pastry dough and freeze on a second baking sheet.

4. Place a 10″ pot lid over each square and cut out 2 perfect circles, keeping the dough on the cookie sheets. Freeze the 2 circles once more on each baking sheet for 15 minutes. It will then be easier to transfer the circles of dough onto a jelly-roll pan without losing their shape.

5. Transfer one of the cold circles to a jelly-roll pan and spread the leek filling over it, leaving ¾″ edge free all around. Brush the free edge with cold water. Cover the leek filling with the second circle and gently press the top layer of the pastry dough down against the bottom one all the way around the edge to stick the edges together, but be sure the top and bottom circles of dough are flush. Prick the edge with a fork all around on the top piece. Decorate the top of the Puff Pastry by drawing straight lines across it with the back of a knife blade. Be sure the dough is cold when you do this—it's easier to draw lines on cold dough. Draw parallel lines about ¾″ apart all the way across, then turn the pie not quite a quarter turn and repeat. This will give you a diamond shape figure all over the top (see illustration, page 371). Refrigerate or freeze until needed.

Preheat oven to 450°F.

6. Mix 1 egg yolk with ½ tablespoon water and brush it over the refrigerated or frozen pie. Bake for 10 minutes on the middle shelf of the oven, then reduce oven temperature to 400°F. and bake for 30 more minutes, covering the top of the pie with loose foil, if necessary. While baking, butter may ooze out of the pie. It comes from the stuffing—that is why it is important to bake the pie in a jelly-roll pan.

7. Remove the pie from the oven and allow to cool for 20 minutes or so. The flavor of the leeks, like onions, comes through better when they are lukewarm than when they are hot.

Almond Butter Cake (Pithiviers)

In France, there is a town of 10,000 people called Pithiviers, 50 miles south of Paris that is immortalized for this almond butter puff pastry cake. You can buy it in every self-respecting pastry and bakery shop in town. Adept at Puff Pastry, you can make a better one—and you can eat it fresh out of the oven, whereas most Pithiviers bought in a pastry shop have been baked too many hours before they are eaten.

SERVES 6–8

Puff Pastry with 6 turns, page 296	1 tablespoon rum
⅔ cup shelled almonds	1 egg
¼ teaspoon almond extract	4 tablespoons sweet butter
	½ cup sugar

1. Follow the directions for Leeks in Puff Pastry, page 438, to shape the Puff Pastry. But substitute the Almond Butter Cream, page 317.

2. Pulverize the almonds in a blender or in the food processor, add ¼ teaspoon almond extract, 1 tablespoon rum, 1 egg, 4 tablespoons sweet butter and ½ cup sugar. Turn on the machine for 10 seconds or so to mix all ingredients. Freeze for 30 minutes before filling the pastry with it following the directions of Leeks in Puff Pastry.

Lentil Purée

Purées of lentils, split peas, page 38, and white beans, page 286, are the perfect accompaniment for roasted meats and fowls.

I highly recommend the extra work of forcing the purée through a fine-mesh sieve. The difference is remarkable, not only in aspect, but in taste.

Special kitchen utensil. A 6½-quart Dutch oven.

SERVES 10

2 carrots	½ teaspoon dried thyme
2 medium-size onions	1 bay leaf
2 whole cloves	1 rib celery with a few leaves, cut in 3 pieces
1 parsnip	
1 pound lentils	2 teaspoons salt
About 5 cups water	Freshly ground black pepper
Several sprigs of parsley	4 tablespoons sweet butter

1. Peel the carrots and cut in ¼″ thick slices. Peel the onions and stick a clove in each one. Peel the parsnip and cut into large pieces.

2. Put the lentils in a 6½-quart Dutch oven, cover generously with water (about 5 cups), and bury the vegetables in the lentils. Add the parsley, thyme, bay leaf, celery, 2 teaspoons salt, and freshly ground pepper. Bring to a boil slowly; then cover and simmer over medium-low heat for 1 hour, or until the lentils are tender. Stir once in a while.

3. Drain the lentils, reserving the liquids for later. Purée the lentils, carrots, onions (cloves removed), celery, and parsnip through the food mill or in the food processor or electric blender. If the purée is very dry, add some of the cooking liquid. (I generally put in about a cup of liquid.) Then force the purée through a fine-mesh sieve (see illustration, pages 36–37). It will remove the skins of the lentils, which are indigestible. Can be prepared ahead of time to this point. Reheat the purée in a covered pan set in a water bath (see illustration, page 35) or in a double boiler, and whisk the purée once in a while while reheating.

4. When the purée is hot, take off the heat and whisk in the 4 tablespoons butter, 1 tablespoon at a time. Taste and correct seasonings with more salt and pepper to enhance the flavors.

Celery Root Purée

The best time to buy celery root, sometimes called celeriac or celery knob, is in late autumn and early winter. Later the celery roots are very big and they are sometimes bitter.

Special kitchen utensils. A stainless steel paring knife; a 6½-quart Dutch oven.

SERVES 6

3 pounds celery root	1½ teaspoons salt
1 clove garlic	Freshly ground black pepper
1 cup milk	4 tablespoons (½ stick) sweet
½ cup cream	butter

1. Using a stainless steel knife, peel the celery roots. Cut in small cubes and cover with cold water in a 6½-quart Dutch oven. Add 1 garlic clove and 1 tablespoon salt. Bring the water to a boil, cover, and cook until tender (about 30 minutes).

2. Drain the celery root. Purée through a food mill or in a food processor fitted with the metal blade. Add 1 cup milk and mix thoroughly. Force

through a fine-mesh sieve (see pages 36–37). Mix in ½ cup cream until the texture is that of mashed potatoes. Season gradually with 1½ teaspoons salt and freshly ground pepper. Taste and correct the seasonings.

3. Reheat in a water bath, covering the pan. Just before eating the purée, off the flame, whisk in 4 tablespoons sweet butter, 1 tablespoon at a time. Taste once more to correct seasonings with salt.

Caramelized Apples and Pears

Caramelized Apples and Pears cut down the strong taste of venison (see page 445) for those who are perhaps a little timid to eat meat with a wild flavor.

Special instruction. Around Christmastime, buy Cortland, Northern Spies, or Stayman apples—or Golden Delicious apples as the last resort. Choose Bosc or Anjou pears.

Special kitchen utensils. Two 12″ cast-iron skillets.

SERVES 6–8

5 pears	⅔ cup sugar
5 apples	2 teaspoons pear brandy
8 tablespoons sweet butter	2 teaspoons applejack or Calvados

1. Peel and split the pears in half lengthwise. Cut each half of the pear crosswise into ¾″ thick slices. Peel and core and quarter the apples, then cut them into ½″ thick slices.

2. Melt 4 tablespoons butter in each of two 12″ cast-iron skillets with the apples in 1 skillet and the pears in the other one. Sprinkle ⅓ cup sugar over each fruit and sauté over medium heat, shaking the skillets once in a while, and turning the fruits with a metal spatula to keep them from scorching. First, the fruits will render their juices and evaporate, and then the fruits will start to caramelize. (It takes about 20 minutes to caramelize.) Sprinkle 2 teaspoons of pear brandy over the pears and 2 teaspoons of applejack or Calvados over the apples.

Note. The caramelized fruits can be puréed in a food mill or food processor for delicious apple or pear sauce.

Roasted Saddle of Lamb

I roast a saddle of lamb in an unorthodox way: upside down for 30 minutes, then right side up for 15 more minutes. Why? One evening, in class, a student roasted the saddle upside down without realizing it. When I looked in the oven and saw the roast in that position, I quickly turned it right side up for the last 15 minutes and what a marvel—it was cooked perfectly.

Roasted the classic way—that is, right side up—the loins are generally slightly overcooked and the fillets (also called tenderloins) are too rare. Whereas, that evening with the roast upside down, the skirts (which are generally under the roast and not on top as they were that evening) prevented the fillets from overcooking, but they were just the right pink throughout. The loins at the bottom for the first 30 minutes stayed rare, and when the roast was turned upside up, the loins continued cooking just for 15 more minutes and were just pink throughout. Since that evening, I always have roasted a saddle of lamb this way! Why don't you try it?

Special instructions. The anatomy of a saddle consists of 2 loins, 2 fillets, and 2 skirts. Throughout most of the year, a saddle trimmed weighs around 4–5 pounds; only in late April or May can the saddle of spring lamb weigh less than 3 pounds. If so, roast the saddle for 15 minutes upside down at 450°F. and 15 minutes right side up at 400°F. Let stand 10 minutes at room temperature before carving.

Special kitchen utensil. A 12″ cast-iron skillet or a roasting pan 16″ x 12″ x 1½″.

SERVES 6

1 clove garlic	½ teaspoon salt
1 teaspoon dried thyme	Freshly ground black pepper
5-pound saddle of lamb, trimmed	1 cup chicken stock
2 tablespoons vegetable oil	2 tablespoons sweet butter

Preheat oven to 450°F.

1. Peel the garlic clove and cut into small slivers. Coat the slivers of garlic with thyme. Cut off all the fat on top of the meat (if the skirts become detached, just tie them to the roast with strings). Make incisions in the 2 loins, skirts, and fillets and bury the garlic slivers in the meat. Tie the saddle with several strings.

2. Place the roast in a roasting pan or a 12" cast-iron skillet skirt side up (i.e., upside down); dribble 2 tablespoons vegetable oil over it; roast on the middle rack of the oven for 15 minutes.

3. After 15 minutes, drop the temperature of the oven to 400°F. Sprinkle ½ teaspoon salt and freshly ground pepper over the roast. Baste the meat with the pan juices every 10 minutes for 30 minutes. After 15 minutes, turn the roast over to brown the top of the loins.

4. Remove the meat from the oven and check its internal temperature with a meat thermometer. (Use a quick-reading kind rather than the sort that remains in the meat while it cooks.) For a medium-rare roast, the temperature should read 130°F. Do not touch the bone; it will give an incorrect reading, since bones get very hot and transmit heat. Wait 10 minutes before carving. The roast will still cook and go to 135°F.

5. Now you must work fast. Carve the meat on a cutting board grooved around the edges. Bone the 2 loins in 1 piece each. Don't be afraid— against the bone the meat looks very rare, but it quickly loses that aspect when you cut each loin into ½" thick slices. Cut the skirts into strips. Bone the 2 fillets and slice each into 3 pieces.

6. Scrape the roasting pan with 1 cup chicken stock and the juices that run out of the roast. Reduce to ½ cup. Taste for seasonings and correct with salt and pepper. Then whisk in 2 tablespoons butter off the flame. Serve in a preheated sauceboat.

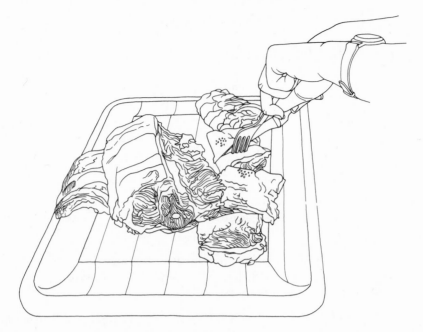

In this recipe, the saddle is cooked rare to medium-rare, but it is also very good cooked longer. Just add 30–45 minutes to the cooking time. The given roasting time is for half a saddle about 4½–5 pounds, 10″ long and with the loins each 2½″–3″ in diameter. Sometimes, the racks are shorter with thicker loins. If so, roast 15 minutes longer than called for in the recipe.

7. *Optional.* The sauce can be enriched with dried morels and cream, see page 447.

Roasted Saddle of Venison

I marinate the saddle for 48 hours in wine and aromatic vegetables. Just follow step 1 for Oxtail Stew, page 190. Then, drain the saddle. Dry it with paper towels. Combine the marinade liquid and its vegetables in a 3-quart pan and cook until the liquids reduce to 2 cups. Smear 5 tablespoons soft butter all over the saddle. Roast it upside down as for a lamb saddle (see illustration, opposite) in a 450°F. preheated oven for 15 minutes. Add 1 cup of the reserved marinade liquid and the vegetables to the roast. Lower the temperature to 425°F. Roast for 15 minutes at 425°F. basting once in a while, then turn the saddle right side up, add the remaining cup of marinade liquid and continue roasting for 15 more minutes. Follow steps 4, 5 and 6 for Saddle of Lamb to carve and finish the sauce.

Morel Sauce for
Roasted Saddle of Lamb or Venison

1 ounce dried morels
1 cup water
2 tablespoons butter
½ cup heavy cream

Pan juices from Roast Saddle of
Lamb, page 443, or Roast
Saddle of Venison, page 445

1. Soak the morels in water for 1 hour. Drain and reserve the morel liquid. Be sure to wash them again under running cold water to remove any sand that might be left on the stems. Quarter them.

2. Melt 2 tablespoons butter in a small skillet and sauté the morels for 3 minutes. Add ½ cup heavy cream and ¼ cup strained morel liquid. Cover and cook for 5 minutes.

3. Add to the pan juices from the lamb or venison roast and bring back to a boil. Boil, stirring, until the liquids thicken slightly. Turn off the heat. Taste and correct seasonings with salt and pepper.

Finger–Size Chocolate Eclairs

For a buffet dinner, these small éclairs make a great dessert. There is no need for plates; they are so small they can be eaten in one bite. I prefer a chocolate butter cream filling to the standard custard filling.

Special instructions. Bake the cream puff dough a day ahead of time and keep the unfilled éclairs in closed plastic bags, but do not refrigerate. Or bake the dough several days before and freeze the éclairs in foil. Prepare the chocolate butter cream 1–2 days ahead of time. Fill and ice the éclairs the day of the buffet.

Special kitchen utensils. Two cookie sheets 14″ x 17″.

MAKES ABOUT 60 SMALL ECLAIRS

Cream Puff Dough, page 49
1 teaspoon sugar

Glaze: 1 egg yolk beaten with
½ tablespoon water

For the butter cream

4 egg yolks
¾ cup sugar
6 tablespoons water
24 tablespoons (3 sticks) sweet
  butter
4 tablespoons praline cream (see
  page 409 to buy it) or 4 tablespoons ground hazelnuts

6 ounces bittersweet chocolate
  (Lindt or Tobler)
1 tablespoon dark rum (Myers's)

For the chocolate icing

¼ cup heavy cream
2 ounces bittersweet chocolate
2 tablespoons dark rum (Myers's)

1. Prepare the Cream Puff Dough, following the quantities of ingredients
   and the instructions, page 49, but add 1 teaspoon sugar with the butter
   and water and substitute ⅛ teaspoon salt for the ½ teaspoon in the master recipe.

   Preheat oven to 400°F.

2. To shape the éclairs: Butter 2 cookie sheets and dust them with flour.
   With your index finger, trace about sixty 2″ long and ½″ wide lines with
   a 1″ space between them on the 2 prepared cookie sheets. Transfer the
   Cream Puff Dough to a pastry bag fitted with a ½″ tube (illustration,
   page 51). Pipe small éclairs following the lines traced on the baking
   sheets; finish each éclair by cutting off the dough with the tube against
   the cookie sheet. Dip a fork in cold water; with the back of the fork,

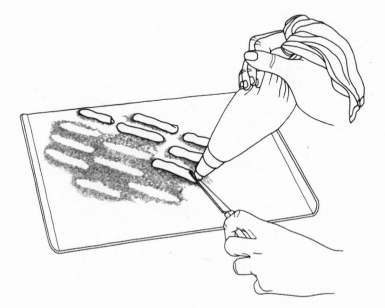

gently flatten each éclair a little. Brush with an egg glaze (1 egg yolk and ½ tablespoon water beaten together). Bake on the middle and middle-top shelves of the oven for about 20 minutes. Check one of the éclairs; open it—it should be just a little moist, not completely dry inside. (One of the problems with éclairs is that sometimes they are too dry—but you must cook them enough; otherwise, they will deflate once they are out of the oven.)

3. Let the éclairs cool completely. Keep them in a closed plastic bag un-refrigerated until the next day or freeze in aluminum paper for several days.

4. For the butter cream: Follow the instructions on page 52, but remem-ber to use the amount of ingredients noted in this recipe. Substitute chocolate and praliné paste or ground hazelnuts for the crystallized gin-ger called for in the Butter Cream recipe.

The day of the buffet

5. If the éclairs are frozen, preheat the oven to 350°F. and bake the frozen éclairs still wrapped in foil until they are warmed through. Then cut the éclairs as you would to open a book.

6. Whip the cold chocolate butter cream to soften it and transfer it to a pastry bag fitted with a serrated tube. Pipe the chocolate butter cream into the bottom part of the éclairs and fold the top back on. Refrigerate the éclairs to firm up the filling.

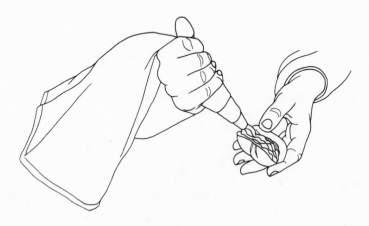

7. *Prepare the chocolate icing.* Bring ¼ cup heavy cream to a boil. Off the flame, melt the 2 ounces chocolate, broken into pieces, in the hot cream and mix. Then add 2 tablespoons rum. The chocolate icing should be runny. If it is prepared ahead of time, reheat when ready to ice the éclairs because it will be too thick to ice them.

8. *To ice the éclairs.* Pour the warm chocolate icing on a warm plate and dip the tops of the éclairs into it; hold the éclairs upside down for 20 seconds or so to let the icing firm up.

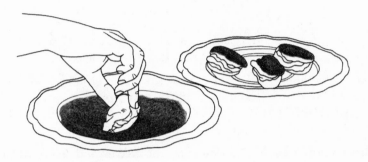

9. Serve as soon as possible after the éclairs are finished. You can put them back in the refrigerator; however, the icing will lose its shiny finish.

Chocolate Truffles

Chocolate truffles are all chocolate and no truffle—they merely look rather like truffles. Typically, they are served around Christmastime. They are excessively rich and will satisfy even the most rabid chocolate addicts. It is crucial to use the best chocolate you can get.

Special instructions. Truffles are made in 2 stages: (1) Make a chocolate and cream filling, flavored with a liqueur and praline cream or with ground hazelnuts. The chocolate filling has a special name in France. It is called a ganache. (2) When the filling is cold, it is coated with melted chocolate and dipped in cocoa. There will be an excess of dipping chocolate and cocoa, but you must have enough to work with. I generally use the remaining chocolate, mixed with ½ tablespoon Crisco, for hot chocolate drinks. The cocoa can be reused. I like to shape the truffles by hand to get a round shape.

MAKES 36 TRUFFLES

For the filling

⅔ cup heavy cream
6 ounces bittersweet chocolate
    (Lindt or Tobler)
4 tablespoons praline cream (see
    page 409 to order) or ground
    hazelnuts
1 tablespoon Grand Marnier,
    Cognac, or rum

For the coating

8 ounces bittersweet chocolate
    (Lindt or Tobler)
¼ cup confectioner's sugar
1½ cups cocoa

1. Bring the cream to a boil. Off the flame, add 6 ounces of chocolate broken into small pieces and stir until the chocolate is melted.

2. Add 4 tablespoons praline cream (or substitute ground hazelnuts) along with 1 tablespoon Grand Marnier, Cognac, or rum, and whisk until blended. Transfer the chocolate filling to a baking pan and freeze to harden (around 30 minutes).

3. Remove the chocolate mixture from the freezer and shape it into little balls about the size of a big cherry by rolling it in your hands. Place on waxed paper and refrigerate for 1 hour.

4. *To dip the chocolate truffles.* Melt 8 ounces of chocolate in a water bath and heat it only to the point of body temperature. Test it by dipping your finger in the chocolate and quickly touching it to your lips; if it feels neither warm nor cool to your lips, it is the right temperature. It must remain at this temperature for all the dipping, so you will have to keep testing and juggling it in and out of the hot water. If the chocolate gets stiff and grainy, smooth it with 1 tablespoon Crisco. Reheat.

5. Remove the truffles from the refrigerator. Using a small spoon, dip each truffle into the melted chocolate and coat it well all over. Place each truffle on a cookie sheet covered with waxed paper. Sprinkle confectioner's sugar over the truffles. Refrigerate for 15 minutes.

6. Sift 1½ cups of cocoa into a small deep bowl. Dip each truffle into cocoa; shake off excess cocoa in a sieve. Transfer to a cake rack just until you have finished coating all the truffles. Place each truffle in a paper candy cup and refrigerate them. Remove from refrigerator at least 15 minutes before eating.

Paris-Brest: A Triple-Filling
Cream Puff Cake

A traditional Paris-Brest is filled with whipped cream. It is excellent if the cream is of superb quality, but I like to make it more festive with a triple filling consisting of a butter cream mixed with pastry cream and an Italian meringue filling. The Paris-Brest then becomes a very special dessert for special occasions, like Christmas or birthdays for instance. It's a grand review of several techniques learned throughout the book.

Special instructions. All the work can be done ahead of time. Follow this timetable; otherwise, there is too much work to do in 1 day:

- Stage 1. Two days ahead of time, prepare the fillings. Notice that the butter cream and the Italian meringue both require a sugar syrup at the soft-ball stage.
- Stage 2. The morning of the dinner, bake the cream puff cake. Fold the 3 fillings together.
- Stage 3. About 3 hours before eating the cake, fill it. Refrigerate until dessert time.

Special kitchen utensil. An 8″ pot lid to shape the rings for the cake.

SERVES 8–10

For the butter cream

3 egg yolks
½ cup sugar
4 tablespoons water
16 tablespoons (2 sticks) sweet
    butter
2 tablespoons praline cream
    (see page 409 to order) or
    ground hazelnuts

For the Pastry Cream Custard

1½ tablespoons flour
1½ tablespoons cornstarch
⅓ cup sugar
2 large egg yolks
1 cup milk
2 tablespoons (¼ stick) sweet
    butter
1 tablespoon Frangelico liqueur

For the Italian meringue

2 egg whites
½ cup sugar
4 tablespoons water

For the cake

Cream Puff Dough, page 49
1 teaspoon sugar
Glaze: 1 egg yolk mixed with
    1 tablespoon milk
Confectioner's sugar

Stage 1: Two days ahead of time

1. *The butter cream.* Beat the egg yolks in an electric beater at medium speed while cooking the syrup. Combine sugar and water in a pan. Cook the syrup until the soft-ball stage (220°F.). Quickly pour the syrup into the egg yolks. Beat for 3 minutes. Refrigerate for 30 minutes. (For detailed instructions, see recipe, page 252.) Add 2 tablespoons praline cream or ground hazelnuts into the butter cream.

2. *For the Pastry Cream Custard.* Sift flour and cornstarch together and mix with 1/3 cup sugar. Beat the egg yolks in a separate bowl. Boil 1 cup of milk; pour half the boiling milk into the sugar-flour mixture. Vigorously whisk the egg yolks into the mixture. Boil the remaining milk again and pour the mixture into the boiling milk. Continue cooking, whisking vigorously, until the custard is very thick, about 30 seconds. Cool. Whisk in 2 tablespoons butter and 1 tablespoon liqueur. Refrigerate until needed.

3. *For the meringue.* This is a meringue made with beaten egg whites to which a syrup at the soft-ball stage is added; the two components are beaten together until stiff for a very shiny meringue. Beat the egg whites in an electric mixer or with an electric hand mixer for about 5 minutes until the whites are soft-peaked. Stop and prepare the soft-ball syrup as follows:

4. Have on hand next to your stove a 2-quart mixing bowl filled halfway with cool tap water and a soupspoon. Combine 1/2 cup sugar and 4 tablespoons water into a small 1-quart saucepan. Over medium heat, stir the sugar and water until the sugar is all dissolved. Note that when the syrup is cooking, the bubbles on the boiling surface will get smaller and smaller as the syrup thickens. After 3 minutes, start testing the syrup (illustration, page 253). Scoop out a quarter of a spoonful of syrup, quickly drop the spoon in the cold water, and with your free hand in the water, shape a small soft ball. If you can shape a soft ball, quickly turn off the heat, hold the pan with a potholder and quickly pour the syrup into the egg whites while the machine is on and beat until stiff and shiny. With a hand electric beater, it is more awkward, but it can be done. Pour with your right hand and beat with your left hand; secure the mixing bowl on a wet potholder. (To remedy a soft-ball stage syrup that has cooked to a hard-ball stage, stir 1/4 cup boiling water into the hard syrup to thin it out and cook it once more to the soft-ball stage.)

Stage 2: The morning of the dinner

5. *Prepare the Cream Puff Dough.* Follow the directions, page 49, adding 1 teaspoon sugar to the water and butter at step 2 and substituting

⅛ teaspoon salt for ½ teaspoon in the recipe. Butter 2 cookie sheets and dust them lightly with flour. With your index finger, draw a circle around an 8″ pot lid on one of the cookie sheets. Fit a pastry bag with a plain ½″ tube. Have an egg glaze ready: 1 egg yolk mixed with 2 teaspoons water. Fill the pastry bag with the Cream Puff Dough and pipe the dough on the drawn circle, then pipe another circle just inside, next to the first circle, touching it all around. Lastly, pipe a third circle, straddling on top of the 2 circles. With the leftover Cream Puff Dough, pipe small puffs on the same cookie sheet, or make small 4″ Paris-Brest. Brush an egg glaze (1 egg yolk mixed with 1 tablespoon milk) over the Paris-Brest and puffs.

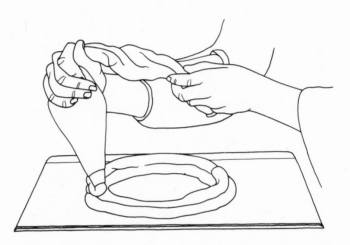

Preheat oven to 400°F.

6. Bake the Paris-Brest cake on the middle shelf of the oven for about 40 minutes, cover the top with foil after 30 minutes. With an electric oven, open up the door slightly for the last 10 minutes to let the steam escape. It is not necessary with a gas oven.

7. Let cool completely and freeze the small puffs or small Paris-Brest for another dessert.

8. Remove the 3 fillings from the refrigerator and whisk each one to aerate it. With a rubber spatula, fold the custard, then the Italian meringue, into the butter cream with gentle strokes in order not to deflate the fillings.

Stage 3: About 3 hours before dessert time

9. Fit a pastry bag with ½″ fluted tube and fill the bag with the combined fillings.

10. Slice the cake horizontally just below the top of the 2 bottom rings and fill the bottom part of the rings with the fillings. Put the top ring back on. Refrigerate until dessert time.

11. At the last minute, sprinkle liberally with confectioner's sugar and serve.

Index

A NOTE ABOUT THE AUTHOR

Born in Paris, Lydie Marshall came to this country as a
teenager and was raised in Cleveland, Ohio. She was grad-
uated from Western Reserve University and New York
University. From 1964–1971 she taught French and Spanish
at St. John's University. At the end of that year she started
her cooking school, A La Bonne Cocotte, in New York's
Greenwich Village. She and her professor husband spend
their winters in New York and summers in the Drôme,
in southeastern France.

A NOTE ON THE TYPE

This book was set on the Linotype in a type face called
Baskerville. The face is a facsimile reproduction of types
cast from molds made for John Baskerville (1706-1775)
from his designs. The punches for the revived Linotype
Baskerville were cut under the supervision of the English
printer George W. Jones. John Baskerville's original face
was one of the forerunners of the type style known as
"modern face"—a "modern" of the period A.D. 1800.

Composed by Maryland Linotype Composition Co., Inc.,
Baltimore, Maryland

Binding pattern from a cloth named after "Lydie" in
the Souleiado Collection at Pierre Deux Fabrics

Design by Dorothy Schmiderer